BASIC
ENGLISH
BRUSHUP

D1534561

BASIC
ENGLISH
BRUSHUP

R. KENT SMITH

UNIVERSITY OF MAINE

JOHN LANGAN

ATLANTIC COMMUNITY COLLEGE

CAROLE MOHR

TOWNSEND PRESS   Marlton, NJ 08053

Books in the Townsend Press Writing Series:
BASIC ENGLISH BRUSHUP
BASIC ENGLISH BRUSHUP, SHORT VERSION
ENGLISH BRUSHUP
BASIC WRITING SKILLS WITH READINGS
WRITING SKILLS WITH READINGS
A BASIC READER FOR COLLEGE WRITERS
THE TOWNSEND THEMATIC READER

Send book orders and requests for desk copies or supplements to:

Townsend Press
1038 Industrial Drive
Berlin, New Jersey 08009

For even faster service, call us at our toll-free number:

1-800-772-6410

Or FAX your request to:

1-609-753-0649

ISBN 0-944210-72-4

Contents

Preface to the Instructor

Basic English Brushup is a comprehensive and engaging guide to the English skills needed by basic writing students. It offers the following features.

1   **Inclusiveness.** Part One of the book describes the goals of effective paragraph writing and provides activities and writing assignments to help students reach those goals. Parts Two to Seven offer a full treatment of the rules of grammar, mechanics, and usage.

   Coverage includes areas that some other writing and grammar workbooks neglect; examples include verb tenses, pronoun forms, sentence variety and style, numbers and abbreviations, dictionary use, and proofreading. Full coverage means the convenience of having within the covers of one text all the basic writing materials that instructors and students are likely to need.

2   **Ease of use.** All of the following make the book easy for students to understand and use:

   • A clear, inviting two-color design with ample white space and very readable print

   • Explanations in simple, familiar language, with a real emphasis on clarity and without excessive grammatical terminology

   • Brief previews in chapters 4–27 to provide a quick sense of what each chapter is about

   • A friendly and helpful tone of voice that never speaks down to students but treats them as adults

   • Self-contained chapters so that students can be assigned just those skills they need

   • A special binding that allows the book to lie flat for convenient use

3   **Abundant practice.** The book is based on the assumption that students learn best when clear explanations are followed by abundant practice. The ample practice materials in each skills chapter are followed by three to five easily graded mastery tests. These tests, which progress from sentence- to paragraph-level items, are perforated and can be removed for easy scoring. The final test in each chapter provides the kind of close proofreading and revising that students need to do on their own papers.

4   **Engaging materials.**   The lively and engaging examples and practice materials in the text will maintain student interest. In particular, the final mastery tests for chapters 4–27 consist of high-interest selections on a wide variety of topics: the need for human touch, sharks, the dangers of pregnancy, turkey behavior, the holiday of Kwanzaa, mental illness, Babe Ruth, tigers, the reign of Ivan the Terrible, the discovery of chocolate, and so on.

5   **Superior supplements.**   The following are available at no charge to instructors adopting the book:

- An *Instructor's Edition* that is identical to the student text except that it includes answers to all the practices and tests

- A combined *Instructor's Manual and Test Bank* that includes teaching hints, diagnostic and achievement tests, a full answer key, and a bank of additional mastery tests

- A *Student Answer Key* consisting of answers for all the activities in Part One and to the practices and tests in the rest of the book. Upon request, a key will be provided for each book that is ordered.

- A software package titled *English Skills Software* that consists of thirty-four computer mastery tests as well as computerized diagnostic and achievement tests

In short, *Basic English Brushup* is designed to serve as a core worktext for any basic writing class. Its many features and supplements make it ideally suited to the diverse needs of today's students.

Acknowledgments

Our appreciation goes to those instructors whose insightful comments on other Townsend Press basic writing books helped as we worked on *Basic English Brushup*. We especially acknowledge the team of developmental writing teachers at Corning Community College. We thank as well Janet M. Goldstein for her design and editing skills and Beth Johnson for her help in developing practice materials in the text.

R. Kent Smith
John Langan
Carole Mohr

Introduction to the Student

Do you feel uneasy when you sit down to write? Perhaps you are preparing a job application letter, working on a college paper, writing a report on the job, or sending a note to a relative or friend. Are you uncertain, for example, about the best way to begin or about just where to place punctuation marks?

If you have doubts when expressing yourself on paper, this book is for you. *Basic English Brushup* will help you learn the essentials of effective writing. Step by step, you will master the core of rules you need to become a confident writer.

Here is how the book is organized:

Part One begins with a chapter that is a guide to writing effective paragraphs. You can practice the principles described in the first chapter by doing the activities in the second chapter. Your instructor may direct you to all or just certain exercises, depending on your needs.

The third chapter provides a series of writing assignments as well as some basic information on punctuation and paper form to review before you begin the assignments. Every so often, your instructor may ask you to write a paragraph. It is only by applying the rules of grammar, punctuation, and usage *in actual writing* that you can truly master them. You will find the topics for writing to be both interesting and meaningful.

Parts Two to Seven present the rules of grammar, punctuation, and usage that you need to do college-level work. Your instructor will help you identify those skills to which you should give your attention. Each chapter is self-contained, and each begins with a preview that provides a good sense of what the chapter is about. After reading the preview, carefully study the explanations and examples and work through the practices in the chapter. At the end of each chapter are three to five tests that will help you master the skill in question.

Basic English Brushup has been designed to benefit you as much as possible. Its format is inviting, its explanations are clear, and its many activities, practices, tests, and assignments will help you learn through doing. *It is a book that has been created to reward effort*, and if you provide that effort, you can make yourself a competent and confident writer. We wish you luck.

R. Kent Smith
John Langan
Carole Mohr

1 / A Brief Guide to Effective Writing

This chapter will show you how to write an effective paragraph. The principles you learn here will help you write longer papers as well. Answered in turn are the following questions:

1 Why does your attitude about writing matter?

2 What is a paragraph?

3 What are the goals of effective writing?

4 How do you reach the goals of effective writing?

WHY DOES YOUR ATTITUDE ABOUT WRITING MATTER?

Your attitude about writing is an important part of your learning to write well. To get a sense of just how you regard writing, read the following statements. Put a check beside those statements with which you agree. This activity is not a test, so try to be as honest as possible.

_____ 1. A good writer should be able to sit down and write a paper straight through without stopping.

_____ 2. Writing is a skill that anyone can learn with practice.

_____ 3. I'll never be good at writing because I make too many spelling, grammar, and punctuation mistakes.

_____ 4. Because I dislike writing, I always start a paper at the last possible minute.

_____ 5. I've always done poorly in English, and I don't expect that to change.

Now read the comments on the next page about the five statements. The comments will help you see if your attitude is hurting or helping your efforts to become a better writer.

1. *A good writer should be able to sit down and write a paper straight through without stopping.*

    The statement is not true. Writing is, in fact, a process. It is not done in one easy step, but in a series of steps, and seldom at one sitting. If you cannot do a paper all at once, that simply means you are like most of the other people on the planet. It is harmful to carry around the false idea that writing should be an easy matter.

2. *Writing is a skill that anyone can learn with practice.*

    This statement is absolutely true. Writing is a skill, like driving or word processing, that you can master with hard work. If you want to learn to write, you can. It is as simple as that. If you believe this, you are ready to learn how to become a competent writer.

    Some people hold the false belief that writing is a natural gift which some have and others do not. Because of this belief, they never make a truly honest effort to learn to write—and so they never learn.

3. *I'll never be good at writing because I make too many spelling, grammar, and punctuation mistakes.*

    The first concern in good writing should be content—what you have to say. Your ideas and feelings are what matter most. You should not worry about spelling, grammar, and punctuation rules while working on content.

    Unfortunately, some people are so self-conscious about making mistakes that they do not focus on what they want to say. They need to realize that a paper is best done in stages, and that the rules can and should wait until a later stage in the writing process. Through review and practice, you will eventually learn how to follow the rules with confidence.

4. *Because I dislike writing, I always start a paper at the last possible minute.*

    This is all-too-common behavior. You feel you are going to do poorly, and then behave in a way to insure you will do poorly! Your attitude is so negative that you defeat yourself—not even allowing enough time to really try.

    Again, what you need to realize is that writing is a process. Because it is done in steps, you don't have to get it right all at once. If you allow yourself enough time, you'll find a way to make a paper come together.

5. *I've always done poorly in English, and I don't expect that to change.*

    How you may have performed in the *past* does not control how you can perform in the *present*. Even if you did poorly in English in high school, it is in your power to make it one of your best subjects in college. If you believe writing can be learned and then work hard at it, you *will* become a better writer.

In conclusion, your attitude is crucial. If you believe you are a poor writer and always will be, chances are you will not improve. If you realize you can become a better writer, chances are you will improve. Depending on how you allow yourself to think, you can be your own best friend or your own worst enemy.

WHAT IS A PARAGRAPH?

A **paragraph** is a series of sentences about one main idea, or **point**. A paragraph typically starts with a point, and the rest of the paragraph provides specific details to support and develop that point.

Consider the following paragraph written by a student named Wanda.

A Terrible Roommate

Taking in Helen as a roommate was a mistake. For one thing, Helen was a truly noisy person. She talked loudly, she ate loudly, and she snored loudly. She never just watched TV, listened to the radio, or put a cassette in the stereo. Instead, she did all three at once. I would walk into the apartment with my hands clapped over my ears and turn off the first noisemaking machine I reached. Then I would hear her cry out, "I was listening to that." Secondly, Helen had no sense of privacy. If she wanted to speak to me, she would find me no matter where I was or what I was doing. She walked in on me while I was dressing. She sat down on my bed for a chat while I was napping. Once she even wandered in while I was taking a bath. And finally, Helen had too many visiting relatives. There were over ten of them, and they all felt perfectly at home in our apartment. I often came into the apartment after an evening out and practically tripped over one of Helen's sisters, cousins, or nephews asleep on our living room floor. When they visited, they would stay for days, eating our groceries and tying up the bathroom and telephone. Helen is gone now, and I've had to take a second job to handle the rent. It's worth it.

The above paragraph, like many effective paragraphs, starts by stating a main idea, or point. In this case, the point is that taking in Helen as a roommate was a bad idea. A point is a general idea that has an opinion injected into it.

In our everyday lives, we constantly make points about all kinds of matters. We express such opinions as "That was a terrible movie" or "My psychology instructor is the best teacher I have ever had" or "My sister is a generous person" or "Eating at that restaurant was a mistake" or "That team should win the playoff game" or "Waitressing is the worst job I ever had" or "Our state should allow the death penalty" or "Cigarette smoking should be banned everywhere." In *talking* to people, we don't always give the reasons for our opinions. But in *writing*, we *must* provide the reasons to support our ideas. Only by supplying solid evidence for any point that we make can we communicate effectively with readers.

An effective paragraph, then, must not only make a point but must support it with **specific evidence**—reasons, examples, and other details. Such specifics help prove to readers that the point is a reasonable one. Even if readers do not agree with the writer, at least they have in front of them the evidence on which the writer has based his or her opinion. Readers are like juries; they want to see the evidence so that they can make their own judgments.

➤ Take a moment now to examine the evidence that Wanda has provided to back up her point about Helen as a roommate. Complete the following outline of Wanda's paragraph by summarizing in a few words her reasons and the details that develop them. The first reason and its supporting details are summarized for you as an example.

Point: Taking in Helen as a roommate was a mistake.

> *Reason 1:* Noisy person
>
> *Details that develop reason 1:* Talked, ate, snored, and played things loudly.
>
> *Reason 2:* _____
>
> *Details that develop reason 2:* _____
>
> _____
>
> *Reason 3:* _____
>
> *Details that develop reason 3:* _____
>
> _____

As the outline makes clear, Wanda provides three reasons to support her point about rooming with Helen: (1) Helen was noisy, (2) she had no sense of privacy, and (3) she had too many visiting relatives. Wanda also provides vivid details to back up each of her three reasons. Her reasons and descriptive details enable readers to see why she feels that rooming with Helen was a mistake.

To write an effective paragraph, then, aim to do what Wanda has done: begin by making a point, and then go on to support that point with specific evidence.

WHAT ARE THE GOALS OF EFFECTIVE WRITING?

Now that you have considered an effective student paragraph, it is time to look at four goals of effective writing:

1 Make a point. It is often best to state that point in the first sentence of your paper, just as Wanda has in her paragraph about her roommate. The sentence that expresses the main idea, or point, of a paragraph is called the **topic sentence**. Activities on pages 25–28 in the next chapter of this book will help you learn how to write a topic sentence.

2 Support the point. To do so, you need to provide specific reasons, examples, and other details that explain and develop the point. The more precise and particular your supporting details are, the better your readers can "see," "hear," and "feel" them. Activities on pages 20–25 and 29–42 in the next chapter of this book will help you learn how to be specific in your writing.

3 Organize the support. There are two common ways to organize the support in a paragraph. You can use either a listing order or a time order. At the same time, you should use suitable signal words, known as **transitions**.

a. Listing order. The writer organizes the supporting evidence in a paper by providing a list of two or more reasons, examples, or other details. Often the most important or interesting item is saved for last because the reader is most likely to remember the last thing read.

Transition words that show a listing order include the following:

for one thing	secondly	another	next	last of all
first of all	also	in addition	moreover	finally

➤ The paragraph about Helen uses a listing order: it lists three reasons why Helen was a bad roommate, and each of those three reasons is introduced by one of the above transitions. In the spaces below, write in the three transitions:

_____   _____   _____

The first reason in the paragraph about Helen is introduced with *for one thing*; the second reason by *secondly;* and the third reason by *finally.*

b. Time order. Supporting details are presented in the order in which they occurred. *First* this happened; *next* this; *after* that, this; and so on. Many paragraphs, especially ones that tell stories or give a series of directions, are organized in a time order.

Transition words that show time relationships include the following:

first	before	after	when	then
next	during	now	while	

➤ Read the playful paragraph on the next page. It is organized in a time order. See if you can underline the six transition words that show the time relationships.

There are a few steps to follow if you want to be sure you are not hired for a job. First, go to the job interview in your basketball clothes. In fact, bring your basketball along. That will make it very clear that you're just stopping in on the way to someplace more important. If you can possibly arrange it, be accompanied by a couple of your buddies. While you're being interviewed, they can hang around the reception area, commenting on what a dump the office is. During the interview, sigh loudly at the interviewer's stupid questions. Ask if you can smoke. Clip your nails. Demand to know what the job pays. After you hear what the salary is, express disbelief at the low figure. Comment that a real cheapskate must run the company. Then explain that you're only waiting for work to tide you over, and that your cousin will be getting you a really high-paying job at his place. Finally, tell the interviewer not to call you too early with a decision. Explain that you party late every night and only get out of bed around noon.

The writer makes the main point of the paragraph in the first sentence: "There are a few steps to follow if you want to be sure you are not hired for a job." The support for this point is the suggested things to do at the interview. Those actions are presented in the order in which they are meant to occur. The time relationships between some are highlighted by these transitions: *first, while, during, after, then,* and *finally.*

More About Transitions

Transitions are words and phrases that make clear the relationships between ideas. They are like signposts that guide travelers, showing them how to move smoothly from one spot to the next. Be sure to take advantage of transitions. They will help organize and connect your ideas, and they will help your readers follow the direction of your thoughts.

➤ To see how transitions help, put a check beside the item in each pair that is easier to read and understand.

_____ I begin each day by writing down a list of the things I need to do. I decide which items are most important.

_____ I begin each day by writing down a list of the things I need to do. Then I decide which items are most important.

_____ One way to lose friends is to always talk and never listen. It is a mistake to borrow money and never pay it back.

_____ One way to lose friends is to always talk and never listen. Another mistake is to borrow money and never pay it back.

In each pair, the second item is easier to read and understand. In the first pair, the time word *then* makes the relationship between the sentences clear. The writer first gets down a list of things to do and *then* decides on which are most important. In the second pair, the listing word *another* makes it clear that the writer is going on to a second way to lose friends.

Activities on pages 42–47 will give you practice in the use of listing order and time order, as well as transitions, to organize the supporting details of a paragraph.

4 Write error-free sentences. If you use correct spelling and follow grammar, punctuation, and usage rules, your sentences will be clear and well written. But by no means must you have all that information in your head. Even the best of writers need to use reference materials to be sure their writing is correct. So keep a good dictionary and grammar handbook nearby when you write your papers.

In general, however, save them for after you've gotten your ideas firmly down on paper. You'll see in the next part of this guide that Wanda made a number of sentence errors as she worked on her paragraph. But she simply ignored them until she got to a later draft of her paper, when there was time enough to make the needed corrections.

HOW DO YOU REACH THE GOALS OF EFFECTIVE WRITING?

Even professional writers do not sit down and automatically, in one draft, write a paper. Instead, they have to work on it a step at a time. Writing a paper is a process that can be divided into the following steps:

Step 1: Getting Started Through Prewriting

Step 2: Preparing a Scratch Outline

Step 3: Writing the First Draft

Step 4: Revising

Step 5: Proofreading

These steps are described on the following pages.

Step 1: Getting Started Through Prewriting

What you need to learn, first, are strategies for working on a paper. These strategies will help you do the thinking needed to figure out both the point you want to make and the support you have for that point.

There are several **prewriting strategies**—ones that you use before writing the first draft of your paper.

- Freewriting
- Questioning
- Clustering
- List making

Freewriting

Freewriting is just sitting down and writing whatever comes into your mind about a topic. Do this for ten minutes or so. Write without stopping, and without worrying in the slightest about spelling, grammar, or the like. Simply get down on paper all the information about the topic that occurs to you.

Below is the freewriting done by Wanda on problems with her roommate Helen. Wanda had been given the assignment, "Write about a problem with a friend, family member, or roommate." Wanda felt right away that she could write about her roommate. She began prewriting as a way to explore her topic and generate details on it.

Example of Freewriting

One thing I would like to write about is my roommate. What a charakter. I learned my lesson with her, I am going to think twice before taking on a roomate again. She folowed me everywhere. Once when I was taking a bath. She didnt like to be alone. I could be taking a nap and she would just walk right in, I'd wake up and there she would be. Talking away. I had to lock doors all the time. To my bedroom and to my bathroom. Then I hurt her feelings. She did pay her rent on time. I'll say that for her. And she was a good cook. But other things were too much. She was on the phone a lot. She had more family than anyone I ever knew. It seemed like they were living their. I got sick and tired of all the people around. She even had keys made up for them and gave them the keys! I really blowed up with her when that happen. There were always dishes in the sink. I would do mine, she not hers. She was a messy person. Cloths all over her bedroom. Stuff was always turned on. She liked things noisee. The TV was always blaring when I walked in. Give me a break, woman. I got back from a crazy day at school wanting some peace and quite. But what do I get? I needed to get her out of my life.

Notice that there are spelling, grammar, and punctuation problems in Wanda's freewriting. Wanda is not worried about such matters, nor should she be. She is just concentrating on getting ideas and details down on paper. She knows that it is best to focus on one thing at a time. At this stage, she just wants to write out thoughts as they come to her, to do some thinking on paper.

You should take the same approach when freewriting: explore your topic without worrying at all about being "correct." Figuring out what you want to say should have all your attention in this early stage of the writing process.

Questioning

Questioning means that you think about your topic by writing down a series of questions and answers about it. Your questions can start with words like *what, when, where, why,* and *how.*

Here are some questions that Wanda might have asked while developing her paper:

Example of Questioning

- *Why did I have a problem with Helen?* She was hard to live with.
- *How was she hard to live with?* Followed me around everywhere; I had no privacy. Also, she was noisy.
- *When did I have no privacy?* When I got back from school and wanted to be quiet and alone; when her relatives came.
- *Where did I have no privacy?* In my bedroom while I was napping; when her relatives were covering the floor when I walked in.
- *When was she noisy?* When I got back from school and when I'd try to study at night.
- *Where was she noisy?* The noise could be heard anywhere in the apartment.

Clustering

Clustering is another strategy that can be used to generate material for a paper. It is helpful for people who like to do their thinking in a visual way.

In **clustering**, you begin by stating your subject in a few words in the center of a blank sheet of paper. Then as ideas come to you, put them in ovals, boxes, or circles around the subject and draw lines to connect them to the subject. Put minor ideas or details in smaller boxes or circles, and use connecting lines to show how they relate as well.

Keep in mind that there is no right or wrong way of clustering. It is a way to think on paper about how various ideas and details relate to one another. On the next page is an example of clustering that Wanda could have done to develop her ideas.

Example of clustering

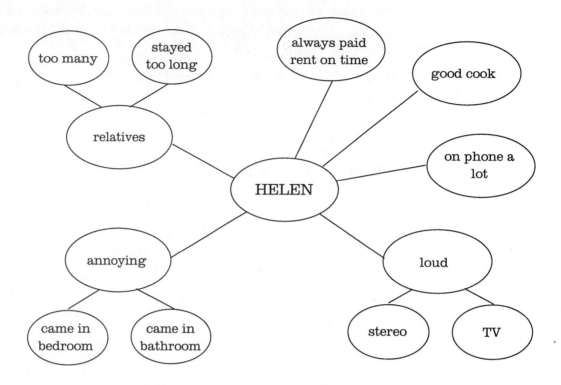

Notice that the clustering, like the freewriting, includes details that do not end up in the final paragraph. Wanda decided later not to develop the idea that Helen spent a lot of time on the phone. And she realized that the details about Helen's paying the rent on time and being a good cook were not relevant to her point. It is natural for a number of such extra or unrelated details to appear as part of the prewriting process. The goal of prewriting is to get a lot of information down on paper. You can then shape, add to, and subtract from your raw material as you take your paper through the series of writing drafts.

List making

In **list making**, a strategy also known as **brainstorming**, you make a list of ideas and details that could go into your paper. Simply pile these items up, one after another, without worrying about putting them in any special order. Try to accumulate as many details as you can think of.

After Wanda did her freewriting about her roommate, she made up the following list of details.

Example of list making

Helen was always around
followed me into the bathroom

came into the bedroom when I was sleeping
walked in on me while I was dressing
I couldn't be alone when I wanted to
started locking doors behind me
talked a lot on the phone
talked when I was going out the door to school
had a lot of relatives
three sisters and they all visited
also cousins she was close to
I would come home and relatives would be there
sometimes they were there and Helen wasn't
she had keys made for some of them
ate out sometimes because no room to cook in kitchen
lot of cooking smells in the house
a very good cook
never charged me for food she bought
also good in paying her rent on time
but hard to relax around
played TV all the time
played stereo at the same time
everything about Helen was loud
even her clothes were loud

One detail led to another as Wanda expanded her list. Slowly but surely, more supporting material emerged that she could use in developing her paper. By the time she was done with her list, she was ready to plan an outline of her paragraph and to write her first draft.

Important Notes About Prewriting Strategies

Some writers may use only one of the above prewriting strategies. Others may use bits and pieces of all four of them. Any one strategy can lead to another. Freewriting may lead to questioning or clustering, which may then lead to a list. Or a writer may start with a list and then use freewriting or questioning to develop items on the list. During this early stage of the writing process, as you do your thinking on paper, anything goes. You should not expect a straight-line progression from the beginning to the end of your paper. Instead, there probably will be a constant moving back and forth as you work to discover your point and just how you will develop it.

Keep in mind that prewriting can also help you choose from among several topics. Wanda might not have been so sure about which person to write about. Then she could have made a list of possible topics—names of people with whom she has had problems. After selecting two or three names from the list, she could have done some prewriting on each to see which seemed most promising. After finding a likely topic, Wanda would have continued with her prewriting activities until she had a solid main point and plenty of support.

Finally, remember that you are not ready to begin writing a paper until you know your main point and many of the details that can be used to support it. Don't rush through prewriting. It's better to spend more time on this stage than to waste time writing a paragraph for which you have no solid point and too little interesting support.

Step 2: Preparing a Scratch Outline

A **scratch outline** is a brief plan for the paragraph. It shows at a glance the point of the paragraph and the support for that point. It is the logical backbone upon which the paper is built.

This rough outline often follows freewriting, questioning, clustering, and/or list making. Or it may gradually emerge in the midst of these strategies. In fact, trying to outline is a good way to see if you need to do more prewriting. If a solid outline does not emerge, then you know you need to do more prewriting to clarify your main point or its support. Once you have a workable outline, you may realize, for instance, that you want to do more list making to develop one of the supporting details in the outline.

In Wanda's case, as she was working on her list of details, she suddenly discovered what the plan of her paragraph could be. She went back to the list, crossed out items that she now realized did not fit, and added the comments shown below and on the next page.

Example of a list with added comments

I had a bad roommate—three reasons:

Helen was always around ⎤
followed me into the bathroom
came into the bedroom when I was sleeping
walked in on me while I was dressing   *Nosy*
I couldn't be alone when I wanted to
started locking doors behind me ⎦
~~talked a lot on the phone~~
~~talked when I was going out the door to school~~
had a lot of relatives ⎤
three sisters and they all visited
also cousins she was close to
I would come home and relatives would be there   *Too many relatives*
sometimes they were there and Helen wasn't
she had keys made for some of them
ate out sometimes because no room to cook in kitchen ⎦
~~lot of cooking smells in the house~~
~~a very good cook~~
~~never charged me for food she bought~~
~~also good in paying her rent on time~~

but hard to relax around
played TV all the time
played stereo at the same time
everything about Helen was loud
even her clothes were loud

Loud person (Noisy)

Under the list, Wanda was now able to prepare her scratch outline:

Example of a scratch outline

I had a bad roommate.

1. Too noisy

2. Too nosy (no sense of privacy)

3. Too many relatives (put last—worst reason)

After all her preliminary writing, Wanda sat back pleased. She knew she had a promising paper—one with a clear point and solid support. Wanda was now ready to write the first draft of her paper, using her outline as a guide.

Step 3: Writing the First Draft

When you do a first draft, be prepared to put in additional thoughts and details that didn't emerge in your prewriting activity. And don't worry if you hit a snag. Just leave a blank space or add a comment such as "Do later" and press on to finish the paper. Also, don't worry yet about grammar, punctuation, or spelling. You don't want to take time correcting words or sentences that you may decide to remove later. Instead, make it your goal to develop the content of your paper with plenty of specific details.

Here is Wanda's first draft:

First draft

Last fall, I decided that I needed to save money by sharing my apartment with someone. I put an ad in the paper and chose the first person who called which was Helen. She was the loudest person I have ever known over the age of five. She talked loud, and she was a noisy eater. When you tried to sleep at night you sure knew what a loud snorer she was. The only other person who snored that loud was my father, and he would wake up everyone in the family. The TV was always on, it was loud. The same thing with the stereo. There was always noise when I walked into the apt. I would have to tell her to turn something off. Then she would compane I was too demandin. Helen never gave me much privicy. She would come into the bedroom when I was naping. I'd be aware that someone was standing there. As soon as I woke she would start talking. ADD MORE DETAILS LATER. Her relatives seemed to come out of the woodwork. I'd walk in and they'd be covering the chairs and sofa and carpet. They were frendly people but too much. They'd be eating in the kitchen. Or watching TV. Or be in the bathroom when I wanted to go in. All this was too much.

After Wanda finished the draft, she was able to put it aside until the next day. You will benefit as well if you can allow some time between finishing a draft and starting to revise.

Step 4: Revising

Revising is as much a stage in the writing process as prewriting, outlining, and doing the first draft. **Revising** means that you rewrite a paper, building upon what has been done to make it stronger and better. One writer has said about revision, "It's like cleaning house—getting rid of all the junk and putting things in the right order." A typical revision means writing at least one or two more drafts.

Here is Wanda's second draft.

Second draft

Taking in Helen as a roomate was a mistake. For one thing Helen was noisy. She talked and ate loudly, and she snored loudly. She never just had on the TV, listened to the radio, or a cassete in the tape deck. She did all three at once. I would walk into the apt. with my hands over my ears and turn off the first noisy machine I reached. I would hear her cry out I was listening to that. The second bad thing about Helen was that she had no sense of privicy. She walked in on me when I was dressing. She sat down on my bed for a chat while I was naping. She even came into the bathroom once when I was taking a bath. The third thing about Helen was that she had too many relatives. I counted over ten and they all came to the apartment. After a night out I would come in and trip over relatives asleep on the living room floor. Relatives would stay eating grocerys and tying up the bathroom and telephone. Helen is gone now, and I've had to take a second job to handle the rent.

Notice that in redoing the draft, Wanda started by clearly stating the point of her paragraph. Also, she inserted clear transitions to set off the three reasons why Helen was a bad roommate. She omitted the detail about her father snoring, which was not relevant to a paragraph focusing on Helen. She added more details, so that she would have enough support for each of her three reasons. She also began to correct some of her spelling mistakes and added a final sentence to round off the paragraph.

Wanda then went on to revise the second draft. Since she was doing her paper on a word processor, she was able to print it out quickly. She double-spaced the lines, allowing room for revisions, which she added in longhand as part of her third draft. (Note that if you are not using a word processor, you may want to do each draft on every other line of a page, so that there is room to revise. Also, write on only one side of a page, so that you can see your entire paper at one time.) Shown below are some of the changes that Wanda made in longhand as she worked on her third draft.

Part of third draft

roommate
Taking in Helen as a ~~roomate~~ was a mistake. For one thing, Helen

a truly   person.   loudly, she
was ∧noisy. She talked ~~and~~ ate loudly, and she snored loudly. She never

watched   put   Instead, s
just ~~had on~~ the TV, listened to the radio, or ∧a cassete in the tape deck. ∧$he

apartment   clapped
did all three at once. I would walk into the ~~apt.~~ with my hands ∧over my

noisemaking   Then
ears and turn off the first ~~noisy~~ machine I reached. ∧I would hear her cry

*   Secondly,*
out, " I was listening to that. " ~~The second bad thing about~~ Helen ~~was that~~

privacy
~~she~~ had no sense of ~~priviey~~. . . .

After writing out the above and other changes, Wanda typed them into her word processor and printed out the almost-final draft of her paper. She was now ready to do a careful proofreading.

Step 5: Proofreading

Proofreading, the final stage in the writing process, means checking a paper carefully for spelling, grammar, punctuation, and other errors. You are ready for this stage when you are satisfied with your choice of supporting details, the order in which they are presented, and the way they and your topic sentence are worded.

At this point in her work, Wanda used her dictionary to do final checks on her spelling. She used a grammar handbook to be sure about her grammar, punctuation, and usage. Wanda also read through the paper carefully, looking for typing errors, omitted words, and any other errors she may have missed before. Such proofreading is often hard to do—students have spent so much time with their work, or so little, that they want to avoid proofing. But done carefully, this important final step will insure that your paper looks as good as possible.

Some Proofreading Hints

One helpful trick at this stage is to read your paper out loud. You will probably hear awkward wordings and become aware of spots where the punctuation needs to be improved. Make the changes needed for your sentences to read smoothly and clearly.

Another helpful technique is to take a sheet of paper and cover your paragraph so that you can expose and check carefully just one line at a time.

A third strategy is to read your paper backward, from the last sentence to the first. Doing so helps keep you from getting caught up in the flow of the paper and missing small mistakes, which is easy to do since you're so familiar with what you meant to say.

(Pages 403–418 will give you practice in proofreading for specific problems.)

A LOOK AHEAD

The next chapter provides a series of activities to help you master three of the four goals in effective writing: (1) making a point, (2) supporting the point with specific details, and (3) organizing the support. Chapter 3 is mainly a series of writing assignments. All of the other chapters that follow deal with grammar, mechanics, and usage. These chapters will help you with the fourth goal of effective writing—producing error-free sentences.

CHAPTER REVIEW

Answer the true-false or multiple choice question or fill in the missing word. Doing so will help you check your understanding of the material presented in this chapter.

1. *True or false?* __T__ Writing is a skill that anyone can learn with practice.

2. An effective paragraph is one that
   a. makes a point.
   b. provides specific support.
   (c.) makes a point *and* provides specific support.
   d. none of the above.

3. A topic sentence expresses the ____*main idea* (or: *point*)____ of a paragraph.

4. Prewriting can help a writer find
   a. a good topic to write about.
   b. a good main point to make about the topic.
   c. enough details to support the main point.
   (d.) all of the above.

5. *True or false?* __T__ During the freewriting process, you should not concern yourself with spelling, punctuation, or grammar.

6. One prewriting technique that everyone should use at some stage of the writing process is to prepare a plan for the paragraph known as a(n) ____*scratch outline*____.

7. When you start writing, your first concern should be
   a. spelling.
   (b.) content.
   c. grammar.
   d. punctuation.

8. Two common ways of organizing a paragraph are using a ____*time*____ order and a ____*listing*____ order.

9. The words *first, next, then, also, another,* and *finally* are examples of signal words, commonly known as ____*transitions*____.

10. The purpose of proofreading is to check a paper for errors in
    a. grammar.
    b. punctuation.
    c. usage and spelling.
    (d.) all of the above.

2 / Practice in Effective Writing

The following series of activities will strengthen your understanding of the writing guidelines presented in the first chapter. Through practice, you will gain a better sense of the goals of effective writing and how to reach those goals. You will also help prepare yourself for the writing assignments in the next chapter, which you may be asked to do while working through the rest of the book.

Your instructor may ask you to do the series of activities in sequence, from beginning to end, or may select the activities that are most suited to your particular needs.

1 UNDERSTANDING GENERAL VERSUS SPECIFIC

A paragraph is made up of a main idea, which is general, and the specific ideas that support it. So to write well, you must understand the difference between general and specific ideas.

It is helpful to realize that you use general and specific ideas all the time in your everyday life. For example, in planning your food shopping, you may tell yourself, "I need some vegetables. I guess I'll buy green peppers, tomatoes, and onions." In such a case, *vegetables* is the general idea, and *green peppers, tomatoes,* and *onions* are the specific ideas.

Or if you are looking for a part-time job, you may think, "What features do I want for that job? I want an hourly pay of at least six dollars, hours from one to five in the afternoon, and a travel time each way of no more than thirty minutes." In this case, *the desired features of a part-time job* is the general idea, and *pay, hours,* and *travel time* are the specific ideas.

Or if you are talking to a friend about a math teacher you feel is poor, you may say, "She acts bored in class, she often arrives late, and she never returns homework." In this case, the general idea is *the math teacher is poor*, and the specific ideas are the three reasons you named.

The four activities here will give you experience in recognizing general-specific relationships. They will also provide a helpful background for all the information and activities that follow.

➤ Activity 1

Each group of words consists of one general idea and four specific ideas. The general idea includes all the specific ideas. Underline the general idea in each group.

Example cooking   dusting   vacuuming   <u>chore</u>   washing dishes

1. wrench   drill   hammer   screwdriver   <u>tool</u>   pliers

2. bruise   fracture   <u>injury</u>   scrape   cut

3. <u>crime</u>   robbery   kidnapping   murder   rape

4. gas   food   <u>expense</u>   rent   taxes

5. come here   stop   go   <u>command</u>   hurry

6. sneakers   boots   high heels   sandals   <u>footwear</u>

7. <u>entertainment</u>   television   concerts   movies   card games

8. long lines   stuck doors   junk mail   slow waiters   <u>annoyances</u>

9. <u>time savers</u>   microwave ovens   take-out food   high-speed trains   express mail

10. nail biting   tardiness   smoking   interrupting   <u>bad habits</u>

➤ Activity 2   *Answers will vary.*

In each item below, one idea is general and the others are specific. The general idea includes the specific ones. In the spaces provided, write in two more specific ideas that are covered by the general idea.

Example   *General:* beverage
           Specific: iced tea, water, __*soda*__ , __*grape juice*__

1. *General:* snacks
   Specific: pretzels, popcorn, _____*fruit, nuts, chips*_____

2. *General:* subject
   Specific: English, biology, _____*history, Spanish, psychology*_____

3. *General:* sports
   Specific: baseball, soccer, _____*football, basketball, tennis*_____

4. *General:* cooking methods

   Specific: boil, steam, _____, *fry, bake, sauté* _____

5. *General:* reading material

   Specific: textbook, comic book, *newspaper*, *magazine, novel* ___

6. *General:* seafood

   Specific: clams, lobster, _____ *shrimp, tuna, scallops* ____

7. *General:* emotion

   Specific: anger, embarrassment, _____, *fear, love, pride* ___

8. *General:* negative personal qualities

   Specific: greed, cowardice, _____ *meanness*, *violence, jealousy* __

9. *General:* positive personal qualities

   Specific: reliability, determination, *kindness, generosity, friendliness* ___

10. *General:* greetings

    Specific: "How are you," "Hello," *"Hi," "Good morning," "Hey there"* ___

➤ **Activity 3**

Read each group of specific ideas below. Then circle the letter of the general idea that tells what the specific ideas have in common. Note that the general idea should not be too broad or too narrow. Begin by trying the example item, and then read the explanation that follows.

Example   *Specific ideas:* egg salad; tuna salad; bacon, lettuce, and tomato; peanut butter and jelly

The general idea is:
a. foods.
b. sandwich fillings.
c. salads used as sandwich fillings.

Explanation

It is true that the specific ideas are all food, but they have in common something even more specific—they are all common sandwich fillings. Therefore answer *a* is too broad, and the correct answer is *b*. Answer *c* is too narrow because it doesn't cover all of the specific ideas. While two of them are salads used as sandwich fillings, two of them are not salads.

1. *Specific ideas:* Easter, Thanksgiving, Valentine's Day, New Year's Day

   The general idea is:
   a. days.
   (b.) holidays.
   c. religious holidays.

2. *Specific ideas:* hide and seek, tag, jacks, hopscotch

   The general idea is:
   a. games.
   b. toys.
   (c.) children's games.

3. *Specific ideas:* runny nose, coughing, sneezing, sore throat

   The general idea is:
   (a.) cold symptoms.
   b. symptoms.
   c. throat problems.

4. *Specific ideas:* yes, no, maybe, OK

   The general idea is:
   a. negative answers.
   b. positive answers.
   (c.) answers.

5. *Specific ideas:* OPEN, STOP, FIRE EXIT, YIELD

   The general idea is:
   a. words.
   (b.) words on signs.
   c. words on traffic signs.

6. *Specific ideas:* leaking toilet, no hot water, broken window, roaches

   The general idea is:
   a. problems.
   b. kitchen problems.
   (c.) apartment problems.

7. *Specific ideas:* tornado, earthquake, sunrise, spring

   The general idea is:
   a. natural disasters.
   (b.) natural events.
   c. events.

8. *Specific ideas:* big and small, short and tall, fat and lean, kind and mean

   The general idea is:
   a. words.
   b. descriptions of sizes.
   (c.) opposites.

9. *Specific ideas:* count to ten, take a deep breath, go for a walk

   The general idea is:

   a. actions.
   (b.) ways to calm down.
   c. ways to calm down just before a test.

10. *Specific ideas:* putting sticky tape on someone's chair, putting a "kick me" sign on someone's back, putting hot pepper in someone's cereal

    The general idea is:

    a. jokes.
    (b.) practical jokes.
    c. practical jokes played on teachers.

➤ Activity 4   *Wording of answers may vary.*

In the following items, the specific ideas are given but the general ideas are unstated. Fill in the blanks with the unstated general ideas.

Example   *General idea:* _____*Bodies of water*_____

   Specific ideas: sea   ocean
                     lake   river

1. *General idea:* _____*Breakfast foods*_____

   Specific ideas: doughnuts   bacon and eggs
                     cereal   pancakes

2. *General idea:* _____*Games*_____

   Specific ideas: chess   checkers
                     Monopoly   dominoes

3. *General idea:* _____*Breads*_____

   Specific ideas: rye   six-grain
                     whole wheat   pumpernickel

4. *General idea:* _____*Jobs*_____

   Specific ideas: salesperson   welder
                     hair stylist   insurance agent

5. *General idea:* _____*White things*_____

   Specific ideas: snow   milk
                     wedding dress the President's house

6. *General idea:* _____*Insults*_____

   Specific ideas: "Your mother stinks."   "You look like an ape."
                     "Your father's a bum."   "Your car is a real junk heap."

7. *General idea:* _____ Common objects of fear _____

   Specific ideas: snakes   heights
                      flying in an airplane   being in small spaces

8. *General idea:* _____ Compliments _____

   Specific ideas: "I like your dress."
                      "Your new haircut looks terrific."
                      "You look great in red."
                      "You did a fine job on last week's paper."

9. *General idea:* _____ Things to do for a wedding _____

   Specific ideas: order the invitations   get the tuxedos
                      get the bride's gown   find a photographer

10. *General idea:* _____ Steps in making pizza _____

    Specific ideas: Roll the dough in a circle.
                       Cover the dough with tomato sauce.
                       Cover the sauce with mushrooms and onions.
                       Then add grated mozzarella cheese.

2   UNDERSTANDING THE PARAGRAPH

A **paragraph** is made up of a main idea and a group of related sentences that develop that main idea. The main idea often appears in a sentence known as the **topic sentence**.

It is helpful to remember that the topic sentence is a *general* statement. The other sentences provide specific support for the general statement.

➤ **Activity**

Each group of sentences below could be written as a short paragraph. Circle the letter of the topic sentence in each case. To find the topic sentence, ask yourself, "Which is a general statement supported by the specific details in the other three statements?"

Begin by trying the example item below. First circle the letter of the sentence you think expresses the main idea. Then read the explanation.

Example   a. If you stop carrying matches or a lighter, you can cut down on impulse smoking.
               b. If you sit in no-smoking areas, you will smoke less.
               c. You can behave in ways that will help you smoke less.
               d. By keeping a record of when and where you smoke, you can learn the most tempting situations and then avoid them.

Explanation

Sentence *a* explains one way to smoke less. Sentences *b* and *d* also provide specific ways to smoke less. In sentence *c*, however, no one specific way is explained. The words "ways that help you smoke less" refer only generally to such methods. Therefore sentence *c* is the topic sentence; it expresses the author's main idea. The other sentences support that idea by providing examples.

1. a. "I couldn't study because I forgot to bring my book home."
   b. "I couldn't take the final because my grandmother died."
   c. Students use some common excuses with instructors.
   d. "I couldn't come to class because I had a migraine headache."

2. a. The brakes are badly worn.
   b. My old car is ready for the junk pile.
   c. The car floor has rusted through, and water splashes on my feet from a wet highway.
   d. My mechanic says its engine is too old to be repaired, and the car isn't worth the cost of a new engine.

3. a. Tobacco is one of the most addictive of all drugs.
   b. Selling cigarettes ought to be against the law.
   c. Non-smokers are put in danger by breathing the smoke from others' cigarettes.
   d. Cigarette smoking kills many more people than all illegal drugs combined.

4. a. Part-time workers are easily laid off.
   b. Most part-time workers get no fringe benefits.
   c. The average part-timer earns three dollars less an hour than a full-timer.
   d. Part-time workers have second-class status.

5. a. The last time I ate at the diner, I got food poisoning and was sick for two days.
   b. The city inspector found roaches and mice in the diner's kitchen.
   c. Our town diner is a health hazard and ought to be closed down.
   d. The toilets in the diner often back up, and the sinks have only a trickle of water.

3 UNDERSTANDING THE TOPIC SENTENCE

As already explained, most paragraphs center around a main idea that is often expressed in a topic sentence. An effective topic sentence does two things. First, it gives the topic of the paragraph. Second, it expresses the writer's attitude or opinion or idea about the topic. For example, look at the following topic sentence:

- Falling in love involves enormous risks.

In this topic sentence, the topic is *falling in love*; the writer's idea about the topic is that falling in love *involves enormous risks*.

➤ Activity

For each topic sentence below, underline the topic and double-underline the point of view that the writer takes toward the topic.

Examples   Our vacation turned out to be a disaster.

The daily life of students is filled with conflicts.

1. Gambling can be addictive.

2. My mother has always been generous.

3. Politicians are often self-serving.

4. The national speed limit should be raised.

5. Serious depression has several warning signs.

6. Insects serve many useful purposes.

7. Doctors are often insensitive.

8. Our dreams may contain symbols.

9. Owning a pet has a number of benefits.

10. High school students should be required to wear uniforms.

4 IDENTIFYING TOPICS, TOPIC SENTENCES, AND SUPPORT

The following activity will sharpen your sense of the differences among topics, topic sentences, and supporting sentences.

➤ Activity

Each group of items below includes one topic, one main idea (expressed in a topic sentence), and two supporting details for that idea. In the space provided, label each item with one of the following:

> *T* — for the topic
> *MI* — for the main idea
> *SD* — for the supporting details

1. _SD_ Staying in the sun too long can cause sunstroke.

   _SD_ People develop skin cancer after years of working on their suntans.

   _T_ Time in the sun.

   _MI_ Spending time in the sun can be dangerous.

2. _SD_ One pitcher smooths the dirt on the pitcher's mound before he throws each pitch.

   _SD_ One infielder sits in the same spot on the dugout bench during every game.

   _MI_ Some baseball players think that certain superstitious habits help them win games.

   _T_ Superstitious baseball players.

3. _SD_ The creakings of a house settling may sound like a monster coming out of a grave.

   _MI_ Nighttime noises can be frightening to children.

   _SD_ Gusts of wind rattling a bedroom window can sound like invaders about to break in.

   _T_ Noises at night.

4. _SD_ Imagine your former sweetheart wearing a diaper or covered with smelly garbage.

   _T_ Recovering from a broken romance.

   _MI_ Certain methods can help you recover from a broken romance.

   _SD_ Each time you find yourself thinking of the other person, stop yourself by banging a fist on the table.

5. _MI_ TV has begun to deal with sex in a more realistic way.

   _SD_ Couples on TV now openly discuss topics such as birth control.

   _SD_ Bedroom scenes are now being shown in detail on some TV shows.

   _T_ TV's treatment of sex.

5 RECOGNIZING SPECIFIC DETAILS I

Specific details are examples, reasons, particulars, and facts. Such details are needed to support and explain a topic sentence effectively. They provide the evidence needed for us to understand, as well as to feel and experience, a writer's point.

Here is a topic sentence followed by two sets of supporting sentences. Which set provides sharp, specific details?

Topic sentence: Some poor people must struggle to make meals for themselves.

a. They gather up whatever free food items they can find in fast-food restaurants and take them home to use however they can. Instead of planning well-balanced meals, they base their diet on anything they can buy that is cheap and filling.

b. Some add hot water to the free packets of ketchup they get at McDonald's to make tomato soup. Others buy cans of cheap dog food and fry it like hamburger.

Explanation

The second set provides specific details: instead of a general statement about "free food items they find in fast-food restaurants and take . . . home to use however they can," we get a vivid detail we can see and picture clearly: "free packets of ketchup they get at McDonald's to make tomato soup."

Instead of a general statement about how the poor will "base their diet on anything they can buy that is cheap and filling," we get exact and vivid details: "Others buy cans of cheap dog food and fry it like hamburger."

Specific details are often like the information we find in a movie script. They provide us with such clear pictures that we could make a film of them if we wanted to. You would know just how to film the information given in the second cluster. You would show a poor person breaking open a McDonald's packet of ketchup and mixing it with water to make a kind of tomato soup. You would show someone opening a can of dog food and frying its contents like hamburger.

In contrast, the writer of the first cluster fails to provide the specific information needed. If you were asked to make a film based on the first cluster, you would have to figure out for yourself just what particulars you were going to show.

When you are working to provide specific supporting information in a paper, it might help to ask yourself, "Could someone easily film this information?" If the answer is "yes," you probably have good details.

➤ **Activity**

Each topic sentence below is followed by two sets of supporting details. Write *S* (for *specific*) in the space next to the set that provides specific support for the point. Write *G* (for *general*) next to the set that offers only vague, general support.

1. *Topic sentence:* My roommate is a messy person.

   _G_ a. He doesn't seem to mind that he can't find any clean clothes or dishes. He never puts anything back in its proper place; he just drops it wherever he happens to be. His side of the room looks as if a hurricane had gone through.

   _S_ b. His coffee cup is covered inside with a thick layer of green mold. I can't tell you what color his easy chair is; it has disappeared under a pile of dirty laundry. When he turns over in bed, I can hear the crunch of cracker crumbs beneath his body.

   Hint: Which supporting set could you make a film of?

2. *Topic sentence:* Roberta is very aggressive.

   _G_ a. Her aggressiveness is apparent in both her personal and professional life. She is never shy about extending social invitations. And while some people are turned off by her aggressive attitude, others are impressed by it and enjoy doing business with her.

   _S_ b. When she meets a man she likes, she is quick to say, "Let's go out sometime. What's your phone number?" In her job as a furniture salesperson, she will follow potential customers out onto the sidewalk as she tries to convince them to buy.

3. *Topic sentence:* Our new kitten causes us lots of trouble.

   _S_ a. He has shredded the curtains in my bedroom with his claws. He nearly drowned when he crawled into the washing machine. And my hands look like raw hamburger from his playful bites and scratches.

   _G_ b. It seems he destroys everything he touches. He's always getting into places he doesn't belong. Sometimes he plays too roughly, and that can be painful.

4. *Topic sentence:* My landlord is a softhearted person.

   _G_ a. Even though he wrote them himself, he sometimes ignores the official apartment rules in order to make his tenants happy.

_S_ b. Although the lease agreement states, "No pets," he brought my daughter a puppy after she told him how much she missed having one.

5. *Topic sentence:* The library is a distracting place to try to study.

_S_ a. It's hard to concentrate when a noisy eight-person poker game is going on on the floor beside you. It's also distracting to overhear remarks like, "Hey, Baby, what's your mother's address? I want to send her a thank-you card for having such a beautiful daughter."

_G_ b. Many students meet in the library to do group activities and socialize with one another. Others go there to flirt. It's easy to get more interested in all that activity than in paying attention to your studies.

6   RECOGNIZING SPECIFIC DETAILS II

➤ Activity

At several points in the following paragraphs you are given a choice of two sets of supporting details. Write *S* (for *specific*) in the space next to the set that provides specific support for the point. Write *G* (for *general*) next to the set that offers only vague, general support.

Paragraph 1

My daughter's boyfriend is a good-for-nothing young man. After knowing him for just three months, everyone in our family is opposed to the relationship.

For one thing, Russell is lazy.

_G_ a. He is always finding an excuse to avoid putting in an honest day's work. He never pitches in and helps with chores around our house, even when he's asked directly to do so. And his attitude about his job isn't any better. To hear him tell it, he deserves special treatment in the workplace. He thinks he's gone out of his way if he just shows up on time.

_S_ b. After starting a new job last week, he announced this Monday that he wasn't going to work because it was his <u>birthday</u>—just as if he is somebody special. And when my husband asked Russell to help put storm windows on the house next Saturday, Russell answered that he uses his weekends to catch up on sleep.

Another quality of Russell's which no one likes is that he is cheap.

___S___ c. When my daughter's birthday came around, Russell said he would take her out to Baldoni's, a fancy Italian restaurant. Then he changed his mind. Instead of spending a lot of money on a meal, he said, he wanted to buy her a really nice pair of earrings. So my daughter cooked dinner for him at her apartment. But there was no present, not even a little one. He claims he's waiting for a jewelry sale at Macy's. I don't think my daughter will ever see that "nice gift."

___G___ d. He makes big promises about all the nice things he's going to do for my daughter, but he never comes through. His words are cheap, and so is he. He's all talk and no action. My daughter isn't greedy, but it hurts her when Russell says he's going to take her someplace nice or give her something special and then nothing happens.

Worst of all, Russell is mean.

___G___ e. Russell seems to get special pleasure from hurting people when he feels they have a weak point. I have heard him make remarks that to him were just funny but that were really very insensitive. You've got to wonder about someone who needs to be ugly to other people just for the sake of being powerful. Sometimes I want to let him know how I feel. Everyone in the family is waiting anxiously for the day when my daughter will see Russell the way the rest of us see him.

___S___ f. When my husband was out of work, Russell said to him, "Well, you've got it made now, living off your wife." After my husband glared at him, he said, "Why're you getting sore? I'm just kidding." Sometimes he snaps at my daughter, saying things like "Don't make me wait—there are plenty of other babes who would like to take your place." At such times I want to blow off his head with a bazooka. Everyone in the family is waiting anxiously for the day when my daughter will see Russell the way the rest of us see him.

Paragraph 2

Many adult children move back in with their parents for some period of time. Although living with Mom and Dad again has some advantages, there are certain problems that are likely to arise.

One common problem is that children may expect their parents to do all the household chores.

___G___ a. They never think that they should take on their share of work around the house. Not only do they not help with their parents' chores; they don't even take responsibility for the extra work that their presence creates. Like babies, they go through the house making a mess that the parents are supposed to clean up. It's as if they think their parents are their servants.

_S_ b. They expect meals to appear on the table as if by magic. After they've eaten, they go off to work or play, never thinking about who's going to do the dishes. They drop their dirty laundry beside the washing machine, assuming that Mom will attend to it and return clean, folded clothes to their bedroom door. And speaking of their bedroom, every day they await the arrival of Mom's Maid Service to make the bed, pick up the floor, and dust the furniture.

Another problem that frequently arises is that parents forget their adult children are no longer adolescents.

_G_ c. Parents like this want to know everything about their adult children's lives. They don't think their kids, even though they are adults, should have any privacy. Whenever they see their children doing anything, they want to know all the details. It's as though their children are still teenagers who are expected to report all their activities. Naturally, adult children get irritated when they are treated as if they were little kids.

_S_ d. They may insist upon knowing far more about their children's comings and goings than the children want to share. For example, if such parents see their adult son heading out the door, they demand to know: Where is he going? Who will he be with? What will he be doing? What time will he be back? In addition, they may not let their adult child have any privacy. If their daughter and a date are sitting in the living room, for instance, they may join them there and start peppering the young man with questions about his family and his job, as if they were interviewing him for the position of son-in-law.

Finally, there may be financial problems when an adult child returns to live at home.

_S_ e. Having an extra adult in the household creates extra expenses. But many adult children don't offer to help deal with those extra costs. Adult children often eat at home, causing the grocery bill to climb. They may stay in a formerly unused room, which now needs to be heated and lit. They produce extra laundry to be washed. They use the telephone, adding to the long-distance bill. For all these reasons, adult children should expect to pay a reasonable room and board fee to their parents.

_G_ f. It's expensive to have another adult living in the household. Adult children would be paying a lot of bills on their own if they weren't staying with their parents. It's only fair that they share the expenses at their parents' house. They should consider all the ways that their living at home is increasing their parents' expenses. Then they should insist upon covering their share of the costs.

7 PROVIDING SPECIFIC DETAILS

➤ Activity   _Answers will vary._

Each of the sentences that follow contains a general word or words, set off in _italic_ type. Substitute sharp, specific words in each case.

Example   Before dinner I had _several things to do_.

Before dinner I had to wash the lunch dishes, do some homework,

and call a garage about getting my car serviced.

1. To pass the time in the hospital waiting area, I browsed through some _reading matter_.

    old Life and Reader's Digest magazines and a copy of the Los Angeles Times

    _____

2. When my marriage broke up, I felt _various emotions_.

    fear, sadness, and relief _____

    _____

3. In the car accident I suffered _a number of injuries_.

    a broken arm, a sprained neck, and bruises all along the left side of my body

    _____

4. At the carnival we went on _several rides_.

    the merry-go-round, roller coaster, and Ferris wheel _____

    _____

5. While watching TV I like to eat _salty snacks_.

    pretzels, popcorn, and peanuts _____

    _____

6. The cafeteria offered *several choices* for dessert.

   fruit salad, blueberry pie, and chocolate bread pudding

7. Before we play cards, remove those *things* from the table.

   dishes, napkins, flowers, and books

8. My brother's room has *a lot of electronic equipment.*

   a stereo, small TV, VCR, and two radios

9. *Bugs* invaded our kitchen and pantry this summer.

   Carpenter ants, silverfish, and roaches

10. All last week, *the weather was terrible.*

    it poured almost constantly, thundering, lightning, and even hailing much of the

    time

8 SELECTING DETAILS THAT FIT

The details in your paper must all clearly relate to and support your main point. If a detail does not support your point, leave it out. Otherwise, your paper will lack unity. For example, see if you can circle the letters of the **two** sentences that do *not* support the topic sentence below.

Topic sentence: Rita is a kind friend.

   a. When one of her friends is sick, Rita offers to help out by doing any needed grocery shopping.
   b. She has been known to go back to a store the day after buying something to return the excess change a clerk mistakenly gave her.
   c. Rita remembers her friends' birthdays and often arranges some sort of celebration.
   d. Although she makes a modest salary, Rita donates generously to various charities.
   e. She listens to her friends' troubles with patience and understanding.

Explanation

> Returning money to a store clerk is not support for the idea that Rita is a kind *friend*, so sentence *b* does not support the topic sentence. Also, while Rita's donations to various charities (sentence *d*) help show she is generous, they do not support the idea of her being a kind friend. The other three statements all clearly back up the topic sentence—they are about how Rita treats her friends kindly.

➤ Activity

Circle the **two** items that do *not* support the topic sentence in each group below.

1. *Topic sentence:* I'm a perfect example of someone who has "math anxiety."

   (a.) Fear of math is almost as widespread as fear of public speaking.

   b. I feel dread every time I sit down to take our Friday math quiz.

   c. During the math midterm, I "froze" and didn't even try to answer most of the questions.

   (d.) I also have a great deal of anxiety when I sit down to write a paper.

   e. I turned down a salesclerk job because I would have had to figure out how much change customers should get back.

2. *Topic sentence:* Carpooling has various benefits for students.

   a. Their gas and parking expenses are lower in a car pool.

   (b.) Recent government regulations require some workers to use a car pool.

   c. Students who are not driving can study or sleep on the way.

   d. Traveling with other students provides companionship and support.

   (e.) Car pools become more popular during hard economic times.

3. *Topic sentence:* Drinking coffee can have unpleasant effects.

   (a.) Some people don't like the taste of decaffeinated coffees.

   b. Coffee in the evening can interfere with sleep at night.

   (c.) As addictions go, coffee is less dangerous than tobacco.

   d. Too much coffee can cause the hands to shake.

   e. Drinking too much coffee can lead to a faster heartbeat and lightheadedness.

4. *Topic sentence:* Some people have very poor telephone manners.

   a. They never identify themselves, but just begin the conversation.

   (b.) They often make their calls on cordless phones.

(c.) They have an unlisted telephone number.

d. They talk to people around them at the same time that they're talking on the phone.

e. They often call around 6 p.m., which is most people's dinner hour.

5. *Topic sentence:* Convenience stores live up to their name.

a. Convenience stores are close to home.

(b.) At certain times of the day, there may be only one clerk available to both serve people and handle the cash register.

(c.) Some convenience-store chains sell products under their own brand name.

d. Convenience stores are open till late or all night.

e. Parking is right outside.

9   PROVIDING DETAILS THAT FIT

➤ **Activity 1**   *Answers will vary.*

Each topic sentence below is followed by one item of support. See if you can add a second item in each case. Make sure your item truly supports the topic sentence.

1. *Topic sentence:* Lunch at that cafeteria is terrible.

a. The french fries are always lukewarm and soggy.

b. *The soups are watery.* _____

2. *Topic sentence:* My little sister's room was a mess.

a. Two of her dresses were lying on the floor, unbuttoned and inside out.

b. *Crayons were spread all over, some crushed from being stepped on.* ___

3. *Topic sentence:* The student lounge is an impossible place to try to study.

a. A television is always blaring in one corner of the lounge.

b. *Frisbees are often sailing through the air.* _____

4. *Topic sentence:* I had to deal with some rude behavior today.

a. A teacher cut me off in the middle of a question.

b. *Someone drove his car headfirst into the parking space I was trying to back into.* ___

5. *Topic sentence:* When I want people to like me, I do several things.

    a. I ask them a lot of questions about themselves, such as what they're taking in school.

    b. *I share personal information about myself with them.* _____

_____

➤ Activity 2   *Answers will vary.*

See if you can add two items of support for each of the topic sentences below.

1. *Topic sentence:* The car was extensively damaged in the accident.

    a. The windshield and the driver's side windows were shattered.

    b. *The driver's door was bent into a bowl shape.* _____

    c. *The left front wheel was ripped into strips.* _____

2. *Topic sentence:* I spent the night preparing for the history exam.

    a. From 10 p.m. to 2 a.m., I studied all the notes I took in class.

    b. *From 2 to 5 a.m., I reviewed my study notes based on the textbook.* _____

    c. *For the next two hours, Ken and I tested each other on important points.* _____

3. *Topic sentence:* My parents were very strict when I was growing up.

    a. I was allowed to watch TV for one hour a day, period.

    b. *No candy was allowed in the house.* _____

    c. *I had to do the dishes every night before going out.* _____

4. *Topic sentence:* Yesterday there was a robbery at the bank where I work.

    a. Two men wearing aviator sunglasses pointed guns at us.

    b. *They made all the customers, including a woman in a wheelchair, lie down on the floor on their stomachs.* _____

    c. *One of them handed me a huge cotton sack and yelled, "Fill this up! Now!"* _____

5. *Topic sentence:* There was a lot of storm damage in the town.

    a. Half of the basements in the town were flooded.

    b. *Winds knocked out storefront windows, allowing heavy rains to damage the rugs and wood floors.* _____

    c. *Lightning slashed through the fifty-foot oak in the park.* _____

10 PROVIDING DETAILS IN A PARAGRAPH

➤ Activity   *Answers will vary.*

The following paragraph needs specific details to back up its three supporting points. In the spaces provided, write two or three sentences of convincing details for each supporting point.

An Unpleasant Eating Experience

My family and I will never eat again at the new neighborhood restaurant. First of all, the service was poor. _____
We waited for ten minutes before getting menus. Then it took another ten

minutes before our orders were taken. I hate to tell you how long it took to get

our food—another twenty minutes.

_____

Second, the prices were very high. _____
A simple Greek salad cost $9.50, and a tuna salad sandwich cost $7.50. We

were even charged for refills of hot tea.

_____

_____

Most of all, the food was not very good. _____
The lettuce in our salads looked like it had been rescued from a dumpster. The

tuna sandwich contained so much mayonnaise that it leaked with every bite.

Believe it or not, even the water had a foul taste.

_____

11 OMITTING AND GROUPING DETAILS WHEN PLANNING A PAPER

One common way to develop material for a paper is to make up a list of details about your topic. The next steps are to (1) omit details that don't truly support your topic and (2) group together remaining details in logical ways. The ability to omit details that don't fit and to group together related details is part of learning how to write effectively.

See if you can figure out a way of putting the following details into three groups. Put an *A* in front of the details that go with one group, a *B* in front of the details that go with a second group, and a *C* in front of the details that make up a third group. Cross out the four details that do not relate to the topic sentence.

Topic sentence: The vacation was a disaster.

_____ Rental agent a cousin of mine

_____ The house a real disappointment

_____ Bedrooms the size of closets

_____ Rain four of the seven days we were there

_____ Daughter badly sunburned on one hazy day

_____ Dismal weather

_____ Glorious sunset only the last night we were there

_____ Air very humid

_____ Husband caught a virus and had days of digestive problems

_____ House not close to the lake but a half-mile hike

_____ Air conditioning did not work

_____ Too cold to go out in the evenings

_____ Large color television that worked well

_____ Medical problems

_____ Son badly cut his finger and had to get stitches at local hospital

_____ Landlord was sympathetic and gave us a discount

Explanation:

After thinking about the list for a while, you probably realized that the details about the house form one group: the house was a disappointment because its bedrooms were the size of closets, it was not close to the lake, and the air conditioning did not work. Details about the bad weather form another group: a lot of rain, humid air, and cold evenings. Finally, there are details about medical problems: a bad sunburn, a virus, and a cut finger.

The main idea—that the vacation was a disaster—can be supported with three kinds of evidence: a disappointing rental house, dismal weather, and medical problems. The other four items in the list do not logically go with any of these three groups and so should be omitted.

The two activities that follow will give you practice in omitting and grouping details.

➤ **Activity 1**

See if you can figure out a way of putting the following details into three groups. Put an *A* in front of the details that go with one group, a *B* in front of the details that go with a second group, and a *C* in front of the details that make up a third group. Cross out the four details that do not relate to the topic sentence.

Topic sentence: My return to school at the age of 38 has created special challenges for my family.

_A_ School means extra work for my husband, Jack.

_A_ Jack has to help kids with their homework.

____ ~~The children have been on the honor roll at school all year.~~

_B_ Often impossible for me to be with the kids when they're sick.

_B_ Could not attend my daughter's birthday party this year.

_B_ School cuts into my time with my children.

_C_ Jack gets tired of hearing stories of fellow students he doesn't know.

____ ~~Most of my fellow students are in their 20's.~~

_A_ Jack has to bathe children and put them to bed.

_C_ He worries I will get a "crush" on my teacher.

_A_ Cooking dinner is something Jack now must do.

_C_ No quiet time after dinner for Jack and me to talk about our day.

_C_ School sometimes creates a strain between Jack and me.

_B_ I haven't been to one of my son's Little League games.

____ ~~My employer pays most of my tuition.~~

____ ~~Jack once took an accounting course at the same college I attend.~~

➤ **Activity 2**

Follow the directions for Activity 1.

Topic sentence: Living at home while going to school can be a very good idea.

__A__   Home a quieter place to study than a noisy college dorm.

__A__   It can produce better grades.

_____   ~~Some students live at apartments near a college.~~

__B__   It can be good for the relationship between a student and parents.

__B__   Parents can begin to know student as an adult instead of a child.

__B__   Parents and student will more easily find time just to talk.

__C__   Parents usually charge a low fee for room and board.

_____   ~~Some students live at home until they marry.~~

__C__   Living at home means not paying to furnish an apartment or dorm room.

__C__   It's economical to split the grocery bill with parents.

__C__   It can be cheaper to live at home than on one's own.

_____   ~~Students living at home will need a car or access to buses that go to school.~~

__A__   At home, students aren't distracted by campus social activities.

__A__   College roommates may encourage more goofing off than studying.

_____   ~~College activities can help students meet new friends.~~

__B__   Students can begin to appreciate parents as people, not just as parents.

12   USING TRANSITIONS

As already stated, transitions are signal words that help readers follow the direction of the writer's thought. To see the value of transitions, look at the two versions of the short paragraph below. Check the version that is easier to read and understand.

_____   To study a textbook more effectively, follow a few helpful steps. Preview the reading, taking a couple of minutes to get a quick sense of what the selection is about. Read and mark the selection, using a highlighter pen to set off important points. Write up a set of study notes that summarize the most important ideas in the selection. Go over and over the ideas in your notes until you know the material.

____ To study a textbook more effectively, follow a few helpful steps. First, preview the reading, taking a couple of minutes to get a quick sense of what the selection is about. Next, read and mark the selection, using a highlighter pen to set off important points. Then write up a set of study notes that summarize the most important ideas in the selection. Finally, go over and over the ideas in your notes until you know the material.

You no doubt chose the second version. The time transitions—*first, next, then, finally*—emphasize the order in which the steps are to be done. The transitions also make clear when one step ends and the other begins.

➤ Activity

The following paragraphs use a listing order or a time order. Fill in the blanks with appropriate transitions from the box above each paragraph. Use every transition once.

In addition	First of all	Finally

1. My blind date with Walter was truly dreadful. ____*First of all*____, he was the rudest date I've ever had. Although he'd said he would pick me up at 7, he showed up at 7:35. Then he just sat in the driveway, gunning his engine. When he realized I wasn't going to walk out to the car, he came to the door and shouted through it, "Hey! You ready or what?" ____*In addition*____, he was just plain dumb. Throughout the evening, I tried everything to get a conversation going. But whenever I mentioned a book, a movie, a sport, or a news event, he would say, "Never heard of it." ____*Finally*____, he was cheap. When we sat down in the restaurant, he handed me a menu and said, "Don't order anything over five dollars." I learned a valuable lesson from my date with Walter— always bring enough money so you can take a bus home.

Then	While	After	When

2. To relieve the stress I feel after a day of work and school, I take the following steps. To start with, I get off the bus a mile from my apartment. I find a brisk walk helps me shake off the dragged-out feeling I often have at the day's end. _____*When*_____ I get home, I make myself a cup of tea and lie down on the couch with my feet up. _____*While*_____ I lie there, I often look through a catalog and imagine having the money to buy all the nice things I see. _____*Then*_____, if I've had an especially hard day, I run a deep bath with plenty of nice-smelling bath oil in it. _____*After*_____ a good long soak in the hot water, I find the cares of the day have drifted away.

Another	Last of all	For one thing

3. There are several reasons why high schools should require students to wear uniforms. _____*For one thing*_____, uniforms would save money for parents and children. It would be a big relief for everyone if they could simply buy two or three inexpensive uniforms, instead of constantly shelling out for designer jeans and other high-priced clothes. _____*Another*_____ advantage of uniforms is that students would not have to spend time worrying about clothes. They would get up every day knowing what they were wearing to school, so they could concentrate more on schoolwork and less on making a fashion statement. _____*Last of all*_____, uniforms would make the division between rich and poor students less obvious. If wealthy students didn't show off their expensive clothes, and students from modest backgrounds didn't feel second-rate because of their lower-cost wardrobes, everyone would get along better.

Before	As	While	Then	When

4. An incident happened yesterday that made me very angry. I got off the bus and started walking the four blocks to my friend's house. _____*As* (or *While*)_____ I walked along, I noticed a group of boys gathered on the sidewalk about a block ahead of me. _____*When*_____ they saw me, they stopped talking. Suddenly nervous, I thought about crossing the street to avoid them. But as I came nearer and heard them start to whistle, a different feeling came over me. Instead of being afraid, I was suddenly angry. Why should I have to worry about being hassled just because I was a woman? I stared straight at the boys and continued walking. _____*Then*_____ the remarks started. "Oooh, baby. Looking fine today," said one. I ignored him. Next another one made a dirty remark about my underwear. _____*Before*_____ I knew what I was doing, I turned on him. "Do you have a mother? Or any sisters?" I demanded. He looked astonished and didn't answer me. I went on. "Is it OK with you if men speak to them like that? Doesn't it bother you that they can't walk down the street without some creep bothering them?" _____*While* (or *As*)_____ I was speaking, the other boys backed away. The one I was facing gave a nervous-sounding laugh, then backed away too. I kept walking. An hour later, I was still shaking with anger.

13 ORGANIZING DETAILS IN A PARAGRAPH

The supporting details in a paragraph must be organized in a meaningful way. The two most common methods of organizing details are to use a listing order and a time order. The activities that follow will give you practice in both methods of organization.

➤ Activity 1

Use *listing order* to arrange the scrambled list of sentences below. Number each supporting sentence 1, 2, 3, . . . so that you go from the least to the most important item.

Note that transitions will help by making clear the relationships between sentences.

Topic sentence: My after-school job has provided me with important benefits.

___2___ Since the job is in the morning, it usually keeps me from staying up too late.

___6___ Without the money I've earned, I would not have been able to pay my tuition.

___3___ A second value of the job is that it's helped me make new friends.

___1___ For one thing, it's helped me manage my time.

___4___ One of my co-workers loves baseball as much as I do, and we've become sports buddies.

___5___ The biggest advantage of the job is that it's allowed me to stay in school.

➤ Activity 2

Follow the directions for Activity 1.

Topic sentence: There are several reasons people daydream.

___2___ Some production line workers, for instance, might dream about running the company.

___3___ Being without something also leads to daydreaming.

___6___ For example, an angry student might dream about dropping his instructor out of a classroom window.

___4___ A starving person will dream about food, or a poor person will dream about owning a house or car.

___1___ One cause of daydreaming is boring jobs that are bearable only when workers imagine themselves doing something else.

___5___ A final reason for daydreaming is to deal with angry feelings.

➤ Activity 3

Use *time order* to arrange the scrambled sentences below. Number the supporting sentences in the order in which they occur in time (1, 2, 3 . . .).

Note that transitions will help by making clear the relationships between sentences.

Topic sentence: There are several steps you can take to find an apartment.

___1___ Check the classified ads and two or three real estate offices for apartments within your price range and desired location.

___5___ When you have chosen your apartment, have a lawyer or a person who knows leases examine your lease before you sign it.

___2___ Then make up a list of the most promising places.

___4___ As you inspect each apartment, make sure that faucets, toilets, stove, and electrical outlets are working properly.

___3___ After you have a solid list, visit at least five of the most promising apartments.

➤ Activity 4

Follow the directions for Activity 3.

Topic sentence: The story of a man named Gary can be an inspiration to many.

___2___ By age seventeen he regularly came to school drunk.

___4___ Gary's moment of truth came at age twenty-five, when he barely escaped death in a drunk-driving incident.

___6___ After an intensive three-month treatment, he was free of alcohol for the first time in over ten years.

___1___ Gary began stealing liquor from his parents when he was fourteen.

___7___ He took advantage of being alcohol-free and returned to college and received a degree.

___8___ Now he works as a counselor in the same treatment center that gave him his second chance.

___3___ In his early twenties, he realized he was completely dependent on alcohol.

___5___ Soon after the accident, he committed himself to a local alcohol-recovery center.

14 PREWRITING

These activities will give you practice in some of the prewriting strategies you can use to generate material for a paper.

Answers will vary.

➤ Activity 1: Freewriting

On a sheet of paper, freewrite for several minutes on the best or worst job you ever had. Don't worry about grammar, punctuation, or spelling. Without stopping, try to write about whatever comes into your head concerning your best or worst job.

➤ Activity 2: Questioning

On another sheet of paper, answer the following questions about your job.

- When did you have the job?
- Where did you work?
- What did you do?
- Whom did you work for?
- Why did you like or dislike the job? (Give one reason and some details that support that reason.)
- What is another reason you liked or disliked the job? What are some details that support the second reason?
- Can you think of a third reason you liked or did not like the job? What are some details that support the third reason?

➤ Activity 3: Clustering

In the center of a blank sheet of paper, write "best job" or "worst job" and circle it. Then, around the circle, add reasons and details about the job. Use a series of boxes, circles, or other shapes, along with connecting lines, to set off the reasons and details. In other words, try to think about and explore your topic in a very visual way.

➤ Activity 4: List Making

On separate paper, make a list of details about the job. Don't worry about putting them in a certain order. Just get down as many details about the job as occur to you. The list can include specific reasons you liked or did not like the job and specific details supporting those reasons.

15 OUTLINING, DRAFTING, AND REVISING A PAPER

Here you will get practice in the writing steps that follow prewriting: outlining, drafting, and revising the paper.

Answers will vary.

➤ Activity 1: Scratch Outline

Based on the list you have prepared, see if you can prepare a scratch outline made up of the three main reasons you liked or did not like the job.

_____ was the best (*or* worst) job I ever had.

Reason 1: _____

Reason 2: _____

Reason 3: _____

➤ Activity 2: First Draft

Now write a first draft of your paper. Begin with your topic sentence stating that a certain job was the best or worst one you ever had. Then state the first reason why it was such a job, followed by specific details that support that reason. Next, state the second reason, followed by specific details supporting that reason. Finally, state the third reason, followed with support.

Don't worry about grammar, punctuation, or spelling. Just concentrate on getting down on paper the details about the job. You may find it helpful to look at the first draft by Wanda (pages 15–16) on why Helen was a terrible roommate.

➤ Activity 3: Revising the Draft

Ideally, you will have a chance to put the paper aside for a while before doing the second draft. In your second draft, try to do all of the following:

- Add transition words such as *first of all, another, and finally* to introduce each of the three reasons you liked or disliked the job.
- Omit any details that do not truly support your topic sentence.
- Add more details as needed, making sure you have plenty of specific support for each of your three reasons.
- In general, improve the flow of your writing.
- Be sure to include a final sentence that rounds off the paper, bringing it to a close.

➤ Activity 4: Proofreading

When you have your almost-final draft of the paper, proofread it in the following ways:

- Using your dictionary (or a spell-check program on your word processor), check any words that you think might be misspelled.

- Drawing upon the suggestions in the proofreading chapter (pages 403–411), check your paper for sentence-skills mistakes.

- Read the paper aloud, listening for awkward wordings and places where the meaning is unclear. Make the changes needed for the paper to read smoothly and clearly. Even better, see if you can get another person to read the draft aloud to you. The spots that this person has trouble reading are spots where you may have to do some rewriting.

- Take a sheet of paper and cover your paper, so that you can expose and carefully check one line at a time. Or, read the paper backwards, from the end of the paragraph to the beginning. Look for typos, omitted words, and other remaining errors.

Don't fail to do a careful proofreading. You may be tired of working on the paper at this point, but you want to make the extra effort needed to make the paper as good as possible. A final push can mean the difference between a higher and a lower grade.

3 / Paper Basics and Writing Assignments

The paragraph writing assignments in this chapter serve two purposes. First, they will help you apply the basic writing principles that you learned in the previous two chapters. Second, they will give you practice in the rules of grammar, punctuation, mechanics, and usage presented in the rest of this book. It is only by applying the basic writing principles and rules in actual writing that you can truly master them.

SENTENCE AND PAPER BASICS

As you work your way through *Basic English Brushup*, your writing will become more and more skillful. Following, however, is some basic information on grammar and paper format to review before you begin the writing assignments.

Beginning a Sentence

Begin each sentence with a **capital letter**.

- **M**y four brothers share one bedroom.
- **A**bout 20 percent of the Earth is permanently frozen.
- **W**e record movies overnight and watch them on the weekends.

Ending a Sentence

The Period (.)

Use a **period** at the end of a statement, a mild command, or an indirect question.

- The children jumped over all the rain puddles.
  (A statement)
- Hand me the red pen.
  (A mild command)
- I wonder if there will be a surprise quiz today.
  (An indirect question)

The Question Mark (?)

Use a **question mark** after a sentence that asks a question.

- Are you ready for the exam**?**
- How did the car get scratched**?**
- "Can I have your phone number**?**" Susanne asked Phil.

Indirect questions tell the reader about questions, rather than asking them directly. They end with periods, not question marks.

- The teacher asked if we were ready for the exam**.**
- I wonder how the car got scratched**.**
- Susanne asked Phil if she could have his phone number**.**

The Exclamation Point (!)

Use an **exclamation point** after a word or statement that expresses extreme emotion or that gives a strong command.

- Help**!**
- Wow**!**
- I just got a huge raise**!**
- Cut that out**!**

Note: Exclamation points lose their power if they are used too frequently. Use them only when you wish to emphasize strong emotion.

➤ Practice 1

Above each line, add the capital letter needed. Also add the missing period, question mark, or exclamation point at the end of the sentence.

   Example   *W*
                  *W*ill we see each other again?

1. *M*
   *m*y car has trouble starting on cold mornings.

2. *H*
   *h*ow many courses are you taking this semester?

3. *T*
   *t*hat helicopter is going to crash!

4. *P*
   *p*lease fill out an application, and then take a seat.

5. *C*
   *c*an I use your computer?

6. *I*
   *i*ced tea was first served at the 1904 World's Fair.

7. *W*
   *w*atch out for that barbed wire!

8. *M*
   ꭓy brother asked if he could use my computer.

9. *D*
   ꭰoes it feel like it's going to rain?

10. *N*
    ꭒot a single student has dropped out of the class.

Preparing a Paper

Following are important guidelines for preparing a paper.

The Title

Most of your school papers will begin with a title. The title of a typed paper should be about an inch and a half from the top of the page. The title of a handwritten paper should be on the top line of the first page. For example, here are the title and the opening part of a paper about the author's brother.

	A Shy Brother
	My older brother is the shyest person I know. Whenever
	there are more than two people in a group, he will stop talking.
	He has never raised his hand to answer a question in class…

Looking at the above correctly written example, identify each of the following statements as either true (**T**) or false (**F**).

_____ 1. The title should be set off in quotation marks.

_____ 2. The title should have a period after it.

_____ 3. The title should be capitalized.

_____ 4. The title should be centered on the page.

_____ 5. A line should be skipped between the title and the first sentence.

You should have answered *false* for the first two items and *true* for the last three. Here is a checklist that summarizes how to handle a title:

- Type the title about an inch and a half below the top of the first page. For handwritten papers, put the title on the top line of the first page.

- Center the title.

- Do not use quotation marks around the title or put a period after the title.

- Capitalize each word in the title. (The only exceptions are small words such as *of, in,* or *for* in the middle of a title.)
- Skip a line between the title and the first sentence of the paper.

Indenting the First Line

The first line of a paragraph should be indented—that is, set in—about one-half inch from the left-hand margin. (Note the indentation of the first line of the paper on the shy brother.) Do not indent the other sentences in a paragraph.

Margins

Leave enough margin on all four sides of a paper to avoid a crowded look. The standard margins are about an inch and a half on the top and left side of the paper and an inch on the right and at the bottom.

Other Guidelines

1 Use full-sized paper (8½ by 11 inches).

2 Write or type on only one side of the paper.

3 Ideally, type your paper using double-spacing. But if you are writing by hand, do the following:

- Use blue or black ink—never pencil.
- Use wide-lined paper, or write on every other line of narrow-lined paper.
- Write letters and punctuation marks as clearly as you can, taking care to distinguish between small and capital letters.

4 If your instructor so requests, include a cover page on which you put your name, the date, and the title and section number of your course.

➤ Practice 2

What **five** corrections are needed in the student paper shown below? Rewrite the paper on the lines provided, adding the corrections. Then explain the corrections in the five numbered spaces on the next page.

	Family meetings
	My family has found various ways to get along well. One way is having
	family meetings. We meet twice a month to discuss and handle our
	problems before they get out of hand. This has saved the members of
	my family a great deal of aggravation. For instance, when my brother...

	A corrected version of the paper: *Family Meetings*
	My family has found various ways to get along well.
	One way is having family meetings. We meet twice a month to
	discuss and handle our problems before they get out of hand.
	This has saved the members of my family a great deal of
	aggravation. For instance, when my brother. . .

1. *The title should be centered.*

2. *The second word in the title should be capitalized.*

3. *A line should be skipped after the title.*

4. *The paragraph's first line should be indented.*

5. *There should be a margin on the right side.*

WRITING ASSIGNMENTS

Writing is best done on topics about which you have information, and in which you have interest. To ensure that you have a choice of topics, following are ten groups of three writing assignments. Your instructor may ask you, for example, to write on your choice of one of the three topics in Group A. As the semester proceeds, he or she may ask you to write paragraphs on your choice of topics from additional groups as well.

Group A

1   Hometown.   If a friend wrote to you asking whether your hometown would be a good place for him or her to move to, what would be your response? Write a one-paragraph letter to your friend explaining the advantages or disadvantages of living in your hometown. Begin your remarks with a specific recommendation to your friend; it will serve as the topic sentence of the paragraph. Cover such matters as employment, recreation, housing, schools, and safety. Be sure your details are as specific and descriptive as you can make them. To connect your ideas, use transitions such as *in addition, furthermore, on the other hand*, and *however*.

2   Leaving Home. Sooner or later most young people leave the home they have grown up in to begin life on their own. While the feeling of independence may be thrilling, flying the coop also involves numerous problems. Write about one problem that many people are likely to meet when they live away from home for the first time, such as a problem with finances, household and personal chores, or loneliness. Explain the problem in detail, using examples throughout. To make your examples persuasive and interesting, take sufficient prewriting time to create a list of realistic and colorful details that you can draw upon.

3   Best or Worst Childhood Experience.   Some of our most vivid memories are of things that happened to us as children, and these memories don't ever seem to fade. In fact, many elderly people say that childhood memories are clearer to them than things that happened yesterday. Think back to one of the best or worst experiences you had as a child. Try to remember the details of the event—sights, sounds, smells, textures, tastes.

You might begin by freewriting for ten minutes or so about good or bad childhood experiences. That freewriting may suggest to you a topic you will want to develop.

After you have decided on a topic, try to write a clear sentence stating what the experience was and whether it was one of the best or worst of your childhood. For example, "The time I was beaten up coming home from my first day in fifth grade was one of my worst childhood moments."

You may then find it helpful to make a list in which you jot down as many details as you can remember about the experience. Stick with a single experience, and don't try to describe too much. If a week you spent at summer camp was an unpleasant experience, don't try to write about the entire week. Just describe one horrible moment or event.

When you write the paper, use a time order to organize details: first this happened, then this, next this, and so on.

As you write, imagine that someone is going to make a short film based on your paragraph. Try to provide vivid details, quotations, and pictures for the filmmaker to shoot.

Group B

1   A Certain Song or Movie.   Is there a certain song or movie that is especially memorable to you? If so, mention the title of the song (the title should be in quotation marks) or movie (the title should be underlined or in italics), and write about the time when the song or movie became so meaningful to you. To be convincing, you will need to include numerous details and clear explanations.

2   A Special Place or Object.   Write a paragraph describing either a place or an object you respond to with strong emotion, such as love, fear, warmth, dread, joy, or sadness. Specific details and vivid description will need to be provided if your emotional reaction is to be understood.

3   A Special Photograph.   We tend to take photographs for granted, but they are magical things. They freeze moments forever, capturing small pieces of time within their borders. Find a photograph that has special meaning for you. Write a paper which describes the photograph and explains why it is special to you.

You might want to first describe the event, place, person or persons that the photograph shows. Then explain the special significance that the photograph has for you. Attach the photograph (or a photocopy of it) to the final draft of your paper.

Group C

1   A Good or Bad Day in Your Life.   Write in detail about a recent good or bad day in your life—your activities, feelings, and experiences during the day. You might begin by making a list of things that you did, felt, saw, thought, heard, and said during that day. Your aim is to accumulate a great many details that you can draw upon later as you begin writing your paper. Making a long list is an excellent way to get started.

Then select and develop those details that best support the idea that the day was a good one or a bad one. Organize your paragraph using a time order—first this happened, then this, next this, and so on.

2   Directions to a Place.   Write a set of specific directions on how to get from the English classroom to your house. Imagine you are giving these directions to a stranger who has just come into the room and who wants to deliver a million dollars to your home. You want, naturally, to give exact directions, including various landmarks that may guide the way, for the stranger does not know the area.

To help you write the paper, first make up a list of all the directions involved. Also, use words like *next, then*, and *after* to help the reader follow clearly as you move from one direction to the next.

3   Problem with a Machine.   We have all had unpleasant experiences with various types of machines. Nothing is more frustrating, for example, than trying to tune in a fuzzy television set in time for a favorite show, obtain a drink from an uncooperative vending machine, or deal with a recurring car problem.

Write a paper about a bad experience you have had with a machine. Use specific details to make your readers understand what your problem was and feel the emotions you felt at the time. To stimulate your memory, here is a brief list of troublemaking machines:

automobile	radio or stereo set	television or VCR
vacuum cleaner	bicycle	computer
hair dryer	motorcycle	washing machine or dryer
lawn mower	vending machine	stove

Group D

1   A Helpful Experience.   Write an account of an experience you have had that taught you something important. It might involve a mistake you made or an event that gave you insight into yourself or others. Perhaps you have had school problems that taught you to be a more effective student, or you have had a conflict with someone that you now understand could have been avoided. Whatever experience you choose to write about, be sure to tell how it has changed your way of thinking.

2   Hindsight.   Occasionally, we call someone a "Monday-morning quarterback." By this we mean that it's easy to say what should have been done after an event (or game) is over. But while we're in the midst of our daily lives, it's hard to know which is the right decision to make or what is the right course of action. We've all looked back and thought, "I wish I'd done . . ." or "I wish I'd said . . ."

Think back to a year or two ago. What is the best advice someone could have given you then? Freewrite for ten minutes or so about how your life might have changed if you have been given that advice.

Then go on to write a paper that begins with a topic sentence something like this, "I wish someone had told me a year ago to cut back a little on my work hours while I'm in college."

3   Things to Accomplish in the Next Year.   Everyone has goals. Some goals, like graduating from college, are realistic; others, like winning a lottery, are mainly fantasy. Think about what you would like to accomplish between today and one year from today. Make the goals realistic ones which you might actually accomplish through determination, persistence, and hard work.

Start by making a list of a number of goals that would make sense for you in the next year. Here is one student's list:

— Get A's or B's in at least half my classes
— Lose ten pounds
— Get a better part-time job
— Take a typing course
— Stay away from people who are bad influences
— Cut down my TV time to ten hours a week
— Focus more on the future and less on old family problems
— Begin an exercise schedule
— Stop smoking

Begin your paper with a general point, such as "There are three goals I intend to accomplish in the following year." Choose the goals from the list you've written, and develop each with specific details. For instance, the student mentioned above developed the idea of getting a better part-time job by writing, "For the past six months I've been working fifteen hours a week at the Burger Hut near my home. I get paid only an hourly rate there. One of my goals is to get another restaurant job where I can make money through tips as well."

Arrange the items in an order that makes sense to you. Save what you feel is the most important goal for last.

Group E

1   A Problem on Campus.   Students on every college campus seem to have certain complaints about their school. They feel there are problems with grades, teachers, buildings, registration procedures, or security, for example. Write a paragraph about a problem on your campus.

You might begin by asking yourself a series of questions: What are some problems on campus? When do they occur? Where do they occur? Why do they occur? How do they affect people? As you answer such questions, you will gradually get a sense of a particular problem you may be able to write about.

State the problem in the first sentence of your paragraph. For example, you could begin with "The school library at Lincoln College is a distracting place to study." Then provide solid supporting details that support your statement. In your concluding sentence, you might mention a possible solution.

2   Parents and Children.   It has been said that the older we get, the more we see our parents in ourselves. Indeed, any of our habits (good and bad), beliefs, and temperaments can often be traced to one of our parents.

Write a paragraph in which you describe three characteristics you have "inherited" from a parent. You might want to think about your topic by asking yourself a series of questions: "How am I like my mother (or father)?" "When and where am I like her (or him)?" "Why am I like her (or him)?"

One student who did such a paper used as her topic sentence the following statement: "Although I hate to admit it, I know that in several ways I'm just like my mom." She then went on to describe how she works too hard, worries too much, and judges other people too harshly. Another student wrote, "I resemble my father in my love of TV sports, my habit of putting things off, and my reluctance to show my feelings." Be sure to include examples for each of the characteristics you mention.

3   Students and Jobs.   Increasingly, educators are concerned about the time that many students spend working in part-time jobs each week, as opposed to time spent studying or involved in extracurricular activities. Examine the issue yourself by writing a paragraph that begins with and supports this point: "Full-time students should not work more than fifteen hours a week."

Before you begin, consider various aspects of this issue. How much time do students need to make the most of school? What can be the problems that result from working, say, thirty hours a week? What do most students do with their earnings? Jot down a series of notes as you think about this issue, and decide upon three separate reasons why students should not work more than fifteen hours a week. As you go on to write the first draft of your paragraph, introduce each of your reasons with transitions such as *first of all, another danger of working too many hours*, and *last of all*.

Group F

1   Giving Advice.   Provide written advice to either a high school or a college student (or to someone else, if you prefer), basing your remarks upon one of the following statements:

- "Be grateful for luck, but don't depend upon it."

- Success is not something to wait for; it's something to work for."

Be sure to use examples (which can be either fanciful, realistic, funny, serious—or whatever type fits your purpose) so the preceding statement is made clear, meaningful, and, if you can, entertaining to the person for whom your remarks are intended.

2   Avoiding Responsibility.   M. Scott Peck, the author of several best-selling self-help books, has written, "The extent to which people will go psychologically to avoid assuming responsibility for personal problems, while always sad, is sometimes almost ludicrous." Think of times you have observed people blaming other people or circumstances for their own problems. Then write a paragraph that begins with the following topic sentence:

- I have seen someone refuse to take responsibility for his (*or* her) own problem.

Then go on to support that statement with an example. As you develop that example, be sure to explain what the person's problem was, how he had helped create it, and how he blamed other people or circumstances rather than accept responsibility for it.

As you think of how to develop your paragraph, ask yourself questions such as these:

- Whom do I know who usually seems to be in one kind of trouble or another?

- Does that person always seem to blame others for his or her problems?

- What are some specific problems that person has in his or her life?

- How has he or she helped to create the problems?

- Whom or what does the person blame for those problems?

3   Dealing with a Problem.   M. Scott Peck states that the only way to solve a problem is to solve it—in other words, to take responsibility for the problem and find a solution. When did you accept the responsibility for a problem in your own life and figure out a solution for it? Write about what happened. Be sure to answer the following questions:

- How was the problem affecting my life?

- When did I realize that I was (in part) responsible for the problem?

- What solution for the problem did I come up with?

- What happened after I put my solution to work?

In selecting a topic for this assignment, think about various kinds of problems you may have experienced: problems getting along with other people, money problems, marriage problems, problems completing work on time, difficulties holding a job, excessive use of alcohol or other drugs, trouble with the law, and so on. Then ask yourself which of these problems you have accepted responsibility for and solved. Once you have thought of a topic, you might begin with a statement like one of the following:

- This past year, I began to take responsibility for my continuing marriage problems.

- I recently faced the fact that I have a drinking problem and have taken steps to deal with it.

- After years of scraping together just enough money to get from one week to the next, I've acted to deal with my money problems.

This statement could then be supported with one or more examples of the problem, a description of how and when the writer realized the problem, and a detailing of the steps the writer has taken to deal with the problem.

Group G

1   A Key Experience in School.   Write a paragraph about one of your key experiences in grade school. Use concrete details—actions, comments, reactions, and so on—to help your readers picture what happened. To select an event to write about, try asking yourself the following questions:

- Which teachers or events in school influenced how I felt about myself?

- What specific incidents stand out in my mind as I think back to elementary school?

Once you know which experience you'll write about, use freewriting to help you remember and record the details. Here is one student's freewriting for this assignment.

> In second grade, Richard L. sat next to me, a really good artist. When he drew something, it looked just like what it was meant to be. He was so good at choosing colors, the use of crayons, watercolors. His pictures were always picked by teacher to be shown on bulletin board. I still remember his drawing of a circus, acrobats, animals, clowns. Many colors and details. I felt pretty bad in art, even though I loved it and couldn't wait for art in class. One day the teacher read story about a boy who looked at the mountains far away, wondering what was on the other side, mountains were huge, dark. After reading, it was art time. "Paint something from the story" teacher said. I painted those mountains, big purple brown mountains with watercolor dripping to show uneven slopes and coloring of sunset, a thin crooked slice of very blue sky at top. Next day I sat down at my desk in the morning. Then I saw my picture was on the bulletin board! Later teacher passed by me, bent down, put hand on my shoulder and whispered good job, lovely painting. Made me feel capable, proud. The feeling lasted a long time.

Once the details of the experience are on paper, you will be free to concentrate on a more carefully constructed version of the event. The author of the above freewriting, for instance, needed to think of a topic sentence. So when writing the first draft, she began with this sentence: "A seemingly small experience in elementary school encouraged me greatly." Writing drafts is also the time to add any persuasive details you may have missed at first. When working on her second draft, the author of the above added at the end: "I felt very proud, which gave me confidence to work harder in all my school subjects."

Before writing out your final version, remember to check for grammar, punctuation, and spelling errors.

2   Learning a New Skill.   Have you faced the problem of learning a new skill or performing a task that, at first, seemed almost impossibly difficult? Write a paragraph in which you discuss the steps you went through to finally learn this skill or accomplish this task.

Here are some sample topic sentences:

- Despite my early fears, I am now almost as comfortable with English as I am with Spanish.

- At the age of thirty-seven, I finally learned to cook for myself, but not without some ugly disasters.

- Adding a regular exercise routine to my life seemed impossible last year, but I have actually done it.

- Although it wasn't long ago that computers seemed beyond me, I have finally joined the computer generation.

3   Finding Time for Reading.   A number of authors have described how a parent or teacher has helped them become regular readers—and how that habit of reading then led to enormous positive changes in their lives. Most of us, however, don't have someone around to insist that we do a certain amount of personal reading every week. In addition, many of us don't seem to have a great deal of free time for reading. How can adults find time to read more? Write a paragraph listing several ways adults can add more reading to their lives.

A good prewriting strategy for this assignment is list making. Simply write out as many ways as you can think of. Don't worry about putting them in any special order. You will select and organize the strategies you wish to include in your paper after accumulating as many ideas as you can. Here is an example of a prewriting list for this paper:

Ways adults can increase the amount of time they spend reading

— on the bus to and from work/school

— while eating breakfast

— instead of watching some TV

— choose motivating materials (articles, books about hobbies, problems, etc.)

Feel free to use items from the above list, but add at least one or two of your own points to include in your paper.

Group H

1   An Embarrassing Moment.   In a paragraph, tell about a time you felt ashamed or embarrassed. Provide details that show clearly what happened. Explain what you and the other people involved said and did. Also, explain how you felt and why you were so uncomfortable.

For example, the paragraph might begin with a sentence like this:

- I was deeply ashamed when I was caught cheating on a spelling test in fifth grade.

The paragraph could continue by telling how the writer cheated and how he was caught; how the teacher and other students looked, spoke, and acted; what the writer did when he was caught; and what emotions and thoughts the writer experienced throughout the incident.

Below are some other topic sentence possibilities. Develop one of them or a variation on one of them. Feel free as well to come up with and write about an entirely different idea.

- My first formal date was the occasion of an embarrassing moment in my life.

- To this day, I wince when I think of an incident that happened to me at a family party.

- I can still remember the shame I felt in my teenage body when I had to use the shower room at school.

- An event that occurred in high school makes my cheeks glow hot and red even today.

2   A Fear of Looking Foolish.   Write a paragraph about how the fear of looking foolish affected your behavior in grade school or high school. Choose an example of a time you acted in a particular way because you were afraid of being ridiculed. Describe how you behaved, and be sure to explain just what kind of embarrassment you were trying to avoid.

Your paragraph might begin with a topic sentence like one of the following:

- Not wanting other students to turn on me, I joined them in making fun of a high school classmate who was very overweight.

- My mother's idea of how I should dress caused me a great deal of embarrassment in school.

- Because I didn't want to admit that I needed glasses, I had a lot of problems in fifth grade.

3   Feeling Out of Place.   Write about a time that you felt out of place, as though you didn't belong. Maybe you found yourself in a foreign country. Or maybe you were in a new school, a new neighborhood, a new job, or a new group of people. To think about how to develop this paper, ask yourself questions like these:

- What brought me into the situation?
- What about the situation made me feel like an outsider?
- What did the people around me do or say?
- What did I imagine other people were thinking about me?
- What thoughts and emotions were running through me?
- How did my feeling like an outsider affect the way I acted?

As you write this assignment, be sure to include plenty of concrete details to help the reader understand your experience. Tell exactly where the incident took place, who else was there, what you and others did and said, and what thoughts and feelings you were experiencing.

Group I

1   A Special Person.   Who has helped you the most in your quest for an education? Write a paper explaining who this person is and how he or she has helped you. Here are some possible topic sentences for this paper:

- My best friend has helped me with my college education in several ways.
- If it weren't for my father, I wouldn't be in college today.
- It was my aunt who impressed upon me the importance of a college education.

To develop support for this paper, try listing the problems you faced and the ways this person has helped you deal with each problem. Alternatively, you could do some freewriting about the person you're writing about.

2   Reaching a Goal.   Write a paragraph telling of something you wanted very badly, but were afraid you would not be able to attain. Describe the struggles you had to overcome to get to your goal. How did you finally reach it? Include some details that communicate how strongly you wanted the goal and how difficult it was to reach. In thinking about a topic for this paper, you may wish to consider the following common goals:

- A certain job
- Enough money for college
- A passing grade
- Quitting smoking or drugs
- Overcoming an illness

Once you've decided on the goal you wish to write about, use it to write a topic sentence, such as any of the following:

- After several false starts, I finally quit smoking.
- It took me a year of saving and seeking financial assistance to get enough money to attend college.
- After two years of medical treatment and support, I feel I have learned to live with my illness.
- Following a careful budget, I was finally able to afford to . . .

To develop supporting material for your topic sentence, try freewriting. For example, here is part of one person's freewriting about the struggle to quit smoking:

> The first time I tried to quit, it lasted a short time. Only a month or less. I made the mistake of not getting rid of all the cigarettes in the house, I kept a few here and there for emergencies. But there should be no emergencies when you quit. Once I took a few puffs on a cigarette I found in the silverware drawer. It was all over—I ran out that day to buy a pack. I told myself I would smoke only one or two cigarettes a day until I was ready to really quit. That type of promise is always a lie because I can't really control myself once I start smoking. It's either all or nothing, and for me, even a puff or two isn't nothing. It wasn't long before I started thinking about quitting again. I was coughing a lot and several news stories were about people with lung cancer and the father of someone in my apartment building died of lung cancer. Also I read in a magazine that smoking causes wrinkles. Finally, about a year ago . . .

3   Career Plans.   What career plans have you made so far? Write a paragraph about how you expect college to prepare you for a specific job. If you haven't decided quite yet, write about the possibilities. In your paragraph, tell readers about your interests and their relationship to the career or careers you have in mind. Also discuss your evaluation of job opportunities in your career. Your topic sentence will be a general statement about your career goals, such as any of these:

- I am aiming for a nursing career, which I believe is a realistic goal.
- Because of my artistic talent and the opportunities for designers, I've decided to major in graphic arts.
- I am aiming for a double degree, in business and in cooking, because I hope one day to have my own restaurant—a business that is always needed.

Group J

1   Being One's Own Worst Enemy.   "A lot of people are their own worst enemies" is a familiar saying. We all know people who hurt themselves. Write a paragraph describing someone you know who is his or her own worst enemy. In your paper, introduce the person and explain his or her hurtful behaviors. You may wish to conclude your paragraph with suggestions for that person. A useful way to gather ideas for this paper is to combine two prewriting techniques—outlining and listing. Begin with an outline of the general areas you expect to cover. Here's an outline that may work:

—Introduce the person
—Describe the hurtful behavior(s)
—Suggest changes

Once you have a workable outline, then use list making to produce specific details for each outline point. For example, here are one person's lists for the points in the outline:

Person
— Vanessa
— Just graduated high school
— Works at a department store
— Wants to go to college, but needs money

Hurtful behaviors
— Just moved into own apartment, which takes much of monthly income—could have stayed at home
— Spends a lot of money on clothing
— Makes no effort to find financial aid for school

Changes
— Stop spending so much and start saving
— Get information from school financial aid offices

2   A Time for Courage.   Write about a time when you had to have courage. Think of an action that frightened you, but that you felt you needed to take anyway. Perhaps you were afraid to ask someone out on a date, or to say no when someone asked you to do something you felt was wrong, or to perform a dangerous activity. In your paper, describe the frightening situation that faced you and how you made the decision to act with courage. Then tell what happened—the actions that you took, the responses of those around you, significant things people said, and how things turned out.

For example, you might begin with a statement like this:

• When I was in junior high, it required courage for me to resist the temptation to shoplift with my favorite cousin.

That passage would then continue with a description of what the cousin did and said, how the writer found the courage to say no to the idea, how the shoplifting cousin reacted, and how the writer felt throughout the whole process.

As you describe the incident, use time transition words to make the sequence of events clear, such as "*At first* I didn't think I could do it. *Later*, however, I had an idea."

3   A Matter of Survival.   Someone has written, "There are times for each of us when simple survival becomes a deadly serious matter. We must then learn to persist—to struggle through each day." What has been your worst struggle? Write a paper describing the problem, what you had to do to deal with it, and how things worked out. You may also wish to comment on how you'd handle the problem today if you had to face it again.

As you work on the drafts for this paper, consider including the following to add interest and clarity:

• Exact quotations of what people said
• Descriptions of revealing behavior, actions, and physical characteristics
• Time transitions to clarify relationships between events

4 / Subjects and Verbs

A sentence expresses a complete thought. Subjects and verbs are the basic parts of any sentence. This chapter explains the following:

1   Subjects

- The little **children** waited for the school bus.
- **Mac and Lucy** are twins.

2   Verbs

- The little children **waited** for the school bus.
- Mac and Lucy **are** twins.
- People **should** never **argue** during a job interview.

3   Prepositional phrases

- Several students **in the class** asked questions **about the final exam**.

SUBJECTS

The **subject** of a sentence is the person, place, thing, or idea that the sentence is about. The subject can be called the "who or what" word. To find the subject, ask yourself, "Who or what is this sentence about?" or "Who or what is doing something in this sentence?"

For example, look at the following two sentences:

- People applauded.

  People is what the sentence is about; they are the ones who are doing something. So *people* is the subject of the sentence.

- Gloria wrote her answers on the blackboard.

  To find out the subject of this sentence, ask yourself, "Who is the sentence about?" or "Who is doing something in the sentence?" The answer is *Gloria.* That's who wrote her answers on the blackboard. So *Gloria* is the subject of the sentence.

A subject will always be either a noun or a pronoun. A **noun** is the name of a person, place, thing, or idea. A **pronoun** is a word—such as *I, you he, she, it, we,* or *they*—that stands for a noun.

> ※ For more information on nouns and pronouns, see "Parts of Speech," pages 419–422.

Descriptive Words

A subject is often accompanied by one or more words that describe it. See if you can find the subjects of the following sentences and the words that describe them.

- A very large truck stalled on the bridge.
- Some tomatoes are yellow.
- Two young boys were playing catch in the alley.

In the first sentence, *truck* is the subject. The words *a, very,* and *large* describe the word *truck*. In the second sentence, *tomatoes* is the subject, and *some* describes it. In the third sentence, the subject is *boys*; the words describing that subject are *two* and *young*.

> ※ For more information on descriptive words (also known as adjectives and adverbs), see "Adjectives and Adverbs," pages 227–236, and "Parts of Speech," pages 426–427.

➤ **Practice 1**   *Answers will vary.*

Add an appropriate word to each blank. The word that you insert will be the subject of the sentence. It will tell *who* or *what* the sentence is about.

1. A _____ *burglar* _____ crept through the dark house.

2. Only three _____ *oranges* _____ are left in the refrigerator.

3. The _____ *lizard* _____ swam across the river.

4. David's gold _____ *chains* _____ glittered in the sunlight.

5. My _____ *sister* _____ reminded me to wear suntan lotion.

6. Several _____ *puppies* _____ were crowded into the small cage.

7. _____ *Julie* _____ ate the raspberries right from the box.

8. _____ *English* _____ is my favorite school subject.

9. Without a sound, a _____ *hawk* _____ grabbed the field mouse by the neck.

10. My mother never went to college. _____ *She* _____ has always felt bad about that.

The Subject and Prepositional Phrases

The subject of a sentence is never part of a prepositional phrase. A **prepositional phrase** is a group of words that begins with a preposition (a word like *in, from, of,* or *with*) and ends with a noun or pronoun (the object of the preposition). Following are some common prepositions you should know:

Common Prepositions

about	before	down	like	to
above	behind	during	of	toward
across	below	except	off	under
after	beneath	for	on	up
among	beside	from	over	with
around	between	in	since	without
at	by	into	through	

Here are a few examples of prepositional phrases:

- in the house
- of the world
- from the bakery
- with your permission

Now look at the sentence below. What is the subject? Write your answer here: _____

- A bunch of green grapes fell onto the supermarket floor.

The answer is *bunch*, but many people would be tempted to choose *grapes*. In this case, however, *grapes* is part of the prepositional phrase *of green grapes*, so it cannot be the subject.

As you look for the subject of a sentence, it may help to cross out the prepositional phrases. For example, look at the following sentences. In each sentence, find the prepositions and cross out the prepositional phrases. Then underline the subject. After finding each subject, read the explanation that follows.

- The sick man, with shaking hands, poured the pills from the brown bottle.

The prepositions are *with* and *from*. Cross out *with shaking hands* and *from the brown bottle*, and you are left with the sentence *The sick man poured the pills*. Ask yourself, "Who poured the pills?" The answer, *man*, is the subject of the sentence.

- A student in the class fell asleep during the long lecture.

In and *during* are prepositions. You should have crossed out the prepositional phrases *in the class* and *during the long lecture*. When you do this, you are left with the sentence *A student fell asleep.* Ask yourself, "Who fell asleep?" The answer, *student*, is the subject of the sentence.

※ For more information on prepositions, see "Parts of Speech," page 425.

➤ **Practice 2**

Cross out the one prepositional phrase in each sentence. Then underline the subject of the sentence.

Example   The ~~pack~~ ~~of cookies~~ disappeared quickly.

1. The <u>blueberries</u> ~~in this pie~~ are bitter.

2. ~~On weekends,~~ <u>Al</u> works overtime.

3. The <u>woman</u> ~~with a pierced nose~~ is my hairdresser.

4. <u>Leaves</u> ~~from our neighbor's tree~~ covered our lawn.

5. ~~During the school play,~~ our <u>daughter</u> lost her voice.

6. <u>Some</u> ~~of the roof shingles~~ are loose.

7. ~~Like her father,~~ <u>Abby</u> adores baseball.

8. The <u>dust</u> ~~under your bed~~ contains tiny creatures.

9. <u>One</u> ~~of my best friends~~ is a computer programmer.

10. ~~From my bedroom window,~~ <u>I</u> can watch my neighbor's TV.

A Note on Singular and Plural Subjects

In addition to spotting subjects, you should note whether a subject is **singular** (one) or **plural** (more than one). Most plural subjects simply end in *s*:

Singular: The **car** in front of us is speeding.

Plural: The **cars** in front of us are speeding.

Some plural subjects are irregular:

Singular: The **child** was crying.

Plural: The **children** were crying.

A **compound subject** is two or more subjects connected by a joining word such as *and.* Compound subjects are usually plural.

Compound: The **car** and the **truck** in front of us are speeding.

※ For more information on compound subjects, see "Subject-Verb Agreement," pages 132–133.

➤ **Practice 3**

Underline the subject or subjects of each sentence. Then in the space on the left, write **S** if the subject is singular and **P** if the subject is plural.

Example   *P*   Love and hate are closely related emotions.

_P_ 1. My best friend and her husband are moving to Dallas.

_P_ 2. Books are often the best companions.

_S_ 3. The noise of the fireworks frightens the baby.

_P_ 4. The guitarist and drum player do not like one another.

_S_ 5. The aroma of barbecued ribs tempts almost everyone.

_P_ 6. Three men in my family are named Michael.

_S_ 7. This envelope has a postmark from Chicago.

_P_ 8. My oven and refrigerator are out of order right now.

_S_ 9. A deck of cards is useful for many different games.

_P_ 10. Every summer, tourists and mosquitoes descend on the Florida coast.

VERBS

Every complete sentence contains a verb. In general, there are two types of verbs: action verbs and linking verbs.

Action Verbs

Action verbs express action; they tell what the subject is doing. You can find an action verb by asking, "What does the subject do?" Look again at this sentence:

• People applauded.

You remember that *people* is the subject of this sentence. What did they do? They *applauded.* So *applauded* is the verb of the sentence. It is an action verb.

Now look at the following sentences, and read the explanations.

• Gloria wrote her answers on the blackboard.

Gloria is the subject of this sentence. What did Gloria do? She *wrote*, so *wrote* is the action verb. (Like subjects, verbs cannot be part of a prepositional phrase. So when looking for the verb in this sentence, you can eliminate the words *on the blackboard*.)

• The balloons drifted slowly to earth.

In this sentence, *balloons* is the subject. What did they do? They *drifted. Drifted* is the verb of the sentence.

➤ **Practice 4**   *Answers will vary.*

Write a word into each blank. The word that you insert will be an action verb. It will tell what the subject does or did.

1. A mosquito _____*hovered*_____ over the sleeping boy.

2. For exercise, I _____*swim*_____.

3. During the biology lecture, Mickey often _____*sleeps*_____.

4. The jury _____*listened*_____ carefully to both sides of the story.

5. For fun, we _____*ran*_____ all the way home from the corner store.

Finding Action Verbs

See if you can underline the action verb in the following two sentences. Then read the explanations.

- The moon disappeared behind the clouds.
- The impatient customer tapped her fingers on the counter.

In looking for the verb in the first sentence, you can eliminate the prepositional phrase *behind the clouds*. That leaves the words *the moon disappeared*. The *moon* is what did something, so it is the subject of the sentence. What did the moon do? It disappeared. So *disappeared* is the action verb.

In the second sentence, you can also eliminate a prepositional phrase: *on the counter*. That leaves *the impatient customer tapped her fingers*. The subject is *customer*—that's who did something. What did the customer do? She tapped. So *tapped* is the action verb in that sentence.

Just as a sentence can contain a compound subject, a sentence can contain a **compound verb**: two or more verbs that have the same subject or subjects. For example, here's another version of one of the sentences above:

- The impatient customer tapped her fingers on the counter and cleared her throat.

In this version, the customer did two things: tapped (her fingers) and cleared (her throat). Therefore, the subject *customer* has a compound verb: *tapped* and *cleared*.

In case you have trouble finding the verb of a sentence, here is one other way to identify a verb:

Try putting a pronoun such as *I, you, he, she, it,* or *they* in front of the word you suspect is a verb. If the word is a verb, the resulting sentence will make sense. Notice, for instance, that for the sentences above, "it disappeared" and "she tapped" make sense.

➤ **Practice 5**

Underline the action verb or verbs in each sentence. You may find it helpful to first identify the subject and to cross out any prepositional phrases.

1. A family of ducks <u>waddled</u> toward the pond.

2. A pot of vegetable soup <u>simmered</u> gently on the stove.

3. After the party, we <u>went</u> to a diner for coffee.

4. Your camera <u>takes</u> nice sharp pictures.

5. The curious child <u>stared</u> silently at the man in the Santa Claus suit.

6. Aunt Lois <u>opened</u> the package and <u>gasped</u> in delight.

7. A German shepherd <u>waited</u> patiently outside the drugstore.

8. The angry bull <u>snorted</u> loudly and <u>charged</u> at the red blanket.

9. Without a word, Paul <u>raced</u> out of the house and into the front yard.

10. Teams of cheerleaders <u>clapped</u> and <u>yelled</u> on opposite sides of the gymnasium.

Linking Verbs

Linking verbs do not show action. **Linking verbs** join (or link) the subject to one or more words that describe the subject. Look at the following examples.

- Before the race, the runners were anxious.

The subject of this sentence is *runners*. The sentence has no action verb—the runners did not *do* anything. Instead, the verb *were* links the subject to a word that describes it: *anxious*. (*Before the race* is a prepositional phrase, and so it cannot contain the subject or the verb.)

- Cara's boyfriend is a good mechanic.

The subject of this sentence is *boyfriend*. The linking verb *is* joins that subject with words that describe him: *a good mechanic*.

Most linking verbs are forms of the verb *be*. Here are forms of *be*, which is the most used verb in the English language:

Forms of the Linking Verb *Be*

am	were	had been
is	will be	will have been
are	have been	
was	has been	

Following are other common words that can be linking verbs.

Other Common Linking Verbs

look	taste	appear
sound	feel	seem
smell	become	

Now see if you can underline the linking verbs in the following two sentences.

- George looks uncomfortable in a suit and tie.
- Sometimes anger is a healthy emotion.

If you underlined *looks* in the first sentence, you were right. *Looks* links the subject, *George*, to words that describe him: *uncomfortable in a suit and tie*.

If you underlined *is* in the second sentence, you were right. *Is* links the subject, *anger*, to words that describe it: *a healthy emotion*.

➤ Practice 6

Underline the one word that is a linking verb in each sentence. You may find it helpful to first cross out any prepositional phrases and then to find the subject.

1. That nurse <u>was</u> kind.

2. The kitchen <u>smells</u> spicy.

3. Lisa and I <u>are</u> roommates.

4. Velvet <u>feels</u> soft and silky.

5. The chocolate cookies <u>taste</u> salty and dry.

6. After jogging, I <u>am</u> always hungry.

7. Those dishes from the dishwasher still <u>look</u> dirty.

8. Since his divorce, Nate <u>seems</u> unhappy.

9. The cashier at our supermarket <u>is</u> a student at Jefferson High School.

10. During the hot, dry summer, the farmers <u>were</u> uneasy about their crops.

Main Verbs and Helping Verbs

Most of the verbs you have looked at so far have been just one word—*wrote, drifted, is, look,* and so on. But many verbs consist of a main verb plus one or more **helping verbs**.

Look at the following two sentences and explanations.

- My sister is joining a drama club.

Sister is the subject of this sentence. She is the person who is doing something. What is she doing? She *is joining* (a drama club). In this sentence, *is* is a helping verb, and *joining* is the main verb.

Joining by itself would not make sense as a verb. It would be incorrect to say, "My sister joining a drama club." Words that end in *-ing* cannot be the verb of a sentence unless they are accompanied by a helping verb.

- Mikey should have given his dog a bath before the pet contest.

In this sentence, *Mikey* is the subject. What should he have done? He *should have given* (his dog a bath). *Should* and *have* are helping verbs. The last verb in the word group, *given*, is the main verb.

Given by itself could not be the verb. It would not be correct to say, "Mikey given his dog a bath."

The helping verbs are listed in the box below.

Helping Verbs

Forms of be:	be, am, is, are, was, were, being, been
Forms of have:	have, has, had
Forms of do:	do, does, did
Special verbs:	can, could, may, might, must, ought (to), shall, should, will, would
(These special verbs are also known as *modals*.)	

Each of the helping verbs can be used alone or in a variety of combinations, such as *have been, may be, might have been,* and *would have been.*

The modals, unlike the other helping verbs, do not change form to indicate tense. In other words, they do not take such endings as *-ed, -s,* and *-ing.* After the modals, always use the basic form of a verb, the form in which a verb is listed in the dictionary (*go, see, work,* and so on).

- You **can** turn in the paper tomorrow.
- We **should** visit Dee in the hospital.

Now see if you can underline the main verbs and the helping verbs in the following two sentences. Then read the explanations.

- Gwen has visited the learning skills lab.
- I will be running in the school's five-mile race.

In the first sentence, *Gwen* is the subject. She is the one who has done something. To find the verb, we can ask, "What did Gwen do?" The answer is *has visited. Has* is the helping verb, and *visited* is the main verb.

In the second sentence, *I* is the subject. What will that subject be doing? He or she *will be running.* So in this sentence, *will* and *be* are helping verbs, and *running* is the main verb.

➤ **Practice 7**

Fill in the blanks under each sentence.

1. As usual, my brother was complaining about his homework.

   Helping verb(s): _____was_____   *Main verb:* _____complaining_____

2. The students will decorate the classroom for the teacher's surprise party.

   Helping verb(s): _____will_____   *Main verb:* _____decorate_____

3. The dental appointment should take about an hour.

   Helping verb(s): _____should_____   *Main verb:* _____take_____

4. Surprisingly, I do enjoy learning grammar.

   Helping verb(s): _____do_____   *Main verb:* _____enjoy_____

5. Margaret has planted parsley and other herbs in her back yard.

   Helping verb(s): _____has_____   *Main verb:* _____planted_____

6. You should have called your mother on her birthday.

   Helping verb(s): ____should have____   *Main verb:* _____called_____

7. The video game machine will accept only quarters.

   Helping verb(s): _____will_____   *Main verb:* _____accept_____

8. That drunk driver could have killed Aunt Esther.

   Helping verb(s): ____could have____   *Main verb:* _____killed_____

9. My girlfriend must have forgotten our date this evening.

   Helping verb(s): ____must have____   *Main verb:* _____forgotten_____

10. The star basketball player at our college might have injured himself seriously.

    Helping verb(s): ____might have____   *Main verb:* _____injured_____

Words That Are Not Verbs

Here is some added information that will help when you look for verbs in a sentence.

1   The verb of a sentence never begins with the word *to*.

- The instructor **agreed** to provide ten minutes for study before the quiz.

  Although *provide* is a verb, *to provide* cannot be the verb of a sentence. The verb of this sentence is *agreed*.

  ※ For more information on verbs that follow the word *to*, see "Sentence Variety and Style," page 280.

2   Certain words—such as *not, just, never, only,* and *always*—may appear between the main verb and the helping verb. Such words are adverbs. They describe the verb, but they are never part of it.

- Our canary **does** not **sing** in front of visitors.
- I **will** never **eat** at that restaurant again.
- You **should** always **wear** your seat belt in a moving vehicle.

  ※ For more information on adverbs, see "Parts of Speech," page 427.

➤ Practice 8

In the space provided, write the complete verb in each sentence.

1. My uncle is not wearing his toupee anymore.

   Complete verb: _____ *is wearing* _____

2. The children hurried to finish their art projects by the end of the class.

   Complete verb: _____ *hurried* _____

3. The noodles should not be boiled more than seven minutes.

   Complete verb: _____ *should be boiled* _____

4. The teacher has promised to return the papers by Friday.

   Complete verb: _____ *has promised* _____

5. Reba will always love her ex-husband.

   Complete verb: _____ *will love* _____

CHAPTER REVIEW

Fill in the correct word or words in each space provided.

1. A _____subject_____ and a _____verb_____ are the basic parts of any sentence.

2. The subject and verb of a sentence are never found in a _____prepositional_____ phrase.

3. *True or false?* __F__ Verbs that join the subject to a word or words that describe the subject are known as helping verbs.

4. Words such as *is, was, smell,* and *seem* are known as _____linking verbs_____.

5. A complete verb can be made up of a _____main_____ verb and one or more helping verbs.

Name_____   Section _____ Date _____

➤ Subjects and Verbs: Test 1

For each sentence, cross out any prepositional phrases. Then underline the subject once and the verb twice. Remember to include any helping verb(s) and also all parts of compound subjects and verbs.

1. Bruce told the joke ~~with a straight face~~.

2. A red kite danced ~~in the gentle breeze~~.

3. My son and daughter are good friends.

4. The plant ~~in the window~~ has died.

5. ~~In some countries~~, snails are a favorite food.

6. ~~For many Americans~~, money is success.

7. Several guests ~~at the party~~ were singing ~~with the band~~.

8. My wife and I always spend our vacation ~~at home~~.

9. ~~After my last final exam~~, I can forget ~~about school~~ ~~for a week~~.

10. Nancy walked ~~to the front~~ ~~of the room~~ and recited a long poem ~~by Robert Frost~~.

Name_____   Section _____   Date _____

Score: (Number right) _____ x 5 = _____%

➤ **Subjects and Verbs: Test 2**

For each sentence, cross out any prepositional phrases. Then, on the lines provided, write the subject(s) and verb(s), including any helping verb(s).

1. The coffee ~~from the leaking pot~~ stained the carpet.

   Subject(s): _____coffee_____   *Verb(s):* _____stained_____

2. My cousins ~~in Louisiana~~ formed a gospel music group.

   Subject(s): _____cousins_____   *Verb(s):* _____formed_____

3. ~~At exactly noon~~, my summer vacation will begin.

   Subject(s): _____vacation_____   *Verb(s):* _____will begin_____

4. A warm sweatshirt ~~with a hood~~ feels good ~~on a chilly day~~.

   Subject(s): _____sweatshirt_____   *Verb(s):* _____feels_____

5. The source ~~of heating and cooling for the house~~ is a heat pump.

   Subject(s): _____source_____   *Verb(s):* _____is_____

6. The cardboard boxes ~~by the river~~ are home ~~to several people~~.

   Subject(s): _____boxes_____   *Verb(s):* _____are_____

7. ~~For my little brother and sister~~, happiness is a McDonald's restaurant.

   Subject(s): _____happiness_____   *Verb(s):* _____is_____

8. Retrievers and sheepdogs do not bite very often.

   Subject(s): Retrievers . . . sheepdogs   *Verb(s):* _____do bite_____

9. The rug-cleaning people should have been here ~~by now~~.

   Subject(s): _____people_____   *Verb(s):* _____should have been_____

10. ~~After work~~, Dena and I ate dinner and studied ~~at her apartment~~.

   Subject(s): _____Dena . . . I_____   *Verb(s):* _____ate . . . studied_____

Name_____ _____ Section _____ Date _____

Score: (Number right) _____ x 5 = _____ %

➤ Subjects and Verbs: Test 3

For each sentence, cross out the prepositional phrase or phrases. Then, on the lines provided, write the subject(s) and verb(s), including any helping verb(s).

1. ~~Between you and me~~, I dislike Rita. Her opinion ~~of herself~~ is too high.

    a. *Subject(s):* _____I_____   *Verb(s):* _____dislike_____

    b. *Subject(s):* _____opinion_____   *Verb(s):* _____is_____

2. An ambulance passed me ~~at top speed~~. ~~After a minute~~, a fire truck followed ~~with its siren screaming~~.

    a. *Subject(s):* _____ambulance_____   *Verb(s):* _____passed_____

    b. *Subject(s):* _____truck_____   *Verb(s):* _____followed_____

3. A cheese omelet and ravioli are today's lunch specials. The soup ~~of the day~~ is vegetable beef.

    a. *Subject(s):* _____omelet . . . ravioli_____   *Verb(s):* _____are_____

    b. *Subject(s):* _____soup_____   *Verb(s):* _____is_____

4. Most ~~of the students in this class~~ hold part-time jobs. ~~In addition~~, several ~~of them~~ have children ~~at home~~.

    a. *Subject(s):* _____Most_____   *Verb(s):* _____hold_____

    b. *Subject(s):* _____several_____   *Verb(s):* _____have_____

5. My mother and father met ~~in September~~ and married ~~in October~~. They have been happy together ~~for twenty-five years~~.

    a. *Subject(s):* _____mother . . . father_____   *Verb(s):* _____met . . . married_____

    b. *Subject(s):* _____They_____   *Verb(s):* _____have been_____

Name_____   Section _____   Date _____

Score: (Number right) _____ x 5 = _____%

➤ Subjects and Verbs: Test 4

For each sentence, cross out the prepositional phrase or phrases. Then, on the lines provided, write the subject(s) and verb(s), including any helping verb(s).

1. The handwriting ~~on this essay~~ looks terrible. ~~In the future~~, you should type your essays.

   a. *Subject(s):* ___handwriting___   *Verb(s):* ___looks___

   b. *Subject(s):* ___you___   *Verb(s):* ___should type___

2. Many passengers talked or slept ~~during the long bus trip~~. Others read ~~in the dim light~~.

   a. *Subject(s):* ___passengers___   *Verb(s):* ___talked . . . slept___

   b. *Subject(s):* ___Others___   *Verb(s):* ___read___

3. Our district elected Lani ~~to city council~~. Her election surprised many people.

   a. *Subject(s):* ___district___   *Verb(s):* ___elected___

   b. *Subject(s):* ___election___   *Verb(s):* ___surprised___

4. The small country store sells groceries and serves simple lunches. The same woman has owned it ~~for forty years~~.

   a. *Subject(s):* ___store___   *Verb(s):* ___sells . . . serves___

   b. *Subject(s):* ___woman___   *Verb(s):* ___has owned___

5. ~~On Sunday nights~~, we usually play games ~~with friends~~. Checkers and poker are two ~~of our favorite games~~.

   a. *Subject(s):* ___we___   *Verb(s):* ___play___

   b. *Subject(s):* ___Checkers . . . poker___   *Verb(s):* ___are___

Name_____   _____ Section _____ Date _____

Score: (Number right) _____ x 2.5 = _____ %

➤ Subjects and Verbs: Test 5

A. In each of the **ten** sentences in this paragraph, cross out any prepositional phrases. Then, underline all the subjects once and the verbs twice. Remember to include any helping verb(s) and also all parts of compound subjects and verbs.

[1]Sharks, ~~with their pointed snouts and fearsome teeth~~, terrify most people. [2]However, ~~of the 375 or so different types of sharks~~, few have attacked people. [3]Most sharks will attack only when ~~in danger~~. [4]The great white shark is one ~~of the most dangerous sharks to humans~~. [5]Many people know and fear this shark ~~from its role~~ ~~in the movie *Jaws*~~. [6]It can grow ~~to over twenty feet~~ ~~in length~~. [7]The coloring ~~of the great white shark~~ is a camouflage ~~in the water~~. [8]The color ~~of its belly~~ is white. [9]~~From underneath~~, the white belly blends ~~with the bright sky~~ overhead. [10]Seals, smaller fish, and people often do not see the great white shark ~~in time~~.

B. Follow the directions given in Part A.

[1]~~Of all the animals~~ ~~on Earth~~, a human baby is the most helpless. [2]Only a small part ~~of the baby's growth~~ occurs ~~before birth~~. [3]The rest ~~of the development~~ happens ~~after delivery~~. [4]~~By contrast~~, snakes and lizards are ready ~~for survival~~ ~~from the moment~~ ~~of their birth~~. [5]Elephants, antelopes, and camels can run ~~with the herd~~ a few hours ~~after birth~~. [6]Chimpanzees and other slow-growing mammals need to depend ~~on their parents~~ ~~for several years~~. [7]But the human body takes ~~about eighteen years~~ to develop. [8]Our slow development may seem ~~like a disadvantage~~.

(Continues on next page)

[9]However, <u>it</u> <u>has</u> a positive side. [10]~~During our years of dependence on older humans~~, <u>we</u> <u>learn</u> to use our minds more skillfully than any other animals ~~on the planet~~.

5 / Verb Tenses

All verbs have various **tenses**—forms that indicate the time the sentence is referring to. This chapter explains the following about verb tenses:

1   The four principal verb parts that are the basis for all of the tenses

2   The most common verb tenses in English

Six main tenses:	present, past, future
	present perfect, past perfect, future perfect
Three progressive tenses:	present progressive, past progressive, future progressive

THE FOUR PRINCIPAL PARTS OF VERBS

Each verb tense is based on one of the four principal parts of verbs. Following are explanations of each of those verb parts.

1   **Basic Form**   The basic form is the form in which verbs are listed in the dictionary. It is used for the present tense for all subjects except third-person singular subjects.

   • I **ask** questions in class.

   Third-person singular verbs are formed by adding -*s* to the basic form.

   • Sue **asks** questions in class.

2   **Past Tense Form**   The past tense of most verbs is formed by adding -*ed* or -*d* to the basic form.

   • We **asked** the teacher to postpone the test.
   • I **named** my son after my grandfather.

3   Present Participle   The present participle is the *-ing* form of a verb. It is used in the progressive tenses, which you will learn about later in the chapter.

- Jack **is asking** the teacher something in the hallway.
- I **am naming** my next child after my grandmother.

4   Past Participle   The past participle of a verb is usually the same as its past tense form. The past participle is the form that is used with the helping verbs *have, has,* and *had* and with *am, is, are, was,* or *were.*

- The teachers **have asked** us to study in groups.
- I **was named** after my mother.

Here are the principal parts of three regular verbs:

Basic Form	Past Tense Form	Present Participle	Past Participle
work	worked	working	worked
smile	smiled	smiling	smiled
wonder	wondered	wondering	wondered

Irregular verbs, which have irregular forms for the past tense form and past participle, are explained in the next chapter, starting on page 103.

SIX MAIN TENSES

There are six main tenses in English. They are **present, past, future, present perfect, past perfect,** and **future perfect.**

Look at the following chart. It shows the six basic tenses of the verb *work.*

Tense	Example
Present	I **work.**
Past	I **worked.**
Future	I **will work.**
Present Perfect	I **have worked.**
Past Perfect	I **had worked.**
Future Perfect	I **will have worked.**

These tenses are explained in more detail on the pages that follow.

Present Tense

Verbs in the **present tense** express present action or habitual action. (A habitual action is one that is often repeated.)

- Our dog **smells** the neighbor's barbecue.

  Smells expresses a present action.

- Jay **works** as a waiter on weekends.

  Works expresses a habitual action.

The forms of present tense verbs are shown with the verb *work* in the box below. Notice the difference between the singular third-person form and the other present tense forms.

Present Tense Forms

	Singular	Plural
First person	I work	we work
Second person	you work	you work
Third person	he, she, it work**s**	they work

Present tense verbs for the third-person singular end with an *-s*. Here are some other sentences in the present tense with subjects that are third-person singular:

- She **reads** about a book a week.
- It **takes** me a month to read a book.
- Dan **drives** an hour to school every day.
- His old car **averages** only ten miles a gallon.

A third-person subject is *he, she, it*, or any single person or thing other than the speaker (first person) or the person spoken to (second person).

➤ Practice 1

A. Fill in the present tense of *smile* for each of the following:

	Singular		Plural
First person	I ___smile___	we ___smile___
Second person	you ___smile___	you ___smile___
Third person	he, she, it ___smiles___	they ___smile___

B. Fill in each space with the present tense form of the verb shown in the margin.

drill   1. The dentist _____*drills*_____ the cavity as his assistant watches.

practice   2. Ling _____*practices*_____ her typing every day.

ring   3. Those church bells _____*ring*_____ on the hour.

make   4. He suddenly _____*makes*_____ a U-turn.

dig   5. Some workers _____*dig*_____ through the stones and rubble.

trim   6. I _____*trim*_____ my fingernails before playing the piano.

clean   7. Dinah _____*cleans*_____ her apartment every Saturday.

tell   8. The nurse _____*tells*_____ the patient to make a fist.

discover   9. My sister often _____*discovers*_____ loose change in her coat pockets.

remember   10. The children _____*remember*_____ the fights their parents used to have.

Past Tense

Verbs in the **past tense** express actions that took place in the past.

- Last year, Jay **worked** as a messenger.
- One day our dog **chased** a raccoon.

The past tense is usually formed by adding *-ed* or *-d* to the end of the basic form of the verb. In the above sentences, the *-ed* and *-d* endings are added to the basic forms of the verbs *work* and *chase*.

Note: People sometimes drop the *-ed* or *-d* ending in their everyday speech. They then tend to omit those endings in their writing as well. For example, someone might say

- I finish the paper an hour before class.

instead of

- I **finished** the paper an hour before class.

In written English, however, the *-ed* or *-d* ending is essential.

➤ Practice 2

Fill in each space with the past tense form of the verb shown in the margin.

seem   1. The movie _____seemed_____ to end suddenly.

sail   2. The ship _____sailed_____ to the Bahamas last week.

wonder   3. Alisha _____wondered_____ where she had put her car keys.

knock   4. Last night someone _____knocked_____ on the door.

name   5. Jean _____named_____ the spotted puppy Freckles.

jump   6. My little son _____jumped_____ up when I entered the room.

talk   7. The students _____talked_____ easily with the new instructor.

check   8. I _____checked_____ the air in my car tires before I went on vacation.

wipe   9. The man _____wiped_____ the lipstick off his cheek with his shirt sleeve.

play   10. Stan _____played_____ his guitar in a concert last summer.

Future Tense

Verbs in the **future tense** describe future actions.

• Next summer, Jay **will work** at a camp.

The future tense is formed by adding the word *will* or *shall* to the basic form of the verb.

➤ Practice 3

Fill in the space with the future tense form of the verb shown in the margin.

play   1. Stan _____will play_____ his guitar in a concert tonight.

plant   2. The lumberjacks _____will plant_____ new trees here next spring.

iron   3. I _____will iron_____ my shirt before going to work tomorrow.

attend   4. Penny _____will attend_____ San Antonio Community College in the fall.

circle   5. The instructor _____will circle_____ any errors she finds in your paper.

Present Perfect Tense (*have* or *has* + past participle)

The **present perfect** tense describes an action that began in the past and either has been finished or is continuing at the present time.

- I **have written** five pages of notes on the textbook chapter.
- Jay **has worked** at a number of jobs over the years.

The present perfect tense is formed by adding the correct form of the helping verb *have* to the past participle of the verb. Here are the present tense forms of *have*:

Present Tense Forms of *Have*

	Singular	Plural
First person	I have	we have
Second person	you have	you have
Third person	he, she, it has	they have

➤ **Practice 4**

Fill in each space with the present perfect tense form of the verb shown in the margin. One is done for you as an example.

pour 1. The hostess _____*has poured*_____ iced tea for most of her guests.

live 2. My roommate _____*has lived*_____ in three different countries.

check 3. Because I will be driving a long distance, I _____*have checked*_____ the air in my car tires.

boil 4. The chef _____*has boiled*_____ the eggs for the salad and is now slicing them.

mix 5. The children _____*have mixed*_____ together in one box the pieces of three different puzzles.

Past Perfect Tense (*had* + past participle)

The **past perfect** tense describes an action that was completed in the past before another past action.

- Jay **had worked** as a messenger before he located a better job as a waiter.

The past perfect tense is formed by adding *had* to the past participle of a verb.

➤ Practice 5

Fill in the space with the past perfect tense form of the verb shown in the margin. Add *had* to the past participle of the verb. One is done for you as an example.

promise 1. Zora _____*had promised*_____ to go to the meeting before she realized it was on her birthday.

struggle 2. The man _____*had struggled*_____ in several part-time jobs before returning to college.

ask 3. My sister _____*had asked*_____ two other men to the dance before inviting Dan.

intend 4. I _____*had intended*_____ to study after dinner, but then my boss called and asked me to work tonight.

invite 5. Hector _____*had invited*_____ his friends to his apartment before he knew that his roommate was ill.

Future Perfect Tense (*will have* + past participle)

The **future perfect** tense describes an action that will be completed before some time in the future.

- Jay **will have worked** at a half dozen different jobs before college graduation.

The future perfect tense is formed by adding *will have* to the past participle of a verb.

➤ Practice 6

Fill in the space with the future perfect tense form of the verb shown in the margin. Add *will have* to the past participle of the verb. One is done for you as an example.

complete 1. I _____*will have completed*_____ five exams by the end of finals week.

attend 2. By graduation day, I _____*will have attended*_____ five parties.

finish 3. You eat so slowly that I _____*will have finished*_____ my ice cream before you begin your spaghetti.

hire 4. The company _____*will have hired*_____ several new employees by May.

design 5. By the end of the summer, my mother _____*will have* _____*designed*_____ and sewed my wedding dress.

THE PROGRESSIVE TENSES

As their names suggest, the progressive tenses express actions still in progress at a particular time. They are made by adding a form of the helping verb *be* to the *-ing* form of the verb, the present participle.

Present Progressive Tense (*am, are,* or *is* + present participle)

The **present progressive** tense expresses an action taking place at this moment or that will occur sometime in the future.

- Jay **is working** at the restaurant today.
- I **am going** to get home late tonight.

The present progressive tense is formed by adding the correct present tense form of the helping verb *be* to the *-ing* form of the verb.

Present Tense Forms of *Be*

	Singular	*Plural*
First person	I am	we are
Second person	you are	you are
Third person	he, she, it is	they are

➤ Practice 7

Below are five sentences with verbs in the present tense. Cross out each verb and change it to the present progressive in the space provided. One is done for you as an example.

1. The child ~~plays~~ with the puppy. _____ *is playing*

2. The microwave ~~beeps~~ loudly. _____ *is beeping*

3. The roses in the garden ~~bloom~~. _____ *are blooming*

4. I ~~practice~~ my speech tonight. _____ *am practicing*

5. The visitors ~~pace~~ in the hospital lobby. _____ *are pacing*

Past Progressive Tense (*was* or *were* + present participle)

The **past progressive** tense expresses an action that was in progress at a certain time in the past.

- Jay **was working** yesterday.

The past progressive tense is formed by adding the correct past tense form of *be* to the *-ing* form of the verb.

Past Tense Forms of *Be*

	Singular	*Plural*
First person	I was	we were
Second person	you were	you were
Third person	he, she, it was	they were

➤ **Practice 8**

Below are five sentences with verbs in the past tense. Cross out each verb and change it to the past progressive in the space provided. One is done for you as an example.

1. The child ~~played~~ with the puppy. _____ *was playing* _____

2. The microwave ~~beeped~~ loudly. _____ *was beeping* _____

3. The roses in the garden ~~bloomed~~. _____ *were blooming* _____

4. I ~~practiced~~ my speech last night. _____ *was practicing* _____

5. The visitors ~~paced~~ in the hospital lobby. _____ *were pacing* _____

Future Progressive Tense (*will be* + present participle)

The **future progressive** tense expresses an action that will be in progress at a certain time in the future.

- Jay **will be working** tomorrow.

The future progressive tense is formed by adding *will be* to the *-ing* form of the verb.

➤ **Practice 9**

Below are five sentences with verbs in the future tense. Cross out each verb and change it to the future progressive in the space provided. One is done for you as an example.

1. The child ~~will play~~ with the puppy. _____ *will be playing* _____

2. The microwave ~~will beep~~ loudly. _____ *will be beeping* _____

3. The roses in the garden ~~will bloom~~. _____ *will be blooming* _____

4. I ~~will practice~~ my speech tonight. _____ *will be practicing* _____

5. The visitors ~~will pace~~ in the hospital lobby. _____ *will be pacing* _____

A Note on *-ing* Verbs

Look at the following word groups:

- Jay working tonight.
- The visitors pacing in the hospital lobby.

The above word groups express incomplete thoughts because their verbs are incomplete. The *-ing* form of a verb cannot stand by itself as the verb of a sentence—it must be accompanied by a helping verb:

- Jay **is working** tonight.
- The visitors **were pacing** in the hospital lobby.

➤ Practice 10

The verb in each of the following sentences is incomplete. Correct each incomplete thought by adding *is, are, was,* or *were* in the space provided.

1   Oscar _____*is*_____ playing the clarinet in his school band this year.

2. You _____*were*_____ giggling in your sleep last night.

3. The girl reported that even though she _____*was*_____ screaming, no one helped her.

4. If you look down the street, you'll see that five boys _____*are*_____ standing on the corner.

5. The customers _____*were*_____ complaining about the long wait until a waitress offered them free cups of coffee.

A SUMMARY OF THE NINE MOST COMMON VERB TENSES

Summarized in the chart on the next page, for the regular verb *call*, are the nine most common tenses in English.

The Nine Most Common Verb Tenses

Present	I **call** my grandmother Nana. My mother **calls** her Babe.
Past	A number of employees **called** in sick today.
Future	Because the flu is going around, more **will** probably **call** in sick tomorrow.
Present perfect	Rebecca **has called** the radio station at least ten times to request her favorite song.
Past perfect	No one **had called** Mitchell "Shorty" for years until he attended his grade-school reunion.
Future perfect	When you finish your first day as a telemarketer, you **will have called** forty potential customers.
Present progressive	Ken **is calling** the restaurant right now to make a reservation for dinner.
Past progressive	He **was calling** a different restaurant when I came in, but I urged him to call my favorite one.
Future progressive	Mom **will be calling** when she arrives home and realizes she left her purse here.

CHAPTER REVIEW

Fill in the correct word or words in each space provided.

1. There are six basic tenses in English. They are the present, past, _____*future*_____, present perfect, _____*past perfect*_____, and future perfect tenses.

2. The past tense of regular verbs is formed by adding __*-ed*__ or __*-d*__ to the basic form of the verb.

3. The _____*future*_____ tense is formed by adding the word *will* (or *shall*) before the basic form of the verb.

4. The present and past _____*perfect*_____ tenses are formed by adding a form of the helping verb *have* (*have, has,* or *had*) to the past participle of the verb.

5. The (*past, past perfect,* or *past progressive*?) _____*past perfect*_____ tense describes an action that was completed in the past before another past action.

6. The present progressive tense is formed by adding the correct form of the helping verb *be* to the (*-s, -ing,* or *-ed*?) _____*-ing*_____ form of the verb.

Name_____ Section _____ Date _____

Score: (Number right) _____ x 10 = _____%

➤ Verb Tenses: Test 1

A. In each space, write the **present tense** form of the verb in the margin.

Examples   *plan*   Carl _____*plans*_____ to enter the contest.

   attend   The students _____*attend*_____ a meeting on the new dress code.

soar   1. The hawk _____*soars*_____ above the corn field.

listen   2. The jurors _____*listen*_____ to the witness.

think   3. Leona _____*thinks*_____ she passed her English exam.

B. In each space, write the **past tense** form of the verb in the margin.

Example   *promise*   My son _____*promised*_____ to wash my car on Saturday.

scratch   4. The prisoner _____*scratched*_____ his initials on the cell wall.

arrive   5. The bus _____*arrived*_____ at our hotel at 7:15 a.m.

float   6. Five orange slices _____*floated*_____ on top of the red punch.

struggle 7. The campers _____*struggled*_____ through the thick underbrush near the camp.

C. In each space, write the **future tense** form of the verb in the margin.

Example   *check*   The nurse _____*will check*_____ your blood pressure each day.

blossom   8. Those trees _____*will blossom*_____ into fluffy white clouds.

stand   9. Everyone _____*will stand*_____ when the judge enters the courtroom.

wear   10. Johnny _____*will wear*_____ a dinosaur costume to the party.

Name_____ Section _____ Date _____

Score: (Number right) _____ x 10 = _____ %

➤ Verb Tenses: Test 2

A. In each space, write the **present perfect tense** form of the verb in the margin.

Examples   *walk*   Bernice _____*has walked*_____ over twenty miles this week.

look   I _____*have looked*_____ all over for my glasses.

wash   1. The students _____*have washed*_____ nearly seventy cars to raise money for their class trip.

gain   2. Rodney _____*has gained*_____ ten pounds in his first year of college.

learn   3. We _____*have learned*_____ about the civil rights movement in our history class this semester.

noticed   4. I _____*have noticed*_____ changes in you since you started going to the gym.

B. In each space, write the **past perfect tense** form of the verb in the margin.

Example   *walk*   Before her heart attack, Bernice seldom _____*had walked*_____ for exercise.

argue   5. Fritz _____*had argued*_____ with a friend before the car accident.

warn   6. Before planting a bomb in the warehouse, the criminal _____*had warned*_____ the FBI.

manage   7. Chelsea _____*had managed*_____ to clean the entire house by the time her parents got home last evening.

C. In each space, write the **future perfect tense** form of the verb in the margin.

Example   *walk*   By the end of this month, Bernice _____*will have walked*_____ over one hundred miles.

work   8. I _____*will have worked*_____ fifty-five hours by the end of the week.

interview   9. By the time she writes her paper, Jodi _____*will have interviewed*_____ six nurses.

watch   10. By the end of the day, the children _____*will have watched*_____ five hours of television.

Name_____ Section _____ Date _____

Score: (Number right) _____ x 10 = _____%

➤ Verb Tenses: Test 3

A. In each space, write the **present progressive tense** form of the verb in the margin.

Examples *try* I _____*am trying*_____ to build up my self-confidence.

sleep It's so hot out that Ralph _____*is sleeping*_____ in his cool basement.

eat The squirrels _____*are eating*_____ all the bird food.

polish 1. Hank _____*is polishing*_____ his car again.

think 2. You _____*are thinking*_____ of ways to avoid an argument.

go 3. The students _____*are going*_____ to watch the eclipse of the moon.

plant 4. I _____*am planting*_____ fifty red tulips along the driveway.

B. In each space, write the **past progressive tense** form of the verb in the margin.

Examples *sleep* Ralph _____*was sleeping*_____ when the siren blared.

whisper Some people in the theater _____*were whispering*_____ all during the movie.

wait 5. Theo _____*was waiting*_____ for me to pick him up at the movie.

find 6. Companies _____*were finding*_____ coal in this area in the early 1900s.

cry 7. When I got home from school, my son _____*was crying*_____.

C. In each space, write the **future progressive tense** form of the verb in the margin.

Example *use* In the future, farmers _____*will be using*_____ fewer and fewer chemicals.

visit 8. We _____*will be visiting*_____ California next summer.

discuss 9. The senators _____*will be discussing*_____ the President's tax bill today.

work 10. The actress _____*will be working*_____ on a movie during her vacation from her television series.

Name_____ Section _____ Date _____

Score: (Number right) _____ x 12.5 = _____%

➤ Verb Tenses: Test 4

Complete each short paragraph below by filling in the verbs described.

1. Dean *(a)* _____*played*_____ a lot of soccer when he was in high school. After graduation, he continued to enjoy soccer. Next week, he *(b)* _____*will be playing*_____ in a county-wide tournament.

   a. Fill in the past tense form of *play*.
   b. Fill in a future progressive tense verb by combining *will be* with the present participle of *play*.

2. My friend Rita is married to a man who is a career officer in the Navy. Before she was married, she *(a)* _____*had moved*_____ only twice in her life. But in the eight years of their marriage, Rita and her husband *(b)* _____*have moved*_____ seven times.

   a. Fill in a past perfect tense verb by using *had* plus the past participle of *move*.
   b. Fill in a present perfect tense verb by using *have* plus the past participle of *move*.

3. The jury *(a)* _____*is listening*_____ to closing arguments in the case today. By the time the members of the jury retire to decide the verdict, they *(b)* _____*will have listened*_____ to ten days of testimony.

   a. Fill in a present progressive verb by combining *is* with the present participle of *listen*.
   b. Fill in a future perfect tense verb by using *will have* plus the past participle of *listen*.

4. For two weeks last month, Allbrands Appliances *(a)* _____*was* _____*advertising*_____ a very cheap price for a microwave oven. But when I went in, they tried to sell me a much more expensive model. When I insisted that I wanted the one they *(b)* _____*had advertised*_____, they shrugged and said, "We don't have any."

   a. Fill in a past progressive tense verb by using *was* plus the present participle of *advertise*.
   b. Fill in a past perfect tense verb by combining *had* and the past participle of *advertise*.

Name_____ Section _____ Date _____

Score: (Number right) _____ x 10 = _____%

➤ Verb Tenses: Test 5

Complete the selection below by filling in each verb that is described in the following list and the list on the next page.

---

1. Fill in a present progressive tense verb by using *is* plus the present participle of *run*.
2. Fill in the correct present tense form of *cheer*.
3. Fill in a future tense verb by using *will* plus the basic form of *moan*.
4. Fill in a present perfect tense verb by combining *have* with the past participle of *borrow*.
5. Fill in a present progressive tense verb by using *am* plus the present participle of *think*.

Of all American farm animals, turkeys get the least respect. One reason is their appearance. Turkeys have enormous feathery ruffs around their backsides, practically no wings, and strange red things drooping from their chins. Then there is the sound they make. It's hard to take an animal seriously when it (1) _____*is running*_____ around saying "Gobble gobble gobble." In addition, there's the Thanksgiving connection. Sure, we may (2) _____*cheer*_____ at the sight of the roast turkey on the Thanksgiving table, surrounded by gravy and sweet potatoes. But the next day we (3) _____*will moan*_____, "Turkey again!" as we look ahead to a solid week of turkey sandwiches, turkey hash, and turkey soup. We look down on the turkey so much that we (4) _____*have borrowed*_____ its name to describe someone we don't like. "He's a turkey," we say.

But all these reasons for making fun of the turkey do not excuse making up a false story about it. The story I (5) _____*am thinking*_____ of is one that a number of schoolchildren have heard reported as fact.

(Continues on next page)

6. Fill in a past progressive tense verb by using *was* plus the present participle of *rain*.

7. Fill in the past tense form of *look*.

8. Fill in the correct present tense form of *need*.

9. Fill in a present perfect verb tense by using *have* plus the past participle of *cause*.

10. Fill in a future progressive tense verb by using *will be* plus the present participle of *find*.

It usually goes something like this: "You remember last week when it (6) _____*was raining*_____ so hard? A bunch of my uncle's turkeys (7) _____*looked*_____ up into the sky at the rain until they drowned!" Turkeys may not be smart, but they are not guilty of that behavior.

Here's the real story: For the first eight or nine weeks of life, a baby turkey is covered with down rather than feathers. Therefore, it (8) _____*needs*_____ special protection from cold and wet weather. Wild turkey mothers are smart enough to hustle their babies to safety when it rains. But farm turkeys are a different story. Generations of being cared for by humans (9) _____*have caused*_____ them to become pretty helpless, not to say dumb. The mother turkeys have lost the instinct to protect their babies from the rain. As a result, the babies die from exposure to harsh weather. So part of the story is true. After the next heavy rain, farmers across the country (10) _____*will be finding*_____ dead baby turkeys out in the farmyard. It's not a pretty sight, but give them a little respect. At least they didn't drown.

6 / Irregular Verbs

This chapter explains the difference between regular and irregular verbs. Then it gives you practice with some common irregular verbs.

1   Regular Verbs

Basic Form	Past Tense Form	Past Participle
work	worked	worked
smile	smiled	smiled

2   Irregular Verbs

Basic Form	Past Tense Form	Past Participle
hide	hid	hidden
swim	swam	swum

REGULAR VERBS

Most English verbs are **regular**. That is, they form their past tense and past participle by adding *-ed* or *-d* to the basic form, as shown in this chart:

Basic Form	Past Tense Form	Past Participle
ask	ask**ed**	ask**ed**
raise	raise**d**	raise**d**

Note: The present participle of both regular and irregular verbs is formed simply by adding *-ing* to the basic form *(asking, raising)*.

IRREGULAR VERBS

Irregular verbs, however, do not follow the pattern of adding *-ed* or *-d* to the basic form of the verb. Instead, their past tense forms and past participles are formed in other ways. On the next two pages are some of the most common irregular verbs. Review them enough to become familiar with them.

Common Irregular Verbs

Basic Form	Past Tense Form	Past Participle
be	was, were	been
become	became	become
begin	began	begun
blow	blew	blown
break	broke	broken
bring	brought	brought
catch	caught	caught
choose	chose	chosen
come	came	come
cut	cut	cut
do	did	done
draw	drew	drawn
drink	drank	drunk
drive	drove	driven
eat	ate	eaten
fall	fell	fallen
feel	felt	felt
find	found	found
fly	flew	flown
freeze	froze	frozen
get	got	got, gotten
give	gave	given
go	went	gone
grow	grew	grown
have	had, has	had
hide	hid	hidden
keep	kept	kept
know	knew	known
lay *(put)*	laid	laid
leave	left	left
lend	lent	lent
lie *(recline)*	lay	lain
lose	lost	lost
make	made	made
read	read	read
ride	rode	ridden
rise	rose	risen
run	ran	run
say	said	said
see	saw	seen
sell	sold	sold
set *(place)*	set	set
shake	shook	shaken
sit *(take a seat)*	sat	sat
sleep	slept	slept

Basic Form	Past Tense Form	Past Participle
speak	spoke	spoken
spend	spent	spent
steal	stole	stolen
swim	swam	swum
take	took	taken
teach	taught	taught
tell	told	told
think	thought	thought
throw	threw	thrown
wear	wore	worn
win	won	won
write	wrote	written

If you think a verb is irregular, and it is not in the above list, look it up in your dictionary. If it is irregular, the principal parts will be listed. For an example of how a dictionary lists the principal parts of irregular verbs, see "Dictionary Use," page 435.

➤ Practice 1

In each item, the present tense of an irregular verb is shown in *italic* type. Fill in the missing **past tense form** in the *a* slot and the **past participle** in the *b* slot. Refer to the above chart as necessary. One item is done for you as an example.

1. I often *freeze* candy bars so that they'll take longer to eat. Last week I (a) _____*froze*_____ several Snickers Bars. In the past year, I probably have (b) _____*frozen*_____ a dozen kinds of candy bars.

2. My cousin *drives* a city bus. He (a) _____*drove*_____ a taxi cab for years before that. In fact, he has (b) _____*driven*_____ for a living all of his adult life.

3. In fifteen minutes, Larry can *draw* a lifelike portrait of anybody. Once, a picture he (a) _____*drew*_____ was published in the newspaper. He works in a little booth at the mall, surrounded by all of the portraits he has (b) _____*drawn*_____.

4. Nadia's parents *speak* Spanish at home. She (a) _____*spoke*_____ only Spanish until she was four. However, for the last twelve years, she has (b) _____*spoken*_____ English in school.

5. Emma *takes* yoga lessons. She *(a)* _____took_____ her first class ten years ago. Yoga makes her feel so good that she has *(b)* _____taken_____ the classes ever since.

6. People often *become* lost in a strange city. When Fran drove to visit her sister in Chicago, she *(a)* _____became_____ confused by a detour. Once she had *(b)* _____become_____ hopelessly lost, she telephoned her sister for help.

7. I *ride* roller coasters every chance I get, but my wife refuses to join me. She *(a)* _____rode_____ one once many years ago. When I ask her to give it another chance, she says, "I have *(b)* _____ridden_____ one, and I hated it. Why would I want to try it again?"

8. My sister reminded me, "Please *bring* paper plates to the picnic." Unfortunately, I *(a)* _____brought_____ some flimsy ones that bent and proceeded to spill food all over people's laps. Luckily, someone else had *(b)* _____brought_____ some heavy cardboard plates.

9. Elizabeth cannot *make* up her mind about her sales job. On Monday, she *(a)* _____made_____ the decision to quit. On Tuesday, she told her boss. On Wednesday, she decided she had *(b)* _____made_____ a mistake and begged for her job back. By Thursday, she wanted to quit again.

10. My uncle *knows* everything about cars. When my car wouldn't start last week, he *(a)* _____knew_____ exactly what was wrong. "You should have *(b)* _____known_____ better than to leave the radio on all evening," he scolded me.

➤ Practice 2

Write the correct form of each verb in the space provided. Keep in mind the following:

- The past tense form of irregular verbs never ends with *-ed*.
- If the sentence does not include a helping verb, choose the past tense form.
- If the sentence includes a helping verb, choose the past participle.

wrote, written   1. The recipe was _____written_____ on the back of an envelope.

selled, sold   2. Ken _____sold_____ his car and now rides his bicycle to work.

wore, worn   3. My favorite blue sweater finally has _____worn_____ out.

ate, eaten   4. A mouse has _____eaten_____ a hole through this bag of dogfood.

lost, losted   5. You could tell by the runner's face that he had _____lost_____ the race.

fell, fallen   6. Before the driver could stop, three large boxes had _____fallen_____ from the back of his truck.

broke, broken   7. When I _____broke_____ my leg, my friends scribbled cheerful messages on the cast.

spended, spent   8. Nathan _____spent_____ most of his teenage years dressed in black and alone in his bedroom.

began, begun   9. The concert had already _____begun_____, but people were still coming to their seats.

hid, hided   10. The news told about a person who foolishly _____hid_____ some money in a microwave oven.

went, gone   11. Sandy has _____gone_____ to a counselor every week since her parents' divorce.

stole, stealed   12. Some neighborhood kids _____stole_____ the flags on all of the mailboxes on our block.

risen, rose   13. By the time the sun had _____risen_____, Margie had already run two miles.

taught, teached 14. The deli manager _____taught_____ the new workers how to slice meat, make potato salad, and use the food scale.

sleeped, slept   15. Since starting her new job, Susan has not _____slept_____ well.

chose, chosen   16. Juanita has _____chosen_____ the color gray for her bridesmaids' dresses.

shaked, shook   17. The elevator _____shook_____ suddenly and then came to a complete stop between the eighth and ninth floors.

throwed, threw   18. The teenagers were fined when they _____threw_____ water balloons out of the hotel window.

became, become   19. Rob did not _____become_____ a firefighter until he had passed several written and physical exams.

drank, drunk   20. Our guests have _____drunk_____ every drop of juice, soda, and milk that was in the house.

Three Problem Verbs

Three common irregular verbs that confuse many writers are *be*, *do*, and *have*. Here are the correct present tense and past tense forms of these three verbs.

	Present Tense		*Past Tense*	
Be	I am	we are	I was	we were
	you are	you are	you were	you were
	he, she, it is	they are	he, she, it was	they were
Do	I do	we do	I did	we did
	you do	you do	you did	you did
	he, she, it does	they do	he, she, it did	they did
Have	I have	we have	I had	we had
	you have	you have	you had	you had
	he, she, it has	they have	he, she it had	they had

➤ Practice 3

Write the correct form of each verb in the space provided.

has, have   1. Alice _____has_____ the same pants in three colors.

are, is   2. Few people realize that pigs _____are_____ intelligent animals.

do, does   3. Every morning before breakfast, my grandfather _____does_____ fifty push-ups.

was, be   4. By halftime, I _____was_____ sure we would lose the game.

do, does   5. In art class, the children _____do_____ self-portraits with crayons and finger paints.

are, be   6. Local merchants _____are_____ worried about the mall being built outside of town.

has, have   7. Gang members often _____have_____ to perform dangerous stunts to become a part of the group.

was, were	8. During the nineteenth century, children ___*were*___ often forced to work twelve-hour days.
did, done	9. The doctor ___*did*___ eight tests on his patient before concluding that she had a cold.
was, were	10. The salesman ___*was*___ annoyed when a customer put a new pair of shoes on bare feet.
are, is	11. My mother ___*is*___ working part-time as a telephone salesperson.
has, have	12. Those sneakers ___*have*___ glow-in-the-dark stripes.
was, were	13. Because Dionne ___*was*___ the first customer at the new store, she won passes to a weekend concert.
has, have	14. No one ___*has*___ ordered the frog legs on the menu.
am, be	15. I ___*am*___ always ready for a game of cards.
has, have	16. The veteran pilot ___*has*___ landed planes in snow, hail, and thick fog.
do, does	17. My parents ___*do*___ not seem to care that I'm very depressed, and that depresses me more.
did, done	18. Even though I ___*did*___ the reading for the course, I still felt lost in class.
was, were	19. Martin Luther King, Jr., ___*was*___ a believer in protest without violence.
was, were	20. We ___*were*___ relieved to see the doctor come out of the operating room with a smile on his face.

Don't and Doesn't

The words *do not* can be combined into one word: *don't*. The words *does not* can also be combined into one word: *doesn't*. Here is how *don't* and *doesn't* are used for the first, second, and third person:

Present Tense Forms of *To Do* + Not

	Singular	Plural
First person	I don't	we don't
Second person	you don't	you don't
Third person	he, she, it doesn't	they don't

Note that *doesn't* (like *does*) is used only for the third-person singular.

➤ **Practice 4**

Complete each sentence by filling in either *don't* or *doesn't*.

1. Olivia _____*doesn't*_____ use any makeup.

2. These cans _____*don't*_____ have labels on them.

3. We _____*don't*_____ go to the movies much.

4. That fire escape _____*doesn't*_____ look sturdy.

5. You _____*don't*_____ remember my name.

6. I _____*don't*_____ enjoy traveling.

7. Alfonso _____*doesn't*_____ have a car this week.

8. My cat _____*doesn't*_____ like cat food.

9. My neighbors _____*don't*_____ recycle their newspapers.

10. The boss _____*doesn't*_____ believe in giving compliments to the employees.

CHAPTER REVIEW

Fill in the correct word or words in each space provided.

1. The past tense of a(n) _____*regular*_____ verb is formed by adding *-ed* or *-d* to the present form.

2. _____*Irregular*_____ verbs do not follow the usual pattern for the past tense and the past participle.

3. Complete the missing present tense forms of the following verbs:

   I am   I do   I have
   you are   you do   you have
   he, she, it __*is*__   he, she, it __*does*__   he, she, it __*has*__

4. *Do not* can be contracted into the word _____*don't*_____.

5. *Does not* can be contracted into the word _____*doesn't*_____.

Name_____ Section _____ Date _____

➤ Irregular Verbs: Test 1

For each sentence below, fill in the correct form of the verb in the space provided.

grew, growed

1. The fairy tale was about a magic beanstalk that _____*grew*_____ higher than the clouds.

drived, drove

2. The family _____*drove*_____ away without paying for their take-out food.

did, done

3. Charles often _____*did*_____ his grandmother's shopping for her.

flew, flown

4. The hot-air balloons had _____*flown*_____ straight into a dangerous storm.

chose, chosen

5. The children already have _____*chosen*_____ teams for the kickball game.

did, done

6. Many students have _____*done*_____ poorly on the final exam.

telled, told

7. When I let Katy know my secret, she _____*told*_____ everyone she knew.

read, readed

8. Last night, Yoshio _____*read*_____ an entire mystery novel before going to bed.

went, gone

9. The sign on the barber shop door said, "Closed. I have _____*gone*_____ fishing."

wrote, written

10. The pen pals had _____*written*_____ to each other for years, but they had never met in person.

Name_____ Section _____ Date _____

Score: (Number right) _____ x 10 = _____ %

➤ Irregular Verbs: Test 2

For each sentence below, fill in the correct form of the verb in the space provided.

rided, rode   1. My sister _____*rode*_____ a horse over the mountain trail.

had, haved   2. Meg _____*had*_____ a job interview with a catering firm last Saturday.

drank, drunk   3. Everyone who had _____*drunk*_____ from that well got a stomachache.

shaked, shook   4. My father _____*shook*_____ the chicken in a bag with bread crumbs and spices.

leaved, left   5. When the carpenters finished their work, they _____*left*_____ behind piles of sawdust.

hid, hidden   6. It was rumored that the old man had _____*hidden*_____ money inside his pillow.

did, done   7. I was the cook, and my roommate _____*did*_____ the cleaning up.

keeped, kept   8. During the war, the soldier _____*kept*_____ a picture of his mother in his shirt pocket.

freezed, frozen   9. My aunt has _____*frozen*_____ eight quarts of strawberries so that she can make pies this winter.

was, were   10. We _____*were*_____ amazed when our gray dog had five tiny white and black puppies.

Name_____   _____ Section _____ Date _____

➤ Irregular Verbs: Test 3

Each short passage below contains an error in the past tense and in the past participle of an irregular verb. Find the **two** errors and cross them out. Then write the correct form of each verb in the space provided.

1. Last Sunday, Grandma invited a dozen people over for dinner. After everything was ~~ate~~, the men started to go watch TV. "Hold it," said Grandma. "If you ~~eaten~~, you help clean up."

   a. _____eaten_____

   b. _____ate_____

2. It is dangerous to shake a baby. Many babies who have been ~~shook~~ have suffered brain injuries. The adults who ~~shaked~~ these babies seldom meant to cause such harm.

   a. _____shaken_____

   b. _____shook_____

3. I have always ~~gave~~ my little children household chores. This month, my son sets the table, and my daughter does some dusting. Last month, they both ~~done~~ some weeding in the back yard.

   a. _____given_____

   b. _____did_____

4. In the winter, I drink about a quart of orange juice a week. But last week when it was so hot, I ~~drinked~~ that much in a day. Once all the orange juice was ~~drank~~, I started in on ice water and cold soda.

   a. _____drank_____

   b. _____drunk_____

5. It really can be more fun to give than to receive. Yesterday I ~~gived~~ my niece a ring of mine that she had always loved. When she saw what I had ~~gave~~ her, her face lit up.

   a. _____gave_____

   b. _____given_____

➤ Irregular Verbs: Test 4

Each short passage below contains **two** irregular verb errors. Find these errors and cross them out. Then write the correct form of each verb in the space provided.

1. "Try to fall in love with a rich woman," my mother urged me. But I ~~falled~~ for a starving artist. When I ~~telled~~ her I had fallen in love with a poor woman, she sighed, "Your father did the same thing."

   a. _____*fell*_____

   b. _____*told*_____

2. Randy ~~losed~~ forty pounds by drinking a diet shake instead of eating meals. But in a year, he gained it all back. Kay, on the other hand, became thin by changing her eating habits and exercising. She dropped pounds more slowly, but she has ~~keeped~~ them off.

   a. _____*lost*_____

   b. _____*kept*_____

3. Hawks ~~has~~ keen eyesight. Once I saw a hawk dive from the top of a tall tree to capture a field mouse. The bird had ~~saw~~ the tiny creature running through the tall grass.

   a. _____*have*_____

   b. _____*seen*_____

4. The two doctors in this office usually see about twenty-five patients each day. But yesterday they ~~seen~~ more than forty. Most of the patients ~~was~~ sick with the flu. Both doctors are planning to take a vacation after the flu season is over.

   a. _____*saw*_____

   b. _____*were*_____

5. My aunt ~~be~~ a big fan of Elvis Presley. Every time she hears "Love Me Tender," she becomes misty-eyed. Last year, she and my uncle ~~gone~~ on a trip to Graceland, Elvis's home. While there, she bought "Elvis Lives" bumper stickers for herself and all her friends.

   a. _____*is*_____

   b. _____*went*_____

Name_____ _____ Section _____ Date _____

Score: (Number right) _____ x 10 = _____%

➤ Irregular Verbs: Test 5

The following passage contains **ten** errors in irregular verbs. Cross out each error. Then in the space above the line, write the correct form of each verb. (If a helping verb is used, then a past participle is needed.)

Most of the time, I enjoy my work as a bartender. I've had the same

gone
job for four years and am pretty good at it. I have never ~~went~~ to

taught
bartending school. Instead, another bartender ~~teached~~ me what I needed

to know. Last night was a pretty typical evening. Soon after I started my

shift, a group of lawyers came in. They were celebrating their success

shook
with an important case. I ~~shooked~~ up a pitcher of martinis and gave them

were
a pitcher of beer as well. They ~~was~~ friendly and pleasant, and we all

traded jokes. When they left two hours later, I had a nice tip. Luckily, the

drunk
driver of the group had ~~drank~~ just one beer and then had coffee the rest

of the night.

Later, I watched a guy alone at the bar. He had ordered only one

seen
drink, but I have ~~saw~~ enough of drinkers to guess that he was already

drunk before he came in. "How you doing tonight, sir?" I asked him. "I'm

knew
OK," he mumbled. "Give me another drink." I ~~known~~ from his voice and

the way his eyes looked that he had already had too much. I didn't want

to embarrass him, so I lowered my voice and said, "Maybe you ought to

have a soda or a cup of coffee this time. It's on the house." He glared at

rose
me and ~~rised~~ from his barstool. "Are you saying I'm drunk?" he shouted. I

sat
managed to calm him down a bit, but then he ~~sitted~~ down—and missed

(Continues on next page)

the stool. When that happened, he realized how drunk he had ~~became~~ *become*

and let me call a taxi for him. I was relieved.

That's the life of a bartender—some fun, some worry, and a lot of

work.

7 / More About Verbs

This chapter explains three things you should know about verb tense:

1   Consistent verb tense

Inconsistent verb tense: We parked the car and **head** toward the movie theater.

Consistent verb tense: We parked the car and headed toward the movie theater.

2   The passive and active voices

Passive voice: I **was visited** last week by a former neighbor.

Active voice: A former neighbor visited me last week.

3   Nonstandard and standard verbs

Nonstandard verbs: Every week, Mandy **volunteer** at a nursing home near her apartment. She often **read** to residents there.

Standard verbs: Every week, Mandy volunteers at a nursing home near her apartment. She often reads to residents there.

CONSISTENT VERB TENSE

In your writing, avoid illogical or needless shifts in tense. For example, if you are writing a paper with the action in the past tense, don't shift suddenly to the present for no reason. Look at the examples below:

Inconsistent verb tense: In my nightmare, a hairy spider **crawled** up the side of my bed and **races** quickly onto my pillow.

There is no reason for the writer to shift suddenly from the past tense (*crawled*) to the present tense (*races*). The inconsistency can be corrected by using the same tense for both verbs:

Consistent verb tense: In my nightmare, a hairy spider **crawled** up the side of my bed and **raced** quickly onto my pillow.

➤ **Practice 1**

In each short passage, there is **one** illogical or unneeded change in verb tense. Cross out the incorrect verb. Then write the correct form of that verb on the line provided.

_____*crashed*_____ 1. The ice skater moved smoothly through her routine. On her last jump, however, she lost her balance and ~~crashes~~ to the ice with a thud.

_____*heat*_____ 2. On many farms, machines milk the cows. The farmers then send the fresh milk to a processing plant. Workers there ~~heated~~ the milk at high temperatures. The intense heat removes bacteria.

_____*picked*_____ 3. When Tina saw flames and smoke coming from her kitchen, she reacted quickly. She ~~picks~~ up her kitten and her purse. Then she rushed out into the fresh air.

_____*crossed*_____ 4. Soldiers in the Civil War fought in bloody battles during the day. But at night, they often ~~cross~~ "enemy" lines for a friendly visit.

_____*prepared*_____ 5. Melba took an inexpensive vacation this summer. She called parks and museums in the area to find out the cheapest times to visit. To save money, she ~~prepares~~ picnic lunches for her visits.

_____*promised*_____ 6. My roommate was very annoyed with me last week. I ~~promise~~ him that he could borrow my car, but I forgot to leave him the keys.

_____*delivers*_____ 7. Arlo works for a small greeting card company. He writes poems for the wedding cards. Then he ~~delivered~~ the cards to the art department, where an artist sketches pictures of wedding bells or flowers.

_____*surged*_____ 8. Last summer, my father went water skiing. After about five attempts, he skied around the entire lake. But when a large wave from another boat ~~surges~~ by, he flipped into the water head first.

_____*stays*_____ 9. My sister complains at the drop of a hat. She often runs to her room in a rage. She ~~stayed~~ there for hours feeling sorry for herself.

_____*disappeared*_____ 10. Last night, I went on the worst date ever. My date, Martin, showed up an hour late. During dinner, all he talked about was himself. Then, just before the waitress brought our check, he ~~disappears~~. I paid the bill and took a taxi home.

THE PASSIVE AND ACTIVE VOICES

The subject of a sentence usually performs the action of the verb. In such cases, the verb is in the **active voice**. For example, look at the following sentence:

- My father **planted** the Japanese maple tree in the front yard.

The verb in this sentence is *planted*. Who performed that action? The answer is *father*, the subject of the sentence. Therefore, the verb is in the active voice. Now look at this version of that sentence:

- The Japanese maple tree in the front yard **was planted** by my father.

The verb in this sentence is *was planted*. The subject of the sentence, *tree*, did not perform the action. The tree was acted upon, by the father. When the subject of a sentence is acted upon, the verb is in the **passive voice**.

Passive verbs are formed by combining a form of *to be (am, is, are, was, were)* with the past participle of a verb (which is usually the same as its past tense form). For example, in the sentence above, *was* plus the past participle of *plant* results in the passive verb *was planted*. Here are some other passive verbs:

Form of *to be*	+	past participle	=	passive verb
am	+	pushed	=	am pushed
is	+	surprised	=	is surprised
was	+	delayed	=	was delayed

In general, write in the active voice. Because it expresses action, it is more energetic and effective than the passive voice. Use the passive voice when you wish to emphasize the receiver of the action or when the performer of the action is unknown.

Here are some more examples of sentences with active and passive verbs:

Active: Our landlord's son **mows** our backyard every week.

The subject of the sentence, *son*, performs the action of the sentence, *mows*.

Passive: Our backyard **is mowed** every week by our landlord's son.

The subject of the sentence—*backyard*—does not act. Instead, it is acted upon. (The passive verb is a combination of *is* plus the past participle of *mow*.)

Active: My sister **wrecked** her new car in an accident last night.

The subject of the sentence, *sister*, is the one who acted—she *wrecked* the car.

Passive: My sister's new car **was wrecked** in an accident last night.

The subject of this sentence, *car*, does not do anything. Something is done to it.

➤ Practice 2

Underline the verb in each sentence. Then circle the **A** in the margin if the verb is active. Circle the **P** in the margin if the verb is passive.

Example   A Ⓟ   The car window <u>was shattered</u> by a poorly aimed baseball.

Ⓐ **P**   1. My mother <u>calls</u> me almost every day.

A Ⓟ   2. Rice <u>is consumed</u> every day by people all over Asia.

Ⓐ **P**   3. Certain breeds of dog <u>bite</u> more often than others.

Ⓐ **P**   4. The cashier <u>counted</u> the change out carefully.

A Ⓟ   5. The injured man <u>was rushed</u> to the emergency room.

A Ⓟ   6. The parade <u>was headed</u> by two young girls twirling batons.

Ⓐ **P**   7. The audience <u>cheered</u> at the play's end.

A Ⓟ   8. Several flights <u>were delayed</u> because of a snowstorm.

Ⓐ **P**   9. The Yellow Pages <u>provide</u> lots of useful information.

A Ⓟ   10. The words "No Trespassing" <u>were painted</u> in red letters on the fence.

Rewriting from the Passive to the Active Voice

Keep in mind that in the active voice, the subject performs the action. Here's a sentence with a passive verb. See if you can rewrite the sentence using the active voice.

Passive voice: Our roof was damaged by the storm.

Active voice: _____

In the passive version of the sentence, the subject *(roof)* was acted upon by the storm. The storm is what did the action. To write an active version of the sentence, you should have made *storm* the subject: *The storm damaged our roof.*

➤ Practice 3

The following sentences are written in the passive voice. For each sentence, underline the verb. Then rewrite the sentence in the active voice, changing the wording as necessary.

Example   Fruits and vegetables <u>are painted</u> often by artists.

Artists often paint fruits and vegetables.

1. The cat <u>was named</u> Leo by my son.

   My son named the cat Leo.

2. Soccer <u>is played</u> by children all over the world.

   Children all over the world play soccer.

3. The book report <u>was prepared</u> hastily by Sean.

   Sean prepared the book report hastily.

4. Some students <u>were pushed</u> around by the gym teacher.

   The gym teacher pushed some students around.

5. Shipping labels <u>are printed</u> quickly by the computer.

   The computer prints shipping labels quickly.

6. A nest <u>was constructed</u> in our mailbox by some robins.

   Some robins constructed a nest in our mailbox.

7. The alarm clock <u>was invented</u> by an American.

   An American invented the alarm clock.

8. The pizza restaurant <u>was closed</u> by the health inspector.

   The health inspector closed the pizza restaurant.

9. My telephone <u>was used</u> for a long-distance call by Jana without my permission.

   Jana used my telephone for a long-distance call without my permission.

10. Many annoying insects, such as mosquitoes, <u>are consumed</u> by spiders.

    Spiders consume many annoying insects, such as mosquitoes.

NONSTANDARD AND STANDARD VERBS

Nonstandard expressions such as *they ain't, we has, I be* or *he don't* are often part of successful communication among family members and friends. In both college and the working world, however, standard English is widely accepted as the norm for speaking and writing.

Nonstandard and Standard Verb Forms

The chart below shows both nonstandard and standard forms of the regular verb *like*. Practice using the standard forms in your speech and writing.

	Nonstandard Forms		**Standard Forms**	
Present tense	I likes	we likes	I lik**e**	we lik**e**
	you likes	you likes	you lik**e**	you lik**e**
	he, she, it like	they likes	he, she, it lik**es**	they lik**e**
Past tense	I like	we like	I lik**ed**	we lik**ed**
	you like	you like	you lik**ed**	you lik**ed**
	he, she, it like	they like	he, she, it lik**ed**	they lik**ed**

Notes:

1   In standard English, always add *-s* or *-es* to a third-person singular verb in the present tense.

Nonstandard: Rex dislike his new job in Utah, and he miss his San Diego friends.

Standard: Rex dislike**s** his new job in Utah, and he miss**es** his San Diego friends.

2   Always add the ending *-ed* or *-d* to a regular verb to show it is past tense.

Nonstandard: As children, Melba and her brother enjoy their piano lessons but hate practicing.

Standard: As children, Melba and her brother enjoy**ed** their piano lessons but hat**ed** practicing.

➤ **Practice 4**

In each blank below, write the standard form of the verb in parentheses.

1. When the skinny boxer saw his huge opponent, he *(decide/decided)* _____decided_____ he was against violent sports.

2. At the family reunion last week, people *(greet/greeted)* _____greeted_____ each other with kisses.

3. Every week, Betty *(make/makes)* _____makes_____ soup from the leftovers she finds in her refrigerator.

4. The movie was so bad that everyone *(laugh/laughed)* _____laughed_____ at the "scary" parts.

5. The twins *(wish/wishes)* _____wish_____ that their parents would get back together.

6. Lester *(play/plays)* _____plays_____ the saxophone better than anyone I've ever heard.

7. Two nights a week, my mother and aunt *(attend/attends)* _____attend_____ night classes.

8. Before she left on her vacation, Cindy *(water/watered)* _____watered_____ her plants, canceled her newspaper, and ate the leftovers in her refrigerator.

9. In bed, my brother always *(pull/pulls)* _____pulls_____ the covers over his head.

10. At high tide during yesterday's storm, powerful waves *(pound/pounded)* _____pounded_____ the shore.

CHAPTER REVIEW

Answer each question by writing **T** (for *true*) or **F** (for *false*) in the space provided.

1. *True or false?* __T__ When writing, one should avoid needless shifts in tense.

2. *True or false?* __F__ When writing, one should never use the passive voice.

3. *True or false?* __T__ In the active voice, the subject of the sentence performs the action of the verb.

4. *True or false?* __T__ In standard English, one should always use *-ed* or *-d* endings to show past tense of regular verbs.

Name_____ Section _____ Date _____

➤ More About Verbs: Test 1

A. In each short passage, there is **one** illogical or needless shift in verb tense. Cross out the incorrect verb. Then write the correct form of that verb on the line provided.

_____*ended*_____   1. The gangster movie started with a car chase, featured a half dozen gun fights, and ~~ends~~ with the death of half the characters.

_____*worked*_____   2. Josh wanted to attend college, but his parents couldn't afford to send him. So he ~~works~~ for two years after high school graduation. With the money he saved, he attended a community college.

_____*watched*_____   3. Officer McFry worked the night shift last night. He patrolled the western part of the city. He also ~~watches~~ traffic at the intersection on Front Street. McFry returned home around 6:30 a.m.

_____*play*_____   4. Our service group meets at a nursing home once a month. We visit with the patients and plan fun activities for them. We sing, ~~played~~ card games, and do craft projects.

B. The following sentences are written in the passive voice. In each sentence, underline the verb. Then rewrite the sentence in the active voice, changing the wording as necessary.

5. That delicious chocolate cake <u>was baked</u> by Sidney.

   *Sidney baked that delicious chocolate cake.*_____

6. Rock music <u>is played</u> at top volume by our neighbors.

   *Our neighbors play rock music at top volume.*_____

7. The highest score on the test <u>was earned</u> by Clarita.

   *Clarita earned the highest score on the test.*_____

C. In each blank below, write the standard form of the verb in parentheses.

8. The children *(look / looked)* _____*looked*_____ under the sofa cushions and found eighty-three cents.

9. At home, my wife is always in jeans, but she *(wear / wears)* _____*wears*_____ suits and dresses to work.

10. When he was younger, my uncle *(play / played)* _____*played*_____ saxophone with a dance band.

Name_____ Section _____ Date _____

Score: (Number right) _____ x 10 = _____%

➤ More About Verbs: Test 2

A. In each short passage, there is **one** illogical or needless shift in verb tense. Cross out the incorrect verb. Then write the correct form of that verb on the line provided.

_____*sprayed*_____ 1. As we walked into the department store, a well-dressed woman from the cosmetics department approached us. Before we could protest, she ~~sprays~~ a cloud of musky-smelling perfume in our direction.

_____*delivered*_____ 2. My friends worked at odd jobs this past summer. Carlos worked at a zoo, cleaning out the bird cages. Jenny worked at Pizza Hut. She ~~delivers~~ pizzas every night of the week.

_____*appear*_____ 3. White flowers blossom on the apple trees every spring. Then tiny green apples ~~appeared~~. Finally, the apples turn into sweet red fruit.

_____*included*_____ 4. On the first Thanksgiving, pilgrims celebrated their survival through the winter. They served many foods, but turkey was not one of them. The menu ~~includes~~ duck, goose, seafood, and eels.

B. Each of the following sentences is written in the passive voice. Rewrite each in the active voice, changing the wording as necessary.

5. Directions to the hotel were provided by a taxi driver.

   *A taxi driver provided directions to the hotel.*_____

6. The dinner table was always cleared by the children.

   *The children always cleared the dinner table.*_____

7. Much air pollution is caused by cars and factories.

   *Cars and factories cause much air pollution.*_____

C. In each blank below, write the standard form of the verb in parentheses.

8. Before he leaves for work each morning, Duncan *(make/makes)* _____*makes*_____ coffee and pours it into a Thermos.

9. When they were teenagers, Kate and Nellie often *(trade/traded)* _____*traded*_____ secrets.

10. My cat *(know/knows)* _____*knows*_____ which bedroom window is mine, and he scratches at it to get my attention.

Name_____ Section _____ Date _____

➤ More About Verbs: Test 3

A. (1–4.) In the short paragraph below, there are **four** illogical or needless shifts in verb tense. Cross out each incorrect verb and, above it, write the correct form of the verb.

Tony and Roxanne's house was in need of some care. One autumn

day, they had nothing else important to do, so that morning they woke up

                       pulled
early and went to work. While Tony raked the leaves, Roxanne ~~pulls~~ the

weeds that grew along the sidewalk. She then scraped loose paint off the

porch stairs while he tied the old newspapers into bundles for recycling.
   painted
Tony ~~paints~~ the porch stairs. Roxanne washed the windows. Together,
   planted
they ~~plant~~ a small tree to replace one that died the winter before. Moving

inside the house, Tony scrubbed the kitchen and bathroom floors.

Roxanne vacuumed and dusted in every room. Then Tony delivered the

newspapers and a load of aluminum cans to the recycyling center and
returned
~~returns~~ with a pizza for dinner.

B. (5–7.) Cross out the **three** sentences in the following paragraph that are in the passive voice. Then write in an active version of each sentence, changing the wording as necessary.

In 1963, Betty Friedan wrote the book *The Feminine Mystique*. In it,

Friedan spoke of what she called "the problem without a name." ~~The~~
Friedan described the problem as women's growing sense of emptiness with
~~problem was described by Friedan as women's growing sense of~~
their lives as housewives and mothers.
~~emptiness with their lives as housewives and mothers.~~ *The Feminine*

Mystique showed how our society kept women "in their place." ~~An uproar~~
The book caused an uproar throughout society.
~~was caused throughout society by the book.~~ It helped to jump-start the

(Continues on next page)

women's-rights movement. Some women greeted the book with relief. ~~It~~
Others attacked it.
~~was attacked by others.~~ Betty Friedan became a heroine to many, and a

villain to others. Today many people consider her the mother of the

modern women's-rights movement.

C. (8–10.) There are **three** nonstandard verb forms in the following paragraph. Cross out each incorrect verb and, above it, write the standard form of the verb.

The color of surgeons' uniforms has changed through the years.

Until 1914, surgeons wore white uniforms. However, bright red blood

against the white cloth disturbed people—especially patients. So
changed
manufacturers ~~change~~ the color of surgical uniforms to spinach green.

Since the end of World War II, operating rooms have had a new type of
started
lighting. In response, surgeons ~~start~~ to wear a color called "misty green."

Since about 1960, many surgeons have switched to "seal blue," a gray-
shows
blue color. Seal blue ~~show~~ up well on the TV monitors that demonstrate

surgical techniques to medical students.

8 / Subject-Verb Agreement

In a correctly written sentence, the subject and verb **agree (match) in number**. Singular subjects have singular verbs, and plural subjects have plural verbs.

In simple sentences of few words, it's not difficult to make the subject and verb agree:

$$S \quad V \qquad\qquad\qquad\qquad S \quad V$$

- Our *baby* **sleeps** more than ten hours a day. Some *babies* **sleep** even longer.

However, not all sentences are as straightforward as the above examples. This chapter will explain three types of situations that can cause problems with subject-verb agreement:

1 Words between the subject and the verb

2 Verb coming before the subject

3 Special singular and plural subjects

    a Compound subjects

    b Collective nouns

    c Indefinite pronoun subjects

    d Relative pronoun subjects: *who, which, that*

WORDS BETWEEN THE SUBJECT AND THE VERB

A verb often comes right after its subject, as in this example:

- The sealed *boxes* **belong** to my brother.

    (Here and in the rest of the chapter, the *subject* is shown in *italic type*, and the **verb** is shown in **boldface type**.)

However, at times the subject and verb are separated by a prepositional phrase. You may remember that a **prepositional phrase** is a group of words that begins with a preposition and ends with a noun or pronoun. *In, on, for, from, of, to* and *by* are common prepositions. (A longer list of prepositions is on page 425.) Look at the following sentence:

- The sealed *boxes* in the closet **belong** to my brother.

In this sentence, the subject and verb are separated by the prepositional phrase *in the closet*. In such cases, you must be careful to make the verb agree with the subject—not with a word in the prepositional phrase.

Following are more examples with explanations.

- The *tomatoes* in this salad **are** brown and mushy.

   Because the subject, *tomatoes*, is plural, the verb must also be plural. The prepositional phrase, *in this salad*, has no effect on the subject and verb agreement.

- That silk *flower* by the candles **looks** real.

   Because the subject, *flower*, is singular, it needs the singular verb *looks*. *By the candles* is a prepositional phrase.

- *Books* about baseball **fill** my son's room.

   The plural subject *books* takes the plural verb *fill*. *About baseball* is a prepositional phrase.

   ※ The separation of subjects and verbs by prepositional phrases is also discussed on pages 69–70 in "Subjects and Verbs."

➤ Practice 1

Underline the subject of each sentence. Then in the space provided, write the correct verb in the margin. (If you have trouble finding a subject, try crossing out the prepositional phrase before the verb.)

taste, tastes   1. The <u>flakes</u> in this cereal _____ *taste* _____ like sawdust.

is, are   2. The <u>woman</u> with the dark sunglasses _____ *is* _____ our mayor.

speaks, speak   3. Many <u>people</u> in Europe _____ *speak* _____ several languages.

is, are   4. The red-haired <u>boy</u> by the swings _____ *is* _____ my son.

sleep, sleeps   5. A <u>person</u> in my classes _____ *sleeps* _____ through most of the lectures.

is, are   6. The <u>lights</u> across the river _____ *are* _____ reflected in the dark water.

charge, charges   7. The <u>stores</u> near campus _____ *charge* _____ too much for most items.

is, are   8. The <u>writing</u> in these romance novels _____ *is* _____ truly terrible.

appear, appears   9. The <u>doors</u> to the apartment _____ *appear* _____ to have been forced open.

serves, serve   10. The <u>yard</u> between our houses _____ *serves* _____ as a softball field.

VERB COMING BEFORE THE SUBJECT

The verb follows the subject in most sentences:

- *Ed* **passed** the course.
- A *rabbit* **lives** in my back yard.
- The *plane* **roared** overhead.

However, in some sentences, the verb comes *before* the subject. To make the subject and verb agree in such cases, look for the subject after the verb. Then decide if the verb should be singular or plural. Sentences in which the verb comes first include questions.

- What **was** your *score* on the test?

   The verb *was* is singular. It agrees with the singular subject *score*. *On the test* is a prepositional phrase. The subject of a sentence is never in a prepositional phrase.

The verb also comes first in sentences that begin with such words as *there is* or *here are*.

- There **are** *ants* in the sugar jar.

   The verb of this sentence is the plural verb *are*, so the subject should be plural as well. You can find the subject by asking, "What are in the sugar jar?" The answer, *ants*, is the subject.

- Here **is** the *menu*.

   The subject of this sentence is *menu*, which needs a singular verb.

The verb may also come before the subject in sentences that begin with a prepositional phrase.

- On that shelf **are** the *reports* for this year.

   The sentence begins with the prepositional phrase *on that shelf*, which is followed by the plural verb *are*. You can find the subject by asking, "What are on that shelf?" The answer is the subject of the sentence: *reports*. The subject and verb agree—they are both plural.

Here's another helpful way to find the subject when the verb comes first: Try to rearrange the sentence so that the subject comes first. The subject may be easier to find when the sentence is in the normal order. For the sentences above, you would then get:

- Your *score* on the test **was** what?
- *Ants* **are** in the sugar jar.
- The *menu* **is** here.
- The *reports* for this year **are** on that shelf.

> ### ➤ Practice 2

Underline the subject of each sentence. Then, in the space provided, write the form of the verb that agrees with the subject. (If you have trouble finding the subject, try crossing out any prepositional phrases.)

is, are   1. Here _____are_____ some <u>messages</u> for you.

is, are   2. What _____is_____ your middle <u>name</u>?

stands, stand   3. Beside the stream _____stands_____ a low wooden <u>fence</u>.

grows, grow   4. In that little garden _____grow_____ twenty <u>herbs</u>.

was, were   5. There _____were_____ black <u>clouds</u> in the sky this morning.

is, are   6. Where _____is_____ the <u>box</u> for these crayons?

lies, lie   7. On the table in the dining room _____lies_____ a <u>letter</u> for you.

is, are   8. There _____are_____ good <u>reasons</u> to hire older workers.

is, are   9. Why _____is_____ <u>Rolf</u> sitting outside in the car?

rests, rest   10. On the bench outside the mall _____rest_____ two tired <u>shoppers</u>.

SPECIAL SINGULAR AND PLURAL SUBJECTS

Compound Subjects

A **compound subject** is made up of two nouns connected by a joining word. Subjects joined by *and* generally take a plural verb.

- *Running* and *lifting* weights **are** good ways to keep in shape.
- *Fear* and *ignorance* **have** a lot to do with hatred.

However, when a compound subject is connected by *or, nor, either . . . or,* or *neither . . . nor,* the verb must agree with the part of the subject that is closer to it.

- My *aunts* or my *mother* usually **hosts** our family gatherings.

  The singular noun *mother* is closer to the verb, so the singular verb *hosts* is used.

- Either *he* or *his parents* **were** home that night.

- Either *his parents* or *he* **was** home that night.

  In the first sentence, the plural noun *parents* is closer to the verb, so the verb is plural. In the second sentence, the singular noun *he* is closer to the verb, so the verb must be singular.

• Neither the *teacher* nor the *students* **are** to blame for the shortage of textbooks.

The plural noun *students* is closer to the verb, so the verb is plural.

➤ **Practice 3**

In each sentence, underline the compound subject. Then, in the space provided, write the correct form of the verb in the margin. (If the subjects are connected by *or* or *nor*, look at the part of the compound subject that is closer to the verb.)

smells, smell   1. Either the trash <u>can</u> or your <u>socks</u> _____*smell*_____ horrible.

lives, live   2. The <u>children</u> and <u>Kara</u> _____*live*_____ in a houseboat.

tastes, taste   3. Neither the <u>fish</u> nor the <u>vegetables</u> _____*taste*_____ fresh in this restaurant.

sounds, sound   4. French <u>fries</u> or a baked <u>potato</u> _____*sounds*_____ good to me for dinner.

donates, donate   5. Her <u>sisters</u> or <u>she</u> usually _____*donates*_____ a cake or cookies to the community bake sale.

seems, seems   6. Neither <u>Polly</u> nor her <u>brothers</u> _____*seem*_____ surprised by their parents' announcement.

is, are   7. Some <u>flowers</u> or a <u>bush</u> _____*is*_____ needed by the driveway.

goes, go   8. <u>Bananas</u> and peanut <u>butter</u> _____*go*_____ well together.

is, are   9. <u>Jogging</u> or <u>walking</u> _____*is*_____ a good way to relieve stress.

babysits, babysit 10. Either my <u>grandparents</u> or my <u>father</u> _____*babysits*_____ for me every Friday.

Collective Nouns

A **collective noun** refers to a group of persons or things that are thought of as one unit. Collective nouns are usually considered singular. Following are some examples.

Collective Nouns

audience	committee	group	quartet
band	couple	herd	society
class	family	jury	team

- The *family* **lives** on Russell Avenue.

Family refers to a single unit, so the singular verb *lives* is used. However, if a collective noun refers to the individual members of the group, a plural pronoun is used.

- The *family* **are** Republicans, Democrats, and Independents.

Since one unit cannot have three different political views, *family* in this sentence clearly refers to the individual members of the group, so the plural verb *are* is used. To emphasize the individuals, some writers would use a subject that is clearly plural:

- The *members* of the family **are** Republicans, Democrats, and Independents.

➤ Practice 4

In each sentence, underline the subject and decide if it needs a singular or plural verb. Then fill in the correct form of the verb in the margin.

is, are

1. The <u>jury</u> _____*is*_____ going to announce its verdict this morning.

has, have

2. The reunion <u>committee</u> _____*has*_____ to decide where to hold the annual banquet.

is, are

3. This noisy <u>audience</u> _____*is*_____ spoiling the movie for me.

takes, take

4. The <u>couple</u> _____*take*_____ separate vacations: she likes to hike, and he likes to lie on the beach.

marches, march

5. Every year, the <u>band</u> _____*marches*_____ in the town's Thanksgiving parade.

Indefinite Pronoun Subjects

Indefinite pronouns are pronouns that do not refer to a specific person or thing. The ones in the box below are always singular.

Singular Indefinite Pronouns

each	anyone	anybody	anything
either	everyone	everybody	everything
neither	someone	somebody	something
one	no one	nobody	nothing

In the following sentences, the subjects are singular indefinite pronouns. Each of the verbs is therefore also singular.

- *Each* of the puppies **is** cute in its own way.
- *Neither* of the boys **knows** his true father.
- Despite the rules, nearly *everyone* in my apartment building **owns** a pet.

Note that the following indefinite pronouns are always plural:

Plural Indefinite Pronouns

both	many	several
few	other	

- *Both* of the puppies **are** cute in their own ways.

The following indefinite pronouns are singular or plural, depending on their context:

Indefinite Pronouns That Can Be Singular or Plural

all	more	none
any	most	some

- *Most* of his outfit **is** white.

  Most here refers to one thing—the outfit, so the singular verb *is* is used.

- *Most* of the salespeople **are** friendly.

  Most here refers to several salespeople, so the plural verb *are* is used.

➤ Practice 5

Underline the subject of each sentence. Then, in the space provided, write the form of the verb that agrees with the subject.

is, are   1. <u>Everybody</u> at my new school _____*is*_____ friendly.

feels, feel   2. <u>Neither</u> of those mattresses _____*feels*_____ comfortable.

knows, know   3. <u>Nobody</u> in my family _____*knows*_____ how to swim.

is, are   4. <u>Some</u> of the money in the cookie jar _____*is*_____ missing.

is, are   5. <u>Some</u> of the cookies _____*are*_____ missing too.

needs, need   6. <u>Each</u> of the children _____*needs*_____ some attention.

wants, want   7. <u>Several</u> of the best ballplayers _____*want*_____ to leave the team.

goes, go   8. <u>Everything</u> in that box _____*goes*_____ to the neighborhood garage sale.

is, are   9. <u>All</u> of my best friends _____*are*_____ older than I.

is, are   10. <u>All</u> of the coconut cream pie _____*is*_____ gone.

Relative Pronoun Subjects: *who, which, that*

The relative pronouns *who, which,* and *that* are singular when they refer to a singular noun. They are plural when they refer to a plural noun.

- I met a woman *who* **is** from China.

- I met two women *who* **are** from China.

    In the first sentence above, *who* refers to the singular word *woman*, so the verb is singular too. In the second sentence, *who* refers to the plural word *women*, so the verb must be plural.

- My car, *which* **is** only a year old, already needs a new battery.

    Which refers to *car*, a singular noun, so the singular verb *is* is used.

- My boss collects old wind-up toys *that* still **work**.

    That refers to the plural noun *toys*, so the plural verb *work* is used.

    ※ For more information on relative pronouns, see "Parts of Speech," page 422.

➤ Practice 6

In each sentence, underline the noun that the relative pronoun refers to. Then fill in the correct form of the verb in the margin.

gives, give   1. We have planted several <u>shrubs</u>, which _____*give*_____ some privacy to our back yard.

gives, give   2. We have planted a <u>hedge</u>, which _____*gives*_____ some privacy to our back yard.

is, are   3. Rhoda dislikes all <u>foods</u> that _____*are*_____ good for her.

is, are   4. Rhoda dislikes all <u>food</u> that _____*is*_____ good for her.

was, were   5. The soles of my <u>shoes</u>, which _____*were*_____ covered with mud, left black footprints on the sidewalk.

was, were   6. The sole of my right <u>shoe</u>, which _____*was*_____ covered with mud, left black footprints down the sidewalk.

is, are   7. Lenny goes out with a <u>woman</u> who _____*is*_____ twice his age.

is, are   8. Lenny goes out with <u>women</u> who _____*are*_____ twice his age.

speaks, speak   9. My daughter's favorite playmate is a little <u>girl</u> who _____*speaks*_____ no English.

speaks, speak   10. My daughter's favorite playmates are two little <u>girls</u> who _____*speak*_____ no English.

CHAPTER REVIEW

Answer each question by writing **T** (for *true*) or **F** (for *false*) in the space provided.

1. *True or false?* __F__ The subject of a sentence is often found in a prepositional phrase.

2. *True or false?* __T__ A subject may come before or after its verb.

3. *True or false?* __F__ Compound subjects joined by *or* or *nor* always need plural verbs.

4. *True or false?* __T__ A collective noun is usually singular.

5. *True or false?* __T__ Indefinite pronouns such as *anyone* and *everybody* are always singular.

6. *True or false?* __T__ The indefinite pronoun *both*, like *many*, is always plural.

7. *True or false?* __F__ Indefinite pronouns such as *most* and *all* are always plural.

8. *True or false?* __T__ A relative pronoun subject (*who, which,* or *that*) is either singular or plural, depending upon the noun it refers to.

Name_____ Section _____ Date _____

➤ Subject-Verb Agreement: Test 1

For each sentence, fill in the correct form of the verb in the margin.

is, are   1. Here _____ is _____ a parking space.

belongs, belong   2. The bones in the backyard _____ belong _____ to our neighbor's dog.

likes, like   3. My neighbors are people who _____ like _____ their privacy.

is, are   4. Why _____ are _____ the lights off?

draws, draw   5. Everyone in our art class _____ draws _____ with a charcoal stick.

itches, itch   6. Each of these sweaters _____ itches _____ .

hurries, hurry   7. Through the airport _____ hurry _____ travelers from all over the world.

gets, get   8. Our group _____ gets _____ together every Friday night to play bridge.

is, are   9. There _____ are _____ sad expressions on the students' faces.

is, are   10. In my English class, either a novel or short stories _____ are _____ assigned every week.

Name_____ Section _____ Date _____

Score: (Number right) _____ x 10 = _____%

➤ Subject-Verb Agreement: Test 2

For each sentence, fill in the correct form of the verb in the margin.

was, were   1. What _____were_____ the reasons for the workers'
                        strike?

plays, play   2. Someone in the apartment upstairs _____plays_____
                        a guitar late at night.

is, are   3. Some cookies or a cake _____is_____ needed
                        for dessert.

was, were   4. Among the guests _____was_____ a private
                        detective.

seems, seem   5. The questions on this test _____seem_____
                        unfair to me.

has, have   6. The jury _____have_____ conflicting opinions.

was, were   7. The students and their teacher _____were_____
                        sitting in a circle.

is, are   8. There _____are_____ many hungry people in
                        America's cities.

makes, make   9. The mayor is a woman who _____makes_____
                        things happen in our town.

was, were   10. Neither the children nor their father _____was_____
                        aware that someone was at the door.

Name_____ Section _____ Date _____

➤ Subject-Verb Agreement: Test 3

Each of the following passages contains **two** mistakes in subject-verb agreement. Find these two mistakes and cross them out. Then write the correct form of each verb in the space provided.

1. Few people ~~recalls~~ seeing baby pigeons. The reason is simple. Baby pigeons in the nest ~~eats~~ a huge amount of food each day. Upon leaving the nest, they are close to the size of their parents.

   a. _____ *recall* _____

   b. _____ *eat* _____

2. Everything in the mall stores ~~are~~ on sale today. Customers from all over are crowding the aisles. There ~~is~~ terrific bargains in many departments.

   a. _____ *is* _____

   b. _____ *are* _____

3. The children and their mother ~~is~~ disappointed in the frozen dinner. The peas look wrinkled and dry. Mounds of soggy stuffing ~~covers~~ a tiny piece of meat.

   a. _____ *are* _____

   b. _____ *cover* _____

4. The members of the swimming team ~~paces~~ nervously beside the pool. Finally, an official blows a whistle. Into the pool ~~dive~~ a swimmer who has large tan arms. He paddles quickly through the water.

   a. _____ *pace* _____

   b. _____ *dives* _____

5. There are three paths through the woods. There ~~is~~ narrow, rocky parts on two of the paths. The hikers take the easiest one. Around a bend, someone spots a snake. It is lying in the middle of the path, sunning itself. One of the hikers ~~fear~~ snakes. He refuses to go on.

   a. _____ *are* _____

   b. _____ *fears* _____

Name_____ Section _____ Date _____

Score: (Number right) _____ x 10 = _____%

➤ Subject-Verb Agreement: Test 4

Each of the following passages contains **two** mistakes in subject-verb agreement. Find these two mistakes and cross them out. Then write the correct form of each verb in the space provided.

1. Our friends in the country ~~gets~~ rid of the insects in their yard without using poisonous sprays. Instead, they use chickens. The chickens happily ~~eats~~ most of the insects. Our friends also get to enjoy fresh eggs.

   a. _____get_____

   b. _____eat_____

2. The house or the barn ~~need~~ to be painted this year. Next year, the other building will be painted. Also, both buildings, which ~~is~~ very old, need repairs.

   a. _____needs_____

   b. _____are_____

3. "Here ~~rests~~ the bones of evil Ned Sloan. The memory of his evil deeds ~~have~~ not died."

   a. _____rest_____

   b. _____has_____

4. One of my professors always listens patiently to students. Each of his students ~~feel~~ free to ask questions. Also, the tests in his class ~~is~~ always fair and clear.

   a. _____feels_____

   b. _____are_____

5. The rain forests of South America ~~is~~ home to many species of frogs. Nobody among the world's scientists ~~know~~ exactly how many. More types are being discovered all the time.

   a. _____are_____

   b. _____knows_____

Name_____ Section _____ Date _____

Score: (Number right) _____ x 10 = _____%

➤ Subject-Verb Agreement: Test 5

The following selection contains **ten** errors in subject-verb agreement. Cross out each wrong verb, and write the correction above the line.

Graceful and beautiful, tigers are on almost everyone's list of

is
favorite animals. A TV special about tigers ~~are~~ almost guaranteed an

audience. The tiger den at the zoo is forever surrounded by eager fans.

Sadly, the tiger may be too popular for its own good. Thousands of

tigers once roamed parts of Asia. However, their numbers have dropped

sharply. In this century, the tigers of Java, Bali, and the Caspian Sea

have   *knows*
region ~~has~~ become extinct. No one ~~know~~ the exact number of tigers living

are
today. There ~~is~~ probably about 150 Siberian tigers. For the South China

tiger, there may be as few as thirty. Today, there may be more tigers in

zoos than living in the wild.

What is happening to all the tigers? They are being killed by hunters

make
who ~~makes~~ a lot of money doing so. Wealthy people in many parts of the

enjoy
world ~~enjoys~~ having a beautiful tiger-skin rug in their homes. But rugs

are not the only reason for killing tigers. In many parts of Asia, the tiger

is believed to possess strong medicine. Tiger-bone potions are thought to

lengthen life and cure rheumatism. Tiger whiskers are believed to give

are
great strength. Pills from the eye of the tiger ~~is~~ supposed to cure epilepsy.

sell
Pharmacies throughout Asia ~~sells~~ wines, powders, creams, and other

products that come from the bodies of tigers.

(Continues on next page)

In most countries, neither the sale nor purchase of tiger products *is* ~~are~~ legal today. But in many cases, nobody in those countries *enforces* ~~enforce~~ the laws. According to one journalist who recently visited Taiwan, "The only difference now is the tiger medicines are kept behind the counter, instead of being out on an open shelf."

9 / Sentence Types

This chapter describes the four basic kinds of sentences in English: simple, compound, complex, and compound-complex sentences.

Simple sentence:	My ten-year-old daughter cooked dinner tonight.
Compound sentence:	Mat grew a moustache, but his wife hates it.
Complex sentence:	Although Tina and Art love each other, they argue constantly.
Compound-complex sentence:	After the rain started, the air cooled down, so we turned off the air conditioner.

The chapter provides practice in all four sentence types. It also presents two types of words you can use to connect ideas together in one sentence:

1 Joining words (for compound sentences)

- Mat grew a moustache, **but** his wife hates it.

2 Dependent words (for complex sentences)

- **Although** Tina and Art love each other, they argue constantly.

THE SIMPLE SENTENCE

A **simple sentence** has a subject and a verb and expresses one complete thought.

- The alarm sounded.
- A jet soared through the darkening sky.
- The tourist should have packed her sunglasses.

A simple sentence may have more than one subject:

- Shorts and T-shirts sway on the clothesline.

   In this sentence, *shorts* and *T-shirts* are the subjects. There is only one verb: *sway*.

A simple sentence may have more than one verb:

- The children splashed and squealed in the swimming pool.

  In this sentence, both *splashed* and *squealed* are the verbs. There is only one subject: *children.*

A simple sentence may even have several subjects and verbs:

- Every weekend, Gary, Sam, and Rita go to the movies, eat at a Chinese restaurant, and dance at a club.

  There are three subjects in this sentence: *Gary, Sam,* and *Rita.* There are also three verbs: *go, eat,* and *dance.*

Note that some grammar books describe a simple sentence as an *independent clause.* A **clause** is simply a group of words having a subject and a verb. A clause may be *independent*—expressing a complete thought and therefore able to stand alone. Or it may be *dependent*—not expressing a complete thought and not able to stand alone.

➤ Practice 1   *Answers will vary.*

A. Complete the simple sentences below by filling in one or more subjects and/or one or more verbs.

1. _____*Purple*_____ is my favorite color.

2. The batter _____*hit*_____ the ball.

3. The _____*waiter*_____ gave me regular coffee instead of decaf.

4. The thoughtless driver _____*threw*_____ a paper cup onto the highway.

5. _____*Papers*_____ and _____*leaves*_____ were blowing across the empty parking lot.

6. _____*Liver*_____ and _____*cabbage*_____ are my least favorite foods.

7. A suitcase _____*fell*_____ off the van and _____*rolled*_____ into a ditch.

8. On rainy Saturday mornings, the children _____*eat*_____ cookies and _____*watch*_____ cartoons on television.

9. _____*Alice*_____ and I often exercise and _____*shop*_____ together.

10. _____*Nick*_____ and _____*Fran*_____ went to a movie and then _____*ate*_____ dinner at a local diner.

B. Write three simple sentences. One should have two subjects, and another should have two verbs.

1. _____ *Answers will vary.* _____

   _____

2. _____

   _____

3. _____

   _____

THE COMPOUND SENTENCE

A **compound sentence** is made up of two or more complete thoughts. For instance, look at the following simple sentences:

- Rose wants chili for dinner.
- She forgot to buy beans.

By using a comma and a joining word, we can combine these two simple sentences into one compound sentence:

- Rose wants chili for dinner, **but** she forgot to buy beans.

The process of joining together two ideas of equal importance in a sentence is known as *coordination*.

Joining Words

In the above example, the simple sentences have been connected by using a comma plus the joining word *but*. There are seven such joining words. Those words (also known as *coordinating conjunctions*) are listed in the chart below. These seven joining words are the only words that can join independent statements into compound sentences.

Joining Words

and	means *in addition*
but	means *however*
so	means *as a result*
for	means *because*
yet	means *however*
or	is used to indicate alternatives
nor	is used to indicate a second negative statement

Look at the following uses of the joining words:

- The driver failed to signal, and he went through a stop sign.

  And means *in addition:* The driver failed to signal; *in addition*, he went through a stop sign.

- I was very tired, but I still had two hours of homework.

  But means *however:* I was very tired; *however*, I still had two hours of homework.

- The meal was not hot, so we sent it back to the kitchen.

  So means *as a result:* The meal was not hot; *as a result*, we sent it back to the kitchen.

- I work at home, for I want to be with my two young children.

  For means *because:* I work at home *because* I want to be with my two young children.

- My brother loves cooking, yet he decided to major in business.

  Yet means *however:* My brother loves cooking; *however*, he decided to major in business.

- You can ride with us to the game, or you can go in someone else's car.

  Or introduces an alternative choice: You can ride with us to the game. *Alternatively*, you can go with someone else.

- Eli does not eat meat, nor does he eat fish.

  Nor introduces a negative statement that has been added to the first negative statement: Eli does *not* eat meat. He also does *not* eat fish.

Punctuation note: In a compound sentence, a comma comes right after the first complete thought and before the joining word.

➤ Practice 2   *Answers will vary.*

Complete each of the following sentences by adding a second complete thought. Remember that a complete thought must contain a subject and a verb.

1. The class was cancelled, so _____*we decided to go out for coffee.*_____

2. I gave our dog a bath, for _____*her coat was muddy.*_____

3. The beef barley soup smelled delicious, but _____*it tasted like dishwater.*_____

   _____

4. Kay went to the store during her break, and _____
   she did all her grocery shopping.

5. I did not pass the test, nor _____*did I pass the course.*_____

6. Sheila promised to meet me at the mall at ten, yet _____
   she didn't arrive until 11:15.
   _____

7. You could work as a waitress this summer, or _____
   you could take a summer school course.
   _____

➤ Practice 3   *Answers may vary.*

A. Use a comma and a suitable joining word to combine each pair of simple sentences into a compound sentence. Choose from the following joining words:

         and   **but**   **so**

1. The city workers are on strike.
   The streets are lined with garbage bags.

   The city workers are on strike, so the streets are lined with garbage bags.
   _____

2. The television was on.
   No one was watching it.

   The television was on, but no one was watching it.
   _____

3. The room is painted yellow.
   It has big, sunny windows.

   The room is painted yellow, and it has big, sunny windows.
   _____

4. A storm was approaching quickly.
   The campers found shelter in a cave.

   A storm was approaching quickly, so the campers found shelter in a cave.
   _____

5. Dean likes whole-wheat toast for breakfast.
   Chris prefers sugar-coated cereal.

   Dean likes whole-wheat toast for breakfast, but Chris prefers sugar-coated
   cereal.

B. Write three compound sentences of your own. Use three different joining words.

1. _____ *Answers will vary.* _____

   _____

2. _____

   _____

3. _____

   _____

THE COMPLEX SENTENCE

As you have already learned, a compound sentence is made up of two or more complete thoughts. Each thought could stand alone as a simple sentence. A **complex sentence**, on the other hand, includes one independent statement and at least one dependent statement, which cannot stand alone. Look at the following example:

- Although nearby trees were blown down, our house escaped the tornado.

The second statement in this sentence is independent. It can stand alone as a simple sentence:

- Our house escaped the tornado.

The first statement, however, cannot stand alone. It is dependent—it depends on the rest of the sentence to finish the thought:

- Although nearby trees were blown down

Dependent statements begin with dependent words, such as *although*. They also include a subject and a verb. (The subject of the dependent statement above is *trees*; the verb is *were blown*.)

Now look at another sentence:

- As the kidnapper made demands on the phone, police surrounded the building.

This is also a complex sentence. One part can stand independently as a simple sentence: *Police surrounded the building*. The other part of the sentence has a subject and a verb, but it begins with a dependent word and cannot stand alone: *as the kidnapper made demands on the phone*.

Here's another complex sentence. See if you can spot the independent and dependent parts of the sentence.

- Paula will not sell her home in the country even if she gets a job in the city.

Paula will not sell her home in the country is the independent part of the sentence. The dependent part begins with the dependent words *even if* and cannot stand alone: *even if she gets a job in the city.*

Dependent Words

In the above examples, the dependent words *although, as,* and *even if* make the statements they introduce dependent. The chart below lists common dependent words.

Dependent Words

after	even if	unless	wherever
although	even though	until	whether
as	if	when	while
because	since	whenever	
before	though	where	

Look at the following examples again to understand how to punctuate complex sentences.

- **As** the kidnapper made demands on the phone, police surrounded the building.
- Paula will not sell her home in the country **even if** she gets a job in the city.

Punctuation note: Notice that when the dependent statement comes first, it is followed by a comma. When the dependent idea comes last, it is generally not separated from the rest of the sentence by a comma.

➤ Practice 4   *Answers will vary.*

Underline the dependent word(s) in each of the following sentences. Then complete each dependent statement. (Every dependent statement should have a subject and a verb.)

1. Dolores cried <u>when</u> _____ *her boyfriend asked her to marry him.* _____

2. <u>Although</u> _____ *I was offered a free ticket to the game* _____, I was too tired to go.

3. Lynn took a shower <u>after</u> _____ *she worked out at the gym.* _____

4. <u>Because</u> _____ *I wanted to do some last-minute studying* _____, I set my alarm for 5 a.m.

5. I was paid for a full week of work <u>even though</u> _____
_____ *I worked only three days.* _____

6. Until *he was fourteen*, Bobby was not allowed to stay at home alone.

7. If *you go to the convenience store*, you should get a quart of milk.

8. Since *I want to buy a car*, I am saving extra money each month.

9. José did some research in the library before *he began writing his draft.*

10. Because *the tickets cost twenty-five dollars*, we decided not to go to the rock concert.

➤ **Practice 5**   *Answers may vary.*

A. Combine each pair of simple sentences into a complex sentence. To change a simple sentence in each pair into a dependent statement, add one of these dependent words:

after   although   because   since   when   while

Put a comma after a dependent clause when it starts a sentence, as in the following example.

Example   The sweater is old and faded.
It is my favorite.

Although the sweater is old and faded, it is my favorite.

1. The travelers slept in their station wagon.
All the motels in the area were full.

The travelers slept in their station wagon because all the motels in the area were full.

2. The campers slept.
Raccoons tore apart their backpacks.

While the campers slept, raccoons tore apart their backpacks.

3. The band finally began to play.
We had sat through an hour of recorded music.

The band finally began to play after we had sat through an hour of recorded music.

4. There is a playoff game in the city.
Traffic is jammed for miles.

When there is a playoff game in the city, traffic is jammed for miles.

5. His wife died.
   Mr. Albertson has been lonely.

   Since his wife died, Mr. Albertson has been lonely.

   _____

6. A fan just moves the air.
   An air conditioner cools it.

   While a fan just moves the air, an air conditioner cools it.

   _____

7. My father and mother are separated.
   They do not plan to divorce.

   Although my father and mother are separated, they do not plan to divorce.

   _____

8. The test was over.
   We decided to get something to eat.

   After the test was over, we decided to get something to eat.

   _____

9. Julie asked Leonard out on a date.
   Her legs were trembling.

   When Julie asked Leonard out on a date, her legs were trembling.

   _____

10. We're trying not to waste paper.
    We usually use cloth napkins.

    Because we're trying not to waste paper, we usually use cloth napkins.

    _____

B. Fill in the blanks to write three complex sentences of your own. If the dependent idea comes first in a sentence, follow it with a comma.

1. Because _____ *Answers will vary.* _____

   _____

2. _____ after

   _____

3. When _____

   _____

THE COMPOUND-COMPLEX SENTENCE

There is yet one more type of sentence, the compound-complex sentence. As its name suggests, the **compound-complex sentence** is a combination of two of the other types of sentences. Like the compound sentence, it includes two independent statements. Like the complex sentence, it contains at least one dependent statement. Here is an example:

- When the children's parents were out of town, the babysitter had parties, and the children watched TV until midnight.

The two independent statements in this sentence are *the babysitter had parties* and *the children watched TV until midnight*. They are connected by the joining word *and*. Together they could make a compound sentence: *The babysitter had parties, and the children watched TV until midnight.*

The dependent statement is *when the children's parents were out of town*. It begins with the dependent word *when*. Combined with either of the two independent statements, it would make a complex sentence, for example: *When the children's parents were out of town, the babysitter had parties.*

➤ Practice 6

First read each sentence to get a sense of its overall meaning. Then insert a logical joining word and a logical dependent word in each sentence. Choose from the following:

> *Joining words:*   **so, for, but, or**
> *Dependent words:* **although, unless, because, when**

1. _____*Although*_____ I like animals very much, I am away from home a great deal, _____*so*_____ I do not own a pet.

2. The German shepherd was huge, _____*but*_____ it was afraid of practically everything _____*because*_____ it had been treated cruelly as a puppy.

3. _____*When*_____ the Sunday TV football games are over, we often go to eat at a nearby diner, _____*or (or and)*_____ sometimes we send out for a pizza.

4. I adore my grandparents, _____*but*_____ I don't see them often _____*because*_____ they live in Italy.

5. _____*Unless*_____ there is an emergency, you should not wake me from my nap, _____*for*_____ I really need some sleep.

※ For information on using a variety of sentence types in your writing, see "Sentence Variety and Style," pages 273–290.

➤ Practice 7   *Answers will vary.*

Combine each group of simple sentences into a compound-complex sentence. Choose from the following joining words and dependent words:

Joining words: **and, but, so**
Dependent words: **although, because, after, when, while**

Example   The bus came in sight.
Connie shouted "Goodbye."
She rushed out the door.

When the bus came in sight, Connie shouted "Goodbye," and she

rushed out the door.

1. Ken became a father.
He knew little about babies.
He learned a lot fast.

    When Ken became a father, he knew little about babies, but he learned a lot

    fast.

2. I need to improve my grades.
I will take more notes in class.
I will spend more time studying each night.

    Because I need to improve my grades, I will take more notes in class, and I will

    spend more time studying each night.

3. We poured tomato juice on the dog's fur.
We shampooed him.
He had been sprayed by a skunk.

    We poured tomato juice on the dog's fur, and we shampooed him after he had

    been sprayed by a skunk.

4. Rafael was sleeping on the sofa.
He got an important phone call.
I woke him up.

    While Rafael was sleeping on the sofa, he got an important phone call, so I

    woke him up.

5. There used to be many small stores downtown.
They are gone now.
Only the mall remains.

    Although there used to be many small stores downtown, they are gone now,

    and only the mall remains.

CHAPTER REVIEW

Circle the letter of the correct answer to each question.

1. The statements in a compound sentence are joined together by a
   a. dependent word.
   (b.) comma and a joining word.
   c. semicolon.

2. A dependent statement includes a
   (a.) dependent word.
   b. comma and a joining word.
   c. semicolon.

3. Which sentence is a simple sentence?
   (a.) The coach did a somersault.
   b. When the coach did a somersault, she hurt her back.
   c. The coach did a somersault, and she hurt her back.
   d. After our gymnastics team won the competition, the coach did a somersault, and she hurt her back.

4. Which sentence is a compound sentence?
   a. The coach did a somersault.
   b. When the coach did a somersault, she hurt her back.
   (c.) The coach did a somersault, and she hurt her back.
   d. After our gymnastics team won the competition, the coach did a somersault, and she hurt her back.

5. Which sentence is a complex sentence?
   a. The coach did a somersault.
   (b.) When the coach did a somersault, she hurt her back.
   c. The coach did a somersault, and she hurt her back.
   d. After our gymnastics team won the competition, the coach did a somersault, and she hurt her back.

6. Which sentence is a compound-complex sentence?
   a. The coach did a somersault.
   b. When the coach did a somersault, she hurt her back.
   c. The coach did a somersault, and she hurt her back.
   (d.) After our gymnastics team won the competition, the coach did a somersault, and she hurt her back.

Name_____ Section _____ Date _____

➤ Sentence Types: Test 1

A. Use a comma and a suitable joining word to combine the following pairs of simple sentences into compound sentences. Choose from *and, but,* or *so.*

Answers may vary.

1. Kwan is quite attractive.
   She sees herself as ugly.

   Kwan is quite attractive, but she sees herself as ugly.

2. This coffee is cold.
   It is too strong.

   This coffee is cold, and it is too strong.

3. The book was very expensive.
   I didn't buy it.

   The book was very expensive, so I didn't buy it.

4. Gene laughed throughout the movie.
   His date didn't laugh once.

   Gene laughed throughout the movie, but his date didn't laugh once.

_____

B. Use a suitable dependent word to combine the following pairs of simple sentences into complex sentences. Choose from *although, because, since,* and *when.* Place a comma after a dependent statement when it starts a sentence.

5. Strawberries are expensive.
   I don't often buy them.

   Since strawberries are expensive, I don't often buy them.

6. An elephant's skin is very thick.
   It is sensitive.

   Although an elephant's skin is very thick, it is sensitive.

7. The city pools have been crowded.
   The weather turned hot.

   The city pools have been crowded because the weather turned hot.

8. An egg spins faster.
   It is hard-boiled.

   An egg spins faster when it is hard-boiled.

Name_____ Section _____ Date _____

➤ Sentence Types: Test 2

A. Use a comma and a suitable joining word to combine the following pairs of simple sentences into compound sentences. Choose from *and, but,* or *so.*

Answers may vary.

1. The car runs well.
   Its body is rusty.

   The car runs well, but its body is rusty.

2. The electricity was out.
   We had no candles.

   The electricity was out, and we had no candles.

3. The tea stain didn't wash out of my white skirt.
   I dyed the skirt tan.

   The tea stain didn't wash out of my white skirt, so I dyed the skirt tan.

4. Thirty percent of M&M's are brown.
   Twenty percent of them are red.

   Thirty percent of M&M's are brown, and 20 percent of them are red.

B. Use a suitable dependent word to combine the following pairs of simple sentences into complex sentences. Choose from *although, because, since,* and *when.* Place a comma after a dependent statement when it starts a sentence.

5. Sandra wanted a good novel to read.
   She went to the library.

   Since Sandra wanted a good novel to read, she went to the library.

6. I quickly called the police.
   I heard a scream outside.

   I quickly called the police because I heard a scream outside.

7. Mark seems unfriendly.
   He is really just shy.

   Although Mark seems unfriendly, he is really just shy.

8. The ball game was postponed.
   It began to rain heavily.

   The ball game was postponed when it began to rain heavily.

Name_____   Section _____   Date _____

➤ Sentence Types: Test 3

Combine each group of simple sentences into compound or complex sentences. Combine the first two sentences into one sentence, and combine the last two sentences into another sentence. Use any of the following joining words and dependent words.

Joining words: **and**   **but**   **so**
Dependent words: **after**   **although**   **because**   **when**

Here are two comma hints: (1) Use a comma between two complete thoughts joined by *and, but,* or *so.* (2) Place a comma after a dependent statement when it starts a sentence.   *Answers may vary.*

1. It had rained for three days.
   The sun finally came out.
   We wanted to have a picnic.
   The ground was too wet.

   After it had rained for three days, the sun finally came out. We wanted to have

   a picnic, but the ground was too wet.

2. Roy saw a bright rainbow.
   He ran to get his camera.
   He rushed back to take a picture.
   The rainbow had gone.

   When Roy saw a bright rainbow, he ran to get his camera. He rushed back to

   take a picture, but the rainbow had gone.

3. A long-winded neighbor was at my door.
   I pretended not to be home.
   She rang the bell several times.
   She knocked on the door repeatedly.

   Because a long-winded neighbor was at my door, I pretended not to be home.

   She rang the bell several times, and she knocked on the door repeatedly.

4. Nadine hates her job.
   She won't leave it.
   She likes the pension plan.
   She will stay for twenty years until retirement.

   Although Nadine hates her job, she won't leave it. She likes the pension plan,

   so she will stay for twenty years until retirement.

Name_____ Section _____ Date _____

Score: (Number right) _____ x 12.5 = _____ %

➤ Sentence Types: Test 4

Combine each group of simple sentences into compound or complex sentences. Combine the first two sentences into one sentence, and combine the last two sentences into another sentence. Use any of the following joining words and dependent words.

Joining words:	**and**	**but**	**so**	
Dependent words:	**although**	**because**	**since**	**when**

Here are two comma hints: (1) Use a comma between two complete thoughts joined by *and, but,* or *so.* (2) Place a comma after a dependent statement when it starts a sentence.   *Answers may vary.*

1. The instructor was late to class.
   The classroom was quiet anyway.
   The students were reading their textbooks.
   They were taking an important test that day.

   Although the instructor was late to class, the classroom was quiet anyway. The

   students were reading their textbooks because they were taking an important

   test that day.

2. I had to meet my girlfriend's mother.
   I was very nervous.
   I was afraid of her opinion of me.
   She was very warm and friendly.

   When I had to meet my girlfriend's mother, I was very nervous. I was afraid of

   her opinion of me, but she was very warm and friendly.

3. Sue Lin left Vietnam in a small, crowded boat.
   She wanted freedom so badly.
   Everyone on the boat faced starvation.
   They were finally rescued by a passing ship.

   Sue Lin left Vietnam in a small, crowded boat since she wanted freedom so

   badly. Everyone on the boat faced starvation, but they were finally rescued by

   a passing ship.

4. Jack was tired of his appearance.
   He shaved all the hair off his head.
   He bought new clothing in bright colors.
   He added an earring as well.

   Jack was tired of his appearance, so he shaved all the hair off his head. He

   bought new clothing in bright colors, and he added an earring as well.

Name_____   Section _____   Date _____

➤ Sentence Types: Test 5

Combine the five pairs of italicized simple sentences into compound or complex sentences. Write the new sentences on the lines provided, adding commas as needed. Use any of the following joining words and dependent words. (Remember that there is more than one way of revising these sentences.)   *Answers may vary.*

and	**but**	**so**	**for**	**yet**
because	**even though**	**if**	**after**	

Mental illness has always frightened people. It is so little understood.

Mental illness has always frightened people because it is so little

understood.

_____.

As a result, some attempts to treat mental illness have been very strange and even cruel. *In the Middle Ages, for instance, some mentally ill people were thought to be witches. They were burned alive at the stake.* _____
In the Middle Ages, for instance, some mentally ill people were thought to be

witches, so they were burned alive at the stake. _____.

Later, communities established asylums for the mentally ill. *Offering disturbed people a place to live was better than treating them as witches. These places were not run humanely.* _____
Offering disturbed people a place to live was better than treating them as

witches, but these places were not run humanely. _____.

In colonial Philadelphia, for instance, insane people were chained to the wall in unheated basement cells and displayed like zoo animals. The doctors then believed mentally ill people to be unfeeling.

Some theories of mental illness were racist. *White doctors measured facial features to determine intelligence and mental health. There was no scientific basis for this method.* _____
White doctors measured facial features to determine intelligence and mental

health even though there was no scientific basis for this method. _____.

"Ideal" facial measurements were those typical of a white European person. By those standards, most people of African or Asian descent could

(Continues on next page)

not qualify as mentally healthy. In addition, before the Civil War, doctors came up with a category of mental illness called "drapetomania." Drapetomania was defined as an excessive, insane desire to escape slavery. The new "illness" was a useful one for slaveowners. *A slave would try to run away. The slaveowner could accuse him or her of being crazy.* <u>If a slave would try to run away, the slaveowner could accuse him or her of being crazy.</u>

_____ .

10 / Sentence Fragments

A complete sentence expresses a complete thought. A **sentence fragment** does not.

This chapter explains several common types of sentence fragments:

1   Dependent-word fragments

Fragment: **After he was locked in a jail cell.** The magician Houdini freed himself.

Sentence: After he was locked in a jail cell, the magician Houdini freed himself.

2   Fragments without a subject

Fragment: Karl lowered himself from the van into his wheelchair. **And then rolled up the sidewalk ramp.**

Sentence: Karl lowered himself from the van into his wheelchair and then rolled up the sidewalk ramp.

3   Fragments without a subject and a verb

Fragment: The ice skater glided around the rink. **Picking up bouquets of flowers.**

Sentence: The ice skater glided around the rink, picking up bouquets of flowers.

DEPENDENT-WORD FRAGMENTS

Some fragments contain a subject and a verb, but they do not express a complete thought. Here's an example:

• Since Laura was tired.

Although this word group contains a subject (*Laura*) and a verb (*was*), it is an incomplete thought. The reader wants to know what happens as a result of Laura being tired. Words such as *since* are dependent words. They make a group of words dependent on another idea to complete the thought. For example, we could correct the above fragment like this:

• Since Laura was tired**, she took a nap**.

The words *she took a nap* complete the thought.

Here are two more dependent-word fragments.

- When the man pointed the gun at us.
- After I turned off the television set.

Each of these word groups begins with a dependent word (*when, after*) and expresses an incomplete idea. See if you can add words to each fragment that would complete the thought.

- When the man pointed the gun at us, _____.

- _____ after I turned off the television set.

Here are some ways to complete the above fragments:

- When the man pointed the gun at us, **we gave him our money**.
- **I picked up a book** after I turned off the television set.

When you use a dependent word, take care that the you complete the thought in the same sentence. Otherwise, a sentence fragment may result. Here is a list of common dependent words:

Dependent Words

after	even if	unless	wherever
although	even though	until	whether
as	if	when	while
because	since	whenever	
before	though	where	

➤ **Practice 1**   *Answers will vary.*

This practice will give you a sense of the difference between a dependent-word fragment and a complete sentence. Turn each fragment into a sentence by adding a statement that completes the thought.

1. When I rang the doorbell, *I heard laughter coming from inside the house* .

2. Because Jill forgot her house keys, *she had to call a locksmith* .

3. *Everyone sang along* while the music played.

4. Unless the rash disappears soon, *you'll have to see a doctor* .

5. *I turn the thermostat down* before I go to sleep at night.

6. Although the report was due yesterday, *I got an extension until next week* .

7. If you want to take a vacation, *start saving for it now* .

8. *Fred went back to sleep* after the alarm rang.

9. Since no one was home, _____*the driver left the package with a neighbor*_____.

10. As I walked into the classroom, _____*I tripped and dropped my books*_____.

➤ **Practice 2**

Half of the following items are correct—they are made up of two complete thoughts. The other half include a dependent-word fragment. Identify each correct item with a **C**. Identify each item that contains a fragment with an **F**.

If you are not sure if a word group is a dependent-word fragment, read it by itself. Does it begin with a dependent word? Is it incomplete on its own? If the answer to both questions is yes, it is a dependent-word fragment.

___F___ 1. Although I had a bad headache. I went to work today.

___C___ 2. My brother loves beer. He drinks the kind with no alcohol.

___F___ 3. When you are ready to take a break. There is a coffee shop next door.

___F___ 4. We will meet at Gina's house to study for the test. Unless you have a better idea.

___C___ 5. At work I am constantly on the phone. It seems glued to my hand.

___F___ 6. While babies are cute. They are also a lot of work.

___C___ 7. Montreal is a fascinating city. Many people there speak French.

___F___ 8. After washing the car. We had a water fight with the wet sponges.

___C___ 9. Mom does yoga exercises every day. She wants to keep her body limber.

___C___ 10. The wedding guests danced for almost three hours. Little children and elderly people joined the fun.

Correcting Dependent-Word Fragments

A common way to correct a dependent-word fragment is to connect it to the sentence that comes before or after it. For example:

• Since I had lost my house key. I had to break a window.

Since I had lost my house key is a dependent-word fragment. Because it expresses an incomplete thought, it leaves the reader expecting more. The writer must tell *in the same sentence* what happened as a result of the house key being lost. Correct this fragment by connecting it to the sentence that follows it.

• Since I had lost my house key, I had to break a window.

Punctuation note: Put a comma at the end of a dependent-word group that starts a sentence, as above.

Here is another example to consider:

- School closed early today. Because of a leak in a water main.

Because of a leak in a water main is a dependent-word fragment. It leaves the reader expecting the rest of the thought. Below, the fragment is corrected by connecting it to the sentence that comes before it.

- School closed early today because of a leak in a water main.

  ※ For more information on this type of sentence, see "Sentence Types," pages 150–151.

➤ Practice 3

Underline the dependent-word fragment in each of the following items. Then correct it in the space provided. Remember to add a comma after a dependent word group that begins a sentence.

1. <u>After he bought a cup of coffee.</u> Eric hurried to the office.

   After he bought a cup of coffee, Eric hurried to the office.

2. The batter argued with the umpire. <u>While the crowd booed.</u>

   The batter argued with the umpire while the crowd booed.

3. All the food will spoil. <u>Unless the refrigerator is fixed soon.</u>

   All the food will spoil unless the refrigerator is fixed soon.

4. <u>Because the movie was so violent.</u> Some people left the theater.

   Because the movie was so violent, some people left the theater.

5. Everything was peaceful. <u>Before Martha stormed into the room.</u>

   Everything was peaceful before Martha stormed into the room.

6. <u>When two guests began to argue.</u> The hostess moved the party outside.

   When two guests began to argue, the hostess moved the party outside.

7. <u>Although the cars were damaged in the accident.</u> The passengers were unharmed.

   Although the cars were damaged in the accident, the passengers were unharmed.

8. <u>Since we forgot to buy a battery.</u> Our son can't play with his new toy today.

   Since we forgot to buy a battery, our son can't play with his new toy today.

9. Our leaves blew into the neighbor's yard. <u>Before I found time to rake them.</u>

   Our leaves blew into the neighbor's yard before I found time to rake them.

   _____

10. The police believed the witness. <u>Until he picked the wrong person out of a lineup.</u>

    The police believed the witness until he picked the wrong person out of a lineup.

    _____

More on Dependent-Word Fragments

Some dependent-word fragments begin with the words *who, whose, whom, which,* or *that.* Here are examples:

- Janice had to clean up the mess. That the kids left in the kitchen.
- I passed the math course. Which I had half-expected to fail.
- Yesterday my wife ran into a fellow. Who was her best friend in high school.

This type of fragment is usually best corrected by attaching it to the sentence that comes before it:

- Janice had to clean up the **mess that** the kids left in the kitchen.
- I passed the math **course which** I had half-expected to fail.
- Yesterday my wife ran into a **fellow who** was her best friend in high school.

➤ Practice 4

Underline the dependent-word fragment in each of the following items. Then correct it in the space provided.

1. I bought an expensive coat. <u>Which was made of soft leather.</u>

   I bought an expensive coat which was made of soft leather.

   _____

2. My neighbor is a quiet man. <u>Whose working day begins at midnight.</u>

   My neighbor is a quiet man whose working day begins at midnight.

   _____

3. The dog growled at the toddler. <u>Who was screaming loudly.</u>

   The dog growled at the toddler who was screaming loudly.

   _____

4. The pilot refused to fly the jet. <u>That had ice on its wings.</u>

The pilot refused to fly the jet that had ice on its wings.

_____

5. Mr. Lopez is one demanding teacher. <u>Whom students love.</u>

Mr. Lopez is one demanding teacher whom students love.

_____

FRAGMENTS WITHOUT A SUBJECT

Some fragments do have a verb, but lack a subject. A word group without a subject does not express a complete thought. Here are examples:

- The politician held a smiling baby. Then posed for the photographers.
- The landlord unclogged the drain. And found a dishcloth stuck in the pipe.

In each of the above examples, the first statement is a complete sentence, and the second word group is a fragment. Note that each fragment is missing a subject. The first fragment omits the subject of the verb *posed*. The second fragment omits the subject of the verb *found*.

Correcting Fragments Without a Subject

There are two ways to correct a fragment that is missing a subject:

1   Connect the fragment to the sentence that comes before it. Add a joining word if needed, as in the first example below.

- The politician held a smiling baby **and then** posed for the photographers.
- The landlord unclogged the drain **and found** a dishcloth stuck in the pipe.

In both cases, we've changed a sentence with one subject and one verb to a sentence with one subject and two verbs. The subject of the first sentence is *politician*, and the two verbs are *held* and *posed*. The subject of the second sentence is *landlord*. The two verbs are *drain* and *found*.

The two verbs in each of the above sentences are connected by the joining word *and*. Two verbs that go with the same subject can also be connected by the joining word *but* or *or*. Here's another example of a fragment that has no subject:

- I decided to skip class. Then changed my mind.

The first statement is a sentence. The subject is *I*, and the verb is *decided*. The second word group is a fragment—it contains only a verb, *changed*. We can correct the fragment like this:

- I decided to skip class **but** then changed my mind.

The subject of this sentence is still *I*, but now it has *two* verbs: *decided* and *changed*. The fragment has been connected to the sentence before it with the word *but*.

2   Create a new sentence by adding a subject to the fragment. Normally, you will add a pronoun that stands for the subject of the previous sentence.

- The politician held a smiling baby. Then **he** posed for the photographers.
- The landlord unclogged the drain. **She** found a dishcloth stuck in the pipe.

In the first example above, *he* stands for *the politician*. In the second example, *she* stands for *the landlord*.

➤ Practice 5   *Corrections may vary.*

Underline the fragment without a subject in each of the following items. Then correct it in the space provided, using one of the two methods given above. Use each method at least several times.

1. The woman paid all of her bills. <u>But then had little money left for food.</u>

   The woman paid all of her bills. She then had little money left for food.

   _____

2. The dealer shuffled the cards. <u>And asked the man to choose one.</u>

   The dealer shuffled the cards and asked the man to choose one.

   _____

3. The cries for help grew more and more faint. <u>Then stopped completely.</u>

   The cries for help grew more and more faint. Then they stopped completely.

   _____

4. The wallet has room for paper money and credit cards. <u>But has no place for coins.</u>

   The wallet has room for paper money and credit cards but has no place for coins.

   _____

5. The dog lifted its head to bark at the mailman. <u>And then went back to sleep.</u>

   The dog lifted its head to bark at the mailman and then went back to sleep.

   _____

6. The movie had a catchy soundtrack and popular actors. <u>Yet made little money at the box office.</u>

   The movie had a catchy soundtrack and popular actors yet made little money at the box office.

7. Each morning, the secretary checks the answering machine for messages. <u>Then opens the mail.</u>

   Each morning, the secretary checks the answering machine for messages. Then she (or he) opens the mail.

8. The wide receiver made a terrific run down the field. <u>But then fumbled the football.</u>

   The wide receiver made a terrific run down the field. Then he fumbled the football.

9. I stuck the needle through the hem. <u>And ran it through a thin layer of my finger.</u>

   I stuck the needle through the hem and ran it through a thin layer of my finger.

10. Someone stole a rare bird from the zoo. <u>But soon returned it with a note of apology.</u>

    Someone stole a rare bird from the zoo but soon returned it with a note of apology.

FRAGMENTS WITHOUT A SUBJECT AND A VERB

There are two common kinds of fragments that are missing a subject and a verb.

-ing and to Fragments

When *-ing* appears at or near the beginning of a word group, a fragment may result. Here is an example of an *-ing* fragment:

- Hoping to furnish their new home cheaply. The newlyweds often go to garage sales.

The second statement is a complete sentence. *Newlyweds* is the subject, and *go* is the verb. However, the first word group lacks both a subject and a verb, so it is a fragment. (An *-ing* word cannot by itself be the verb of a sentence. In this case, the *-ing* word group describes the word *newlyweds*.)

A fragment may also result when a word group begins with *to* followed by a basic verb form (as in *to go* or *to be*). Here is an example of a fragment that begins with *to* plus a basic verb form:

- Leo jogged through the park. To clear his mind before the midterm.

The first statement is a complete sentence. The subject is *Leo*, and the verb is *jogged*. However, the second word group is a fragment that lacks both a subject and a verb. (A word that follows *to* cannot be the verb of a sentence. *To clear his mind before the midterm* describes the verb *jogged*.)

Correcting Fragments That Begin with *-ing* or *to*

There are two ways to correct these fragments:

1   Connect the fragment to the sentence that comes before or after it.

- Hoping to furnish their new home **cheaply,** the newlyweds often go to garage sales.
- Leo jogged through the **park to** clear his mind before the midterm.

Punctuation note: When an *-ing* or *to* word group starts a sentence, follow it with a comma.

2   Create a complete sentence by adding a subject and a verb to the fragment. To do so, revise the material as necessary.

- The newlyweds often go to garage sales. **They hope** to furnish their new home cheaply.
- Leo jogged through the park. **He wanted** to clear his mind before the midterm.

➤ Practice 6   *Corrections may vary.*

Underline the *-ing* or *to* fragment in each of the following items. Then correct it in the space provided, using one of the two methods given above. Vary your methods of correction.

1. The owner has opened a take-out window. <u>To attract more customers to the diner.</u>

   The owner has opened a take-out window. She wants to attract more customers

   to the diner.

2. <u>Rising high into the sky.</u> The blue hot-air balloon could be seen for miles.

   The blue hot-air balloon rose high into the sky. It could be seen for miles.

3. <u>To get off the horse.</u> The circus rider did a forward flip.

   To get off the horse, the circus rider did a forward flip.

4. <u>Eating the spinach.</u> I felt bits of sand in my mouth.

   Eating the spinach, I felt bits of sand in my mouth.

5. The dog sat quietly near the baby's high chair. <u>Waiting for crumbs to fall.</u>

   The dog sat quietly near the baby's high chair, waiting for crumbs to fall.

6. The hikers broke branches. <u>To mark the trail for their return trip.</u>

   The hikers broke branches. They wanted to mark the trail for their return trip.

7. The family saves plastic bags and bottles. <u>To take to the recycling center.</u>

   The family saves plastic bags and bottles to take to the recycling center.

8. The man jumped from the fifth floor into the firefighters' net. <u>Praying loudly all the while.</u>

   The man jumped from the fifth floor into the firefighters' net. He was praying loudly all the while.

9. <u>Glancing out the window.</u> Rudy spotted someone taking tomatoes from his garden.

   Glancing out the window, Rudy spotted someone taking tomatoes from his garden.

10. <u>To enter the contest.</u> My sister wrote a jingle for her favorite potato chips.

    To enter the contest, my sister wrote a jingle for her favorite potato chips.

Example Fragments

A second common type of fragment without a subject or a verb begins with words like *including, such as, especially, for example,* and *for instance.* These words introduce an example of something that has already been stated.

- Most English words come from other languages. Including German, Latin, and Greek.

- For a main dish, I often serve beans and grains. For example, lentils with brown rice.

In each of the above, the second word group lacks both a subject and a verb. Each of those fragments begins with a word or words that introduce examples (*including, for example*).

Correcting Example Fragments

There are two ways to correct an example fragment:

1   Add the fragment to the sentence that comes before it.

- Most English words come from other **languages, including** German, Latin, and Greek.

2   Create a new sentence by adding a subject and verb to the fragment. To do so, revise the material as necessary.

- For a main dish, I often serve beans and grains. For example, **I mix** lentils and brown rice.

➤ **Practice 7**

Underline the example fragment in each of the following items. Then correct it in the space provided, using one of the two methods given above.

1. For class, we had to read several novels. <u>Including *Lord of the Flies.*</u>

   For class, we had to read several novels, including <u>Lord of the Flies</u>.

   _____

2. Gary is a rude person at times. <u>For instance, interrupting an instructor during a lecture.</u>

   Gary is a rude person at times. For instance, he interrupts an instructor during

   a lecture.

3. <u>With braces I cannot eat certain foods.</u> Especially popcorn and apples.

   With braces I cannot eat certain foods, especially popcorn and apples.

   _____

4. There are healthier ways to prepare chicken than frying. <u>For example, broiling.</u>

   There are healthier ways to prepare chicken than frying. For example, there is

   broiling.

5. The detective searched the room for clues. <u>Such as old letters, receipts, and ticket stubs.</u>

   The detective searched the room for clues, such as old letters, receipts, and

   ticket stubs.

CHAPTER REVIEW

Fill in the correct word or words in each space provided.

1. To be a sentence, a group of words must express ____*a complete*____ _____*thought*_____.

2. Words such as *because, until,* and *while* are known as _____*dependent*_____ words. Word groups that begin with them depend on another statement to complete the thought.

3. Some fragments have a verb but lack a _____*subject*_____.

4. *-Ing* and *to* fragments lack both a _____*subject*_____ and a _____*verb*_____.

5. Fragments that begin with words like *such as, including,* and *for example* are known as _____*example*_____ fragments.

Name_____   Section _____   Date _____

➤ Sentence Fragments: Test 1

Underline the sentence fragment in each item that follows. Then correct the fragment, using one of the methods described in the chapter.

Corrections may vary.

1. <u>Because we have smoke detectors.</u> We survived the fire.

   Because we have smoke detectors, we survived the fire.

2. The dentist is advertising for an assistant. <u>To replace the fired one.</u>

   The dentist is advertising for an assistant to replace the fired one.

3. <u>Since the movie was on after midnight.</u> We taped it to watch the next day.

   Since the movie was on after midnight, we taped it to watch the next day.

4. Monkeys can be trained. <u>To help people without movement in their arms and legs.</u>

   Monkeys can be trained to help people without movement in their arms and legs.

5. There are many very healthful desserts. <u>Including fruit salad and apple sauce.</u>

   There are many very healthful desserts, including fruit salad and apple sauce.

6. Our neighbor loses her temper with her young children. <u>But is trying to become more patient with them.</u>

   Our neighbor loses her temper with her young children. She is trying to become more patient with them.

7. My grandfather has many interests. <u>For example, playing poker and watching old cowboy movies.</u>

   My grandfather has many interests. For example, he plays poker and watches old cowboy movies.

8. Diane sat down with her boyfriend. <u>Then gently said, "I can't marry you."</u>

   Diane sat down with her boyfriend. Then she gently said, "I can't marry you."

Name_____   Section _____   Date _____

Score: (Number right) _____ x 12.5 = _____%

➤ Sentence Fragments: Test 2

Underline the sentence fragment in each item that follows. Then correct the fragment, using one of the methods described in the chapter.

Corrections may vary.

1. I walked gracefully toward my date. <u>And then tripped on the rug.</u>

   I walked gracefully toward my date and then tripped on the rug.

   _____

2. <u>Rolling slowly backwards.</u> The car in the alley had no driver.

   Rolling slowly backwards, the car in the alley had no driver.

   _____

3. I was very nervous. <u>Because I had not studied for the exam.</u>

   I was very nervous because I had not studied for the exam.

   _____

4. Citrus fruits are full of nutrients. <u>Especially vitamin C.</u>

   Citrus fruits are full of nutrients, especially vitamin C.

   _____

5. <u>To get himself to be on time.</u> James set all the clocks in his apartment ten minutes ahead.

   To get himself to be on time, James set all the clocks in his apartment ten

   minutes ahead.

6. Dana becomes happy over little things. <u>Such as her glow-in-the-dark toothbrush.</u>

   Dana becomes happy over little things. One of them is her glow-in-the-dark

   toothbrush.

7. <u>Before people in town can burn leaves.</u> They have to get a permit.

   Before people in town can burn leaves, they have to get a permit.

   _____

8. <u>When Connie had saved up enough money for a vacation.</u> Her old car broke down and needed expensive repairs.

   When Connie had saved up enough money for a vacation, her old car broke

   down and needed expensive repairs.

Name_____ _____ Section _____ Date _____

Score: (Number right) _____ x 12.5 = _____ %

➤ Sentence Fragments: Test 3

Underline the **two** sentence fragments in each short passage that follows. Then correct each fragment, using one of the methods described in the chapter.   *Corrections may vary.*

1. <u>When people are scared.</u> The hair on their bodies really can "stand on end." Each hair is attached to a tiny muscle. <u>Which can pull the hair straight up.</u> The muscles react together in response to a great fright.

   When people are scared, the hair on their bodies really can "stand on end."

   Each hair is attached to a tiny muscle which can pull the hair straight up.

   _____

   _____

2. Christmas comes earlier each year. <u>Because merchants like to stretch out the buying season.</u> Right after Halloween this year, store owners hung colored lights. <u>And filled their windows with Christmas decorations.</u>

   Christmas comes earlier each year because merchants like to stretch out the

   buying season. Right after Halloween this year, store owners hung colored

   lights and filled their windows with Christmas decorations.

   _____

3. <u>Lasting almost two years.</u> An elephant's pregnancy is the longest of all mammals'. Mother elephants devote much of their time to child care. <u>And nurse their babies up to eight years.</u>

   Lasting almost two years, an elephant's pregnancy is the longest of all

   mammals'. Mother elephants devote much of their time to child care. They nurse

   their babies up to eight years.

   _____

4. Karen hates hospitals. <u>Even though she's a nurse.</u> She says they are full of germs and doctors. <u>Waiting to do horrible things to you.</u>

   Karen hates hospitals even though she's a nurse. She says they are full of

   germs and doctors waiting to do horrible things to you.

   _____

   _____

Name_____   Section _____   Date _____

Score: (Number right) _____ x 12.5 = _____%

➤ Sentence Fragments: Test 4

Underline the **two** sentence fragments in each short passage that follows. Then correct each fragment, using one of the methods described in the chapter.   *Corrections may vary.*

1. Snakes have the reputation of being slimy. <u>But don't deserve their bad image.</u> <u>Being cool and dry.</u> Snakes actually are quite pleasant to touch.

    Snakes have the reputation of being slimy but don't deserve their bad image.

    Being cool and dry, snakes actually are quite pleasant to touch.

    _____

    _____

2. <u>Moving up the mountain at a fast pace.</u> The young hikers were soon exhausted. They were not used to hiking at altitudes. <u>Where the air was thinner.</u>

    Moving up the mountain at a fast pace, the young hikers were soon exhausted.

    They were not used to hiking at altitudes where the air was thinner.

    _____

    _____

3. Honeys vary quite a bit in taste. <u>Depending on their flower source.</u> In many supermarkets you can find several types of honey. <u>Such as clover and wildflower honey.</u>

    Honeys vary quite a bit in taste depending on their flower source. In many

    supermarkets you can find several types of honey. These include clover and

    wildflower honey.

    _____

4. Jodie likes to pamper herself. <u>After she's had a hard day at work.</u> She loves to relax in an extra-hot bubble bath. <u>When she gets out.</u> Her skin is wrinkled like a prune.

    Jodie likes to pamper herself after she's had a hard day at work. . . .

    When she gets out, her skin is wrinkled like a prune.

    _____

    _____

Name_____ _____ Section _____ Date _____

Score: (Number right) _____ x 10 = _____%

➤ Sentence Fragments: Test 5

The following passage contains **ten** sentence fragments. Underline each fragment. Then correct it on or above the line, crossing out unneeded periods, replacing unneeded capital letters with lower-case letters, and so on.

Hardly anyone has enough money. <u>To pay for college without help.</u> To get a scholarship, however, you must be a brain or a terrific athlete, right? The answer is not so simple. <u>And may surprise you.</u>

Good grades or a great sports record is very useful. <u>In getting a scholarship.</u> Nevertheless, you may be eligible for some of the more unusual scholarships available at colleges across the country. <u>Even if you're not an outstanding student or athlete.</u> For instance, the Rochester Institute of Technology offers $1,500 in tuition assistance to 150 students born on June 12, 1979. <u>Which is the date of the 150th anniversary of the school's founding.</u> Harvard University has grants for freshmen with certain last names. <u>Such as Anderson, Baxendale, Borden, Bright, Murphy, and Pennoyer.</u>

<u>If you or a parent have an unusual skill or occupation.</u> You may be eligible for other scholarships. The University of Arizona, for example, will give $500 to any applicant with a grade-point average of at least 2.5. <u>Who has roped calves in a rodeo.</u> Also, Tufts University gives scholarships. <u>To help the children of fishermen.</u> Other scholarships are available to students who have been golf caddies or have worked on Indian reservations.

(Continues on next page)

<u>Depending on various other circumstances in your life.</u> You may be eligible for other scholarships. Juniata College in Pennsylvania, for instance, awards $10,000 each year to a left-handed person.

Corrections

Note: Corrections may vary.

1. *Hardly anyone has enough money to pay for college without help.*
2. *It may surprise you.*
3. *Good grades or a great sports record is very useful in getting a scholarship.*
4. *Nevertheless, you may be eligible for some of the more unusual scholarships available at colleges across the country even if you're not an outstanding student or athlete.*
5. *For instance, the Rochester Institute of Technology offers $1,500 in tuition assistance to 150 students born on June 12, 1979, which is the date of the 150th anniversary of the school's founding.*
6. *These include Anderson, Baxendale, Borden, Bright, Murphy, and Pennoyer.*
7. *If you or a parent have an unusual skill or occupation, you may be eligible for other scholarships.*
8. *The University of Arizona, for example, will give $500 to any applicant with a grade-point average of at least 2.5 who has roped calves in a rodeo.*
9. *Also, Tufts University gives scholarships to help the children of fishermen.*
10. *Depending on various other circumstances in your life, you may be eligible for other scholarships.*

11 / Run-Ons and Comma Splices

This chapter explains the following:

1   Two common sentence errors: run-ons and comma splices

Run-on: I locked my keys in the car the motor was running.

Comma splice: I locked my keys in the car, the motor was running.

2   Four methods of correcting run-ons and comma splices

Add a period and a capital letter: I locked my keys in the car. **T**he motor was running.

Add a comma and a joining word: I locked my keys in the car, **and** the motor was running.

Add a dependent word: **When** I locked my keys in the car, the motor was running.

Add a semicolon: I locked my keys in the car; the motor was running.

RECOGNIZING RUN-ONS AND COMMA SPLICES

A **run-on** is made up of two complete thoughts that are incorrectly run together without a connection between them. Here is an example of a run-on:

- Dolphins have killed sharks they never attack humans.

    The complete thoughts are *dolphins have killed sharks* and *they never attack humans.*

A **comma splice** is made up of two complete thoughts that are incorrectly joined (or spliced) together with only a comma. *A comma alone is not enough to connect two complete thoughts.* Here's an example of a comma splice:

- Dolphins have killed sharks, they never attack humans.

➤ Practice 1

In the blank space by each item, write one of the following:

  C for a sentence that is correct
  RO for a run-on sentence
  CS for a comma splice

For run-on sentences and comma splices, mark the spot between the two thoughts with a slash (/). Look at the examples:

Examples   _RO_ The garage is locked / no one has a key.

    _CS_ The house was covered with ivy, / a stone path led to the front door.

    _C_ When I was alone in the house, I kept hearing noises.

_RO_ 1. Don likes to knit his wife taught him how.

_C_ 2. The bell rang, and the boxers returned to their corners.

_CS_ 3. The bicycle is in the basement, it has two flat tires.

_RO_ 4. Excited fans filled the gym the big game finally began.

_RO_ 5. The patient sat down with his doctor he brought a list of questions to ask.

_CS_ 6. Lisa is lucky, she can eat anything without gaining weight.

_C_ 7. Since it rained during our entire vacation, we played cards and told stories.

_RO_ 8. The bee stung the girl on the toe she should not have taken off her shoes.

_CS_ 9. My sister just got married, she and her husband will live with his parents for a while.

_C_ 10. The waiters served soft drinks to the children, but they offered wine to the adults.

CORRECTING RUN-ONS AND COMMA SPLICES

There are four ways to correct run-ons and comma splices.

Method 1: Use a Period and a Capital Letter

Put each complete thought into its own sentence.

Run-on: The computer hummed loudly the sound was annoying.

Comma splice: The computer hummed loudly, the sound was annoying.

Correct version: The computer hummed loudly. **T**he sound was annoying.

➤ Practice 2

Draw a slash (/) between the two complete thoughts in each run-on or comma splice that follows. Then rewrite the item, using a period and capital letter to divide it into two sentences. Note the example below.

Example   Our neighbor must hate to mow grass / he filled his yard with green stones.

Our neighbor must hate to mow grass. He filled his yard with

green stones.

1. Hamsters are small, / they are also very cute.
   Hamsters are small. They are also very cute.

2. Grape juice spilled on the carpet / it made permanent stains.
   Grape juice spilled on the carpet. It made permanent stains.

3. Kareem's brownies are great, / he adds nuts and chocolate chips.
   Kareem's brownies are great. He adds nuts and chocolate chips.

4. My sister is raising triplets / all three of them have red hair.
   My sister is raising triplets. All three of them have red hair.

5. "Weeds" can be attractive / some are even good to eat.
   "Weeds" can be attractive. Some are even good to eat.

6. The police officers were puzzled by the crime / they found no fingerprints.
   The police officers were puzzled by the crime. They found no fingerprints.

7. There was an accident on the bridge this morning, / traffic was stopped for an hour.
   There was an accident on the bridge this morning. Traffic was stopped for an

   hour.

8. Coupons help shoppers save money / they also help stores to sell products.
   Coupons help shoppers save money. They also help stores to sell products.

9. The television show was canceled after six episodes, / it was not very funny.
   The television show was canceled after six episodes. It was not very funny.

10. Chipmunks have dug many holes in our yard / now it looks like a miniature golf course.
    Chipmunks have dug many holes in our yard. Now it looks like a miniature golf

    course.

Method 2: Use a Comma and a Joining Word

Connect two complete thoughts into one sentence with a comma and a joining word. The most common joining words are *and, but,* and *so.* (The other joining words are *for, yet, or,* and *nor.*)

Run-on:	Dolphins have killed sharks they never attack humans.
Comma splice:	Dolphins have killed sharks, they never attack humans.
Correct version:	Dolphins have killed sharks, **but** they never attack humans.

※ For more information on sentences made up of two complete thoughts connected by a comma and a joining word, see "Sentence Types," pages 147–148.

➤ Practice 3

Draw a slash (/) between the two complete thoughts in each of the run-ons or comma splices that follow. Then rewrite each sentence, using a comma and a logical joining word to connect the two complete thoughts. Choose from the following joining words:

and (which means *in addition*)
but (which means *however*)
so (which means *as a result*)

Note the example.

Example   The applesauce was tart, / the cook added some sugar.
The applesauce was tart, so the cook added some sugar.

1. The garden is overgrown / the fence is falling down.
The garden is overgrown, and the fence is falling down.

2. I called Robin three times last night / she never answered.
I called Robin three times last night, but she never answered.

3. The motorcycle wouldn't start, / the man called a taxi.
The motorcycle wouldn't start, so the man called a taxi.

4. The alarm clock fell on the floor / then it started to ring.
The alarm clock fell on the floor, and then it started to ring.

5. I was out of jelly and butter / I spread yogurt on my toast.
I was out of jelly and butter, so I spread yogurt on my toast.

6. The flowers in that yard look wonderful, / the grass needs cutting.
The flowers in that yard look wonderful, but the grass needs cutting.

7. Gina is allergic to animals / she can't have a pet.

   Gina is allergic to animals, so she can't have a pet.

8. A window was broken, / the jewels had been taken.

   A window was broken, and the jewels had been taken.

9. Mr. Dobbs is friendly with his customers / he is rude to his workers.

   Mr. Dobbs is friendly with his customers, but he is rude to his workers.

10. My back itched in a hard-to-reach place / I scratched it on the doorpost.

    My back itched in a hard-to-reach place, so I scratched it on the doorpost.

Method 3: Use a Dependent Word

Add a dependent word to one of the complete thoughts. The sentence will then have one thought that depends upon the remaining complete thought for its full meaning. Here are some common dependent words:

Dependent Words

after	even if	unless	wherever
although	even though	until	whether
as	if	when	while
because	since	whenever	
before	though	where	

Run-on:　　　　　The roads are covered with ice school has been cancelled.

Comma splice:　　The roads are covered with ice, school has been cancelled.

Correct version:　**Because** the roads are covered with ice, school has been cancelled.

Punctuation note: When a dependent thought begins a sentence, it is followed by a comma.

　※　For more information on sentences made up of one complete thought and one or more dependent thoughts, see "Sentence Types," pages 150–151.

➤ Practice 4

Draw a slash (/) between the two complete thoughts in each of the run-ons or comma splices that follow. Then correct each sentence by adding a dependent word to one of the complete thoughts. Choose from these words:

because   after   since   although   while   if

Remember that if the dependent thought comes at the beginning of the sentence, it must be followed with a comma.

Examples   The couple finished their meal, / they asked to see the dessert menu.

After the couple finished their meal, they asked to see the dessert menu.

I pulled off the road / my eyes would not stay open.

I pulled off the road because my eyes would not stay open.

1. I care for my elderly parents, / I have very little free time.

   Because I care for my elderly parents, I have very little free time.

2. The water began to boil, / I added the ears of corn.

   After the water began to boil, I added the ears of corn.

3. The children swam in the bay, / their parents sunned on the beach.

   The children swam in the bay while their parents sunned on the beach.

4. We will have to leave in exactly ten minutes / we want to see the kickoff.

   We will have to leave in exactly ten minutes if we want to see the kickoff.

5. The forecast is for heavy rain / our neighbor is watering his lawn.

   Although the forecast is for heavy rain, our neighbor is watering his lawn.

6. I finished my written report / I spent the rest of the night studying.

   After I finished my written report, I spent the rest of the night studying.

7. Lauren is going to Spain next summer / she is studying Spanish this year.

   Since Lauren is going to Spain next summer, she is studying Spanish this year.

8. The movie was filmed in black and white, / it is being shown on TV tonight in color.

   Although the movie was filmed in black and white, it is being shown on TV tonight in color.

9. I take the train to my downtown job / finding a space to park can be very difficult.

   I take the train to my downtown job because finding a space to park can be

   very difficult.

10. James ordered two scoops of vanilla ice cream / there were thirty-two flavors available.

    James ordered two scoops of vanilla ice cream although there were thirty-two

    flavors available.

Method 4: Use a Semicolon

A final method of connecting two complete thoughts is to use a semicolon. A semicolon (;) is made up of a period and a comma. It is used between two closely related complete thoughts.

Run-on:	The fish was served with its head still on Fred quickly lost his appetite.
Comma splice:	The fish was served with its head still on, Fred quickly lost his appetite.
Correct version:	The fish was served with its head still on; Fred quickly lost his appetite.

➤ Practice 5

Draw a slash (/) between the two complete thoughts in each run-on or comma splice that follows. Then rewrite the item, using a semicolon to connect the two complete thoughts. Note the example below.

Example   The exam was not easy / there were two hundred multiple-choice items.

The exam was not easy; there were two hundred multiple-choice

items.

1. Dogs run in packs / cats are more solitary animals.
   Dogs run in packs; cats are more solitary animals.

2. The stack of books was too high, / it fell with a crash.
   The stack of books was too high; it fell with a crash.

3. I peered through the front-door peephole / a strange man was standing outside.
   I peered through the front-door peephole; a strange man was standing outside.

4. Thousands of actors go to Hollywood, / few ever become stars.

   Thousands of actors go to Hollywood; few ever become stars.

   _____

5. The auditorium was packed with angry people / the meeting would be an ugly one.

   The auditorium was packed with angry people; the meeting would be an ugly

   one.

Semicolon with a Transitional Word or Words

A semicolon is sometimes used with a transitional word (or words) and a comma to join two complete thoughts.

Run-on:	The fish was served with its head still on as a result, Fred quickly lost his appetite.
Comma splice:	The fish was served with its head still on, as a result, Fred quickly lost his appetite.
Correct version:	The fish was served with its head still on**; as a result,** Fred quickly lost his appetite.

Below are some common transitional words that may be used when correcting a run-on or comma splice.

Common Transitional Words

afterwards	in fact	furthermore
also	in addition	nevertheless
as a result	instead	on the other hand
consequently	meanwhile	otherwise
however	moreover	thus

➤ Practice 6

Draw a slash (/) between the two complete thoughts in each run-on or comma splice that follows. Then correct each item by adding a semicolon and an appropriate transitional word (followed by a comma) between the complete thoughts. Choose from the box of transitional words above.

Example   The air is very stale in the library / the lighting is poor.

The air is very stale in the library; moreover, the lighting is poor.

1. I don't usually like desserts / this pumpkin pie is delicious.

   I don't usually like desserts; however, this pumpkin pie is delicious.

2. Our dog barks all the time, / the landlord has refused to renew our lease.

   Our dog barks all the time; consequently, the landlord has refused to renew our

   lease.

3. The house needs a new septic system, / it should have a new roof.

   The house needs a new septic system; in addition, it should have a new roof.

4. I almost never write to my brother / I call him several times a month.

   I almost never write to my brother; on the other hand, I call him several times a

   month.

5. You should eat a good breakfast / you'll be out of energy before noon.

   You should eat a good breakfast; otherwise, you'll be out of energy before noon.

➤ Practice 7

The passage below contains two comma splices and two run-ons. Rewrite the passage on the lines provided. Correct the first mistake by separating the two complete thoughts with a period. Correct the second mistake by adding the joining word *so*. Correct the third mistake by adding the dependent word *although* and a comma. Correct the fourth mistake by adding a semicolon.

My Human Behavior final exam is next week, I am very worried about passing it. Because I was sick a lot at the start of the semester, I never read many of the chapters in the text. For the past month I've been working full-time, it's hard to find time to study. I will ask the teacher for extra help it may be too late. I do not enjoy feeling so much stress I intend never to fall so far behind in class again.

My Human Behavior final exam is next week. I am very worried about

passing it. Because I was sick a lot at the start of the semester, I never read

many of the chapters in the text. For the past month I've been working full-time,

so it's hard to find time to study. Although I will ask the teacher for extra help,

it may be too late. I do not enjoy feeling so much stress; I intend never to fall so

far behind in class again.

CHAPTER REVIEW

Fill in the correct word or words in each space provided.

1. A _____run-on_____ is made up of two complete thoughts that are incorrectly run together without a connection between them.

2. A _____comma splice_____ is made up of two complete thoughts that are incorrectly joined together with only a comma between them.

3. One way to correct run-ons and comma splices is to add a _____period_____ and a capital letter.

4. Two complete thoughts can be joined together in a sentence by a comma and a _____joining_____ word such as *and, but,* or *so.*

5. Two complete thoughts can be joined together in one sentence by adding a _____dependent_____ word such as *when* or *because.*

6. Two complete thoughts can be joined together in a sentence by a _____semicolon_____ and a transitional word such as *moreover, however,* or *consequently.*

Name_____ Section _____ Date _____

➤ Run-Ons and Comma Splices: Test 1

Draw a slash (/) between the two complete thoughts in each run-on or comma splice. Then rewrite each sentence using the method stated.

A. Use a period and a capital letter to divide the two complete thoughts into two sentences.

1. The cat slept on the windowsill / she was wrapped in warm sunlight.

    The cat slept on the windowsill. She was wrapped in warm sunlight.

    _____

2. Larry is not a good babysitter, / he treats his little brother like an insect.

    Larry is not a good babysitter. He treats his little brother like an insect.

    _____

B. Use a comma and a logical joining word (*and, but,* or *so*) to connect the two complete thoughts.

3. Rick is colorblind / his wife lays out his clothes every morning.

    Rick is colorblind, so his wife lays out his clothes every morning.

    _____

4. The weatherman predicted a sunny day / it is cold and cloudy.

    The weatherman predicted a sunny day, but it is cold and cloudy.

    _____

C. Use a dependent word (*after, although, because,* or *when*) to connect the two complete thoughts.

5. These raisin cookies are delicious, / I can't eat another one.

    Although these raisin cookies are delicious, I can't eat another one.

    _____

6. The engine has cooled / you can add more water to the radiator.

    After (or *When*) *the engine has cooled, you can add more water to the radiator.*

    _____

D. Use a semicolon to connect the two complete thoughts.

7. The wind knocked over a ladder, / the ladder then broke a window.

    The wind knocked over a ladder; the ladder then broke a window.

    _____

8. We decided to leave the restaurant / the food was too expensive.

    We decided to leave the restaurant; the food was too expensive.

    _____

Name_____ Section _____ Date _____

Score: (Number right) _____ x 12.5 = _____%

➤ Run-Ons and Comma Splices: Test 2

A. Use a period and a capital letter to divide the two complete thoughts into two sentences.

1. The hammer and saw began to rust, / they had been left out in the rain.

   The hammer and saw began to rust. They had been left out in the rain.
   _____

2. Pets are more popular today than ever / one reason is people's fear of loneliness.

   Pets are more popular today than ever. One reason is people's fear of

   loneliness.

B. Use a comma and a logical joining word (*and, but,* or *so*) to connect the two complete thoughts.

3. Alan's new apartment is small / it is very comfortable.

   Alan's new apartment is small, but it is very comfortable.

4. Jill couldn't afford to pay her rent / she advertised in the paper for a roommate.

   Jill couldn't afford to pay her rent, so she advertised in the paper for a

   roommate.

C. Use a dependent word (*after, although, because,* or *when*) to connect the two complete thoughts.

5. The party ended, / we had three hours of cleaning up to do.

   After (or When) the party ended, we had three hours of cleaning up to do.
   _____

6. I am more alert in the morning, / early classes are better for me.

   Because I am more alert in the morning, early classes are better for me.
   _____

D. Use a semicolon and a transitional word or words (*as a result, in addition,* or *otherwise*) followed by a comma to connect the two complete thoughts.

7. An accident stopped traffic / a long line of cars built up on the highway.

   An accident stopped traffic; as a result, a long line of cars built up on the

   highway.

8. The floor must be swept and mopped / the carpets must be vacuumed.

   The floor must be swept and mopped; in addition, the carpets must be

   vacuumed.

Name_____ Section _____ Date _____

➤ Run-Ons and Comma Splices: Test 3

There are **two** run-ons or comma splices in each passage, or one of each. Correct them by using one of the following:

1 A period and a capital letter
2 A comma and one of these joining words: *and, but,* or *so*
3 One of these dependent words: *although* and *because*
4 A semicolon

Vary your methods of correction.   *Corrections will vary.*

1. Garlic may smell bad it tastes delicious. It has other good qualities as well. Garlic can help lower cholesterol, it is also supposed to keep vampires away.

   Garlic may smell bad, but it tastes delicious. . . .

   Garlic can help lower cholesterol; it is also supposed to keep vampires away.

   _____

2. The dog raced into the house it was happy to be among people. Its owner bent down to pet it he drew back in disgust. The dog had rolled in something with a horrible smell.

   The dog raced into the house. It was happy to be among people.

   Its owner bent down to pet it, but he drew back in disgust. . . .

   _____

3. Small feet were admired in ancient China, many female infants had their feet tightly bound. The feet then grew into tiny deformed shapes. The women could barely walk their feet were crippled for life.

   Because small feet were admired in ancient China, many female infants had

   their feet tightly bound. . . .

   The women could barely walk. Their feet were crippled for life.

4. Steve had never gone skiing before, he was rather nervous. He looked at the beginners' slope. It looked like a mountain to him a patient instructor helped him to get over his fears.

   Steve had never gone skiing before, so he was rather nervous. . . .

   Although it looked like a mountain to him, a patient instructor helped him to get

   over his fears.

Name_____ Section _____ Date _____

Score: (Number right) _____ x 12.5 = _____%

➤ Run-Ons and Comma Splices: Test 4

There are **two** run-ons or comma splices in each passage, or one of each. Correct them by using one of the following:

1 A period and a capital letter

2 A comma and one of these joining words: *and, but,* or *so*

3 One of these dependent words: *although, because,* or *when*

4 A semicolon and a transitional word or words followed by a comma: *as a result, however,* or *in addition*.

Vary your methods of correction.   *Corrections will vary.*

1. Davie insisted on dressing himself for nursery school. It was a cold winter day, he put on shorts and a tank top. He also put on cowboy boots over his bare feet. He liked his image in the mirror his mother made him change.

   Although it was a cold winter day, he put on shorts and a tank top. . . .

   He liked his image in the mirror; however, his mother made him change.

   _____

2. The four college friends were losing touch with one another they decided to start a "circle" letter. Each woman receives the letter, she adds a page and then sends it on to the next friend. Each person has to write only one letter to keep the other three informed.

   The four college friends were losing touch with one another, so they decided to

   start a "circle" letter. . . . When each woman receives the letter, she adds a page

   and then sends it on to the next friend.

3. Ireland's official language is English some people still speak the old Irish language. Road signs are printed in both Irish and English. The Irish did not want their language to die out, children are now taught Irish in school.

   Ireland's official language is English, but some people still speak the old Irish

   language. . . . The Irish did not want their language to die out; as a result,

   children are now taught Irish in school.

4. The night was dark and spooky a cold wind howled. The babysitter was reading the latest scary Stephen King novel. She finished the book she tried to go to sleep on the couch. However, she soon got up and turned on the TV and most of the lights in the house.

   The night was dark and spooky. A cold wind howled. . . .

   When she finished the book, she tried to go to sleep on the couch.

   _____

Name_____   Section _____   Date _____

Score: (Number right) _____ x 12.5 = _____%

➤ Run-Ons and Comma Splices: Test 5

The following passage contains **four** run-ons and **four** comma splices. Correct each error by adding 1) a period and a capital letter, 2) a comma and a joining word, 3) a dependent word (and, if needed, a comma), or 4) a semicolon alone or followed by a transitional word (or words) and a comma. Vary your methods of correction.

Corrections will vary.

A loving hug, a friendly squeeze, and a playful pat are essential to our mental health. Researchers are learning that affectionate touching is more than just pleasant*;* it is something human beings need deeply.

The need for touch begins at ~~birth, infants~~ *birth. Infants* feel loved when they are gently touched. Touch is at least as important to them as food. Babies can survive near-starvation, *but* they can actually die from lack of affection. Most babies receiving too little touch do not die *; however,* they may develop mental or emotional problems later in life.

Children also need lots of loving touch from their ~~parents, that~~ *parents. That* need changes at around the age of eight. Children will then begin to pull away from some contact, *and* they may say hugging and kissing are "icky." Parents need to respect a child's growing need for independence and privacy. Yet they should also be ready to provide physical attention when the child is ready for it.

Teenagers often feel confused about touching. They may have a strong need for affectionate touch *; on the other hand,* they may be embarrassed to accept it from their parents. Likewise, they may fear being regarded as strange if they touch their friends (unless sex is involved). Teens sometimes turn to

(Continues on next page)

drugs or alcohol when they are hungry for affection but afraid to admit it.

Parents can help a self-conscious teenager by providing as much casual

and friendly touching as the teen can accept.

The need for human touch never ~~ends surveys~~ *ends. Surveys* of successful

marriages show that touching and hugging are key factors in a happy

relationship.

12 / Pronoun Forms

A **pronoun** is a word that can be used in place of a noun.

- • Mel scrubbed the potatoes. Then **he** peeled some carrots.

In the second sentence above, the word *he* is a pronoun that is used in place of the word *Mel*.

※ For more information on pronouns, see "Parts of Speech," pages 420–422.

This chapter explains how to choose the correct pronoun to use in a sentence. It covers the following four areas:

1   Personal pronouns as subjects, objects, and possessives

2   Pronouns with *and* or *or*

3   Pronouns in comparisons

4   *Who* and *whom*

PERSONAL PRONOUNS AS SUBJECTS, OBJECTS, AND POSSESSIVES

Pronouns have different forms, or cases, depending on their use in a sentence. As explained below, they may serve as subjects, objects, or possessives.

Subject Pronouns

Subject pronouns act as the subjects of verbs. Here are the subject forms of personal pronouns:

Subject Pronouns

	First Person	Second Person	Third Person
Singular:	I	you	he, she, it
Plural:	we	you	they

- **I** have an itch.

  I is the subject of the verb *have*.

- **She** always remembers her nieces' birthdays.

  She is the subject of the verb *remembers*.

- **They** agreed to the deal and shook hands.

  They is the subject of the verbs *agreed* and *shook*.

Object Pronouns

Object pronouns act as the objects of verbs or of prepositions. Here is a list of the object forms of personal pronouns:

Object Pronouns

	First Person	*Second Person*	*Third Person*
Singular:	me	you	him, her, it
Plural:	us	you	them

When a pronoun receives the action of a verb, an object pronoun should be used.

- Clara pinched **him**.

  Him receives the action of the verb *pinched*. *Him* tells who was pinched.

- Jeff is addicted to Coca-Cola. He drinks **it** for breakfast.

  It receives the action of the verb *drinks*. *It* tells what Jeff drinks for breakfast.

When a pronoun is the object of a preposition, an object pronoun should be used. Prepositions are words such as *to, for, with,* and *from.* (A longer list of prepositions is on page 69.)

- My sister tossed the car keys to **me**.

  Me is the object of the preposition *to*.

- I gave the children money for hot dogs. For **us**, I packed some sandwiches.

  Us is the object of the preposition *for*.

When the preposition *to* or *for* is understood, an object pronoun must still be used.

- My sister tossed **me** the car keys.

  The preposition *to* is implied before the pronoun *me*.

- Flo knitted **him** a tie.

  The preposition *for* is implied before the pronoun *him*.

Possessive Pronouns

Possessive pronouns show that something is owned, or possessed. Here are possessive forms of personal pronouns:

Possessive Pronouns

	First Person	*Second Person*	*Third Person*
Singular:	my, mine	your, yours	his, her, hers, its
Plural:	our, ours	your, yours	their, theirs

- If Lucille needs a sweater, she can borrow **mine**.

    Mine means *the sweater belonging to me.*

- The house lost most of **its** roof during the tornado.

    Its roof means *the roof belonging to the house.*

- Roger and Emily saw many of **their** friends at the party.

    Their friends means *the friends belonging to Roger and Emily.*

Note: Possessive pronouns never contain an apostrophe.

- During the last storm, our apple tree lost all of **its** blossoms (not "*it's* blossoms").

➤ **Practice 1**

Each sentence contains one pronoun. Underline each pronoun. Then, in the space in the margin, identify the pronoun by writing **S** for a subject pronoun, **O** for an object pronoun, and **P** for a possessive pronoun. The first item is done for you as an example.

O   1. The concert gave <u>me</u> a headache.

P   2. <u>Your</u> father is very friendly.

S   3. <u>They</u> once lived in Texas.

O   4. Read the letter out loud to <u>us</u>.

S   5. Apparently <u>she</u> is somebody famous.

P   6. The door on <u>my</u> closet has a broken hinge.

O   7. A stone almost hit <u>me</u> in the eye.

O   8. Stu gave <u>us</u> nothing but trouble.

P   9. Diane often forgets to take <u>her</u> calculator to math class.

S   10. Next Friday, <u>I</u> will be twenty-eight.

➤ **Practice 2**

Fill in each blank with the appropriate pronoun in the margin. Before making your choice, decide if you need a subject, object, or possessive pronoun.

her, she   1. Over the summer, Melba changed _____*her*_____ hair color, job, and boyfriend.

Me, I   2. _____*I*_____ will treat you to lunch today.

our, us   3. Over the last ten years, twenty-three foster children have lived with _____*us*_____.

your, you   4. You should iron _____*your*_____ shirt before going to the job interview.

we, us   5. Will you join _____*us*_____ at the movies Friday night?

They, Them   6. _____*They*_____ cannot find an apartment they like in this neighorhood.

I, me   7. Richard must give _____*me*_____ a ride to school tomorrow.

him, his   8. When he died at the age of ninety-six, Grandpa still had all of _____*his*_____ teeth.

he, him   9. Jill spotted her son on the playground and brought _____*him*_____ a sandwich.

We, Us   10. _____*We*_____ held a family meeting to decide how to split up household chores.

PRONOUNS WITH *AND* AND *OR*

Deciding which pronoun to use may become confusing when there are two subjects or two objects joined by *and* or *or*. However, the rules remain the same: Use a subject pronoun for the subject of a verb; use an object pronoun for the object of a verb or preposition.

- My brother and **I** loved the Wizard of Oz books.

  I is a subject of the verb *loved*. *Brother* is also a subject of *loved*.

- Our parents often read to my brother and **me**.

  Me is an object of the preposition *to*. *Brother* is also an object of *to*.

You can figure out which pronoun to use by mentally leaving out the other word that goes with *and* or *or*. For instance, in the first example above, omitting the words *my brother and* makes it clear that *I* is the correct pronoun to use: . . . *I loved the Wizard of Oz books*. (You would never say *Me loved the Wizard of Oz books*.)

Try mentally omitting words in the following sentences. Then fill in each blank with the correct pronoun in parentheses.

- The prom was so long ago, I can't remember all of the details. Either Gene or *(I, me)* _____ drove. Furthermore, I can't remember whether Katie Davis went with him or *(I, me)* _____.

The correct choice for the first blank becomes clear when the words *Either Gene or* are omitted: . . . *I drove. I* is the subject of the verb *drove.*

The correct choice for the second blank becomes clear when the words *him or* are omitted: *I can't remember whether Katie Davis went with . . . me. Me* is the object of the preposition *with.*

➤ Practice 3

In each sentence, a choice of a subject or an object pronoun is given in parentheses. In the blank space, write the correct pronoun.

1. Is that package addressed to my husband or *(I, me)* _____ me _____?

2. According to Jess, either *(he, him)* _____ he _____ or his roommate will fix the broken window.

3. The piano is too heavy for Kate and *(she, her)* _____ her _____ to move on their own.

4. Robbie and *(he, him)* _____ he _____ first met when they were in the fourth grade.

5. That strong coffee kept Dad and *(we, us)* _____ us _____ awake for hours.

6. My mother heard that the new position of floor manager will go either to her coworker Ken or *(she, her)* _____ her _____.

7. For many years, *(we, us)* _____ we _____ and Dale have worked at the same company.

8. In the books about the Hardy boys, *(they, them)* _____ they _____ and their detective father work together to solve mysteries.

9. Mark and *(I, me)* _____ I _____ had been arguing loudly when our boss walked into the room.

10. She simply frowned at Mark and *(I, me)* _____ me _____ and left.

PRONOUNS IN COMPARISONS

When pronouns are used in comparisons, they often follow the word *than* or *as.*

- My roommate, Matt, received more valentines than **I**.
- Rhonda's behavior puzzled you as much as **me**.

Words are often omitted in comparisons, to avoid repetition. To see whether you should use a subject or object pronoun, mentally fill in the missing words. In the first sentence above, *I* is the subject of the understood verb *received*.

- My roommate, Matt, received more valentines than **I** [received].

In the second sentence, *me* is the object of the verb *puzzled*. That verb is understood but not stated for the second part of the comparison.

- Rhonda's behavior puzzled you as much as [it puzzled] **me**.

Now try to fill in the correct pronouns in the following comparisons:

- Brad was my first crush. I never adored anyone as much as *(he, him)* _____. I had never met anyone as playful and kind as *(he, him)* _____.

In the first blank above, you should have written the object form of the pronoun, *him: I never adored anyone as much as [I adored] him. Him* is the object of the verb *adored*, which is missing but understood in the sentence.

In the second blank above, you should have written the subject form of the pronoun, *he: I had never met anyone as playful and kind as he [was]. He* is the subject of the understood verb *was*.

➤ Practice 4

In each sentence, a choice of a subject or an object pronoun is given in parentheses. In the blank space, write the correct pronoun.

1. Della has more seniority in the company than *(we, us)* _____we_____.

2. Our argument bothers you as much as *(I, me)* _____me_____.

3. Omar told his teammates he runs faster than *(they, them)* _____they_____.

4. My little brother is five inches taller than *(I, me)* _____I_____.

5. The algebra final worries me more than *(she, her)* _____her_____; she is hardly studying for it.

6. We don't give parties as often as *(them, they)* _____they_____.

7. As a child, I had a pet collie; there was no relative I loved as much as *(he, him)* _____him_____.

8. My family and our neighbors all caught the flu, but we weren't as sick as *(they, them)* _____they_____.

9. Julius bats the ball farther than his sister, but she runs the bases faster than *(he, him)* _____he_____.

10. That buzzing noise in the lamp annoys Dad more than *(we, us)* _____us_____; he has to leave the room.

WHO AND WHOM

Who is a subject pronoun; *whom* is an object pronoun.

- The person **who** owns the expensive car won't let anybody else park it.

  Who owns the expensive car is a dependent word group. *Who* is the subject of the verb *owns*.

- The babysitter **whom** they trust cannot work tonight.

  Whom they trust is a dependent word group. *Whom* is the object of the verb *trust*. The subject of *trust* is *they*.

As a general rule, to know whether to use *who* or *whom*, find the first verb after *who* or *whom*. Decide whether that verb already has a subject. If it doesn't have a subject, use the subject pronoun *who*. If it does have a subject, use the object pronoun *whom*.

See if you can fill in the right pronoun in the following sentences.

- The arrested person is a man *(who, whom)* _____ I once dated.
- The man and woman *(who, whom)* _____ live next door argue constantly.

In the first sentence above, look at the verb *dated*. Does it have a subject? Yes, the subject is *I*. Therefore the object pronoun *whom* is the correct choice: *The arrested person is a man whom I once dated.* *Whom* is the object of the verb *dated*.

In the second sentence above, look at the verb *live*. Does it have a subject? No. Therefore the subject pronoun *who* is the correct choice: *The man and woman who live next door argue constantly.* *Who* is the subject of the verb *live*.

Note: In informal speech and writing, *who* is often substituted for *whom*:

- The babysitter who they trust cannot work tonight.

In formal writing, however, *whom* is generally used. In the practices and tests in this chapter, use the formal approach.

➤ Practice 5

In each blank space, write the correct choice of pronoun.

1. The company hired a secretary *(who, whom)* ____who____ can speak Spanish.

2. My first boss was a man *(who, whom)* ____whom____ I could not please.

3. I admire a man *(who, whom)* ____who____ cries at movies.

4. Chester Arthur is a President *(who, whom)* ____whom____ few Americans remember.

5. Students *(who, whom)* ____who____ cheated on the test were suspended.

Who and *Whom* in Questions

In questions, *who* is a subject pronoun, and *whom* is an object pronoun. You can often decide whether to use *who* or *whom* in a question in the same way you decide whether to use *who* or *whom* in a statement.

- **Who** should go?

The verb after *who* is *should go*, which does not have another subject. Therefore use the subject form of the pronoun, *who*.

- **Whom** should I hire?

I is the subject of the verb *should hire*, so use the object form of the pronoun, *whom*.

➤ Practice 6

Fill in each blank with either *who* or *whom*.

1. *(Who, Whom)* _____Who_____ will do the dishes tonight?

2. *(Who, Whom)* _____Whom_____ were you expecting?

3. *(Who, Whom)* _____Who_____ woke up in the middle of the night?

4. *(Who, Whom)* _____Who_____ is making all that racket?

5. *(Who, Whom)* _____Whom_____ did you just call on the phone?

CHAPTER REVIEW

Fill in the correct word or words in each space provided.

1. A(n) _____subject_____ pronoun serves as the subject of a verb.

2. A(n) _____object_____ pronoun serves as the object of a verb or a preposition.

3. A(n) _____possessive_____ pronoun shows that someone owns something.

4. To use the correct pronoun in a comparison, mentally fill in the missing words to decide if you need a _____subject_____ or an _____object_____ pronoun.

Name_____ Section _____ Date _____

Score: (Number right) _____ x 10 = _____%

➤ **Pronoun Forms: Test 1**

Fill in each blank with the appropriate pronoun from the margin.

She, Her   1. _____*She*_____ got the highest grade on the mid-term exam.

they, their   2. The twins had braces on _____*their*_____ teeth for three years.

we, us   3. We are sure that getting married is the right thing for _____*us*_____.

they, them   4. Since my aunt and uncle enjoy basketball more than I do, I gave the tickets to _____*them*_____.

I, me   5. She and _____*I*_____ have been friends since we were little children.

he, him   6. I don't know whether to believe you or _____*him*_____.

she, her   7. Hector and his sister both speak some Spanish, but Hector is more fluent than _____*she*_____.

he, him   8. We enjoyed no teacher as much as _____*him*_____; he was always interesting.

who, whom   9. Our mayor is a former nun _____*who*_____ decided to enter politics.

who, whom   10. The principal is a young man _____*who*_____ has earned the community's respect.

Name_____   Section _____   Date _____

Score: (Number right) _____ x 10 = _____%

➤ Pronoun Forms: Test 2

Fill in each blank with the appropriate pronoun from the margin.

we, us   1. You are welcome to drive to the meeting with _____ *us* _____.

they, their   2. All of my blue jeans have holes in _____ *their* _____ knees.

I, me   3. My mother changes jobs more frequently than _____ *I* _____.

who, whom 4. The man _____ *whom* _____ the car hit is my uncle.

we, us   5. Next weekend, you and _____ *we* _____ should go to a movie together.

I, me   6. _____ *I* _____ and my dog often hike in the woods for hours at a time.

she, her   7. Sarah's boss said there was no employee he valued as much as _____ *her* _____.

he, him   8. Does that red sports car belong to his parents or _____ *him* _____?

who, whom 9. The mechanic _____ *who* _____ usually works on my car is on vacation.

he, him   10. When the captain's boat capsized, _____ *he* _____ and his crew had a dangerous adventure.

Name_____ Section _____ Date _____

Score: (Number right) _____ x 12.5 = _____%

➤ Pronoun Forms: Test 3

In each of the following short paragraphs, **two** errors have been made in the use of pronouns as subjects and objects. Find the two pronouns that should not have been used, and cross them out. Then write the corrections in the spaces provided.

1. I have to move out of this apartment. I've been waging war against cockroaches, and ~~them~~ are winning. It's my neighbor's fault. Living next door to ~~he~~ is like living near a dump. His kitchen is a motel for roaches, and his "guests" keep visiting me.

   a. _____ *they* _____

   b. _____ *him* _____

2. My wife Rosie and ~~me~~ ride a train to work in the city every day. We and our fellow travelers have formed a little club. The twelve of us eat breakfast together in the train car. We even celebrate our birthdays. When Rosie and I had the flu together, they sent her and ~~I~~ a giant "get well" card.

   a. _____ *I* _____

   b. _____ *me* _____

3. Our new boss is a woman ~~whom~~ deserves the "boss of the year" award. She has given us permission to dress in casual clothing on Fridays. From Monday through Thursday, we all wear our usual "office clothes": suits, ties, dresses, skirts. On Fridays she and ~~us~~ wear jeans, sweaters, and running shoes.

   a. _____ *who* _____

   b. _____ *we* _____

4. All evening I waited for my girlfriend to call. She and ~~me~~ were going on a trip the next day, and I needed to know when she would pick me up. I couldn't call her because she was out with a man ~~whom~~ works with her. As the evening went on I got angrier and angrier at her for not calling. Finally I went to bed. That's when I noticed that my phone was unplugged.

   a. _____ *I* _____

   b. _____ *who* _____

➤ Pronoun Forms: Test 4

In each of the following short paragraphs, **two** errors have been made in the use of pronouns as subjects and objects. Find the two pronouns that should not have been used, and cross them out. Then write the corrections in the spaces provided.

1. Doctors used to appear in cigarette advertising. ~~Them~~ would praise smoking as "relaxing" and "healthful." One ad was especially outrageous. It showed a doctor ~~whom~~ was happily smoking. He said that the cigarette in the ad had "not a cough in a carload."

   a. _____ *They* _____

   b. _____ *who* _____

2. My wife and ~~me~~ have differing musical tastes. My wife loves jazz. To me, however, jazz is just noise. On the other hand, I like to listen to heavy metal bands. For ~~she~~, listening to heavy metal is like being locked in a room with a jackhammer.

   a. _____ *I* _____

   b. _____ *her* _____

3. Ballet dancers are terrific athletes. Few can leap higher than ~~them~~. Many male dancers who have danced for a few years can probably jump between four and five feet off the ground. Some stars, like Mikhail Baryshnikov, reach even higher. Even though he stands only 5 feet 8 inches, a six-foot jump off the ground is easy for ~~he~~.

   a. _____ *they* _____

   b. _____ *him* _____

4. My brother was married to a woman named Cheryl. I had been friends with ~~she~~ for years—we went to the same high school. They've been divorced for years, but Cheryl and ~~me~~ are still close friends. We tell people that we used to be sisters-in-law, but now we're sisters-out-of-the-law.

   a. _____ *her* _____

   b. _____ *I* _____

Name_____ _____ Section _____ Date _____

Score: (Number right) _____ x 10 = _____%

➤ Pronoun Forms: Test 5

The following passage contains **ten** errors in pronoun use. Find the ten pronouns that should not have been used, and cross them out. Above each one, write in the correction.

I am a huge baseball fan, and my father and uncles love the sport as

much as ~~me~~ *I*. When I was a kid, ~~us~~ *we* spent many hours talking baseball

together. George Herman Ruth was the player that meant the most to

them. He was the player ~~whom~~ *who* is better known as "Babe" Ruth. The Babe

spent fifteen years playing for the New York Yankees. During the 1920s

and '30s, Ruth was the best-known athlete in the world. Fans everywhere

waited with anticipation when he stepped up to bat, for he was always a

threat to hit a home run. His career total of 714 home runs was a record

that stayed in the books for decades. A plaque at the Baseball Hall of

Fame calls him the "Greatest drawing card in history of baseball."

Not only was he well known, but he was also extremely well paid. No

athlete earned more than ~~him~~ *he*. His top salary with the Yankees was

$80,000. But his salary was only part of the story. In 1927, for instance,

he hit sixty home runs, which earned ~~he~~ *him* about $300,000 total. That figure

included money he earned from appearing in a movie, endorsing

products, and so on. Advertisers paid Ruth a good fee to endorse ~~they~~ *their*

products. During his entire baseball career, Ruth earned about $3

million. Dad and my uncles calculated that figure would work out to

about $23.8 million today.

(Continues on next page)

To them and ~~I~~ _me_, the Babe was a hero ~~whom~~ _who_ deserved every penny he

got. ~~Them~~ _They_ and ~~me~~ _I_ never tired of talking about the great Yankee slugger.

13 / Pronoun Problems

This chapter explains three common problems with pronouns:

1   Pronoun shifts in number: A pronoun must agree in number with the noun it refers to.

   Incorrect: Each of my sisters has **their** own room.

   Correct: Each of my sisters has her own room.

2   Pronoun shifts in person: Pronouns must be consistent in person. Unnecessary shifts in person (for example, from *I* to *one*) confuse readers.

   Incorrect: **One's** patience runs thin when I am faced with a slow-moving line at the bank.

   Correct: My patience runs thin when I am faced with a slow-moving line at the bank.

3   Unclear pronoun reference: A pronoun must clearly refer to the noun it stands for.

   Incorrect: Michael gave Arnie his car keys. (Whose keys?)

   Correct: Michael gave his car keys to Arnie.

PRONOUN SHIFTS IN NUMBER

A pronoun must agree in number with the noun it refers to, which is also called the pronoun's **antecedent**. Singular nouns require singular pronouns; plural nouns require plural pronouns.

In the following examples, pronouns are printed in **boldface type**; the antecedents are printed in *italic type*.

- The dying *tree* lost all **its** leaves.

   The antecedent *tree* is singular, so the pronoun must be singular: *its*.

- When *Vic* was in the Army, **his** little brother wrote to **him** almost every day.

   The antecedent *Vic* is singular, so the pronouns must be singular: *his* and *him*.

- Do the *neighbors* know that **their** dog is loose?

  The antecedent *neighbors* is plural, so the pronoun must be plural: *their*.

- *Linda and Ted* act like newlyweds, but **they** have been married for years.

  The antecedent *Linda and Ted* is plural, so the pronoun must be plural: *they*.

➤ Practice 1

In each blank space, write the noun or nouns that the given pronoun refers to.

Example   The ridges on our fingertips have a function. They help fingers to grasp things.

They refers to _____ *ridges* _____.

1. The photographer realized she had run out of film.

   She refers to _____ photographer _____.

2. The cat hid its kittens in the hayloft.

   Its refers to _____ cat _____.

3. Kate and Barry don't get along with their stepfather.

   Their refers to _____ Kate and Barry _____.

4. Martin never drinks coffee in the evening. It keeps him awake all night.

   It refers to _____ coffee _____. *Him* refers to _____ Martin _____.

5. Nora is a year older than her brother, but they are both in sixth grade.

   Her refers to _____ Nora _____. *They* refers to _____ Nora and her brother _____.

➤ Practice 2

In the spaces provided for each sentence, write (a) the pronoun used and (b) the noun or nouns that the pronoun refers to.

1. The movie started late, and it was badly out of focus.

   The pronoun _____ it _____ refers to _____ movie _____.

2. Marlene buys most of her clothing at thrift shops.

   The pronoun _____ her _____ refers to _____ Marlene _____.

3. As the horse neared the finish line, his energy ran out.

   The pronoun _____ his _____ refers to _____ horse _____.

4. A man was at the door a minute ago, but now he is gone.

   The pronoun _____*he*_____ refers to _____*man*_____.

5. Carla and Vicki are twins, but they don't look alike.

   The pronoun _____*they*_____ refers to _____*Carla and Vicki*_____.

Indefinite Pronouns

Most pronouns refer to one or more particular persons or things. However, **indefinite pronouns** do not refer to particular persons or things. The following indefinite pronouns are always singular:

Singular Indefinite Pronouns

each	anyone	anybody	anything
either	everyone	everybody	everything
neither	someone	somebody	something
one	no one	nobody	nothing

- *Something* has left **its** muddy footprints on the hood of the car.
- *One* of my sisters has lost **her** job.
- *Everybody* is entitled to change **his or her** mind.

   The indefinite pronouns *something, one,* and *everybody* are singular. The personal pronouns that refer to them must also be singular: *its, her, his or her.*

Note on Gender Agreement: Choose a pronoun that agrees in gender with the noun it refers to. Because *one of my sisters* is clearly feminine, use *her.* But *everybody* includes males and females, so use *his or her.* If *his or her* seems awkward in a sentence, try rewriting the sentence with a plural subject:

- *People* are entitled to change **their** minds.

The following indefinite pronouns are always plural:

Plural Indefinite Pronouns

both	many	several
few	other	

- *Both* of my brothers worked **their** way through college.

   Both, the subject of this sentence, is plural, so the plural pronoun *their* is used.

The following indefinite pronouns are singular or plural, depending on their context:

Indefinite Pronouns That Can Be Singular or Plural

all	more	none
any	most	some

- *Some* of the pie is fine, but **its** crust is burnt.

  Some here refers to one thing—the pie, so the singular pronoun *its* is used.

- *Some* of the students forgot **their** books.

  Some here refers to several students, so the plural pronoun *their* is used.

➤ **Practice 3**

In the spaces provided for each sentence, write (a) the pronoun or pronouns needed and (b) the word that the pronoun or pronouns refer to.

Example   Neither of the boys has had *(his / their)* measles shot yet.

The pronoun needed is ___*his*___. The word it refers to is ___*neither*___.

1. Everything in the office has *(its / their)* own place.

   The pronoun needed is ___*its*___. The word it refers to is ___*everything*___.

2. Neither of my uncles has ever smoked in *(his / their)* life.

   The pronoun needed is ___*his*___. The word it refers to is ___*neither*___.

3. Many restaurants post *(its / their)* menus in the window.

   The pronoun needed is ___*their*___. The word it refers to is ___*restaurants*___.

4. Don't eat anything out of the garden until you've washed *(them / it)*.

   The pronoun needed is ___*it*___. The word it refers to is ___*anything*___.

5. Is anyone brave enough to read *(their / his or her)* essay aloud to the class?

   The pronoun needed is ___*his or her*___. The word it refers to is ___*anyone*___.

6. Both of the girls invited *(her mother / their mothers)* to the mother-daughter luncheon.

   The pronoun needed is ___*their*___. The word it refers to is ___*both*___.

7. Everybody loses *(their / his or her)* temper occasionally.

   The pronoun needed is ___*his or her*___. The word it refers to is ___*everybody*___.

8. Nobody can enter that plant without *(their / his or her)* security badge.

   The pronoun needed is _his or her_. The word it refers to is ____nobody____.

9. Most of the room has been painted, and *(it is / they are)* almost dry.

   The pronoun needed is ____it____. The word it refers to is ____most____.

10. Most of the invitations have been addressed, but *(it still needs / they still need)* to be stamped.

    The pronoun needed is ____they____. The word it refers to is ____most____.

A Note on Collective Nouns

A **collective noun** refers to a group of persons or things considered to be a unit. Collective nouns are usually considered singular. Following are some examples.

Some Collective Nouns

audience	committee	group	quartet
band	couple	herd	society
class	family	jury	team

• The *class* started late, and **it** ended early.

  Class refers to a single unit, so the singular pronoun *it* is used.

However, if a collective noun refers to the individual members of the group, a plural pronoun is used.

• The *class* handed in **their** essays before vacation.

Many writers feel it is awkward to use a collective noun as a plural. They prefer to revise the sentence.

• The class *members* handed in **their** essays before vacation.

PRONOUN SHIFTS IN PERSON

A pronoun that refers to the person who is speaking is called a **first-person pronoun**. Examples of first-person pronouns are *I, me,* and *our*. A pronoun that refers to someone being spoken to, such as *you*, is a **second-person pronoun**. And a pronoun that refers to another person or thing, such as *he, she,* or *it*, is a **third-person pronoun**.

Following are the the personal pronouns in first-, second-, and third-person groupings:

Personal Pronouns

	First person	Second person	Third person
Singular	I, me, my, mine	you, your, yours	he, him, his; she, her, hers; it, its
Plural	we, us, our, ours	you, your, yours	they, them, their, theirs

When a writer makes unnecessary shifts in person, the writing may become less clear. The sentences below, for example, show some needless shifts in person. (The words that show the shifts are boldfaced.)

- The worst thing about **my** not writing letters is that **you** never get any back.

    The writer begins with the first-person pronoun *my*, but then shifts to the second-person pronoun *you*.

- Though **we** like most of **our** neighbors, there are a few **you** can't get along with.

    The writer begins with the first-person pronouns *we* and *our*, but then shifts to the second-person pronoun *you*.

These sentences can be improved by eliminating the shifts in person:

- The worst thing about **my** not writing letters is that **I** never get any back.
- Though **we** like most of **our** neighbors, there are a few **we** can't get along with.

➤ **Practice 4**

Write the correct pronoun in each space provided.

they, we   1. Whenever students are under a great deal of stress, _____*they*_____ often stop studying.

one, you   2. If you want to do well in this course, _____*you*_____ should plan on attending every day.

you, me   3. When I first began to work as a waitress, I was surprised at how rude some customers were to _____*me*_____.

we, you   4. It's hard for us to pay for health insurance, but _____*we*_____ don't dare go without it.

you, I   5. When _____*I*_____ drive on the highway, I get disgusted at the amount of trash I see.

I, you   6. Although I like visiting my Aunt Rita, _____*I*_____ always feel like my visit has disrupted her life.

we, you   7. When we answer the telephone at work, _____*we*_____ are supposed to say the company name.

I, one   8. I would like to go to a school where _____*I*_____ can meet many people who are different from me.

you, they   9. Dog owners should put tags on their dogs in case _____*they*_____ lose their pets.

we, they   10. People often take a first-aid course so that _____*they*_____ can learn how to help choking and heart attack victims.

UNCLEAR PRONOUN REFERENCE

A pronoun must refer clearly to its antecedent—the word it stands for. If the word a pronoun refers to is uncertain, the sentence will be confusing. As shown below, some pronouns are unclear because they have two possible antecedents. Others are unclear because they have no antecedent.

Two Possible Antecedents

A pronoun's reference will not be clear if there are two possible antecedents.

- Eva told her mother that she had received a postcard from Alaska.

  Who received the letter, Eva or her mother?

- I wrote a to-do list with my purple pen, and now I can't find it.

  What can't the writer find, the list or the pen?

An unclear sentence with two antecedents can sometimes be corrected by using the speaker's exact words.

- Eva told her mother, "**I** received (*or:* "**You** received) a postcard from Alaska."

  ※ For an explanation of how to use quotation marks, see pages 373–374 in "Quotation Marks."

In some cases, the best solution is to replace the pronoun with the word it was meant to refer to.

- I wrote a to-do list with my purple pen, and now I can't find **the list** (*or:* **the pen**).

No Antecedent

A pronoun's reference will not be clear if there is no antecedent.

- I just received our cable TV bill. **They** said the Disney Channel is providing a free preview next month.

  Who said there's a free preview? We don't know because *they* has no word to refer to.

- My older brother is a chemist, but **that** doesn't interest me.

  What doesn't interest the writer? The pronoun *that* doesn't refer to any word in the sentence.

To correct an unclear reference in which a pronoun has no antecedent, replace the pronoun with the word or words it is meant to refer to.

- I just received our cable TV bill. **The cable company** said the Disney Channel is providing a free preview next month.

- My older brother is a chemist, but **chemistry** doesn't interest me.

➤ Practice 5

In each sentence below, underline the correct word or words in parentheses.

1. At a local deli, (they / <u>the owners</u>) provide each table with a free bowl of pickles.

2. Joan said the cordless phone is under the red pillow, but I can't find (it / <u>the phone</u>).

3. Rita asked Paula (if she could help with the dishes. /, <u>"Can I help with the dishes?"</u>)

4. In a letter from Publisher's Clearing House, (they / <u>the contest organizers</u>) all but promise that I have already won ten million dollars.

5. When my cousins arrived at the picnic with the homemade pies, (<u>my cousins</u> / they) were very welcome.

➤ Practice 6   *Wordings of revisions may vary.*

Revise each sentence to eliminate the unclear pronoun reference.

1. When Nick questioned the repairman, he became very upset.

    When Nick questioned the repairman, the repairman became very upset.

    _____

2. My parents are expert horseshoe players, but I've never become any good
    at it.

    My parents are expert horseshoe players, but I've never become any good at

    horseshoes.

3. Mary Alice told her sister that her boyfriend was cheating on her.

    Mary Alice told her sister, "My boyfriend is cheating on me." (Or: "Your

    boyfriend is cheating on you.")

4. I bought a stationary bicycle that has a timer, but I never use it.

    I bought a stationary bicycle that has a timer, but I never use the timer. (Or: I

    never use the bicycle.)

5. I went to the hardware store for 100-watt lightbulbs, but they didn't have
    any.

    I went to the hardware store for 100-watt lightbulbs, but the clerks didn't have

    any.

CHAPTER REVIEW

Answer each question by writing **T** (for *true*) or **F** (for *false*) in the space provided.

1. *True or false?* __F__ A pronoun may be singular even if its antecedent is plural.

2. *True or false?* __T__ *Everybody* and *everything* are singular indefinite pronouns.

3. *True or false?* __F__ A collective noun is usually plural.

4. *True or false?* __T__ A writer should not needlessly change from the first person to the second person.

5. *True or false?* __T__ A pronoun's reference will not be clear if the pronoun has two possible antecedents.

Name_____ Section _____ Date _____

Score: (Number right) _____ x 10 = _____%

➤ Pronoun Problems: Test 1

A. In each blank space, write the pronoun that agrees in number with the word or words it refers to.

its, their   1. The school has asbestos in many of _____*its*_____ classrooms.

her, their   2. My mother and her sister often share _____*their*_____ clothing and jewelry.

his or her, their   3. No one in the class remembered _____*his or her*_____ textbook.

her, their   4. Neither of my nieces wants to share _____*her*_____ toys.

B. For each sentence, cross out the pronoun that makes a shift in person. Then, in the space provided, write a pronoun that corrects the shift in person.

_____*us*_____   5. We work at a store where the owners don't provide ~~you~~ with any health insurance.

_____*I*_____   6. I wanted to see the movie star, but ~~one~~ couldn't get past her security guard.

_____*their*_____   7. Members of the gang said they feel the gang is like ~~your~~ family.

C. In each sentence below, underline the correct word or words in parentheses.

8. I stopped by the post office and asked (<u>a postal worker</u>/ them) to hold my mail while I was on vacation.

9. Carrie told Linda (that she had gotten four phone calls that afternoon./ ,<u>"You got four phone calls this afternoon."</u>)

10. I could be a cafeteria server again next semester, but I really hate (it/ <u>working in the cafeteria</u>).

Name _____   Section _____   Date _____

Score: (Number right) _____ x 10 = _____%

➤ Pronoun Problems: Test 2

A. In each blank space, write the pronoun that agrees in number with the word or words it refers to.

his, their   1. Each of my brothers has _____ **his** _____ own television.

its, their   2. Some schools have a day-care center for the children of _____ **their** _____ employees and students.

her, their   3. One of the hens has laid _____ **her** _____ egg on an old blanket in the shed.

his or her, their 4. Everybody in our apartment building was told to lock _____ **his or her** _____ door in the evening.

B. For each sentence, cross out the pronoun that makes a shift in person. Then, in the space provided, write a pronoun that corrects the shift in person.

_____ **me** _____   5. The constant ringing of my telephone often drives ~~one~~ crazy.

_____ **they** _____   6. If people want something from the kitchen, ~~you~~ have to go and get it.

_____ **he (or she)** _____ 7. The newspaper carrier didn't realize that ~~you~~ would have to deliver papers at 5 a.m.

C. In each sentence below, underline the correct word or words in parentheses.

8. Jeanine is a devoted user of coupons at the supermarket, but I can't find the time for (it / <u>collecting coupons</u>).

9. Ian told his father (he was late for his doctor's appointment. / <u>"You're late for your doctor's appointment."</u>)

10. In this letter from the bank, (<u>the customer service manager says</u> / they say) my account is overdrawn.

Name_____   Section _____   Date _____

➤ Pronoun Problems: Test 3

Each of the following passages contains **two** pronoun mistakes. Find these two mistakes and cross them out. Then write the corrections in the spaces provided.   *Wordings of corrections may vary.*

1. First-year students at our school are required to take a math course. ~~You~~ must also pass a computer class. Help is available at a study-skills center. Anyone who brings in ~~their~~ homework receives assistance.

    a. _____*They*_____

    b. _____*his or her*_____

2. Each of the sisters is a successful artist in ~~their~~ own field. Anna creates oil paintings that she sells at several galleries. Clarita makes quilts which she sells from her home. Anna was recently delighted to tell Clarita ~~that she had won a prize for her work.~~

    a. _____*her*_____

    b. _____*, "You have won a prize for your work."*_____

3. My roommate and I are looking for jobs. We didn't realize that ~~you~~ could look for jobs in places other than the newspaper. One of our friends has visited her college's career center. Two other friends have signed up with a job agency where ~~you~~ will learn about jobs in the nearby area.

    a. _____*we*_____

    b. _____*they*_____

4. Nick informed his brother Lloyd ~~that he would take over the family meat packing business.~~ The next day, Nick was found dead. Although Lloyd hired the best lawyer ~~one~~ could find, he was found guilty of butchering his brother.

    a. _____*, "I'm taking over the family meat packing business."*_____

    b. _____*he*_____

Name_____ Section _____ Date _____

Score: (Number right) _____ x 12.5 = _____%

➤ Pronoun Problems: Test 4

Each of the following passages contains **two** pronoun mistakes. Find these two mistakes and cross them out. Then write the corrections in the spaces provided. *Wordings of corrections may vary.*

1. You can make ~~one's~~ own grape juice in a few simple steps. First buy some fresh, ripe grapes. Then put them in a thin cloth and squeeze tightly until all the juice has been drained into a container. ~~We~~ can also add sugar, but you may find that the juice is already sweet enough.

    a. _____*your*_____

    b. _____*You*_____

2. Lew and Mandy usually do the crossword puzzle in the Sunday newspaper. There are always a few clues ~~you~~ have to look up in a dictionary. Whenever one of them figures out a clue, ~~they~~ will yell out the answer.

    a. _____*they*_____

    b. _____*he or she*_____

3. Anybody who plays Bingo at our church women's club knows ~~they~~ must cry "bingo" in order to win. The word comes from an early version of the game in which players had to ring a bell when ~~you~~ had won. The sound of the bell—"bing"—gave the game its name.

    a. _____*she*_____

    b. _____*they*_____

4. Hassan and Pete take a math class together. On Friday, class ended early, so Hassan went with Pete to ~~his~~ favorite coffee shop. However, it was closed. ~~They~~ had hung a sign on the door that said, "Sorry, Gone for a Cup of Tea. Be Back in an Hour."

    a. _____*Pete's* (Or: *Hassan's*)_____

    b. _____*The owners*_____

Name_____ Section _____ Date _____

Score: (Number right) _____ x 10 = _____%

➤ Pronoun Problems: Test 5

The following selection has a total of **ten** errors in 1) pronoun shifts in number, 2) pronoun shifts in person, and 3) unclear pronoun reference. Cross out each error, and write the correction above the line.

Some corrections may vary.

Belinda woke up on Saturday morning feeling very energetic. She

jumped out of bed, determined to make great use of ~~one's~~ *her* free day. Soon

Belinda and her mother were enjoying the breakfast of banana pancakes

~~she~~ *Belinda* had made. As they ate, Belinda enthusiastically explained her plans

for the day. "First I'll drive to the bakery to see if it has any of those

cinnamon rolls we like," she said. "I'll also stop at the gift shop and ask

~~them~~ *the owners* if they're hiring extra help over the holidays. After I get home, I'll

write to Grandma and put a new photograph of myself in ~~it~~ *the letter*."

An hour later, Belinda had still not left home. Earlier that morning,

her brother had taken the family car to do some shopping without even

checking to see if she might need it too. "Anyone who uses the car should

tell the rest of the family before ~~they take~~ *he or she takes* it," said Belinda angrily.

Both of her parents offered ~~his or her~~ *their* opinion that Belinda could use

her own legs to go downtown. "You spend hours exercising in aerobics

class when you could get ~~it~~ *exercise* for free by walking where you want to go,"

said her mother. "After all, it would be only a fifteen- or twenty-minute

walk, and it is a beautiful day."

But Belinda said she simply had to drive. "What if I meet someone I

know, and ~~they see~~ *he or she sees* me walking? It's so embarrassing when I go to school

on Monday and people tease ~~you~~ *me* about not having a car."

(Continues on next page)

Neither of her parents showed sympathy on ~~their faces~~. "If your *his or her face* friends don't like you when you don't have a car," said her father, "then it's time to find new friends."

14 / Adjectives and Adverbs

This chapter explains the following:

1   How to identify adjectives and adverbs

  - The circular *(adjective)* house is magnificent *(adjective)*.
  - The extremely *(adverb)* small boy climbed the rope very *(adverb)* quickly *(adverb)*.

2   How to use adjectives and adverbs in comparisons

  - I'm a **worse** cook than my brother, but our sister is the **worst** cook in the family.

3   How to use two troublesome pairs: *good* and *well, bad* and *badly*

  - I can usually work well and do a good job even when I don't feel well.
  - In addition to his bad attitude, the outfielder has been playing badly.

4   How to avoid double negatives

  Incorrect: I **can't hardly** wait for summer vacation.
  Correct: I can hardly wait for summer vacation.

IDENTIFYING ADJECTIVES AND ADVERBS

Adjectives

An **adjective** describes a noun or pronoun. It generally answers such questions as: What kind of? Which one? How many?

An adjective may come before the noun or pronoun it describes.

  - The **weary** hikers shuffled down the **dusty** road.

    The adjective *weary* describes the noun *hikers*; it tells what kind of hikers. The adjective *dusty* describes the noun *road*; it tells what kind of road.

  - The **green** car has **two** antennas.

    The adjective *green* tells which car has the antennas. The adjective *two* tells how many antennas there are.

An adjective that describes the subject of a sentence may also come after a linking verb (such as *is, be, were,* and *seem*).

- That dog's skin is **wrinkled** and **dry**.

  The adjectives *wrinkled* and *dry* describe the subject, *skin*. They follow the linking verb *is*.

  ※ For more information on linking verbs, see "Subjects and Verbs," pages 73–74.

➤ **Practice 1**   *Answers will vary.*

Complete each sentence with an appropriate adjective. Then underline the noun or pronoun that the adjective describes.

Examples   My _____*new*_____ sweater had shrunk.

The principal was _____*impolite*_____.

1. I'm in the mood for a _____*romantic*_____ movie.

2. This _____*rainy*_____ weather really bothers me.

3. I've never read such a _____*depressing*_____ book.

4. A _____*selfish*_____ person makes a poor boss.

5. My aunt has an unusually _____*soft*_____ voice.

6. The dance at school last night was _____*terrific*_____.

7. My _____*new*_____ pants are at the cleaners.

8. It's too bad that you are so _____*shy*_____.

9. _____*Rose*_____ bushes line the side of the house.

10. Sylvia wrote her sister a(n) _____*angry*_____ letter.

Adverbs

An **adverb** is a word that describes a verb, an adjective, or another adverb. Many adverbs end in *-ly*. Adverbs generally answer such questions as: How? When? Where? How much?

- The chef **carefully** spread raspberry frosting over the cake.

  The adverb *carefully* describes the verb *spread*. *Carefully* tells how the chef spread the frosting.

- The robber stood **there**.

  The adverb *there* describes the verb *stood*. *There* tells where the robber stood.

- Ann was **extremely** embarrassed when she stumbled on stage.

  The adverb *extremely* describes the adjective *embarrassed*. It tells how much Ann was embarrassed.

- That lamp shines **very brightly**.

  The adverb *very* describes the adverb *brightly*. *Very* tells how brightly the lamp shines. The adverb *brightly* describes the verb *shines*; it tells how the lamp shines.

Adverbs with Action Verbs

Be careful to use an adverb—not an adjective—after an action verb. Compare the following:

Incorrect	*Correct*
The boss snored loud at his desk. (*Loud* is an adjective.)	The boss snored **loudly** at his desk.
Speak slow during your lecture. (*Slow* is an adjective.)	Speak **slowly** during your lecture.
The batter swung wild at all the pitches. (*Wild* is an adjective.)	The batter swung **wildly** at all the pitches.

➤ Practice 2

Complete each sentence with the adverb form of the adjective in the margin. (Change each adjective in the margin to an adverb by adding *-ly*.)

    Example   *quick*   Sandra read the book too _____*quickly*_____.

soft   1. Bev spoke _____*softly*_____ to the frightened puppy.

helpless   2. The family watched _____*helplessly*_____ as their house burned.

hurried   3. The two teachers spoke _____*hurriedly*_____ between classes.

shy   4. The little girl peeked _____*shyly*_____ at her new neighbor.

honest   5. A good businessperson deals _____*honestly*_____ with everyone.

slow   6. Signs warn motorists to drive _____*slowly*_____ near the school.

longing   7. The cat stared _____*longingly*_____ at the leftover tuna casserole.

frequent   8. Cable TV channels _____*frequently*_____ show the same movie ten or more times in one month.

kind   9. Our neighbor _____*kindly*_____ offered to feed our pets while we were gone.

serious   10. Many teenagers complain that their parents don't take them _____*seriously*_____.

➤ **Practice 3**

Complete each sentence correctly with either the adverb or adjective in the margin.

rapid, rapidly   1. Felipe spoke _____*rapidly*_____ in Spanish to his grandfather.

rapid, rapidly   2. Their _____*rapid*_____ conversation was difficult for me to follow.

quiet, quietly   3. The frog sat _____*quietly*_____ on a lily pad.

patient, patiently   4. The mother is _____*patient*_____ with her youngster.

patient, patiently   5. Ravi waited _____*patiently*_____ for the elevator to arrive.

willing, willingly   6. How many of you are _____*willing*_____ to sell tickets for the play?

prompt, promptly   7. The invitation asks for a _____*prompt*_____ response.

quick, quickly   8. Come _____*quickly*_____ if you want to see a beautiful rainbow.

cheerful, cheerfully   9. Olga smiled _____*cheerfully*_____ at her customer.

cheerful, cheerfully   10. Her _____*cheerful*_____ smile warmed the room.

USING ADJECTIVES AND ADVERBS IN COMPARISONS

Comparing Two Things

In general, to compare two things, add *-er* to adjectives and adverbs of one syllable.

- Grilling food is **faster** than roasting.

   The adjective *faster* is used to compare two methods: grilling and roasting.

- My mother works **longer** each day than my father.

   The adverb *longer* is used to compare how long two people work each day.

For longer adjectives and adverbs, do not add *-er*. Instead, add the word *more* to compare two things.

- My dog is **more intelligent** than my cat.

   The words *more intelligent* describe the subject *dog*; they are being used to compare two things, the dog and the cat.

- Marie sings **more sweetly** than I do.

   The words *more sweetly* describe the verb *sings*; they are being used to compare the ways two people sing.

➤ **Practice 4**

Write in the correct form of the word in the margin by adding either *-er* or *more*.

Examples   *thin*   Kate is _____*thinner*_____ than her twin sister.

carefully   I prefer to ride with Dan. He drives _____ _____*more carefully*_____ than you.

full   1. This bag of potato chips is _____*fuller*_____ than that one.

affectionate   2. My dog is _____*more affectionate*_____ than my boyfriend.

gray   3. This shirt looks _____*grayer*_____ than it did before I washed it.

neat   4. The inside of my car is _____*neater*_____ than the inside of my apartment.

annoying   5. There are few sounds _____*more annoying*_____ than fingernails scratching a blackboard.

Comparing Three Things

In general, to compare three or more things, add *-est* to adjectives and adverbs of one syllable.

- Grilling food is faster than roasting, but microwaving is **fastest** of all.

  The adjective *fastest* is used to compare three methods: grilling, roasting, and microwaving.

- My mother works longer each day than my father, but in my family, I work **longest**.

  The adverb *longest* is used to compare how long three or more people work each day.

For longer adjectives and adverbs, do not add *-est*. Instead, add the word *most* when comparing three or more things.

- My dog is more intelligent than my cat, but my parrot is the **most intelligent** pet I have ever had.

  Most intelligent is used to compare several animals.

- Among the couples I know, my brother and sister-in-law are the **most happily** married of all.

  Most happily is used to compare how happy many couples are.

➤ **Practice 5**

Write in the correct form of the word in the margin by adding either *-est* or *most*.

Examples   *cold*   The _____coldest_____ it ever gets around here is about zero degrees Fahrenheit.

            delightful   The ___most delightful___ play of the year is now at the Morgan Theater.

young   1. Eliza is the _____youngest_____ of eight children.

important   2. The ___most important___ thing in Julia's life is clothes.

fresh   3. The Metro Mart has the _____freshest_____ vegetables in town.

artistic   4. Of the eighteen students in my class, Juan is the _____most artistic_____ .

difficult   5. My brother enjoys playing the ___most difficult___ video games he can find.

Notes About Comparisons

1   Do not use both an *-er* ending and *more*, or an *-est* ending and *most*.

Incorrect: My uncle's hair is more curlier than my aunt's.

Correct: My uncle's hair is **curlier** than my aunt's.

2   Certain short adjectives and adverbs have irregular forms:

	Comparing two	*Comparing three or more*
bad, badly	worse	worst
good, well	better	best
little	less	least
much, many	more	most

• The grape cough syrup tastes **better** than the orange syrup, but the lemon cough drops taste the **best**.

• Sid is doing **badly** in speech class, but I'm doing even **worse**.

➤ Practice 6

Cross out the incorrect word or words of comparison in each of the following sentences. Then write the correction on the line provided.

Example   _____easier_____   The test was ~~more easier~~ than I expected.

_____worst_____   1. That was the ~~baddest~~ accident I've ever seen.

_____better_____   2. It is ~~gooder~~ to try and fail than not to try at all.

_____older_____   3. My mother is ~~more older~~ than my father.

_____less_____   4. I use ~~lesser~~ oil in my cooking than I used to.

_____sweeter_____   5. This grapefruit is actually ~~more sweeter~~ than that orange.

_____least_____   6. This year we had the ~~most little~~ rain we've had in years.

_____most beautiful_____   7. I think the peacock is the ~~most beautifulest~~ of all birds.

_____worse_____   8. The macaroni salad tastes ~~worser~~ than the potato salad.

_____least_____   9. Cheap Charlie's is the ~~less~~ expensive of all the variety stores in town.

_____less_____   10. I'm on a diet, so put ~~more little~~ mayonnaise on my sandwich than usual.

USING TWO TROUBLESOME PAIRS: *GOOD* AND *WELL*, *BAD* AND *BADLY*

Good is an adjective that often means "enjoyable," "talented," or "positive."

- I had a **good** day.
- Sue is a **good** skier.
- Think **good** thoughts.

As an adverb, *well* often means "skillfully" or "successfully."

- Sue skis **well**.
- The schedule worked **well**.
- Pedro interacts **well** with others.

As an adjective, *well* means "healthy."

- The patient is **well** once again.

Bad is an adjective. *Badly* is an adverb.

- I look **bad**.

  Bad is an adjective that comes after the linking verb *look*. It describes the appearance of the subject of the sentence, *I*.

- I need sleep **badly**.

  Badly is an adverb that describes the verb *need*. It explains how much the sleep is needed.

➤ **Practice 7**

Complete the sentence with the correct word in the margin.

good, well   1. Ike hums really _____**well**_____.

good, well   2. Did you have a _____**good**_____ day at work?

bad, badly   3. I need a haircut _____**badly**_____.

bad, badly   4. My mother has a really _____**bad**_____ headache.

good, well   5. No student did very _____**well**_____ on the algebra test.

bad, badly   6. Luckily, no one was _____**badly**_____ hurt in the accident.

good, well   7. This machine bakes bread very _____**well**_____.

bad, badly   8. After a week on a liquids-only diet, Ben looks really _____**bad**_____.

good, well   9. Keep taking the antibiotic until it's gone, even if you think you are all _____**well**_____.

good, well   10. Working in a nursing home was a _____**good**_____ experience for me.

AVOIDING DOUBLE NEGATIVES

In standard English, it is incorrect to express a negative idea by pairing one negative with another. Common negative words include *not, nothing, never, nowhere, nobody,* and *neither.* To correct a double negative, either eliminate one of the negative words or replace a negative with a positive word.

Incorrect: I **shouldn't** go **nowhere** this weekend.

Correct: I **should** go **nowhere** this weekend.

Correct: I **shouldn't** go **anywhere** this weekend.

Shouldn't means *should not*, so the first sentence above contains two negatives: *not* and *nowhere*. In the first correct sentence, *not* has been eliminated. In the second correct sentence, *nowhere* has been replaced with a positive word.

The words *hardly, scarcely,* and *barely* are also negatives. They should not be paired with other negatives such as *never* and *not*. Correct a double negative containing *hardly, scarcely,* or *barely* by eliminating the other negative word.

Incorrect: I **couldn't scarcely** recognize you.

Correct: I **could scarcely** recognize you.

➤ Practice 8   *Answers will vary.*

Correct the double negative in each sentence by crossing out one of the negative words and writing any additional correction above the line.

Example   I won't ~~never~~ go to that restaurant again.

will
Or: I ~~won't~~ never go to that restaurant again.

ever
1. Don't ~~never~~ stick anything into an electrical outlet.

2. The two sisters ~~don't~~ scarcely speak to one another.

will
3. I ~~won't~~ never believe a word that Vicky says.

anything
4. Some days I feel that I can't do ~~nothing~~ right.

can
5. Ken ~~can't~~ go nowhere without running into one of his ex-wives.

can
6. It's so dark in this room that I ~~can't~~ scarcely read.

should
7. My neighbor ~~shouldn't~~ never have tried to fix the roof on her own.

anything
8. Pete won't say ~~nothing~~ unless he's sure he's right.

would
9. Nobody ~~wouldn't~~ believe what happened to me at work today.

ever
10. That salesperson won't ~~never~~ stop trying, even when a customer starts

walking away.

CHAPTER REVIEW

Fill in the correct word or words in each space provided.

1. Adjectives describe nouns and (*adverbs* or *pronouns*?)
   _____*pronouns*_____.

2. An adjective that describes the subject of a sentence may come after a(n) (*action* or *linking*?) _____*linking*_____ verb.

3. Adverbs describe verbs, adjectives, and (*nouns* or *other adverbs*?)
   _____*other adverbs*_____.

4. Generally, to compare three or more things, add (*-er, more,* or *-est*?)
   _____*-est*_____ to adjectives and adverbs of one syllable.

5. The form of *little* for comparing three or more things is (*less, most little,* or *least*?) _____*least*_____.

Name_____   Section _____   Date _____

Score: (Number right) _____ x 10 = _____%

➤ Adjectives and Adverbs: Test 1

Cross out the adjective or adverb error in each sentence and write the correction in the space at the left.

Example _____*sweeter*_____ This peach is ~~more sweeter~~ than candy.

_____*suddenly*_____ 1. I braked my car ~~sudden~~ to avoid a dog.

_____*good*_____ 2. How did you get to be so ~~well~~ in math?

_____*calmly*_____ 3. Let's try to settle our disagreement ~~calm~~.

_____*faster*_____ 4. To get a job as a secretary, I have to be able to type ~~more faster~~.

_____*nicest*_____ 5. James is the ~~most nicest~~ of all the waiters.

_____*well*_____ 6. I feel pretty good, but the doctor says I'm not ~~good~~ yet.

_____*carefully*_____ 7. Sam printed his name ~~careful~~ across the top of the page.

_____*brightly*_____ 8. Although it is cold, the sun is shining ~~bright~~.

_____*anything*_____ 9. Nobody knows ~~nothing~~ about why the manager was fired.

_____*better*_____ 10. My sister has a ~~more good~~ chance than I do of making the team.

➤ Adjectives and Adverbs: Test 2

Each short paragraph below contains **two** errors in adjective and/or adverb use. Find the errors and cross them out. Then write the correct form of each word or words in the space provided.

1. We eat three different kinds of cereal in my house. One teenager wants the ~~most sweetest~~ sugar-coated cereal he can find. The other doesn't like ~~nothing~~ sweet, so he eats shredded wheat instead. I eat hot oatmeal every morning.

   a. _____ *sweetest* _____

   b. _____ *anything* _____

2. Many people become ~~bad~~ depressed during the winter. Their mood improves ~~quick~~ when they receive natural-light therapy.

   a. _____ *badly* _____

   b. _____ *quickly* _____

3. I can't decide which book to read for my report. *The Old Man and the Sea* is ~~more short~~ than *The Great Gatsby*, so at first I thought I'd read that. But now that I've glanced through *Gatsby*, it seems the ~~most~~ interesting book.

   a. _____ *shorter* _____

   b. _____ *more* _____

4. Mr. Kensington has the ~~goodest~~ sense of humor in his family. For instance, he'll say that his knee is stiff from a war injury. But if you ask him to explain, he'll tell you ~~cheerful~~ that he got old and his knee "wore out."

   a. _____ *best* _____

   b. _____ *cheerfully* _____

5. Nothing is ~~more good~~ on a cold day than cuddling up on the sofa with hot cocoa and a good magazine. But I've got so much studying to do lately that I ~~haven't scarcely~~ time to read anything but textbooks.

   a. _____ *better* _____

   b. _____ *have scarcely* _____

Name_____ Section _____ Date _____

Score: (Number right) _____ x 10 = _____%

➤ Adjectives and Adverbs: Test 3

The selection that follows contains **ten** errors in adjective and/or adverb use. Find and cross out each error, and write the correction above the crossed-out word or words.

Some people think of a pregnant woman as just a container for her

unborn baby to grow within. The truth is, however, that a pregnant

countless
woman and her baby are linked in ~~countlessly~~ ways. Many of the

mother's decisions have a positive or negative effect on the child she

poorly
carries. For example, women who eat ~~poor~~ during their pregnancies are

putting their babies' health at risk. Their babies have a good chance of

being born underweight, and babies with a low birth weight develop

more often
problems much ~~more oftener~~ than normal-weight babies. Certain

illnesses in a pregnant woman are dangerous for an unborn baby as well.

worst
One of the ~~most bad~~ is German measles. If a woman catches German

measles before the eleventh week of her pregnancy, her baby will almost
certainly
~~certain~~ be born deaf and with heart problems.

Medications and drugs that a woman uses during pregnancy can

also hurt her baby. Before a pregnant woman uses any medication, she

should ask her doctor if it is safe for the baby. In the past, it was thought

that an occasional cigarette was OK for a pregnant woman. Now

researchers say tobacco is more dangerous than we thought. Babies born
thinner
to smoking mothers are ~~more thinner~~ than the babies of non-smokers.
worse
They often grow up to be ~~worser~~ students than other children as well

(Continues on next page)

because they may have trouble concentrating. One of the worst things a

pregnant woman can do, however, is drink alcohol. If she does, her baby

is at risk for fetal alcohol syndrome (FAS). Babies with FAS often have

emotional

physical, mental, and ~~emotionally~~ problems. The more a woman drinks,

more serious

the ~~seriouser~~ her baby's FAS is likely to be. But even just one or two

is (Or: *isn't ~~no~~ any*)

drinks a day can be dangerous. Doctors say there ~~isn't~~ no safe amount

that a woman can drink while she is pregnant.

15 / Misplaced and Dangling Modifiers

This chapter explains two common modifier problems:

1   Misplaced modifiers

   Incorrect: The man bought a tie at the department store **with yellow and blue stripes**.

   Correct: The man bought a tie with yellow and blue stripes at the department store.

2   Dangling modifiers

   Incorrect: **Biting my lip**, not laughing was difficult.

   Correct: Biting my lip, I found it difficult not to laugh.

MODIFIERS

A **modifier** is one or more words that describe another word or word group. For example, the modifier below is **boldfaced**, and the word it modifies is underlined.

- My cousin has a <u>cat</u> **with all-white fur**.

The modifier *with all-white fur* describes *cat*. Here are a few more examples:

- The <u>woman</u> **behind the cash register** is my boss.
- I have **nearly** <u>a thousand</u> baseball cards.
- He <u>printed</u> his name **neatly**.

MISPLACED MODIFIERS

A **misplaced modifier** is a modifier that is incorrectly separated from the word or words that it describes. Misplaced modifiers seem to describe words that the author did not intend them to describe. When modifiers are misplaced, the reader may misunderstand the sentence. Generally, the solution is to place the modifier as close as possible to the word or words it describes. Look at the following examples.

Misplaced modifier: Sam bought a used car from a local dealer with a smoky tailpipe.

Corrected version: Sam bought a used <u>car</u> **with a smoky tailpipe** from a local dealer.

In the first sentence above, the modifier *with a smoky tailpipe* is misplaced. Its unintentional meaning is that the local dealer has a smoky tailpipe. To avoid this meaning, place the modifier next to the word that it describes, *car.*

Misplaced modifier: The robin built a nest at the back of our house of grass and string.

Corrected version: The robin built a <u>nest</u> **of grass and string** at the back of our house.

In the first sentence above, the words *of grass and string* are misplaced. Because they are near the word *house,* the reader might think that the house is made of grass and string. To avoid this meaning, place the modifier next to the word that it describes, *nest.*

Misplaced modifier: Take this note to Mr. Henderson's office which Kim wrote.

Corrected version: Take this <u>note</u> **which Kim wrote** to Mr. Henderson's office.

In the first sentence above, the words *which Kim wrote* are misplaced. The words must be placed next to *note,* the word that they are clearly meant to describe.

Following is another example of a sentence with a misplaced modifier. See if you can correct it by putting the modifier in another place in the sentence. Write your revision on the lines below.

Misplaced modifier: I am going to New Orleans to visit my aunt on a train.

_____

_____

The original version of the sentence seems to say that the speaker will visit with his aunt on the train. However, the modifier *on a train* is meant to tell how the speaker *is going* to New Orleans. To make that meaning clear, the modifier needs to be placed closer to the words *am going:* "I <u>am going</u> **on a train** to New Orleans to visit my aunt."

➤ **Practice 1**

Underline the misplaced words in each sentence. Then rewrite the sentence on the line, placing the modifier where its meaning will be clear.

1. I'm returning the shirt to the store <u>that is too small</u>.

    I'm returning the shirt that is too small to the store.

    _____

2. The plants by the lamp <u>with small purple blossoms</u> are violets.

    The plants with small purple blossoms by the lamp are violets.

    _____

3. We watched as our house burned to the ground <u>with helpless anger</u>.

    We watched with helpless anger as our house burned to the ground.

    _____

4. The woman in that boat <u>that is waving</u> is trying to tell us something.

    The woman that is waving in that boat is trying to tell us something.

    _____

5. The bracelet on Roberta's arm <u>made of gold links</u> belongs to her mother.

    The bracelet made of gold links on Roberta's arm belongs to her mother.

    _____

Certain Single-Word Modifiers

Certain single-word modifiers—such as *almost, only, nearly,* and *even*—limit the words they modify. Such single-word modifiers must generally be placed before the word they limit.

> *Misplaced modifier:* Christie almost sneezed fifteen times last evening.

> *Corrected version:*   Christie sneezed **almost** <u>fifteen</u> times last evening.

Because the word *almost* is misplaced, readers might think Christie almost sneezed fifteen times, but in fact did not sneeze at all. To prevent this confusion, put *almost* in front of the word it modifies, *fifteen*. Then it becomes clear that Christie must have sneezed a number of times.

➤ **Practice 2**

Underline the misplaced single-word modifier in each sentence. Then rewrite the sentence on the line below, placing the modifier in front of the word it is meant to limit.

1. Carrie <u>nearly</u> has sixty freckles on her face.

    Carrie has nearly sixty freckles on her face.

    _____

2. Suelyn <u>almost</u> cried through the whole sad movie.

    Suelyn cried through almost the whole sad movie.

    _____

3. I <u>even</u> didn't make one mistake on the midterm test.

    I didn't make even one mistake on the midterm test.

    _____

4. The terrible fall <u>nearly</u> broke every bone in the skier's body.

    The terrible fall broke nearly every bone in the skier's body.

    _____

5. By the end of the war, twenty countries were <u>almost</u> involved in the fighting.

    By the end of the war, almost twenty countries were involved in the fighting.

    _____

DANGLING MODIFIERS

You have learned that a misplaced modifer is incorrectly separated from the word or words it describes. In contrast, a **dangling modifier** has no word in the sentence to describe. Dangling modifiers usually begin a sentence. When a modifier begins a sentence, it must be followed by the word or words it is meant to describe. Look at this example:

> *Dangling modifier:* Sitting in the dentist's chair, the sound of the drill awakened Larry's old fears.

The modifier *sitting in the dentist's chair* is followed by *the sound of the drill*. This word order suggests that the sound of the drill was sitting in the dentist's chair. Clearly, that is not what the author intended. The modifier was meant to describe the word *Larry*. Since *Larry* is not in the sentence, it is not possible to correct the dangling modifier simply by changing its position in the sentence.

There are two methods of correcting a dangling modifier:

Method 1: Follow the Dangling Modifier with the Word or Words It Is Meant to Modify

After the dangling modifier, write the word it is meant to describe, and then revise as necessary. Using this method, we could correct the sentence about Larry's experience at the dentist's office like this:

> *Corrected version:*   Sitting in the dentist's chair, **Larry found that** the sound of the drill awakened **his** old fears.

Now the modifier is no longer dangling. It is followed by the word it is meant to describe, *Larry*. (The boldfaced words are those that have been changed in the revision.)

Following is another dangling modifier. How could you correct it using the method described above? Write your correction on the lines below.

> *Dangling modifier:*   Depressed and disappointed, running away seemed the only thing for me to do.

_____

_____

The dangling modifier in the above sentence is *depressed and disappointed*. It is meant to describe the word *I*, but there is no *I* in the sentence. So you should have corrected the sentence by writing *I* after the opening modifier and then rewriting as necessary: "Depressed and disappointed, **I felt that** running away **was** the only thing for me to do."

➤ Practice 3   *Revisions may vary.*

Underline the dangling modifier in each sentence. Then, on the lines provided, revise the sentence, using the first method of correction.

1. <u>Out of money</u>, my only choice was to borrow from a friend.

   Out of money, I decided that my only choice was to borrow from a friend.

   _____

2. <u>While jogging</u>, a good topic for Anton's English paper occurred to him.

   While jogging, Anton thought of a good topic for his English paper.

   _____

3. <u>Bored by the lecture</u>, Jed's thoughts turned to dinner.

   Bored by the lecture, Jed began thinking about dinner.

   _____

4. <u>Moving around the sun</u>, Earth's speed is more than 66,000 miles per hour.

   Moving around the sun, Earth travels at a speed of more than 66,000 miles per

   hour.

5. <u>Loudly booing and cursing</u>, the fans' disapproval of the call was clear.

   Loudly booing and cursing, the fans clearly showed their disapproval of the

   call.

Method 2: Add a Subject and a Verb to the Opening Word Group

The second method of correcting a dangling modifier is to add a subject and a verb to the opening word group, and revise as necessary. We could use this method to correct the sentence about Larry's experience at the dentist's office.

Dangling modifier: Sitting in the dentist's chair, the sound of the drill awakened Larry's old fears.

Corrected version: **As Larry was** sitting in the dentist's chair, the sound of the drill awakened **his** old fears.

In this revision, the subject *Larry* and the verb *was* have been added to the opening word group.

Following is the dangling modifier that you revised using the first method of correction. How could you correct it using the second method? Write your revision on the lines below.

Dangling modifier: Depressed and disappointed, running away seemed the only thing for me to do.

_____

_____

You should have revised the sentence so that *I* and the appropriate verb are in the opening word group: "**Since I was** depressed and disappointed, running away seemed the only thing for me to do."

➤ Practice 4   *Revisions may vary.*

Underline the dangling modifier in each sentence. Then, on the lines provided, revise the sentence, using the second method of correction.

1. <u>While waiting for an important call</u>, Peg's phone began making weird noises.

    While Peg was waiting for an important call, her phone began making weird

    noises.

2. <u>After being shampooed</u>, Trish was surprised by the carpet's new look.

    After the carpet was shampooed, Trish was surprised by its new look.

    _____

3. <u>Touched by the movie</u>, tears came to my eyes.

    Since I was touched by the movie, tears came to my eyes.

    _____

4. <u>After eating one too many corn dogs</u>, Stella's stomach rebelled.

    After Stella ate one too many corn dogs, her stomach rebelled.

    _____

5. <u>Born on the Fourth of July</u>, Rob's birthday cake was always red, white, and blue.

    Because Rob was born on the Fourth of July, his birthday cake was always

    red, white, and blue.

CHAPTER REVIEW

Circle the letter of the word or words that correctly complete each item.

1. A modifier
   a. illustrates.
   b. describes.
   c. defines.

2. A misplaced modifier can generally be corrected by placing it as close as possible to
   a. the end of the sentence.
   b. the beginning of the sentence.
   c. the word or words being modified.

3. A single-word modifier such as *almost* and *only* must usually be placed
   a. before the word it modifies.
   b. after the word it modifies.
   c. in place of the word it modifies.

4. A modifier is said to be dangling when the sentence does not include
   a. a subject.
   b. the word or words being modified.
   c. a subject and a verb.

5. A dangling modifier usually appears
   a. at the beginning of a sentence.
   b. in the middle of a sentence.
   c. at the end of a sentence.

Name_____ Section _____ Date _____

Score: (Number right) _____ x 12.5 = _____%

➤ Misplaced and Dangling Modifiers: Test 1

A. Underline the misplaced word or words in each sentence. Then rewrite the sentence, placing the modifier where its intended meaning is clear.

1. The customer demanded that the waiter take her order <u>rudely</u>.

   The customer rudely demanded that the waiter take her order.
   _____

2. I peeled the potatoes before I cooked them <u>with a paring knife</u>.

   I peeled the potatoes with a paring knife before I cooked them.
   _____

3. In one week, the cat <u>nearly</u> had caught every mouse in the house.

   In one week, the cat had caught nearly every mouse in the house.
   _____

4. The child playing on the jungle gym <u>with fuzzy orange hair</u> is my nephew.

   The child with fuzzy orange hair playing on the jungle gym is my nephew.
   _____

B. Underline the dangling modifier in each sentence. Then, on the line provided, revise the sentence so that its meaning is clear. *Revisions may vary.*

5. <u>Lying on the sunny beach</u>, thoughts of skin cancer began to enter my mind.

   Lying on the sunny beach, I began having thoughts of skin cancer.
   _____

6. <u>Not meaning to be cruel</u>, George's careless remark hurt Jackie's feelings.

   Although George did not mean to be cruel, his careless remark hurt Jackie's

   feelings.

7. <u>Though not a fan of science fiction</u>, the new *Star Trek* movie, to my surprise, was very enjoyable.

   Though not a fan of science fiction, I found the new <u>Star Trek</u> movie, to my

   surprise, very enjoyable.

8. <u>Exhausted by his first day at school,</u> Sam's eyes closed in the middle of his favorite TV show.

   Exhausted by his first day at school, Sam closed his eyes in the middle of his

   favorite TV show.

➤ Misplaced and Dangling Modifiers: Test 2

Each group of sentences contains **one** misplaced modifier and **one** dangling modifier. Underline the two errors. Then, on the lines provided, rewrite the sentences that contain the errors so that the intended meanings are clear.

Revisions may vary.

1. I mailed a letter to my cousin who lives in Alaska <u>without a stamp</u>. I was embarrassed when the post office sent it back to me a week later. <u>Gluing a stamp on firmly</u>, off it went again.

   I mailed a letter without a stamp to my cousin who lives in Alaska. . . . Gluing

   a stamp on firmly, I sent it off again.

   _____

2. Lin's mother answered the door, and Jim asked if he could speak to Lin <u>politely</u>. <u>Impressed with Jim's manner</u>, the answer was "Certainly. Please come in."

   Lin's mother answered the door, and Jim asked politely if he could speak to

   Lin. Impressed with Jim's manner, her mother answered, "Certainly. Please

   come in."

3. The thunderstorm ended, and Shannon saw the sun burst through the clouds. <u>Searching the sky</u>, a glorious rainbow appeared. It <u>nearly</u> lasted a minute and then faded from view.

   . . . . As she was searching the sky, a glorious rainbow appeared. It lasted

   nearly a minute and then faded from view.

   _____

4. <u>Not meaning to embarrass you</u>, but please answer a question about your birthday present. Will you wear the sweater that I bought for you <u>ever</u>? If you won't, I could exchange it for something else.

   I don't mean to embarrass you, but please answer a question about your

   birthday present. Will you ever wear the sweater that I bought for you? . . .

   _____

5. Most of Ms. Nichol's students were gazing blankly into space one warm spring day. In fact, Ms. Nichol noticed that two students <u>only</u> were paying attention. <u>Clapping her hands together sharply</u>, the students woke up from their daydreams.

   . . . . In fact, Ms. Nichol noticed that only two students were paying attention.

   When Ms. Nichol clapped her hands together sharply, the students woke up

   from their daydreams.

Name_____ Section _____ Date _____

Score: (Number right) _____ x 10 = _____%

➤ Misplaced and Dangling Modifiers: Test 3

A. The following paragraph contains **five** misplaced modifiers. Underline each, and then revise as needed above the line.

Kate and Iris decided to cook a special Italian meal for their boyfriends, Chip and Marty. As the spaghetti sauce simmered on the stove that afternoon, the girls went out to get some final ingredients for the meal. They spotted an Italian bakery a few miles from the house <u>that was new</u>. "Perfect!" said Kate. "We'll get some fresh-baked bread." Soon they had two loaves of Italian bread, fresh and warm from the oven. The aroma filled the car, <u>which was delicious</u>. It drove the girls nearly mad with hunger. Iris pulled a loaf out of the bag. She broke off a hunk of the warm and crusty bread and handed it to Kate. Then she tore off a piece for herself. By the time they were in sight of the house, they <u>almost</u> had eaten all of the bread. So they went back and bought two more loaves from the bakery <u>that survived the trip home</u>. That night, Chip and Marty attacked the delicious meal the girls had prepared <u>with hearty appetites</u>. "But you're eating hardly anything!" Chip exclaimed to Kate and Iris. The two girls smiled at each other. Kate said, "You know how it is. When you cook all day, you kind of lose your appetite."

Revisions *(Note: Revisions may vary.)*

1. *They spotted an Italian bakery that was new a few miles from the house.*
2. *The aroma, which was delicious, filled the car.*
3. *By the time they were in sight of the house, they had eaten almost all of the bread.*
4. *So they went back and bought two more loaves that survived the trip home from the bakery.*
5. *That night, Chip and Marty attacked with hearty appetites the delicious meal the girls had prepared.*

(Continues on next page)

B. The following paragraph contains **five** dangling modifiers. Underline each, and then revise the sentence above the line.

Jay's fishing trip with his buddies was not exactly a success. <u>Driving to the cabin in the mountains</u>, a flat tire was the first stroke of bad luck. Once the gang arrived at the cabin, they found the last renters had left the place in terrible condition. <u>Covered with dirty dishes, empty food containers, food scraps, and newspapers</u>, the guys spent a long time cleaning. They did manage to catch a few trout before suppertime. But that night, bad luck struck again. <u>While frying fish over the campfire</u>, Jay's flannel shirt burst into flames. <u>Thinking quickly</u>, jumping into the nearby lake put the fire out. The guys went to bed early after their unlucky first day. "Surely tomorrow will be better," said Jay as he climbed into his bunk. But he was wrong. <u>Running down the stairs the next morning</u>, a step broke under his weight. He spent the rest of the day in a nearby emergency room, having a cast put on his broken ankle.

Revisions

Note: Revisions may vary.

1. *As they were driving to the cabin in the mountains, a flat tire was the first stroke of bad luck.*
2. *Covered with dirty dishes, empty food containers, food scraps, and newspapers, the cabin took the guys a long time to clean.*
3. *While Jay was frying fish over the campfire, his flannel shirt burst into flames.*
4. *Thinking quickly, Jay jumped into the nearby lake and put the fire out.*
5. *As Jay was running down the stairs the next morning, a step broke under his weight.*

16 / Word Choice

Not all writing problems involve grammar. A sentence may be grammatically correct, yet fail to communicate well because of the words that the writer has chosen. This chapter explains three common types of ineffective word choice:

1 Slang

Slang: My roommate is **something else**.

Revised: My roommate is a very special person.

2 Clichés

Cliché: This semester, I have **bitten off more than I can chew**.

Revised: This semester, I have taken on more work than I can manage.

3 Wordiness

Wordy: It is **absolutely essential and necessary** that you borrow some folding chairs for the party.

Revised: It is essential that you borrow some folding chairs for the party.

SLANG

Slang expressions are lively and fun to use, but they should be avoided in formal writing. One problem with slang is that it's not always understood by all readers. Slang used by members of a particular group (such as teenagers or science-fiction fans) may be unfamiliar to people outside of the group. Also, slang tends to change rapidly. What was *cool* for one generation is *awesome* for another. Finally, slang is by nature informal. So while it adds color to our everyday speech, it is generally out of place in writing for school or work. Use slang only when you have a specific purpose in mind, such as being humorous or communicating the flavor of an informal conversation.

Slang: After a bummer of a movie, we pigged out on a pizza.

Revised: After a **disappointing** movie, we **devoured** a pizza.

➤ **Practice 1**   *Revisions may vary.*

Revise the slang expression (printed in *italics*) in each sentence.

1. Tiffany did not *have a clue about* what was being taught in her algebra class.

   _____ understand _____

2. When my parents see my final grades, I will be *dead meat.*

   _____ in trouble _____

3. Everyone was *grossed out* when the cat brought home a dead rat.

   _____ disgusted _____

4. Exhausted by their trip, the twins *sacked out* as soon as they got home.

   _____ fell asleep _____

5. Freddie is really *in la-la land* if he thinks he can make a living as a juggler.

   _____ fooling himself _____

CLICHÉS

A cliché is an expression that was once lively and colorful. However, because it has been used too often, it has become dull and boring. Try to use fresh wording in place of predictable expressions. Following are a few of the clichés to avoid in your writing:

Common Clichés

avoid like the plague	last but not least	sick and tired
better late than never	light as a feather	sigh of relief
bored to tears	make ends meet	time and time again
easy as pie	pie in the sky	tried and true
in the nick of time	pretty as a picture	under the weather
in this day and age	sad but true	without a doubt

Cliché: My new boss is as sharp as a tack.

Revised: My new boss is **very insightful**.

➤ **Practice 2**   *Revisions may vary.*

Rewrite the cliché (printed in *italics*) in each sentence.

1. Although the box was *light as a feather*, Jeremy refused to carry it.

   _____ extremely light _____

2. *In this day and age*, teenagers face many temptations.

   Today

3. Smoking cigarettes is *playing with fire*.

   very risky

4. On the first day of summer vacation, I felt *free as a bird*.

   carefree

5. Luke must really have been hungry because he *chowed down* three burgers at dinner.

   ate

WORDINESS

Some writers think that using more words than necessary makes their writing sound important. Actually, wordiness just annoys and confuses your reader. Try to edit your writing carefully. First of all, remove words that mean the same as other words in the sentence, as in the following example.

Wordy: Though huge in size and blood red in color, the cartoon monster had a sweet personality.

Revised: Though **huge** and **blood red**, the cartoon monster had a sweet personality.

Huge refers to size, so the words *in size* can be removed with no loss of meaning. *Red* is a color, so the words *in color* are also unnecessary. Following is another example of wordiness resulting from repetitiveness. The author has said the same thing twice.

Wordy: I finally made up my mind and decided to look for a new job.

Revised: I finally **decided** to look for a new job.

Secondly, avoid puffed-up phrases that can be expressed in a word or two instead.

Wordy: Due to the fact that the printer was out of paper, Renee went to a store for the purpose of buying some.

Revised: **Because** the printer was out of paper, Renee went to a store **to buy** some.

In general, work to express your thoughts in the fewest words possible that are still complete and clear. Notice, for example, how easily the wordy expressions in the first box on the next page can be replaced by one or two words. The wordy expressions in the second box can be made concise by eliminating repetitive words.

Wordy Expression	Concise Replacement
a large number of	many
at an earlier point in time	before
at this point in time	now
be in possession of	have
due to the fact that	because
during the time that	while
each and every day	daily
in order to	to
in the event that	if
in the near future	soon
in this day and time	today
made the decision to	decided

Examples of Wordiness due to Repetition

few ~~in number~~

green ~~in color~~

postponed ~~until later~~

small ~~in size~~

~~hurriedly~~ rushed

punched ~~with his fist~~

listened ~~with his ears~~

~~the feeling of~~ sadness

the first paragraph ~~at the beginning~~ of the chapter

See if you can revise the following wordy sentence by 1) replacing one group of words and 2) eliminating two unnecessary words.

Owing to the fact that I was depressed, I postponed my guitar lesson until later.

_____

_____

The wordy expression *owing to the fact that* can be replaced by the single word *because* or *since*. The words *until later* can be eliminated with no loss of meaning. Here's a concise version of the wordy sentence: "Because I was depressed, I postponed my guitar lesson."

➤ **Practice 3**   *Corrections may vary.*

Underline the one example of wordiness in each sentence that follows. Then rewrite the sentence as clearly and concisely as possible.

> **Example**   I realized suddenly that my date <u>had stood me up and was not going to show up</u>.
>
> *I realized suddenly that my date had stood me up.*

1. <u>Due to the fact that</u> Lionel won the lottery, he won't be coming to work today.

   Because Lionel won the lottery, he won't be coming to work today.

   _____

2. My sister <u>went ahead and made the decision</u> to take a job in Maryland.

   My sister decided to take a job in Maryland.

   _____

3. Jeff hid his extra house key and now has forgotten <u>the location where it is</u>.

   Jeff hid his extra house key and now has forgotten where it is.

   _____

4. I do not know <u>at this point in time</u> if I will return to school next semester.

   I do not know now if I will return to school next semester.

   _____

5. <u>Daily exercise every day of the week</u> gives my mother more energy.

   Daily exercise gives my mother more energy.

   _____

CHAPTER REVIEW

Answer each question by circling the letter of the correct answer.

1. Slang should be avoided in
   a. informal writing.
   b. formal writing.
   c. all writing.

2. Slang expressions are usually
   a. used only by teenagers.
   b. dull and boring.
   c. best understood by members of a particular group.

3. Clichés are expressions that are
   a. very hard to understand.
   b. dull from overuse.
   c. both of the above.

4. Wordiness results from
   a. using words that mean the same as other words in the sentence.
   b. using puffed-up phrases where a word or two would do.
   c. both of the above.

Name_____ Section _____ Date _____

Score: (Number right) _____ x 10 = _____%

➤ Word Choice: Test 1

A. Each sentence below contains **one** example of slang or clichés. Underline the error and then rewrite it, using more effective language. *Revisions may vary.*

1. All morning I have been <u>as nervous as a long-tailed cat in a room full of rocking chairs</u>.

   _____*extremely nervous*_____

2. Maddie was <u>slow as molasses</u> getting ready for school this morning.

   _____*very slow*_____

3. I had only one drink at the party, but Jon got totally <u>wasted</u>.

   _____*intoxicated*_____

4. Public interest in the upcoming election seems <u>dead as a doornail</u>.

   _____*to have died out*_____

5. Dad <u>freaked out</u> when I got home at 3 a.m.

   _____*lost his temper*_____

B. Underline the **one** example of wordiness in each sentence that follows. Then rewrite the sentence as concisely as possible. *Revisions may vary.*

6. We were glad to hear the exam had been <u>postponed until a later date</u>.

   *We were glad to hear the exam had been postponed.*_____

   _____

7. I <u>have an unproven suspicion</u> that Harry has been shoplifting.

   *I suspect that Harry has been shoplifting.*_____

8. Please call me <u>at the point in time when</u> you are ready to go.

   *Please call me when you are ready to go.*_____

9. The store opens at 10 <u>a.m. in the morning</u>.

   *The store opens at 10 a.m.*_____

10. Reba forgot her jacket and had to <u>return back again</u> to her house for it.

    *Reba forgot her jacket and had to return to her house for it.*_____

    _____

Name_____ Section _____ Date _____

Score: (Number right) _____ x 10 = _____ %

➤ Word Choice: Test 2

Each item below contains **two** examples of ineffective word choice: slang, clichés, or wordiness. Underline the errors. Then rewrite each underlined part as clearly and concisely as possible.   *Revisions may vary.*

1. Thirty-seven students signed up for the creative writing class, but only twenty-four could be accepted. The other thirteen were really <u>bummed out</u>. They asked the dean to consider opening a second section of the class, but he <u>gave them the cold shoulder</u>.

   a. _____*disappointed*_____

   b. _____*ignored them*_____

2. Wally assembled the big circular track for his son's model train. Then he <u>connected the cars hooking them up together</u>. Finally he threw the switch and watched the train glide around the track. He was <u>as pleased as punch</u> that it all worked perfectly.

   a. _____*connected the cars*_____

   b. _____*pleased*_____

3. The microwave oven I bought from your store is <u>a loser</u>. Although I have followed the manufacturer's instructions, the oven has never worked properly. I expect you to replace the oven <u>in the very near future</u>. If that is not possible, please return my money.

   a. _____*defective*_____

   b. _____*very soon*_____

4. <u>In the event that</u> I decide to get another roommate, I will choose her carefully. My former experiences with roommates have not been very good. Once I lived with someone who <u>ripped off</u> my jewelry. Even worse, another roommate stole my boyfriend.

   a. _____*If*_____

   b. _____*stole*_____

5. The movie I saw last night was advertised as a comedy, but I didn't laugh once. Instead, it completely <u>weirded me out</u>. It showed married people who hated one another and parents who shouted at their children. Why do people <u>in this day and age</u> think it is funny for people to mistreat one another?

   a. _____*confused me*_____

   b. _____*today*_____

Name_____ Section _____ Date _____

Score: (Number right) _____ x 10 = _____%

➤ Word Choice: Test 3

A. The passage below contains **five** examples of slang and clichés. Underline each, and then revise it above the line, using more effective language.

Revisions may vary.

When Jen woke up and saw it was raining for the sixth day in a row,

unusual
she knew she had to think of some <u>way-out</u> activity for her children. They

tired
were <u>sick and tired</u> of jigsaw puzzles, painting, and Play-Dough. Being

depressed
indoors was making them all feel <u>down in the dumps</u>.

So Jen got out her big jar of pennies and called her two children.

"You each count out three hundred pennies," she said. "We'll stop at the

bank and get them changed into dollar bills. Then we'll go to the mall,

and you can spend them however you like."

terrific
The children thought Jen's idea was <u>totally awesome</u>. They spent a

long time counting the pennies and even longer deciding how to spend

was relieved
their money at the mall. On the way home, Jen <u>heaved a sigh of relief</u>

when she saw the sun appear through the clouds. Maybe tomorrow the

children could play outside.

(Continues on next page)

B. There are **five** cases of wordiness in the paragraph that follows. Cross out any unnecessary words. If words need to be replaced, cross them out and revise above the lines.

Revisions may vary.

Apartment-hunting with Ira was a frustrating experience. We started last Saturday at 9 a.m. ~~in the morning~~ and didn't stop until it was dark. We looked at a dozen apartments, some of which I thought were very nice. But Ira rejected them all. One had big sunny windows ~~that let in a lot of sun~~, but Ira felt there were not enough windows ~~in number~~. Another had plenty of windows, but he didn't like the color of the carpet
because
~~that was covering the floor~~. He rejected a third ~~due to the fact that~~ there was a crack in the ceiling. When Ira asked me to help him look at more apartments Monday evening, I said I was too busy. I spent the evening appreciating my own imperfect but comfortable apartment.

17 / Parallelism

This chapter explains **parallelism**, the expression of two or more ideas in matching grammatical form.

Not parallel: I love **to walk**, running, and lifting weights.

Parallel: I love walking, running, and lifting weights.

Not parallel: Nina has a high fever and **a throat that is sore**.

Parallel: Nina has a high fever and a sore throat.

USING PARALLEL FORMS

At times, you will need to present two or more equal ideas in a sentence. You must then be careful to present the ideas in matching form. This matching form is called **parallelism**. Look at the following example.

Not parallel: Dinner consisted of baked potatoes, pork chops that were broiled, and steamed broccoli.

All of the items in the list of foods play an equal role in the sentence, so they should be expressed in parallel form. *Baked potatoes* and *steamed broccoli* are parallel. The adjectives *(baked* and *steamed)* come before the nouns they describe *(potatoes* and *broccoli)*. But the form of *pork chops that were broiled* is different. To achieve parallelism, give the nonparallel item the same form as the others:

Parallel: Dinner consisted of baked potatoes, **broiled pork chops**, and steamed broccoli.

The unmatched idea has been corrected: the adjective *broiled* has been placed before *pork chops*. The sentence now reads clearly and smoothly.

In the above example, the parallel forms are adjective-noun combinations. When using parallelism, note the grammatical forms you are using. Match nouns with nouns, verb forms with the same types of verb forms, and so on. For instance:

- *Nouns:* rain, hail, and sleet
- *Adjectives:* tall, dark, and handsome
- *Prepositional phrases:* over the moon and beyond the rainbow
- *Nouns and past tense verbs:* he washed, she dried
- *-Ing word groups that end in nouns:* singing duets, playing the piano, dancing the tango

➤ **Practice 1**

The one item in each list that is not parallel in form to the other items is crossed out. In the space provided, rewrite that item in parallel form. The first one has been done for you as an example.

1. fresh food
   attractive setting
   ~~service that is fast~~

   fast service

2. screaming children
   ~~dogs that howl~~
   blaring music

   howling dogs

3. slow
   ~~speaks rudely~~
   careless

   rude

4. ~~to hike~~
   swimming
   boating

   hiking

5. noisy neighbors
   high rent
   ~~security that is poor~~

   poor security

6. ~~cleaning of the apartment~~
   paid the bills
   did the laundry

   cleaned the apartment

7. looking good
   ~~to have fun~~
   feeling fine

   having fun

8. healthy soups
   tasty sandwiches
   ~~desserts that are inexpensive~~

   inexpensive desserts

9. under the desk drawers
   ~~the floor of the closet~~
   behind the bedroom curtains

   on the closet floor

10. works at the supermarket
    ~~member of the church choir~~
    coaches the Little League team

    sings in the church choir

WHEN TO USE PARALLELISM

Here are writing situations in which parallelism is appropriate.

1 Use parallelism when presenting a series of items.

Not parallel: On summer weekends, my family spends time hiking, visiting friends, and they go to the movies.

Parallel: On summer weekends, my family spends time hiking, visiting friends, and **going to the movies**.

The sentences list a series of activities. *Hiking* and *visiting* both end in *-ing*. To be parallel, *they go to the movies* must be revised to include an *-ing* word.

Not parallel: The children were arguing in the lobby, talked during the movie, and complained on the ride home.

Parallel: The children **argued in the lobby**, talked during the movie, and complained on the ride home.

Both *talked* and *complained* are past tense verbs. To be parallel, *were arguing in the lobby* needs to be revised to include the past tense form of *argue*.

Not parallel: The speaker had sweaty hands, an upset stomach, and a voice that was nervous.

Parallel: The speaker had sweaty hands, an upset stomach, and **a nervous voice**.

Two of the items in this series (*sweaty hands* and *upset stomach*) have the same word order: an adjective followed by a noun. To be parallel, the third item in the series should have the same order.

2   Use parallelism for pairs of ideas linked by connecting words, such as *and* and *or*. Other connecting words are *either . . . or, neither . . . nor, not only . . . but also*.

Not parallel: My older brother *and* the only sister I have are not coming to my wedding.

Parallel: My older brother *and* **my only sister** are not coming to my wedding.

My older brother and *the only sister I have* are connected by the joining word *and*, so they have equal roles in the sentence. They need to be worded in parallel form.

Not parallel: I can *either* stay at work late tonight *or* tomorrow I could come in to work early.

Parallel: I can *either* stay at work late tonight *or* **come in to work early tomorrow**.

Two choices are joined by the connecting words *either . . . or*. Because the verb *stay* follows the word *either*, the verb *come* must follow the word *or*.

Not parallel: The painters were *not only* late *but also* were messy.

Parallel: The painters were *not only* late *but also* **messy**.

Since the adjective *late* follows *not only*, the adjective *messy* must follow *but also*.

3   Use parallelism in comparisons using *than* or *as*. The things being compared should be presented in parallel form.

Not parallel: It is often kinder to tell a partial truth *than* revealing the whole truth.

Parallel: It is often kinder to tell a partial truth *than* **to reveal the whole truth**.

In the parallel version, the two items being compared begin with *to* plus the basic form of the verb (*to tell* and *to reveal*).

Not parallel: For me, watching sports is *as* dull *as* to stare at the ceiling.

Parallel: For me, watching sports is *as* dull *as* **staring at the ceiling**.

In the parallel version, the two activities being compared are expressed with *-ing* words.

➤ Practice 2

The part of each sentence that needs revising is italicized. On the line, rewrite this part to make it match the other item(s) listed.

1. On hot days I close the windows, turn on the fans, and *am complaining* a lot.

    complain

2. Amos chose a bouquet of white roses, red carnations, and *tulips that were yellow*.

    yellow tulips

3. Smoking and *to spit* are both prohibited on the subway.

    spitting

4. These apples are not only small but also *have a sour taste*.

    sour

5. It is easier to wash dishes every day than *letting* them pile up for a week.

    to let

6. All Elroy asks of a girlfriend is that she be cooperative, honest, and *have lots of money*.

    rich

7. Laura usually either braids her hair or *is putting* it up in a French twist.

    puts

8. My neighbors include a dress designer, a *person who teaches second grade*, and a car salesperson.

    second grade teacher

9. For lunch we were given limp bologna sandwiches, *peanut-butter crackers that were stale*, and warm sugary punch.

    stale peanut-butter crackers

10. Many runaways are lured to the city by the bright lights, *activity going on constantly*, and empty promises.

    constant activity

THE EFFECTS OF PARALLELISM

Parallelism will help your words flow smoothly and clearly. It will help you eliminate awkward language in your papers. In general, parallelism adds power and polish to writing.

Many famous speeches and pieces of writing feature skillful parallelism. The matching form of their words and phrases helps makes them memorable, as with the following two examples.

- "I know not how others may feel, but as for me, give me liberty or give me death!"—Patrick Henry

Would Henry's speech have had the same ring if he'd said, ". . . give me liberty or else I would prefer to die"?

- "That's one small step for man, one giant leap for mankind."—Astronaut Neil Armstrong, upon taking a step onto the moon

Armstrong's words gain power because "one small step for man" and "one giant leap for mankind" have the same form. His statement would have been much less forceful if he had said instead, "That's one small step for man, and a major step forward for mankind in general."

Finally, consider the following use that one student made of parallelism:

- "Some of my best childhood memories are of my parents' New Year's Eve parties. Some guests came in sequins; others showed up in jeans. The spicy aromas of cold cuts and pickles mingled with the sweet scents of after-shaves and cologne."

Those sentences would have been less impressive had the student written, ". . . Some guests came in sequined outfits. Jeans were also worn to the party. Among the foods my parents served were spicy cold cuts and pickles. The sweet scents of after-shaves and cologne filled the house."

➤ Practice 3

Underline the part of each sentence that is not parallel. Then, in the space provided, rewrite this part to make it match the other item(s) listed.

1. My uncle usually wears loud ties, <u>shoes that are scuffed</u>, and wrinkled shirts.

   scuffed shoes

2. Interesting work is as important to me as <u>pay that is good</u>.

   good pay (or _Work that is interesting is as important to me as pay that is good_)

3. For exercise, I either play basketball at the playground or <u>am riding</u> a bike in the park.

   ride

4. Getting the mail, taking out the trash, and <u>dog feeding</u> are Jamal's daily chores.

_____ *feeding the dog* _____

5. The driving rain turned the yard into a swamp, and <u>the highway was</u> a river.

_____ *the highway into* (or *, and it turned the highway into*) _____

6. <u>Bill paying</u>, balancing the checkbook, and cleaning my bathroom are my least-favorite tasks.

_____ *Paying bills* _____

7. Attending class regularly and <u>to take</u> notes carefully are two keys to success in school.

_____ *taking* _____

8. Weekends at our house usually include working in the yard, shopping for groceries, and <u>we go</u> to church.

_____ *going* _____

9. Roast turkey, baked sweet potatoes, and <u>pie made from pumpkin</u> are traditional Thanksgiving foods.

_____ *pumpkin pie* _____

10. Paying college tuition and not studying is as sensible as <u>to buy</u> tickets to a movie and not watching it.

_____ *buying* _____

CHAPTER REVIEW

Fill in the correct word(s) in each space provided.

1. Parallelism should be used when (*two* or *two or more*?) _____ *two or more* _____ equal ideas are presented in a sentence.

2. *True or false?* _T_ In parallel language, items are stated in matching grammatical forms.

3. Parallelism makes writing less (*wordy, awkward,* or *general*?) _____ *awkward* _____.

4. *True or false?* _T_ Parallelism will help your words flow smoothly and clearly.

Name_____ Section _____ Date _____

➤ Parallelism: Test 1

Underline the part of each sentence that is not parallel. Then, in the space provided, rewrite this part to make it match the other item(s) listed.

1. Maribel is not only a terrific singer but also <u>plays the piano very well</u>.

   _____ *a very good piano player* (Or *not only sings terrifically*) _____

2. The movie featured terrible acting, excessive violence, and <u>plot twists that were ridiculous</u>.

   _____ *ridiculous plot twists* _____

3. On a crowded highway, traveling too slow is almost as bad as <u>to drive</u> too fast.

   _____ *driving* _____

4. The sick boy's mother gave him some aspirin, tucked him in bed, and <u>was pouring</u> him a cup of tea.

   _____ *poured* _____

5. Before he left for his trip, Zack brought his dog to the kennel and <u>was cleaning</u> the house.

   _____ *cleaned* _____

6. Every day at work, Carla has to smile constantly, to speak <u>in a cheerful way</u>, and to move quickly.

   _____ *cheerfully* _____

7. People come to the mountain resort for either rich gourmet meals or <u>to eat diet foods</u>.

   _____ *diet foods* _____

8. A steady job, <u>an apartment that is pleasant</u>, and some loyal friends are what my brother needs.

   _____ *a pleasant apartment* _____

9. My doctor advised me to stop smoking and <u>that I should lose some weight</u>.

   _____ *to lose some weight* _____

10. The woman in the <u>slacks with stripes</u>, velvet jacket, and artist's beret is my Aunt Mame.

    _____ *striped slacks* _____

Name_____ Section _____ Date _____

Score: (Number right) _____ x 10 = _____%

➤ Parallelism: Test 2

Each group of sentences contains **two** errors in parallelism. Underline these errors. Then, on the lines below, rewrite each item that doesn't match to make it parallel with the other item or items in the sentence.

1. When Phil left for work, he felt bright and cheerful. But by midafternoon he was coughing, wheezing, and <u>shivers ran throughout his body</u>. He left work, drove home, and <u>was crawling</u> into bed, where he stayed for the next four days.

   a. _____ *shivering* _____

   b. _____ *crawled* _____

2. I never spend money on fancy wrapping paper. When people get a present, they generally want to rip off the paper and <u>be looking</u> at what's inside. So I wrap my gifts in either plain brown grocery bags or <u>Sunday comics that are colorful</u>.

   a. _____ *look* _____

   b. _____ *colorful Sunday comics* _____

3. Failing students can be kinder than <u>to pass</u> them. There is little benefit to passing a student to a level of work he or she can't do. In addition, it is cruel to graduate a student from high school who has neither the communication skills nor the <u>skills at math</u> needed to get along in the world.

   a. _____ *passing* _____

   b. _____ *math skills* _____

4. The little boy drew back from his new babysitter. Her <u>nails, long and red</u>, black eye makeup, and jangling jewelry all frightened him. He was sure she was either a bad witch or <u>a queen that was evil</u>.

   a. _____ *long, red nails* _____

   b. _____ *an evil queen* _____

5. An actress stopped in the middle of a Broadway show and scolded flash photographers in the audience. She said they can either have a photo session or <u>they can be enjoying</u> the show, but they can't do both. The photographers sank down in their seats, <u>their cameras were put away</u>, and quietly watched the show.

   a. _____ *enjoy* _____

   b. _____ *put away their cameras* _____

Name_____ Section _____ Date _____

Score: (Number right) _____ x 10 = _____%

➤ Parallelism: Test 3

There are **ten** problems with parallelism in the following selection. Cross out each part that isn't parallel, and write the correction above the line.

The novel *Les Miserables* was written in the 1800s by French author

hungry
Victor Hugo. It tells the story of Jean Valjean. Poor and ~~being full of~~

~~hunger~~, Valjean stole a loaf of bread one day. He was arrested and
received
~~receiving~~ a sentence of five years as a slave in a galley ship. His attempts

to escape added years to his sentence. In the end, Valjean served nineteen

angry
years for stealing the bread. He left prison bitter, vengeful, and ~~full of~~
softened
~~anger~~. But a surprising event changed Valjean's mind and ~~was softening~~

his heart. The story of what happened is known as "The Bishop's

Candlesticks."

to sleep
Valjean could find nothing to eat and no place ~~for sleeping~~ because

everyone was afraid of him. Finally, he stormed angrily into the house of
asked
a bishop. He demanded a scrap of food and ~~was asking~~ for permission to

sleep in the stable. To Valjean's surprise, the bishop welcomed him kindly
warmly
and ~~in a warm fashion~~. He ate dinner with Valjean and then, taking one

of a pair of silver candlesticks, led Valjean to a comfortable bedroom. The

bishop left Valjean with a candle in the candlestick.

stole
During the night, Valjean sneaked out of bed and ~~was stealing~~ the

knives and forks from the dining room. In the morning, soldiers brought

him and the silver to the bishop's door. The bishop greeted him as a
responded
friend and ~~was responding~~, "I am glad you took the silverware I gave you,

(Continues on next page)

but why didn't you take the silver candlesticks too? I want you to have them." Convinced that Valjean was innocent, the soldiers went away.

Valjean spent the rest of his life helping people, sharing with them, and *showing* ~~he showed~~ them the kindness the bishop had shown him.

18 / Sentence Variety and Style

Writing clearly and correctly is only part of your challenge as a writer. In addition, you should aim to make your sentences varied and interesting. You want to avoid overly repetitive patterns and to emphasize key points. Carefully crafted sentences and paragraphs help readers enjoy the meaning and rhythm of your writing and encourage them to follow your ideas.

This chapter explains a number of ways to add variety and style to your writing:

1   Use compound and complex sentences

2   Use a series of items (adjectives and verbs)

3   Use verbals (infinitives, participles, and gerunds)

4   Use prepositional phrases and *-ly* word groups to begin sentences

5   Use appositives

6   Use relative pronoun word groups

USE COMPOUND AND COMPLEX SENTENCES

Combine simple sentences into compound or complex sentences.

Combine Simple Sentences into Compound Sentences

1   Join two simple sentences with a comma and one of the following joining words: *and, but, so, or, nor, for, yet.*

Two simple sentences: My brother-in-law does landscaping from spring to fall. He works at snow removal in the winter.

One compound sentence: My brother-in-law does landscaping from spring to fall, **and** he works at snow removal in the winter.

2   Join two simple sentences with a semicolon alone or with an appropriate transitional word or words as well. Common transitional words include *afterwards, as a result, however, in addition, instead,* and *on the other hand.* (For a longer list of transitional words, see page 188.)

Two simple sentences:
Twenty students were registered for class. Only eight were present.

One compound sentence with a semicolon:
Twenty students were registered for class; only eight were present.

One compound sentence with a semicolon and a transitional word:
Twenty students were registered for class; **however,** only eight were present.

In compound sentences, the complete ideas receive equal emphasis.

※   For more information on compound sentences, see "Sentence Types," pages 147–148, and "Run-Ons and Comma Splices," pages 184 and 187–188.

➤ Practice 1

A. Use a comma and a suitable joining word to combine each pair of simple sentences into a compound sentence. Choose from the joining words *and, but,* and *so.*

1. The baby goat was cute and fluffy. It had a vicious temper.

   The baby goat was cute and fluffy, but it had a vicious temper.
   _____

2. I have an exam in the morning. I'd better get to bed early.

   I have an exam in the morning, so I'd better get to bed early.
   _____

3. These shoes are comfortable. Their price is reasonable.

   These shoes are comfortable, and their price is reasonable.
   _____

4. Rain began falling heavily. The umpires cancelled the game.

   Rain began falling heavily, so the umpires cancelled the game.
   _____

5. I am afraid of heights. Flying in an airplane doesn't bother me.

   I am afraid of heights, but flying in an airplane doesn't bother me.
   _____

B. Use a semicolon and a transitional word or words to combine each pair of simple sentences into a compound sentence. Use each of the following transitional words once: *as a result, afterward, however, in addition,* and *instead.* Follow the transitional word(s) with a comma.

6. Lilly never uses sugar. She uses honey and maple syrup.

   Lilly never uses sugar; instead, she uses honey and maple syrup.

7. Skiing is a lot of fun. It's too expensive to do often.

   Skiing is a lot of fun; however, it's too expensive to do often.

8. We went to a movie last night. We stopped for ice cream.

   We went to a movie last night; afterward, we stopped for ice cream.

9. Kareem is allergic to wheat. He can't eat anything made with flour.

   Kareem is allergic to wheat; as a result, he can't eat anything made with

   flour.

10. My brother and sister-in-law have three children. They have a foster child.

    My brother and sister-in-law have three children; in addition, they have a

    foster child.

Combine Simple Sentences into Complex Sentences

Use a dependent word to make one of the complete thoughts dependent on the other. Common dependent words are *after, although, because, since, when,* and *while.* A dependent thought that begins a sentence should generally be followed by a comma. (For a longer list of dependent words, see page 151.)

Two simple sentences: The sun is low in the sky. A mural of tree shadows appears on the bedroom wall.

One complex sentence: **When** the sun is low in the sky, a mural of tree shadows appears on the bedroom wall.

In complex sentences, the independent thought is more important than the dependent thought.

※ For more information on complex sentences, see "Sentence Types," pages 150–151.

> ## Practice 2

Combine each pair of simple sentences into a complex sentence. Use each of the following dependent words once: *after, although, because, until,* and *when.* (Follow a dependent thought that comes at the beginning of a sentence with a comma.)

1. The house is beautiful. It seems cold and unfriendly to me.

    Although the house is beautiful, it seems cold and unfriendly to me.

    _____

2. Grandma needs to live in a warm climate. She is moving to Arizona.

    Because Grandma needs to live in a warm climate, she is moving to Arizona.

    _____

3. Several accidents occurred on the new road. A traffic light was installed.

    After several accidents occurred on the new road, a traffic light was installed.

    _____

4. Sam practices his saxophone. The dog howls.

    When Sam practices his saxophone, the dog howls.

    _____

5. I had never eaten a cheesesteak sandwich. I moved to Philadelphia.

    I had never eaten a cheesesteak sandwich until I moved to Philadelphia.

    _____

Use a Variety of Sentence Types

Try to use a variety of sentence types in your writing. Too much of the same kind of sentence can be dull. Also, you can organize your ideas more meaningfully with differing sentence structures. For example, read this paragraph:

> There was a lack of convenient transportation at the beginning of the nineteenth century. The stagecoach was the major form of transportation. It wasn't a very comfortable one. Twelve passengers were crowded into the coach. It traveled at just four miles an hour. Roads were mostly dirt. They were usually either rutted or muddy. These were unpleasant conditions. Many people preferred to stay home.

Notice how choppy the passage is at points. It has a dull rhythm because it is made up entirely of simple sentences. Also, the relationships between ideas aren't clear. On the next page is a revision. Some simple sentences have been combined into compound sentences and a complex sentence, which add interest and meaning to the paragraph.

There was a lack of convenient transportation at the beginning of the nineteenth century. The stagecoach was the major form of transportation, and it wasn't a very comfortable one. Twelve passengers were crowded into the coach, which traveled at just four miles an hour. Roads were mostly dirt, so they were usually either rutted or muddy. Because of these unpleasant conditions, many people preferred to stay home.

➤ Practice 3   *Answers may vary.*

Rewrite the following passage on the lines below by combining the three pairs of italicized sentences. Before making your revisions, read the passage at least a couple of times. Also, feel free to check the list of joining words on page 147 and the list of dependent words on page 151. When revising, remember to add commas where needed.

In nineteenth-century England, many people made a living by "body snatching." *They would sneak into a graveyard. Then they would dig up a fairly fresh body.* They would sell it to a medical school for research. No questions were ever asked. *Bodies for research were almost impossible to come by. Researchers paid a lot of money for them.* A skillful grave robber could live almost as well as the research physicians.

They would sneak into a graveyard, and then they would dig up a fairly fresh

body. When they would sell it to a medical school for research, no questions

were ever asked. Bodies for research were almost impossible to come by, so

researchers paid a lot of money for them.

_____

_____

USE A SERIES OF ITEMS (ADJECTIVES AND VERBS)

A great deal of information can be communicated in one sentence by using a series of items. Adjectives and verbs are often effective in a series.

1   Use a series of adjectives

- The **helpful tax** accountant was a **friendly young** man in a wheelchair.

Punctuation Note: Use commas between two or more adjectives that can be joined by *and*.

- My husband refuses to throw away his **old, ragged** shirt.

A comma should be used between *old* and *ragged* because they can be joined by *and* ("old and ragged shirt").

※ For more information on adjectives, see "Adjectives and Adverbs," pages 227–236.

➤ **Practice 4**

Combine each group of sentences into one sentence by using a series of adjectives. Omit repeated and unnecessary words.

Example   The instructor told a story to the class.
The story was long.
The story was boring.
The class was sleepy.
The class was inattentive.

The instructor told a long, boring story to the sleepy, inattentive

class.

1. In my basement, I have an office.
    The office is well-lit.
    The office is comfortable.

    In my basement, I have a well-lit, comfortable office.

    _____

2. I wrote a letter to my uncle.
    The letter was long.
    The letter was affectionate.
    The uncle is sick.
    The uncle is elderly.

    I wrote a long, affectionate letter to my sick, elderly uncle.

    _____

3. A little girl in a dress sat in a rocking chair.
    The little girl was plump.
    The dress was blue.
    The dress was flowered.
    The rocking chair was wooden.

    A plump little girl in a blue flowered dress sat in a wooden rocking chair.

    _____

4. A woman in a sports car drove down the street.
    The woman was nervous-looking.
    The car was small.
    The car was red.
    The street was narrow.
    The street was slush-filled.

    A nervous-looking woman in a small red sports car drove down the narrow,

    slush-filled street.

5. We watched the otters slide down the riverbank into the water.
The otters were sleek.
The otters were playful.
The river bank was steep.
The river bank was muddy.
The water was clear.
The water was blue.

We watched the sleek, playful otters slide down the steep, muddy riverbank

into the clear blue water.

2   Use a series of verbs

- While we waited for our waiter, he **took** a phone call, **chatted** with the cashier, and **disappeared** into the kitchen.

When two or more verbs go with a single subject, the verb is called a compound verb.

▒ For more information on compound verbs, see "Subjects and Verbs," page 72.

➤ **Practice 5**

Combine each group of sentences into one sentence by using a series of verbs. Omit repeated and unnecessary words.

Example   The last leaf on the tree fluttered in the breeze.
The leaf let go of the branch.
The leaf spiraled to the ground.
The last leaf on the tree fluttered in the breeze, let go of the branch,

and spiraled to the ground.

1. The dog ran to the door.
The dog pushed his nose against the doorbell.
The dog waited to be let in.

The dog ran to the door, pushed his nose against the doorbell, and waited to be

let in.

2. A microwave oven reheats leftovers.
It fries bacon.
It cooks vegetables.
It pops popcorn.

A microwave oven reheats leftovers, fries bacon, cooks vegetables, and pops

popcorn.

3. At the diner, I ordered a triple-decker turkey sandwich.
   I ate half of it.
   I brought the other half home for lunch the next day.

   At the diner, I ordered a triple-decker turkey sandwich, ate half of it, and

   brought the other half home for lunch the next day.

   _____

4. When asked to put the toy down, the child screamed.
   The child held her breath.
   The child kicked.
   The child grasped the toy tightly.

   When asked to put the toy down, the child screamed, held her breath, kicked,

   and grasped the toy tightly.

   _____

5. The tall, muscular man turned pale at the sight of the needle.
   He groaned as it entered his arm.
   He fainted as it was removed.

   The tall, muscular man turned pale at the sight of the needle, groaned as it

   entered his arm, and fainted as it was removed.

   _____

USE VERBALS (INFINITIVES, PARTICIPLES, AND GERUNDS)

As you might guess from their name, **verbals** are words that are formed from verbs. However, they do not function as verbs. There are three kinds of verbals: infinitives, participles, and gerunds. Verbals add variety and interest to writing.

The Infinitive

The **infinitive** is formed by adding the base form of the verb to the word *to*, as in *to go* or *to work*. An infinitive generally describes or explains other words in the sentence. (It may also function as a noun.) To add variety to your writing, try beginning some sentences with infinitive word groups. An infinitive word group that begins a sentence is usually followed by a comma.

- **To reach a goal,** you usually must aim for it.
- **To relax before going to bed,** Leila took a long, hot bath.

➤ **Practice 6**

Combine each pair of sentences below into one sentence that begins with an infinitive word group. To do so, turn one of the sentences into an infinitive word group and add and omit words as necessary. (Follow each infinitive word group with a comma.)

Example   I stretched and ran in place for a few minutes.
I did this to feel more alert.

To feel more alert, I stretched and ran in place for a few minutes.

1. Raul is improving his English.
Raul practices talking with everyone he meets.

To improve his English, Raul practices talking with everyone he meets.

2. It is possible to find time to review your class notes.
Make use of in-between moments, such as time on the bus.

To find time to review your class notes, make use of in-between moments, such

as time on the bus.

3. Alicia mixed water and lemon juice.
She decided to make window cleaner.

To make window cleaner, Alicia mixed water and lemon juice.

4. I made my folding doors move smoothly.
I rubbed cooking oil along the metal grooves.

To make my folding doors move smoothly, I rubbed cooking oil along the metal

grooves.

5. He polished his shoes and ironed his shirt.
He wanted to look good for his interview.

To look good for his interview, he polished his shoes and ironed his shirt.

The Participle

Present participles end in *-ing*. Most **past participles** end in *-ed*. This type of verbal always functions as an adjective. Sometimes a participle comes before the word being described.

- The **snoring** man never heard the burglar enter his home.
- The **painted** desk was bought at a garage sale.

Participles and participle word groups can be used effectively at the beginning of sentences. In that position, they must be followed by the word they describe:

- **Being creative**, I thought of a good reason to put off doing my homework.
- **Delayed again**, Marge came home too late to see her son's Little League game.

Participles and participle word groups can also be effectively used within sentences after the words they describe:

- An old couch, **sagging deeply**, sat on the curb.
- The cake, **decorated like a social security card**, was for someone's sixty-fifth birthday.

➤ Practice 7   *Answers may vary.*

A. Combine each pair of sentences below into one sentence. To do so, turn one of the independent ideas into a present participle (an *-ing* word) or a present participle word group, and add or omit words as necessary.

Example   The child was crying.
He ran to his mother.

The crying child ran to his mother. **Or:** *Crying, the child ran to*

his mother. **Or:** *The child, crying, ran to his mother.*

1. They stared at me.
   They looked as if they had seen a ghost.

   They stared at me, looking as if they had seen a ghost.

2. The cat settled down in a sunny spot by the window.
   It purred quietly.

   The cat, purring quietly, settled down in a sunny spot by the window.

3. George nodded his head.
   He pretended to listen to the long-winded salesman.

   Nodding his head, George pretended to listen to the long-winded salesman.

4. I pulled on a warm hat.
   I prepared to go out in the snowstorm.

   Pulling on a warm hat, I prepared to go out in the snowstorm.

5. Holly scribbled notes frantically.
   She tried to keep up with the rapid lecture.

   Scribbling notes frantically, Holly tried to keep up with the rapid lecture.

   _____

B. Combine each pair of sentences below into one sentence. To do so, turn one of the independent ideas into a past participle or a past participle word group, and add or omit words as necessary.

Example   The actor ran up the aisle to claim his award.
He was overjoyed.

The overjoyed actor ran up the aisle to claim his award.

Or: *Overjoyed, the actor ran up the aisle to claim his award.*

Or: *The actor, overjoyed, ran up the aisle to claim his award.*

6. The workers sat with their mouths open.
   They were stunned.

   The stunned workers sat with their mouths open.

   _____

7. I was bored by the movie.
   I left after finishing my popcorn.

   Bored by the movie, I left after finishing my popcorn.

   _____

8. Ryan played in the schoolyard alone.
   He was excluded from the other children's games.

   Ryan, excluded from the other children's games, played in the schoolyard

   alone.

9. Dad left the hospital room in tears.
   He was pained at the sight of my mother in the oxygen tent.

   Pained at the sight of my mother in the oxygen tent, Dad left the hospital

   room in tears.

10. I was refreshed from a brief nap.
    I went back to studying for my English final.

    Refreshed from a brief nap, I went back to studying for my English final.

    _____

The Gerund

A **gerund** is an *-ing* word (a present participle) that is used as a noun. For variety, use a gerund or a word group that begins with a gerund.

- **Agreeing** with Susan is often easier than arguing with her.
- There is no reason for your **lying**.

➤ Practice 8

Combine each of the following pairs of sentences into one sentence. To do so, turn the second sentence into a gerund. Then add the gerund to the first sentence, revising as necessary.

Example   There is something that can improve everyone's day. It is to smile.

Smiling can improve everyone's day.

1. There is an easy but expensive way to learn geography. That way is to travel.

   Traveling is an easy but expensive way to learn geography.

2. One thing is easier than finding solutions. That is to complain.

   Complaining is easier than finding solutions.

3. There is a sport that Kevin excels in. That sport is to wrestle.

   Wrestling is a sport that Kevin excels in.

4. Many people are nervous about something. That is to speak in public.

   Many people are nervous about speaking in public.

5. There is something that is fun and also good exercise. That something is to dance.

   Dancing is fun and also good exercise.

USE PREPOSITIONAL PHRASES AND -*LY* WORD GROUPS TO BEGIN SENTENCES

As you have already seen, you can add variety to your writing by beginning some sentences with verbals. You can also achieve variety by beginning sentences with prepositional phrases and *-ly* words.

Prepositional Phrases

Begin a sentence with a prepositional phrase. A prepositional phrase begins with a preposition and ends with a noun, the object of the preposition. Common prepositions include *in, on, of, by, from, across, before, under,* and *behind.* (See page 69 for a longer list of prepositions.) When the prepositional phrase comes at the beginning of the sentence, it is generally followed by a comma.

- **In the dark basement,** I heard breathing.

Prepositional phrases are generally found *within* a sentence. As a result, *beginning* a sentence with a prepositional phrase draws attention to a description of the time, the place, or the like. It also allows the writer to place a more dramatic idea at the end. For example:

Preposition within a sentence: I began sneezing uncontrollably **during the love scene**.

Preposition at the beginning: **During the love scene,** I began sneezing uncontrollably.

➤ Practice 9

Combine each pair of sentences into one sentence that begins with a prepositional phrase. To do so, use part of the second sentence at the beginning of the first one. Follow the introductory prepositional phrase with a comma.

Example   A helicopter circled wildly. It circled over our heads.
Over our heads, a helicopter circled wildly.

1. There is a tattoo parlor. It is across from the bowling alley.
   Across from the bowling alley, there is a tattoo parlor.

2. A snake lay hidden. It lay under a rock.
   Under a rock, a snake lay hidden.

3. Eight people live together. They live in that tiny house.
   In that tiny house, eight people live together.

4. Sharon ran out of the room. She ran out before I could say a word.
   Before I could say a word, Sharon ran out of the room.

5. We heard an evil chuckle. We heard it from behind the locked door.
   From behind the locked door, we heard an evil chuckle.

-Ly Words

Begin a sentence with a word ending in -ly. Most words ending in -ly are adverbs. When an -ly word is at the beginning of a sentence, it is usually followed by a comma.

- **Expertly,** Cliff changed the baby's diaper.

As with prepositional phrases, -ly words are generally found within a sentence. The above sentence, for example, might be written: *Cliff changed the baby's diaper expertly.* Here are more examples of sentences that begin with an -ly word:

- **Gradually,** the drops formed a large puddle on the floor.
- **Selfishly,** I ate both deliciously chewy ends of the fresh rye bread.

Beginning with an -ly word generally draws attention to how something is done.

※ For more information on adverbs, see pages 228–229.

➤ **Practice 10**

Combine each pair of sentences into one sentence that begins with an -ly word. To do so, replace the second sentence with an -ly word and put it at the beginning of the first sentence. Follow the introductory -ly word with a comma.

Example   Sandra added the last touches to her painting.
She was careful.

Carefully, Sandra added the last touches to her painting.

1. The cat walked past the sleeping dog.
   It was cautious.

   Cautiously, the cat walked past the sleeping dog.

2. We scraped every bit of paint off the old cupboard.
   We were patient.

   Patiently, we scraped every bit of paint off the old cupboard.

3. Mrs. Gerhart described her family's life in Nazi Germany.
   She was sad.

   Sadly, Mrs. Gerhart described her family's life in Nazi Germany.

4. The boys attacked the huge bowl of popcorn.
   They were hungry.

   Hungrily, the boys attacked the huge bowl of popcorn.

5. Nan began her speech to the class.
   She was nervous.

   Nervously, Nan began her speech to the class.

USE APPOSITIVES

An **appositive** is a word or word group that renames or identifies a noun or pronoun. The appositive follows the word or words it explains.

- Greta Garbo, **a beautiful and adored actress**, retired from filmmaking at the age of thirty-six.
- The only air-conditioning in Ed's car, **a twelve-year-old Volkswagen bug**, was a hole in the floor.

Punctuation Note: When an appositive is not essential to the main meaning of a sentence, it is set off by commas, as above. Most appositives are not essential to the meaning of a sentence. They may add interesting information, but the sentence makes full sense without them. Without its appositive, for example, the first sentence above still makes sense: *Greta Garbo retired from filmmaking at the age of thirty-six.*

> ※ For more information on essential and nonessential material, see "Commas," page 348.

➤ Practice 11

Combine each pair of sentences into one sentence with an appositive. To do so, convert the second sentence into an appositive by removing unnecessary words. Then put the appositive in the first sentence after the word it describes or explains.

Example Tyrannosaurus Rex lived more than 60 million years ago.
Tyrannosaurus Rex was the fiercest dinosaur ever.

Tyrannosaurus Rex, the fiercest dinosaur ever, lived more than 60

million years ago.

1. Earl asked his aunt for a loan.
   His aunt is a successful lawyer.

   Earl asked his aunt, a successful lawyer, for a loan.

2. Vivian's parrot can say many words.
   Her parrot is a beautiful bird.

   Vivian's parrot, a beautiful bird, can say many words.

3. Lena's car has traveled more than 100,000 miles.
   It is a 1980 Honda Accord.

   Lena's car, a 1980 Honda Accord, has traveled more than 100,000 miles.

4. This handmade box has a hidden drawer.
   The box is an antique.

   This handmade box, an antique, has a hidden drawer.

   _____

5. The microwave quickly prepares most of my meals.
   It was a gift from my children.

   The microwave, a gift from my children, quickly prepares most of my meals.

   _____

USE RELATIVE PRONOUN WORD GROUPS

Relative pronouns (*who, whom, whose, which*, and *that*) begin dependent word groups (word groups containing a subject and verb but unable to stand alone as complete thoughts). These word groups describe nouns and pronouns that have already been mentioned.

- My guitar teacher, **who plays with a local band**, is very patient.
- To the cauliflower mixture, add some saffron, **which comes in tiny packets**.

Punctuation Note: When relative pronoun word groups provide nonessential information, as above, they are set off by commas. When they provide essential information, they are not set off by commas.

- The man **who usually sleeps by the steps of City Hall** is not there today.

The boldfaced words above are essential. Without them, we would not know which man is being referred to.

> ※ For more information on essential and nonessential material, see "Commas," page 348.

> ➤ Practice 12

Combine each pair of sentences into one sentence with a relative pronoun word group, revising as necessary. Choose from these relative pronouns: *who, whose, which*, and *that*. (The first three relative pronoun word groups need to be set off with commas.)

Example   My high school principal was a very nice woman.
She was my next-door neighbor.

My high school principal, who was my next-door neighbor, was a

very nice woman.

1. This book is about the author's childhood in China.
   I enjoyed the book very much.

   This book, which I enjoyed very much, is about the author's childhood in China.

   _____

2. My roommate enjoys sharing her room with only one person.
   She comes from a very large family.

   My roommate, who comes from a very large family, enjoys sharing her room

   with only one person.

3. Santos and Bill both liked the movie.
   The movie was in Spanish with English subtitles.

   Santos and Bill both liked the movie, which was in Spanish with English

   subtitles.

4. The person is getting a ticket.
   It's the person whose car is out in front.

   The person whose car is out in front is getting a ticket.

   _____

5. I've decided to enter the marathon.
   It is the marathon that will be run on Saturday.

   I've decided to enter the marathon that will be run on Saturday.

   _____

A Note on Appositives and Relative-Pronoun Word Groups

Appositives and relative-pronoun word groups can often be used interchangeably. They both are used to describe, rename, or explain a noun or pronoun.

Appositive version:	Hazel, **my stepmother**, is also my aunt.
Relative-pronoun version:	Hazel, **who is my stepmother**, is also my aunt.
Appositive version:	My elementary school, **John Hay School**, no longer exists.
Relative-pronoun version:	My elementary school, **which was John Hay School**, no longer exists.

CHAPTER REVIEW

Circle the letter of the correct answer for each item.

1. To combine two simple sentences into a compound sentence, use
   a. a comma and a joining word.
   b. a semicolon and an appropriate transitional word.
   c. either of the above.

2. To combine two simple sentences into a complex sentence, use
   a. a joining word.
   b. a transitional word.
   c. a dependent word.

3. A great deal of information can be communicated in one sentence by using a series of
   a. adjectives.
   b. verbs.
   c. either of the above.

4. The three kinds of verbals are
   a. simple, compound, complex.
   b. joining, transitional, dependent.
   c. infinitives, participles, gerunds.

5. An infinitive is
   a. *to* plus the base form of the verb.
   b. a present participle (an *-ing* word) or a past participle (an *-ed* word) that functions as an adjective.
   c. a present participle (an *-ing* word) that functions as a noun.

6. A gerund is
   a. *to* plus the base form of the verb.
   b. a present participle (an *-ing* word) or a past participle (an *-ed* word) that functions as an adjective.
   c. a present participle (an *-ing* word) that functions as a noun.

7. An appositive
   a. can begin a sentence.
   b. follows the noun it renames or identifies.
   c. both of the above.

8. A relative pronoun word group
   a. can begin a sentence.
   b. describes a noun or pronoun already mentioned in a sentence.
   c. can stand alone as an independent sentence.

Name _____ Section _____ Date _____

Score: (Number right) _____ x 12.5 = _____%

➤ Sentence Variety and Style: Test 1   *Answers may vary.*

A. Use a comma and a suitable joining word to combine each pair of simple sentences into a compound sentence. Choose from the joining words *and, but,* and *so.*

1. Yogurt is delicious. It is low in fat and calories.

   Yogurt is delicious, and it is low in fat and calories.

2. Roberto acts friendly to his coworkers. He says nasty things about them at home.

   Roberto acts friendly to his coworkers, but he says nasty things about them at

   home.

B. Use a semicolon and a transitional word or words (followed by a comma) to combine each pair of simple sentences into a compound sentence. Use each of the following transitional words once: *as a result, however, in addition.*

3. I love to eat. I don't love to cook.

   I love to eat; however, I don't love to cook.

4. Stretching feels wonderful. It's good for your posture.

   Stretching feels wonderful; in addition, it's good for your posture.

5. The newspaper comes out early in the morning. Reporters must work late into the night.

   The newspaper comes out early in the morning; as a result, reporters must

   work late into the night.

C. Combine each pair of simple sentences into a complex sentence. Use each of the following dependent words once: *after, because,* and *while.* Put a comma after any dependent word group that begins a sentence.

6. Rose had a car accident. She was afraid to drive.

   After Rose had a car accident, she was afraid to drive.

7. I'll hold the dog. You put his leash on.

   I'll hold the dog while you put his leash on.

8. My son is allergic to peanuts. He can't eat peanut butter sandwiches.

   Because my son is allergic to peanuts, he can't eat peanut butter sandwiches.

Name_____ Section _____ Date _____

Score: (Number right) _____ x 20 = _____%

➤ Sentence Variety and Style: Test 2   *Answers may vary.*

A. Combine each group of sentences into one sentence by using a series of adjectives and/or verbs. Omit repeated and unnecessary words, and add commas as needed.

1. The rainstorm flooded our basement.
   The rainstorm was sudden.
   The rainstorm was terrible.
   It knocked slates off the roof.
   It uprooted a young tree.

   The sudden, terrible rainstorm flooded our basement, knocked slates off the

   roof, and uprooted a young tree.

2. The truck was speeding.
   The truck was brown.
   The truck skidded on some ice.
   The truck almost hit a police officer.
   The police officer was startled.
   The police officer was young.

   The speeding brown truck skidded on some ice and almost hit a young, startled

   police officer.

3. As I waited to hear whether I'd gotten the job, I cleaned my apartment.
   The job was wonderful.
   The job was in sales.
   I painted my toenails.
   I listened to music.
   I wrote a letter.

   As I waited to hear whether I'd gotten the wonderful sales job, I cleaned my

   apartment, painted my toenails, listened to music, and wrote a letter.

B. Combine each of the following pairs of sentences into one sentence. To do so, turn the second sentence into a gerund (a noun that ends in *-ing*), and revise as necessary.

4. There is a more valuable skill than talking. That is to listen.

   Listening is a more valuable skill than talking.

5. My doctor just wrote a popular article. He wrote about burps.

   My doctor just wrote a popular article about burping.

Name_____ Section _____ Date _____

➤ **Sentence Variety and Style: Test 3**

A. Combine each pair of sentences below into one sentence that begins with an infinitive (*to* + the base form of a verb). Follow the infinitive with a comma.

1. Colonial women used spinning wheels. They did this to make thread.

   To make thread, Colonial women used spinning wheels.

2. I want to keep my car running well. I change the oil frequently.

   To keep my car running well, I change the oil frequently.

B. Combine each pair of sentences below into one sentence that begins with a participle (an *-ing* or *-ed* word that describes) or a participle word group. (Remember that the participle must describe the word that follows it.) Follow the participle or participle word group with a comma.

   Answers may vary.

3. Kathleen read the letter. She gasped in surprise.

   Gasping in surprise, Kathleen read the letter.

4. Nate stood at the corner and looked in all directions. He was confused.

   Confused, Nate stood at the corner and looked in all directions.

   _____

C. Combine each pair of sentences into one sentence that begins with a prepositional phrase. Follow the prepositional phrase with a comma.

5. A car wash is being built. It is being built beside our house.

   Beside our house, a car wash is being built.

6. There are too many stories about fires and murders. The stories are in the news.

   In the news, there are too many stories about fires and murders.

   _____

D. Combine each pair of sentences into one sentence that begins with an *-ly* word. Follow the *-ly* word with a comma.

7. The children sang as they played in the sandbox. They were cheerful.

   Cheerfully, the children sang as they played in the sandbox.

8. I felt along the wall for the light switch. I did so in a slow manner.

   Slowly, I felt along the wall for the light switch.

Name_____   Section _____   Date _____

Score: (Number right) _____ x 12.5 = _____ %

➤ **Sentence Variety and Style: Test 4**

A. Combine each pair of sentences into one sentence with an appositive (a word or words that rename or identify a noun or pronoun).

1. My favorite dessert is on the menu. My favorite dessert is pumpkin pie.

   My favorite dessert, pumpkin pie, is on the menu.

2. The TV show's host smiled at the contestants. The TV show's host was Alex Trebek.

   The TV show's host, Alex Trebek, smiled at the contestants.

3. W.C. Fields had bank accounts in many different names. He was a comedian and actor.

   W.C. Fields, a comedian and actor, had bank accounts in many different names.

4. Sarah looked at her present with astonishment. It was a diamond ring.

   Sarah looked at her present, a diamond ring, with astonishment.

B. Combine each pair of sentences into one sentence with a relative pronoun word group. Choose from these relative pronouns: *who, which, whose,* and *that.* The first three relative pronoun word groups need to be set off with commas.

5. Margo keeps in touch with me through postcards. She is an old friend.

   Margo, who is an old friend, keeps in touch with me through postcards.

6. Birds eat small stones and bits of gravel. The stones and gravel help birds digest their food.

   Birds eat small stones and bits of gravel, which help birds digest their food.

   _____

7. Mrs. Walker is running for mayor. Her husband is my English teacher.

   Mrs. Walker, whose husband is my English teacher, is running for mayor.

   _____

8. The candy store will close next month. The candy store is the one that is on the corner of Main and Tenth.

   The candy store that is on the corner of Main and Tenth will close next month.

   _____

Name_____   Section _____   Date _____

Score: (Number right) _____ x 10 = _____ %

➤ Sentence Variety and Style: Test 5   *Answers will vary.*

A. Combine sentences in the following paragraph so that there is one combination of adjectives and two combinations of verbs. Also, be sure that the final paragraph includes at least one compound sentence and one complex sentence.

> Sue and Miles wanted a vacation. They wanted a vacation that was nice. They wanted one that was quiet. They wanted one that was relaxing. They rented a small lakeside cabin. Their first day there was very peaceful. The situation quickly changed. A large family moved into a nearby cabin. They played music at top volume. They raced around in a speedboat with a loud whining engine. Sue and Miles were no longer very relaxed. They packed up their things. They drove off. They returned to their quiet apartment.

Sue and Miles wanted a nice, quiet, relaxing vacation, so they rented a small

lakeside cabin. Their first day there was very peaceful; however, the situation

quickly changed. A large family moved into a nearby cabin, played music at top

volume, and raced around in a speedboat with a loud whining engine. Because

Sue and Miles were no longer very relaxed, they packed up their things, drove off,

and returned to their quiet apartment.

B. Combine five pairs of sentences in the following paragraph so that it contains at least one of each of the verbals or verbal word groups: infinitives, participles, and gerunds.

> My aunt decided to find a helpful form of exercise. She was suffering from arthritis. She learned that something is very healthful. It is to swim. It works every muscle group in the body without straining the muscles. She took a course for beginners at the YWCA. She did that to learn how to swim. She wore water wings for the first few lessons. She was frightened. She knows how to swim well now. She never wears the water wings anymore. She swims three times a week and feels much better.

My aunt, suffering from arthritis, decided to find a helpful form of exercise. She

learned that swimming is very healthful. It works every muscle group in the

body without straining the muscles. To learn how to swim, she took a course for

beginners at the YWCA. Frightened, she wore water wings for the first few

lessons. Knowing how to swim well now, she never wears the water wings

anymore. She swims three times a week and feels much better.

(Continues on next page)

C. Combine sentences in the following paragraph so that three sentences begin with prepositional phrases and two begin with -*ly* words.

> Nita sells beauty products. She sells them at the present. However, she is more interested in computers. She has taught herself a lot about computers. She did so in her usual thorough manner. Nita applied for jobs with several computer stores. She did that recently. The managers of two of those stores called her. They called within one week. She will go in for one interview tomorrow and another next week. Nita will soon get a new job. She will get it without a doubt.

Presently, Nita sells beauty products. However, she is more interested in computers. In her usual thorough manner, she has taught herself a lot about computers. Recently, Nita applied for jobs with several computer stores. Within one week, the managers of two of those stores called her. She will go in for one interview tomorrow and another next week. Without a doubt, Nita will soon get a new job.

D. Combine sentences in the following paragraph by creating a total of five appositives and relative pronoun word groups.

> Last year, José took a cooking course. José was my roommate at the time. He wanted to improve his kitchen skills. His kitchen skills were very poor. The man who taught the course was Joe Appleman. Joe Appleman is the head chef at the fanciest restaurant in town. That restaurant is called The Black Tulip. At the course, José met a woman. The woman is a professional chef. José's cooking skills aren't much improved, but his eating certainly has. He and that woman got married last month.

Last year, José, my roommate at the time, took a cooking course. He wanted to improve his kitchen skills, which were very poor. The man who taught the course was Joe Appleman, the head chef at the fanciest restaurant in town, The Black Tulip. At the course, José met a woman who is a professional chef. José's cooking skills aren't much improved, but his eating certainly has. He and that woman got married last month.

19 / Spelling Improvement

This chapter explains the following ways to improve your spelling:

1 Use the dictionary
2 Use an electronic spelling checker
3 Keep a personal spelling list
4 Learn commonly confused words
5 Learn some helpful spelling rules

    a I before E rule

    b Silent E rule

    c Y rule

    d Doubling rule

    e Rules for adding *-es* to nouns and verbs that end in *s*, *sh*, *ch*, or *x*

    f Rules for adding *-es* to nouns and verbs ending in a consonant plus *y*

USE THE DICTIONARY

The single most important way to improve your spelling is to get into the habit of checking words in a dictionary. But you may at times have trouble locating a given word. "If I can't spell a word," you might ask, "how can I find it in the dictionary?" The answer is that you have to guess what the letters might be.

Here are some hints to help you make informed guesses.

Hint 1

If you're not sure about the vowels in a word, you will have to experiment. Vowels often sound the same. So try an *i* in place of an *a*, an *e* in place of an *i*, and so on.

Hint 2

Consonants are sometimes doubled in a word. If you can't find your word with single consonants, try doubling them.

Hint 3

Following are groups of letters or letter combinations that often sound alike. If your word isn't spelled with one of the letters in a pair or group shown below, it might be spelled with another in the same pair or group. For example, if it isn't spelled with a *k*, it may be spelled with a *c*.

Vowels				
ai / ay	**au / aw**	**ee / ea**	**ou / ow**	**oo / u**
Consonants				
c / k **c / s**	**f / ph**	**g / j**	**sch / sc / sk**	**s / z**
Combinations				
re / ri **able / ible**	**ent / ant**	**er / or**	**tion / sion**	

➤ **Practice 1**

Use your dictionary and the above hints to find the correct spelling of the following words.

1. divelop _____*develop*_____
2. diferent _____*different*_____
3. sertain _____*certain*_____
4. chearful _____*cheerful*_____
5. sergery _____*surgery*_____
6. skedule _____*schedule*_____
7. fony _____*phony*_____
8. comfortible _____*comfortable*_____
9. mayer _____*mayor*_____
10. paiment _____*payment*_____

11. aukward _____*awkward*_____
12. photografy _____*photography*_____
13. asemble _____*assemble*_____
14. seazon _____*season*_____
15. dependant _____*dependent*_____
16. terrable _____*terrible*_____
17. dezign _____*design*_____
18. rilease _____*release*_____
19. funcsion _____*function*_____
20. awthor _____*author*_____

USE AN ELECTRONIC SPELLING CHECKER

Take advantage of electronic spelling tools. If you work on a computer or electronic typewriter that has a spelling checker, use it before finalizing your papers. Pocket-size electronic spelling checkers are also widely available.

KEEP A PERSONAL SPELLING LIST

In a special place, write down every word you misspell. Include its correct spelling, underline the difficult part of the word, and add any hints you can use to remember how to spell it. If spelling is a particular problem for you, you might even want to start a spelling notebook that has a separate page for each letter of the alphabet. Here's one format you might use:

	How I spelled it	Correct spelling	Hints
	receive	rec<u>ei</u>ve	I before E except after C
	separate	sep<u>a</u>rate	There's A RAT in sepARATe
	a lot	<u>a</u> lot	Two words (like "a little")
	alright	<u>all</u> right	Two words (like "all wrong")

Study your list regularly, and refer to it whenever you write and proofread a paper.

LEARN COMMONLY CONFUSED WORDS

Many spelling errors result from words that sound alike or almost alike but that are spelled differently, such as *brake* and *brake*, *wear* and *where*, or *right* and *write*. To avoid such errors, study carefully the list of words on pages 311–324.

LEARN SOME HELPFUL SPELLING RULES

Even poor spellers can improve by following a few spelling rules. Following are six rules that apply to many words.

I before *E* rule

I before *E* except after *C*
Or when sounded like *A*, as in *neighbor* and *weigh*.

	I *before* E	*Except after* C	*Or when sounded like* A
Examples:	bel**ie**f, ch**ie**f, f**ie**ld	rece**i**ve, c**ei**ling	v**ei**n, **ei**ght

Exceptions to the above rule include: **ei**ther, l**ei**sure, for**ei**gn, sci**e**nce, soci**e**ty

➤ **Practice 2**

A. Complete each word with either *ie* or *ei*.

1. dec_*ei*_ve

2. bel_*ie*_ve

3. br_*ie*_f

4. fr_*ei*_ght

5. c_*ei*_ling

6. pr_*ie*_st

7. cash_*ie*_r

8. w_*ei*_gh

9. p_*ie*_ce

10. r_*ei*_ndeer

B. In each sentence, fill in the blank with either *ie* or *ei*.

11. I rec_*ei*_ved some interesting junk mail today.

12. Many of the people in my n_*ei*_ghborhood are retired.

13. Norma never gave up her bel_*ie*_f in her husband's innocence.

14. What do you like to do in your l_*ei*_sure time?

15. There's a lot of traffic now, so don't ignore this y_*ie*_ld sign.

16. The r_*ei*_gn of Queen Victoria of Great Britain lasted over sixty years.

17. My parents are working hard to ach_*ie*_ve their retirement goals.

18. I have never traveled to any for_*ei*_gn countries.

19. My _*ei*_ghty-year-old grandfather still does a daily twenty pushups.

20. A th_*ie*_f broke into Parker's Bakery last night and stole all the dough.

Silent *E* rule

If a word ends in a silent (unpronounced) *e*, drop the *e* before adding an ending that starts with a vowel. Keep the *e* when adding an ending that begins with a consonant.

	Drop the e *with endings that start with a vowel*	Keep the e *with endings that start with a consonant*
Examples:	like + ed = li**ke**d	love + ly = lov**e**ly
	confuse + ing = confu**s**ing	shame + ful = sham**e**ful
	fame + ous = fa**m**ous	hope + less = hop**e**less
	guide + ance = gui**dance**	manage + ment = manag**e**ment

Exceptions include: notic**e**able, arg**u**ment, jud**g**ment, tr**u**ly

➤ Practice 3

A. Write out each word shown.

1. abuse + ing = _____*abusing*_____

2. hope + ed = _____*hoped*_____

3. have + ing = _____*having*_____

4. desire + able = _____*desirable*_____

5. ridicule + ous = _____*ridiculous*_____

6. sincere + ity = _____*sincerity*_____

B. Write out each word shown.

7. sincere + ly = _____*sincerely*_____

8. peace + ful = _____*peaceful*_____

9. advance + ment = _____*advancement*_____

10. noise + less = _____*noiseless*_____

11. large + ness = _____*largeness*_____

12. grace + ful = _____*graceful*_____

13. bare + ly = _____*barely*_____

C. Write out each word shown.

14. write + ing = _____*writing*_____

15. care + ful = _____*careful*_____

16. safe + ly = _____*safely*_____

17. hire + ed = _____*hired*_____

18. serve + ing = _____*serving*_____

19. notice + able = _____*noticeable*_____

20. excite + ment = _____*excitement*_____

Y rule

Change the final *y* of a word to *i* when:

a The last two letters of the word are a consonant plus *y*. (Keep a *y* that follows a vowel.)

b The ending being added begins with a vowel or is *-ful, -ly,* or *-ness.*

Exception: Keep the *y* if the ending being added is *-ing.*

	Change the y *to* i	*Keep the* y
Examples:	happy + ness = happiness	destroy + s = destroys
	lucky + ly = luckily	display + ed = displayed
	beauty + ful = beautiful	gray + ed = grayed
	try + ed = tried	try + ing = trying
	carry + er = carrier	carry + ing = carrying

➤ **Practice 4**

A. Write out each word shown.

1. rely + ed =   *relied*

2. holy + ness =   *holiness*

3. play + ful =   *playful*

4. cry + ing =   *crying*

5. cry + ed =   *cried*

6. plenty + ful =   *plentiful*

7. lazy + ness =   *laziness*

8. fly + ing =   *flying*

9. angry + ly =   *angrily*

10. betray + ed =   *betrayed*

B. Write out each word shown.

11. stay + ing =   *staying*

    stay + ed =   *stayed*

12. busy + ness =   *business*

    busy + ly =   *busily*

13. silly + er =   *sillier*

    silly + ness =   *silliness*

14. employ + ed =   *employed*

    employ + er =   *employer*

15. bury + ing =   _____ *burying* _____

    bury + ed =   _____ *buried* _____

16. dry + ing =   _____ *drying* _____

    dry + ed =   _____ *dried* _____

17. happy + ly =   _____ *happily* _____

    happy + er =   _____ *happier* _____

18. funny + er =   _____ *funnier* _____

    funny + est = _____ *funniest* _____

19. satisfy + ing = _____ *satisfying* _____

    satisfy + ed = _____ *satisfied* _____

20. annoy + ed =   _____ *annoyed* _____

    annoy + ance = _____ *annoyance* _____

Doubling rule

Double the final consonant of a word before adding an ending when:

a The last three letters of the word are a consonant, a vowel, and a consonant (CVC).

b The word is only one syllable (for example, *stop*) or is accented on the last syllable (for example, *begin*).

c The ending being added begins with a vowel.

	One-syllable words that end in CVC	*Words accented on the last syllable that end in CVC*
Examples:	stop + ed = sto**pp**ed	begin + ing = begi**nn**ing
	flat + er = fla**tt**er	control + er = contro**ll**er
	red + est = re**dd**est	occur + ence = occu**rr**ence

➤ Practice 5

A. First note whether each word ends in the CVC pattern or with another pattern (VVC, VCC, etc.), and write the pattern in the first column. Then add to each word the endings shown.

Word		*Pattern of Last Three Letters*	*-ed*	*-ing*
Examples	trip	*CVC*	*tripped*	*tripping*
	growl	*VCC*	*growled*	*growling*
1. jog		*CVC*	*jogged*	*jogging*
2. learn		*VCC*	*learned*	*learning*

Word	Pattern of Last Three Letters	-ed	-ing
3. slam	CVC	slammed	slamming
4. wrap	CVC	wrapped	wrapping
5. rain	VVC	rained	raining
6. dot	CVC	dotted	dotting
7. flood	VVC	flooded	flooding
8. beg	CVC	begged	begging
9. clip	CVC	clipped	clipping
10. burn	VCC	burned	burning

B. First note whether each word ends in the CVC pattern or with another pattern (VVC, VCC, etc.), and write the pattern in the first column. Then add to each word the endings shown. *If a word ends in CVC, remember to check to see if the final syllable is stressed or not.*

	Word	Pattern of Last Three Letters	-ed	-ing
Examples	admit	CVC	admitted	admitting
	recall	VCC	recalled	recalling
11.	expel	CVC	expelled	expelling
12.	perform	VCC	performed	performing
13.	enter	CVC	entered	entering
14.	omit	CVC	omitted	omitting
15.	murder	CVC	murdered	murdering
16.	prefer	CVC	preferred	preferring
17.	occur	CVC	occurred	occurring
18.	explain	VVC	explained	explaining
19.	submit	CVC	submitted	submitting
20.	reason	CVC	reasoned	reasoning

Rules for adding *-es* to nouns and verbs that end in *s, sh, ch,* or *x*

Most plurals are formed by adding *-s* to the singular noun, but in some cases *-es* is added. For nouns that end in *s, sh, ch,* or *x*, form the plural by adding *-es*.

Examples: kiss + es = kiss**es**   coach + es = coach**es**
                wish + es = wish**es**   tax + es = tax**es**

Most third-person singular verbs end in *-s* (he runs, she sings, it grows). But for verbs that end in *s*, *sh*, *ch*, or *x*, form the third-person singular with *-es*.

Examples: miss + es = miss**es**   catch + es = catch**es**
                wash + es = wash**es**   mix + es = mix**es**

➤ **Practice 6**

Add *-s* or *-es* as needed to each of the following words.

1. bush   *bushes*
2. mix   *mixes*
3. pitch   *pitches*
4. glass   *glasses*
5. carpet   *carpets*
6. crash   *crashes*
7. box   *boxes*
8. watch   *watches*
9. shine   *shines*
10. business   *businesses*

Rules for adding *-es* to nouns and verbs that end in a consonant plus *y*

For nouns that end in a consonant plus *y*, form the plural by changing the *y* to *i* and adding *-es*.

Examples: fly + es = fl**ies**   lady + es = lad**ies**
                canary + es = canar**ies**

For verbs that end in a consonant plus *y*, form the third-person singular by changing the *y* to *i* and adding *-es*.

Examples: pity + es = pit**ies**   marry + es = marr**ies**
                bully + es = bull**ies**

➤ Practice 7

Add -*s* or -*es* as needed to each of the following words. Where appropriate, change a final *y* to *i* before adding -*es*.

1. army   *armies*

2. try   *tries*

3. tray   *trays*

4. hurry   *hurries*

5. attorney   *attorneys*

6. variety   *varieties*

7. chimney   *chimneys*

8. baby   *babies*

9. journey   *journeys*

10. sympathy   *sympathies*

CHAPTER REVIEW

Circle the letter of the correct answer to each question.

1. *E* usually comes before *I*
   a. when they follow *A*.
   b. when the two letters sound like *A*. ⭕

2. When adding an ending that starts with a vowel (such as -*ed* or -*ing*) to a word that ends in *e*, you should usually
   a. drop the *e*. ⭕
   b. keep the *e*.

3. The final *y* of a word may be changed to *i* when the last two letters of the word are
   a. a consonant plus *y*. ⭕
   b. a vowel plus *y*.

4. The doubling rule applies when the last three letters of the word are
   a. a vowel, a vowel, and a consonant.
   b. a consonant, a vowel, and a consonant. ⭕

5. Add -*es* to nouns and verbs that end in
   a. *s*, *sh*, *ch*, *x*, and a consonant plus *y*. ⭕
   b. *s*, *ment*, *x*, double letters, and a vowel plus *y*.

Name_____ Section _____ Date _____

Score: (Number right) _____ x 4 = _____ %

➤ Spelling Improvement: Test 1

Use the spelling rules in the chapter to write out the words indicated.

A. Complete each word with either *ie* or *ei*.

1. gr_*ie*_f   3. n_*ei*_ghbor   5. _*ei*_ther

2. dec_*ei*_ve   4. fr_*ie*_nd

B. Use the silent *e* rule to write out each word shown.

6. time + ed = _____*timed*_____   9. fame + ous = _____*famous*_____

7. time + ly = _____*timely*_____   10. change + ing = _____*changing*_____

8. hope + ful = _____*hopeful*_____

C. Use the *Y* rule to write out each word shown.

11. fry + ed = _____*fried*_____   14. duty + ful = _____*dutiful*_____

12. easy + ly = _____*easily*_____   15. lonely + ness = _____*loneliness*_____

13. stay + ed = _____*stayed*_____

D. Use the doubling rule to write out each word shown.

16. drop + ing = _____*dropping*_____   19. jump + er = _____*jumper*_____

17. pad + ing = _____*padding*_____   20. sad + est = _____*saddest*_____

18. prefer + ed = _____*preferred*_____

E. Add *-s* or *-es* as needed to each of the following words. Where appropriate, change a final *y* to *i* before adding *-es*.

21. box _____*boxes*_____   24. valley _____*valleys*_____

22. enemy _____*enemies*_____   25. porch _____*porches*_____

23. country _____*countries*_____

Name_____ Section _____ Date _____

Score: (Number right) _____ x 4 = _____%

➤ Spelling Improvement: Test 2

Use the spelling rules in the chapter to write out the words indicated.

A. Complete each word with either *ie* or *ei*.

1. conc__*ei*_ve   3. soc_*ie*_ty   5. ch__*ie*_f

2. f_*ie*_ld   4. v__*ei*_n

B. Use the silent *e* rule to write out each word shown.

6. come + ing = ____*coming*____   9. accurate + ly = ____*accurately*____

7. care + less = ____*careless*____   10. choose + ing = ____*choosing*____

8. desire + able = ___*desirable*____

C. Use the *Y* rule to write out each word shown.

11. reply + ed = ____*replied*____   14. glory + ous = ____*glorious*____

12. pray + ing = ____*praying*____   15. study + ed = _____*studied*____

13. carry + ed = ____*carried*____

D. Use the doubling rule to write out each word shown.

16. bark + ing = ____*barking*____   19. mop + ed = _____*mopped*____

17. rob + er = _____*robber*____   20. refer + ing = _____*referring*____

18. commit + ed = __*committed*____

E. Add *-s* or *-es* as needed to each of the following words. Where appropriate, change a final *y* to *i* before adding *-es*.

21. city _____*cities*_____   24. dress _____*dresses*_____

22. branch ____*branches*____   25. puppy _____*puppies*_____

23. subway ____*subways*____

Name _____ Section _____ Date _____

➤ Spelling Improvement: Test 3

Use the spelling rules in the chapter to correct the **ten** misspelled words in
the following passage. Find the ten errors and cross them out. Then in the
spaces above the lines, write the corrections.

In the fall of 1960, Richard M. Nixon and John F. Kennedy were

running
~~runing~~ against one another for President. Most people ~~beleived~~ Nixon
                                                              believed

                                          occurred
would win. But then three events ~~occured~~ that hurt the Nixon candidacy.

The first blow was the historic debate between Nixon and Kennedy on

September 26, less than two months before the election. Nixon was an

intelligent, well-informed politician. Kennedy was less experienced.

However, he was youthful and handsome, while Nixon had just been
                                      underweight
released from the hospital. He was ~~underwieght~~ and pasty-faced. Makeup
      tried
artists ~~tryed~~ to hide his five o'clock shadow, but only made him appear more
                                              luckily
sickly. Nixon performed well in the debate. But ~~luckyly~~ for Kennedy, most

Americans watched the debate on TV, rather than listening to their radios.

The second and third events happened in October. Both damaged

Nixon's hope of carrying the nation's African-American vote. First, a

Nixon campaign official said that if Nixon were elected, he would appoint
                                                    denied
an African-American to his cabinet. But Nixon then ~~denyed~~ any such

guarantee. His standing with African-American voters fell. Soon after
              famous
that, the ~~fameous~~ civil rights leader Martin Luther King, Jr., was

arrested. John Kennedy telephoned King's wife, Coretta. He sent his best
wishes
~~wishs~~ to the King family. Kennedy's brother, Robert, helped arrange

(Continues on next page)

King's release from jail. In response, King encouraged African-Americans

to vote for Kennedy. In fact, King's father, who had ~~earlyer~~ *earlier* said that he

would never vote for a Catholic (Kennedy was Catholic), announced that

he had changed his mind. When Election Day rolled around in November,

African-American voters turned out in record numbers. Kennedy won by

the smallest margin in history—only about 100,000 votes.

20 / Commonly Confused Words

This chapter explains:

1   Homonyms

2   Other confusing words

HOMONYMS

Homonyms are two or more words that have the same sound but different spellings and meanings.

The Big Four

The following four groups of words cause writers the most trouble.

its	*belonging to it*
it's	contraction of *it is*

- **It's** a shame that the shiny car lost **its** muffler and now roars like an old truck.

  (*It is* a shame that the shiny car lost the muffler *belonging to it* and now roars like an old truck.)

  Spelling hint: In ***it's***, the apostrophe takes the place of the *i* in the word *is*.

➤ Fill in each blank with either *its* or *it's*.

1. After five days, the jury finally reached _____*its*_____ verdict.

2. _____*It's*_____ hard to care about a job that's boring and pays poorly.

3. The railroad station has a beautiful sculpture in _____*its*_____ entryway.

4. Since Jennifer doesn't return your calls, _____*it's*_____ clear she is still upset with you.

5. The mall was almost empty after the storm because _____*its*_____ parking lot was still packed with snow.

➤ On each line, write a short sentence using the word shown.

1. *its* _____ *Answers will vary.* _____

2. *it's* _____

their	*belonging to them*
there	(1) *in* or *to that place*; (2) used with *is, are, was, were*, and other forms of the verb *to be*
they're	contraction of *they are*

- Our neighbors are health-food addicts. When we attend parties at **their** home, they serve pizza with broccoli florets on top. **They're** also fond of serving carrot juice. I hope they won't be offended when we don't go **there** very often.

(Our neighbors are health-food addicts. When we attend parties at the home *belonging to them*, they serve pizza with broccoli florets on top. *They are* also fond of serving carrot juice. I hope they won't be offended when we don't go *to that place* very often.)

Spelling hints: *There, where,* and *here*, which all end in *-ere*, all refer to places.

In *they're*, the apostrophe takes the place of the *a* in *are*.

➤ Fill in each blank with either *their, there,* or *they're*.

1. We finally found Roger's contact lens over ____there____ by the desk.

2. My aunt and uncle said ____they're____ going to quit smoking on New Year's Day.

3. The Hoffmans sold ____their____ restaurant and retired to a small town in Ohio.

4. My parents had to work late, but ____they're____ going to meet us for dinner later.

5. Our neighbors tie up ____their____ dog right outside my bedroom window.

➤ On each line, write a short sentence using the word shown.

1. *their* _____ *Answers will vary.* _____

2. *there* _____

3. *they're* _____

to	(1) used before a verb, as in "to serve"; (2) *so as to reach*
too	(1) *overly* or *extremely*; (2) *also*
two	*the number 2*

- I'll take these **two** letters **to** the post office for you, but you'll need **to** put more postage on one of them. It is **too** heavy for only one stamp.

(I'll take these 2 letters *so as to reach* the post office for you, but you'll need *to put* more postage on one of them. It is *overly* heavy for only one stamp.)

Spelling hint: *Too* has one *o*, and it **also** has another one.

➤ Fill in each blank with either *to, too,* or *two*.

1. After you help Rita with her homework, can you help me _____*too*_____ ?

2. Can you give me a ride _____*to*_____ campus tomorrow?

3. This omelet is _____*too*_____ big for one person.

4. I bought _____*two*_____ new tires, so my car should pass inspection.

5. One secret of happiness is learning _____*to*_____ need less instead of more.

➤ On each line, write a short sentence using the word shown.

1. *to* _____*Answers will vary.*_____

2. *too* _____

3. *two* _____

your	*belonging to you*
you're	contraction of *you are*

- **You're** going to need a first-aid kit and high boots for **your** camping trip.

(*You are* going to need a first-aid kit and high boots for the camping trip *belonging to you*.)

Spelling hint: In **you're**, the apostrophe takes the place of the *a* in *are*.

➤ Fill in each blank with either *your* or *you're*.

1. _____*You're*_____ not supposed to dial 911 except in an emergency.

2. _____*Your*_____ roommate left this note for you.

3. I'm afraid I don't appreciate _____*your*_____ sense of humor.

4. Once _____*you're*_____ on Payne Road, it is two miles to Tate's Strawberry Farm.

5. The principal is looking forward to meeting _____*your*_____ parents.

➤ On each line, write a short sentence using the word shown.

1. *your* _____*Answers will vary.*_____

2. *you're* _____

More Confusing Homonyms

brake   (1) *to slow* or *to stop;* (2) *the part of a vehicle used to slow or stop it*

break   (1) *to cause to come apart;* (2) *a temporary stop or rest*

    • If you get a **break** from your work, could you check the **brake** on my bike?

    Spelling hint: That bird can br**eak** a nut with its b**eak**.

➤ Fill in each blank with either *brake* or *break*.

1. No child will be able to _____*break*_____ this toy.

2. I took my lunch _____*break*_____ at 2:00 p.m.

3. The driver didn't _____*brake*_____ until he heard a police siren.

4. Poor _____*brake*_____s have caused numerous car accidents.

5. I had to _____*break*_____ the coconut with a hammer.

buy   *to purchase*

by   (1) *close to;* (2) *no later than;* (3) *through the action of*

    • **Buy** furniture from Sofas Inc. **by** the end of the year, and you won't have to pay until March.

    Spelling hint: I'd like to b**uy** something for **U**.

➤ Fill in each blank with either *buy* or *by*.

1. Why must you _____*buy*_____ such expensive designer jeans?

2. The beautiful mural in the lobby was painted _____*by*_____ a student.

3. An old dog was sleeping on the front porch _____*by*_____ the screen door.

4. We have to turn in our research papers _____*by*_____ the end of the month.

5. My sister is hoping to _____*buy*_____ a home of her own this year.

hear	(1) *to take in by ear;* (2) *to be informed*
here	*in* or *to this place*

      • There is so much noise in **here** that I can't **hear** the announcer's voice.

      Spelling hint: You h**ear** sounds with your **ear**.

➤ Fill in each blank with either *hear* or *here.*

    1. When I asked Sal where he had been, he replied, "_____*Here*_____ and there."

    2. I can _____*hear*_____ a cricket chirping somewhere in this house.

    3. Stay _____*here*_____ while I get the police!

    4. I _____*hear*_____ that there's a new Greek restaurant in town.

    5. The teacher yelled, "Bring that note right _____*here*_____!"

hole	*an empty or hollow spot*
whole	*complete* or *entire*

      • The joking boy told his mother that he hadn't eaten the **whole** doughnut; he had left the doughnut **hole**.

      Spelling hint: A **mole** (four letters) lives in a **hole** (four letters) in the ground.

➤ Fill in each blank with either *hole* or *whole.*

    1. My father insisted that he wanted to hear the _____*whole*_____ story.

    2. There's a huge _____*hole*_____ in our yard where a pool will be built.

    3. Slices of the pie sell for seventy-five cents each, but a _____*whole*_____ pie is only three dollars.

    4. Mary put the _____*whole*_____ egg in the batter even though the recipe said to use only the yolk.

    5. A tunnel in California is actually a long _____*hole*_____ in a huge tree.

knew	(the past tense of *know*) (1) *had understanding, knowledge, or information;* (2) *was or were familiar with*
new	(1) *the opposite of old;* (2) *having arrived recently;* (3) *unfamiliar*

      • The **new** girl in our class **knew** only two people here on her first day of school.

      Spelling hint: If you **kn**ew something, you had **kn**owledge.

➤ Fill in each blank with either *knew* or *new*.

1. The bride insisted on all _____*new*_____ furniture in her house.

2. We followed Jen, who _____*knew*_____ the way to the picnic grounds.

3. The _____*new*_____ fad in men's jeans is baggy and big.

4. Tanya _____*knew*_____ only two people at the party, and she didn't like either of them.

5. Although the woman insisted we had gone to high school together, her face was _____*new*_____ to me.

know   (1) *to have understanding, knowledge, or information;* (2) *to be familiar with*

no   (1) *not any;* (2) *the opposite of yes*

   • Puffing away on a cigar, the man claimed he didn't **know** there was a **no**-smoking sign above his head.

   Spelling hint: If you **kn**ow something, you have **kn**owledge.

➤ Fill in each blank with either *know* or *no*.

1. I _____*know*_____ how to handle rude callers—I hang up.

2. There are _____*no*_____ muffins left in the basket.

3. Glenn claims he doesn't _____*know*_____ how to wash dishes.

4. "_____*No*_____," replied the five-year-old's mother, "you may not have a slingshot."

5. Since you _____*know*_____ Alison better than I do, you should tell her about the dent in her car.

passed   (the past tense of *pass*) (1) *handed to;* (2) *went by;* (3) *completed successfully*

past   (1) *the time before the present;* (2) *by*

   • In the **past**, I have **passed** all my courses, but I may not pass them all this semester.

   Spelling hint: If you need a verb, use ***passed***. The *-ed* at its end shows it is the past tense of the verb *pass*.

➤ Fill in each blank with either *passed* or *past*.

1. Only five minutes have _____*passed*_____ since I last looked at the clock.

2. A bumblebee just flew _____*past*_____ my head.

3. Mick _____*passed*_____ his driver's test on the third try.

4. Unfortunately, one of the cars that Marylou _____*passed*_____ on the highway was a police car.

5. Life was not always as carefree in the _____*past*_____ as some people would like to believe.

peace	(1) *the absence of war;* (2) *calmness or quiet*
piece	*a separate part or portion of something*

  • Danny would not give the babysitter any **peace** until she gave him a **piece** of candy.

  Spelling hints: Have a **pie**ce of **pie**.
  We all want **pea**ce on **ear**th.

➤ Fill in each blank with either *peace* or *piece*.

1. One _____*piece*_____ of the torn love letter was missing.

2. A white dove is often used as a symbol of _____*peace*_____.

3. An open-faced sandwich is made with only one _____*piece*_____ of bread.

4. Broken _____*piece*_____s of antique glass were found by construction workers.

5. The leaders of the city gangs finally agreed to get along with each other in _____*peace*_____.

plain	(1) *not fancy;* (2) *obvious;* (3) *straightforward*
plane	a shortened form of *airplane*

  • It is very **plain** to anyone with eyes that there is too much ice on the wings of this **plane**.

  Spelling hint: The air**plane** landed in the wrong **lane**.

➤ Fill in each blank with either *plain* or *plane*.

1. We waited an hour on the runway before our _____*plane*_____ took off.

2. I prefer a _____*plain*_____ meal of meat and potatoes over any fancy French dish.

3. It soon became _____*plain*_____ to the FBI that the hijacker would not give up.

4. The student pilot took over the controls once the _____*plane*_____ was in the air.

5. Why can't instructions on tax forms be written in _____*plain*_____ English?

principal   (1) *main;* (2) *the person in charge of a school*
principle   *a guideline or rule*

> • Our **principal** believes in the **principle** of giving teachers a great deal of freedom.
>
> **Spelling hint:** Ideally a school princi**pal** should be a **pal**.

➤ Fill in each blank with either *principal* or *principle*.

1. My aunt is the _____*principal*_____ owner of a beauty shop on Mill Avenue.

2. I try to live by the _____*principle*_____ of treating others as I want to be treated.

3. Mr. Larson became _____*principal*_____ of Stanton High School after teaching there for years.

4. The _____*principal*_____ reason the Butlers are moving to California is to be near their grandchildren.

5. Our basketball coach taught us to follow the _____*principle*_____ of being gracious in defeat as well as in victory.

right   (1) *correct;* (2) *the opposite of left;* (3) *a legal or moral privilege*
write   *to form letters and words*

> • I had to **write** my name on the upper **right**-hand corner of each page of the test.
>
> **Spelling hint:** When you **w**rite, you use **w**ords.

➤ Fill in each blank with either *right* or *write*.

1. Please _____*write*_____ to me while you're away at college.

2. I always forget the _____*right*_____ way to fold a diaper.

3. After you pass a big shopping mall, take a _____*right*_____ turn.

4. Before starting my paper, I tried to _____*write*_____ down all the ideas that were in my head.

5. No one has the _____*right*_____ to eat and sleep in this house without doing some household chores.

threw   (the past tense of *throw*) *tossed*
through   (1) *into and out of;* (2) *finished*

> • As the inconsiderate couple drove **through** the tunnel, they **threw** paper cups out of their car.

Spelling hint: You may have a **rough** time getting th**rough** the reading.

➤ Fill in each blank with either *threw* or *through*.

1. My boss _____*threw*_____ a pile of work on my desk at 6 p.m.

2. Please hand in your tests when you are _____*through*_____ with them.

3. I walked _____*through*_____ the shoe store quickly; all the sneakers cost over $50.

4. When it began to rain, we quickly _____*threw*_____ a plastic cloth over our picnic table.

5. As we drove _____*through*_____ the state, we were disappointed by all the ugly billboards.

wear	*to have on* (as with clothing)
where	*in what place* or *to what place*

• Susan planned to **wear** her new sweater, but she couldn't remember **where** it was.

Spelling hint: You w**ear** a fancy earring on your **ear**.

➤ Fill in each blank with either *wear* or *where*.

1. _____*Where*_____ is the Hillside Hotel?

2. Bruce likes to _____*wear*_____ his baseball jersey to school.

3. Each year, I forget _____*where*_____ I stored my Christmas decorations.

4. Vanessa likes to _____*wear*_____ soft pinks, blues, and greens—she looks best in those colors.

5. Before he left on his trip, Earl told us _____*where*_____ to keep his mail and newspapers.

weather	*outside conditions* (rain, wind, temperature, etc.)
whether	*if;* used to introduce alternatives

• **Whether** or not the picnic is a success depends a great deal on the **weather**.

Spelling hint: W**eather** occurs on **earth**.

➤ Fill in each blank with either *weather* or *whether*.

1. Carmen hasn't decided _____*whether*_____ to go to the football game or to study tonight.

2. The _____*weather*_____ in England is rainy much of the time.

3. I wondered _____*whether*_____ I should take biology or chemistry as my science course.

4. Uncle Karl likes rainy, dark _____*weather*_____; it matches his personality.

5. I didn't know _____*whether*_____ I should call the teacher Mrs. Murray or Ms. Murray.

whose	*belonging to whom*
who's	contraction of *who is* or *who has*

- When the call came into the police station, the officer asked, "**Who's** willing to help a woman **whose** pet snake just escaped?"

Spelling hint: The apostrophe in ***who's*** takes the place of the *i* in *is* (for *who is*) or the *ha* in *has* (for *who has*).

➤ Fill in each blank with either *whose* or *who's*.

1. _____*Who's*_____ already seen the new Tom Hanks movie?

2. _____*Who's*_____ driving to the football game?

3. _____*Whose*_____ car is parked behind mine?

4. The chef _____*who's*_____ going to make the food for the party is famous for his tarts.

5. The butcher _____*whose*_____ shop burned down has decided to go back to college.

OTHER CONFUSING WORDS

a	used before words that begin with a consonant sound
an	used before words that begin with a vowel or a silent *h* (as in *hour*)

- Would you like **an** ice-cream cone or **a** shake?

➤ Fill in each blank with either *a* or *an*.

1. _____*An*_____ insect has six legs and a three-part body.

2. I left _____*a*_____ note on the kitchen counter saying when I'd be back.

3. Is that _____*an*_____ alligator you are petting in that photograph?

4. A hush fell over the circus audience when _____*a*_____ tightrope walker fell.

5. Although she worked hard, Louise was shocked to receive such _____*an*_____ honor as "Worker of the Year."

accept   (1) *to receive;* (2) *to agree to take;* (3) *to believe in*

except   (1) *excluding or leaving out;* (2) *but*

> • All the employees **except** the part-timers were willing to **accept** the new contract.

➤ Fill in each blank with either *accept* or *except*.

1. Mrs. Carlotti says she will _____*accept*_____ an appointment to the school board.

2. My daughter likes all types of food _____*except*_____ meat, fish, dairy products, and vegetables.

3. Whatever your decision is, I will _____*accept*_____ it.

4. All of my relatives attended our family reunion _____*except*_____ for an elderly aunt.

5. At the company dinner, Meredith will _____*accept*_____ the award on behalf of our department.

advice   *an opinion meant to be helpful*

advise   *to give an opinion meant to be helpful*

> • Never take the **advice** of someone who **advises** you to act against your conscience.

➤ Fill in each blank with either *advice* or *advise*.

1. "I _____*advise*_____ you to replace your fanbelt," the gas station attendant said.

2. Don't seek _____*advice*_____ from anybody you don't admire.

3. Employment experts _____*advise*_____ people to get training throughout their lives.

4. There's so much conflicting _____*advice*_____ about diet that it's no wonder people are confused about food.

5. My son's kindergarten teacher said the best _____*advice*_____ she could give parents is to read regularly to their children.

affect   *to influence*
effect   *a result*

> • Divorce **affects** an entire family, and its **effects**—both good and bad—last for years.

▶ Fill in each blank with either *affect* or *effect*.

1. Your actions _____*affect*_____ those around you, whether you're aware of it or not.

2. The child spattered red paint on the paper and then stepped back to admire the _____*effect*_____.

3. According to psychologists, the color of the clothes we wear _____*affect*_____s our moods.

4. What will be the economic _____*effect*_____s if the factory closes?

5. The referees did not allow the obnoxious behavior of some fans to _____*affect*_____ their decisions.

desert   *(1) to leave or abandon; (2) a dry region with little or no plant growth*

dessert   *a sweet course eaten at the end of a meal*

> • The children were willing to **desert** the TV set only when **dessert** was served.

▶ Fill in each blank with either *desert* or *dessert*.

1. For me, a real _____*dessert*_____ must contain chocolate.

2. As a result of irrigation, this area is now farmland instead of _____*desert*_____.

3. What causes a parent to _____*desert*_____ his or her children?

4. If I'm not very hungry, I skip the meal and eat _____*dessert*_____.

5. Certain medications can make your mouth feel as dry as a _____*desert*_____.

fewer   used for items that can be counted
less   used for general amounts

> • As our congregation ages, our church is left with **fewer** members and **less** financial support.

➤ Fill in each blank with either *fewer* or *less*.

1. By the 1920s, there were _____*fewer*_____ horses and more cars on the road.

2. When I get too little sleep, I have _____*less*_____ patience than usual.

3. Whose car had _____*fewer*_____ miles on it, yours or Carl's?

4. Two-percent milk has _____*less*_____ fat in it than whole milk.

5. Two-percent milk also contains _____*fewer*_____ calories.

loose	(1) *not tight;* (2) *free; not confined*
lose	(1) *to misplace;* (2) *to not win;* (3) *to be deprived of something one has had*

• If you don't fix that **loose** steering wheel, you could **lose** control of your car.

➤ Fill in each blank with either *loose* or *lose*.

1. I _____*lose*_____ my car keys at least once a week.

2. A _____*loose*_____ shutter was banging against the side of the house.

3. I always _____*lose*_____ when I play chess against my computer.

4. Clyde was warned that he would _____*lose*_____ his job if he were late to work one more time.

5. In our town, it's illegal to allow cats to run _____*loose*_____.

quiet	(1) *silent;* (2) *relaxing and peaceful*
quite	(1) *truly;* (2) *very;* (3) *completely*
quit	(1) *to stop doing something;* (2) *to resign from one's job*

• My boss was **quiet** after I said I might want to **quit** my job but that I wasn't **quite** sure.

➤ Fill in each blank with either *quiet, quite,* or *quit*.

1. The rain had frozen, and the roads were _____*quite*_____ slippery.

2. Let's spend a _____*quiet*_____ evening at home tonight.

3. The waitress began to take my dish, but I wasn't _____*quite*_____ done.

4. My speech teacher told me to _____*quit*_____ saying the word *like* so much, but like, what's wrong with that word?

5. We had enjoyed the glitter and noisy excitement of Las Vegas, but we were glad to be back home in our _____*quiet*_____ little town.

than   a word used in comparisons

then   (1) *at that time;* (2) *next*

- First Dad proved he was a better wrestler **than** I am; **then** he helped me improve.

➤ Fill in each blank with either *than* or *then*.

1. I scrubbed the potatoes, and _____*then*_____ I poked holes in them.

2. Crossword puzzles are more difficult _____*than*_____ word searches.

3. My parents were born in the 1930s. There were no TV sets or computers _____*then*_____.

4. You should learn about the candidates and _____*then*_____ go and vote.

5. The tiny family-owned shop is always more crowded _____*than*_____ the huge supermarket.

use   *to make use of*

used (to) *accustomed* or *in the habit*

- I am **used** to very spicy food, but when I cook for others, I **use** much less hot pepper.

   Spelling hint: Do not forget to include the *d* with "used to."

➤ Fill in each blank with either *use* or *used*.

1. After spending six years in Alaska, I am _____*used*_____ to cold weather.

2. Should I _____*use*_____ a paste or liquid wax on my car?

3. After you get married, will you _____*use*_____ your husband's last name?

4. Being the youngest of four girls, Elaine is _____*used*_____ to wearing hand-me-downs.

5. Because I _____*use*_____ so many stamps in my business, I buy self-sticking stamps.

were   the past tense of *are*

we're   contraction of *we are*

- **We're** going to visit the town in Florida where my grandparents **were** born.

➤ Fill in each blank with either *were* or *we're*.

1. Where _____*were*_____ you when I needed you?

2. _____*We're*_____ having a quiz on Friday.

3. Our relatives _____*were*_____ not surprised to hear of my brother's divorce.

4. I don't think _____*we're*_____ going to have to wait more than five minutes to get seated.

5. The Beatles _____*were*_____ once known as Long John and the Silver Beatles.

CHAPTER REVIEW

Answer each question by writing **T** (for *true*) or **F** (for *false*) in the space provided.

1. *True or false?* __F__   *It's* means "belonging to it."

2. *True or false?* __T__   *Their* means "belonging to them."

3. *True or false?* __F__   *Too* represents the number 2.

4. *True or false?* __T__   *Your* means "belonging to you."

5. *True or false?* __F__   *Right* is what we do with a pen or pencil.

6. *True or false?* __T__   *Than* is a word used to compare.

7. *True or false?* __T__   *Threw* is the past tense of *throw*.

8. *True or false?* __F__   *Where* means "to have on."

9. *True or false?* __T__   *Piece* refers to a part of something.

10. *True or false?* __T__   *Whose* means "belonging to whom."

Name_____ Section _____ Date _____

➤ Commonly Confused Words: Test 1

In each space, write the word in the margin that fits the sentence.

Your, You're
its, it's

1. _____*Your*_____ dog has lost _____*its*_____ flea collar.

Its, It's
brake, break

2. _____*It's*_____ always a good idea to take a _____*break*_____ after an hour of studying.

principal, principle
quiet, quite, quit

3. The _____*principal*_____ of my old high school _____*quit*_____ his job to stay home and take care of his grandchildren.

affect, effect
loose, lose

4. Despite the terrible _____*effect*_____s of the earthquake, people didn't _____*lose*_____ their sense of humor.

hear, here
than, then

5. Hawks can _____*hear*_____ very well, but their eyesight is even sharper _____*than*_____ their hearing.

Who's, Whose
know, no

6. _____*Who's*_____ going to tell Paul that there are _____*no*_____ more tickets to the concert?

Weather, whether
passed, past

7. _____*Whether*_____ you _____*passed*_____ the test or failed it, you will still pass the course.

peace, piece
hear, here

8. "Can we have some _____*peace*_____ and quiet _____*here*_____?" yelled the father of six children.

to, too, two
threw, through

9. My grandparents are going to spend _____*two*_____ months driving in a motor home _____*through*_____ parts of the country.

Their, There, They're
passed, past

10. _____*They're*_____ planning to drive right _____*past*_____ Disney World and go to the Everglades instead.

Name_____ Section _____ Date _____

Score: (Number right) _____ x 5 = _____%

➤ Commonly Confused Words: Test 2

In each space, write the word in the margin that fits the sentence.

were, we're
a, an

1. Tomorrow _____*we're*_____ going to buy _____*an*_____ afghan for Mom.

Its, It's
new, knew

2. _____*It's*_____ clear that the Raders didn't want us to have their _____*new*_____ address.

Whose, who's
hole, whole

3. _____*Whose*_____ baseball has made this large _____*hole*_____ in my garage window?

than, then
to, too, two

4. Not having enough water to drink is more dangerous _____*than*_____ having _____*too*_____ little food.

wear, where
peace, piece

5. Angela couldn't remember _____*where*_____ she had put the _____*piece*_____ of paper with Cory's phone number.

knew, new
threw, through

6. We _____*knew*_____ it would be difficult getting _____*through*_____ the holidays the year after Dad died.

weather, whether
wear, where

7. When I see what the _____*weather*_____ will be tomorrow, I'll decide what to _____*wear*_____ to work.

Than, Then
threw, through

8. Some teens began a fight in the restaurant. _____*Then*_____ the manager came and _____*threw*_____ them out.

right, write
peace, piece

9. It is not easy to _____*write*_____ a treaty that will bring a lasting _____*peace*_____ between the warring countries.

hole, whole
to, too, two

10. The _____*whole*_____ community is working together _____*to*_____ raise the money needed for the repair of the town's water tower.

Name_____ Section _____ Date _____

Score: (Number right) _____ x 10 = _____%

➤ Commonly Confused Words: Test 3

Each passage below contains **two** errors in commonly confused words. Find these errors and cross them out. Then write the correct words in the spaces provided.

1. When I visited a friend in Montreal, he said, "~~Their~~ is more French spoken here ~~then~~ English."

   a. _____*There*_____

   b. _____*than*_____

2. My journalism teacher says that ~~know~~ one has the ~~write~~ to tell lies about a person in the newspaper.

   a. _____*no*_____

   b. _____*right*_____

3. "Who are you ~~too~~ order me around?" asked the angry waiter. "~~Your~~ only the bartender! If you continue, I'm going to quit."

   a. _____*to*_____

   b. _____*You're*_____

4. The librarian gave quite good ~~advise~~ to us freshmen. She said we should get ~~use~~ to taking responsibility for getting our work done on time.

   a. _____*advice*_____

   b. _____*used*_____

5. In the ~~passed~~, I didn't realize that a single ~~peace~~ of cake could have several hundred calories and a great deal of fat. Now I choose my desserts more carefully.

   a. _____*past*_____

   b. _____*piece*_____

Name_____ Section _____ Date _____

Score: (Number right) _____ x 10 = _____%

➤ Commonly Confused Words: Test 4

Each passage below contains **two** errors in commonly confused words. Find these errors and cross them out. Then write the correct words in the spaces provided.

1. There is a good reason to keep your promises. If you ~~brake~~ them, ~~whose~~ going to accept your word in the future?

   a. _____ *break* _____

   b. _____ *who's* _____

2. As we ~~past~~ the same bank a second time, our two children in the back seat groaned. When we saw the bank again, we ~~new~~ we were lost.

   a. _____ *passed* _____

   b. _____ *knew* _____

3. "~~Your~~ going to have to speak loudly," said our host at the retirement home. "Many of us can't ~~here~~ very well."

   a. _____ *You're* _____

   b. _____ *hear* _____

4. It's plain that if you'd ~~by~~ fewer outfits, you'd pay ~~fewer~~ interest on your charge card bill each month.

   a. _____ *buy* _____

   b. _____ *less* _____

5. The workman casually tossed a hammer aside. ~~Than~~ he was horrified to see it break ~~threw~~ the stained-glass window he had just installed.

   a. _____ *Then* _____

   b. _____ *through* _____

Name_____ Section _____ Date _____

Score: (Number right) _____ x 5 = _____ %

➤ Commonly Confused Words: Test 5

The passage below contains **twenty** errors in commonly confused words. Find these errors and cross them out. Then in the spaces above the lines, write the corrections.

quite

Amelia Earhart was ~~quiet~~ famous during her lifetime for being a

daring pilot. After her death—or at least, after what was probably her

death—she became even more famous, as the center of a mystery. After

Earhart graduated from high school in 1915, she earned her pilot's

license and became something of a wanderer. When she flew across the

two

Atlantic Ocean with ~~too~~ men in 1928, the unusual trip made headlines. In

1937, Earhart began her boldest trip yet. With a navigator named Fred

plane

Noonan to assist her, she set out to fly around the world. Their ~~plain~~ took

where

off from Miami, Florida, in June. They flew to New Guinea, ~~wear~~ they

then   *an*

stopped to rest and make repairs. They ~~than~~ took off for ~~a~~ island in the

Pacific on July 1. But on that date, Earhart's radio messages stopped.

hear

Friends waiting to ~~here~~ from her became alarmed. A widespread search

by

~~buy~~ U.S. Navy ships turned up no sign of Earhart or Noonan. The

its

aircraft and ~~it's~~ crew had disappeared.

Since then, many stories have been told to explain what happened

to   *There*

~~too~~ Earhart. She may have simply run out of fuel over the Pacific. ~~Their~~

are plenty of places in the ocean deep enough to conceal a crashed

weather

airplane. Or perhaps she ran into unexpected bad ~~whether~~ that caused

lose

her to ~~loose~~ control of the flight. But another theory says that Earhart

(Continues on next page)

was murdered. In 1937, Japan was building strong military defenses on

were

some Pacific islands. Those defenses ~~we're~~ top secret, unknown to the

world until World War II. Some historians believe that Earhart was

forced down by Japanese troops who were afraid that she had spotted

their   *Whose*

~~there~~ military buildup. ~~Who's~~ theory is correct? After all these years, no

right   *piece*

one knows which is ~~write~~. Not a single ~~peace~~ of her aircraft has been

accept

found. Whichever explanation you ~~except~~, Amelia Earhart remains one of

past

the most famous pilots of the ~~passed~~.

21 / Capital Letters

This chapter presents the main uses of capital letters:

1 The first word in a sentence or direct quotation
2 The word "I" and people's names
3 Family names
4 Names of specific places and languages
5 Names of specific groups
6 Calendar items
7 Brand names
8 Titles
9 Names of specific school courses
10 Names of historic periods and well-known events
11 Opening and closing of a letter

THE FIRST WORD IN A SENTENCE OR DIRECT QUOTATION

Sentences begin with capital letters. The first word of a quoted sentence is also capitalized.

- The ice cream man said, "**T**ry a frozen banana bar. **T**hey're delicious."
- "**I**'m sure they are," Leo replied, "but they're too hard for my dentures."

In the last sentence, the word *but* is not capitalized because it does not start a sentence. It is part of the sentence that begins with the words *I'm sure they are.*

THE WORD "I" AND PEOPLE'S NAMES

Capitalize the word *I* and all parts of people's names.

- Because **I** was the first caller in the radio contest, **I** won a backstage pass to the **B**ruce **S**pringsteen concert.
- **I**'m fond of **C**armen, but **I** don't care for her husband.

Note: A title that comes before someone's name is treated as part of the name.

- **M**ayor **A**nderson spoke to **O**fficer **J**enkins after the burglary.

FAMILY NAMES

Capitalize a word that is used as a substitute for the name of a family member. Also capitalize words like *aunt*, *uncle*, and *cousin* when they are used as part of people's names.

- My biggest fan at the dirt bike competitions was **M**om.
- Go help **G**randfather carry those heavy bags.
- Phil is staying at **U**ncle Raymond's house for the holidays.

But: Do not capitalize words such as *mom* or *grandfather* when they come after possessive words such as *my, her,* or *our.*

- My grandmother lives next door to my parents.
- Phil and his uncle are both recovered alcoholics.

NAMES OF SPECIFIC PLACES AND LANGUAGES

In general, if a place is on a map (including a street map), capitalize it.

- Janice, who is the president of a large corporation in **B**oston, grew up on a farm near **K**okomo, **I**ndiana.

But: Places that are not specifically named should not be capitalized.

- Janice, who is the president of a large corporation in a big city, grew up on a farm near a small city.

The names of languages come from place names, so languages are also capitalized.

- The signs in the airport terminal were written in **S**panish, **E**nglish, and **J**apanese.

NAMES OF SPECIFIC GROUPS

Capitalize names of specific groups, such as races, religions, nationalities, companies, clubs, and other organizations.

- Edward, who is **P**olish-**A**merican, sometimes cooks **C**hinese dishes for his **N**orthside **C**hess **C**lub meetings.
- Arlene, the local president of **M**others **A**gainst **D**runk **D**riving, is a part-time real estate agent for **C**entury 21.

➤ Practice 1

Underline the words that need capitals. Then write those words with capitals in the spaces provided. The number of spaces shows how many capitals are missing in each sentence.

1. <u>my</u> roommate is so lazy that she once refused to get up for a fire drill.

    My

2. <u>the</u> instructor said, "<u>no</u> one knows for sure why dinosaurs became extinct."

    The   *No*

3. While she was in college, <u>anna</u> missed her family in <u>puerto</u> <u>rico</u>.

    Anna   *Puerto*   *Rico*

4. <u>if</u> <u>i'm</u> not back by midnight, call <u>detective</u> <u>harrison</u>.

    If   *I'm*   *Detective*   *Harrison*

5. My mother is <u>mexican</u> and a <u>baptist</u>, while <u>dad</u> is <u>italian</u> and a Catholic.

    Mexican   *Baptist*   *Dad*   *Italian*

6. The ice skating rink at <u>rockefeller</u> <u>center</u> is a popular <u>manhattan</u> attraction.

    Rockefeller   *Center*   *Manhattan*

7. My neighbor, <u>mrs.</u> Fraser, is a driver for <u>domino's</u> <u>pizza</u>.

    Mrs.   *Domino's*   *Pizza*

8. Several <u>asian</u> languages can be heard at a <u>chinese</u> market on <u>fifth</u> <u>avenue</u>.

    Asian   *Chinese*   *Fifth*   *Avenue*

9. My doctor, <u>dr.</u> <u>findley</u>, drove an old convertible to the medical convention.

    Dr.   *Findley*

10. But he flew to the <u>american</u> <u>medical</u> <u>association</u> meeting in <u>hawaii</u>.

    American   *Medical*   *Association*   *Hawaii*

CALENDAR ITEMS

Capitalize the names of days of the week, months, and holidays.

- At first, **T**hanksgiving was celebrated on the last **T**hursday in **N**ovember, but it was changed to the fourth **T**hursday of the month.

- My cousin wants a government job so that he'll get **V**eterans **D**ay and **P**residents' **D**ay off.

But: The names of the seasons (spring, summer, fall, winter) are not capitalized.

- The children love fall and winter because their favorite holidays occur then.

BRAND NAMES

Capitalize the brand name of a product, but not the kind of product it is.

- Every morning Tony has **M**inute **M**aid orange juice and **F**ruit **L**oops cereal with milk.
- My niece will eat only two kinds of meat: **P**erdue chicken and **O**scar **M**ayer hot dogs.

TITLES

Capitalize the titles of books, TV or stage shows, songs, magazines, movies, articles, poems, stories, papers, etc.

- Sitting in the waiting room, Dennis nervously paged through issues of *Life* and *People* magazines.
- Gwen wrote a paper titled "**A V**iew of **A**frican-**A**merican **W**omen" which was based on the book and movie *The Color Purple*.

Note: The words *the, of, a, an, and*, and other little, unstressed words are not capitalized when they appear in the middle of a title. That is why *of* is not capitalized in the title "A View of African-American Women."

> ※ For information on when to italicize (or underline) titles and when to set them off with quotation marks, see pages 377–378 in "Quotation Marks."

NAMES OF SPECIFIC SCHOOL COURSES

Capitalize the names of specific courses, including those with a number.

- This semester, Jody has **D**ance 101, **G**eneral **P**sychology, and **E**conomics 235.

But: The names of general subject areas are not capitalized.

- This semester, Jody has a gym class, a psychology course, and an economics course.

HISTORIC PERIODS AND WELL-KNOWN EVENTS

Capitalize the names of specific periods and famous events in history.

- During the **M**iddle **A**ges, only the nobility and the clegy could read and write.

- The act of protest in which 342 tea chests were thrown into the ocean came to be known as the **B**oston **T**ea **P**arty.

OPENING AND CLOSING OF A LETTER

Capitalize all words in the salutation of a letter.

- Dear Ms. Axelrod: • Dear Sir or Madam:

Capitalize only the first word of the closing of a letter.

- Sincerely yours,   • Yours truly,

➤ Practice 2

Underline the words that need capitals. Then write those words with capitals in the spaces provided. The number of spaces shows how many capitals are missing in each sentence.

1. Kara likes to eat cherry ices on hot summer days in <u>august</u>.

   August

2. Julius munched loudly on <u>fritos</u> in his history class.

   Fritos

3. Rodrigo has <u>biology</u> 101 at the same time that his brother has a literature class.

   Biology

4. My little niece often watches her videotape of *<u>beauty</u> and the <u>beast</u>*.

   Beauty   *Beast*

5. Grandpa heated up some <u>log</u> <u>cabin</u> syrup to pour over his <u>eggo</u> waffles.

   Log   *Cabin*   *Eggo*

6. Paul's essay titled "<u>an</u> embarrassing <u>moment</u>" appeared in the humor section of the student literary magazine.

   An   *Embarrassing*   *Moment*

7. Dear <u>sir</u>:
   Your microwave has been repaired and can be picked up after <u>labor</u> <u>day</u>.
   <u>sincerely</u>,
   Rick's Repairs

   Sir   *Labor*   *Day*   *Sincerely*

8. The story of Dracula has inspired such movies as *<u>love</u> at <u>first</u> <u>bite</u>*.

   Love   *First*   *Bite*

9. Last summer, I had time to read _newsweek_, the daily and _sunday_ newspaper, and several books by Stephen King, including _misery_.

   Newsweek   _Sunday_   _Misery_

10. The <u>great</u> <u>depression</u> began in 1929 on <u>black</u> <u>tuesday</u>, the day the stock market crashed.

   Great   _Depression_   _Black_   _Tuesday_

CHAPTER REVIEW

Answer each question by writing **T** (for _true_) or **F** (for _false_) in the space provided.

1. _True or false?_ ___F___ Capitalize the first word of a sentence but not the first word of a quoted sentence.

2. _True or false?_ ___T___ A title before a name (such as Senator Hartman) should be capitalized.

3. _True or false?_ ___F___ Capitalize the names of seasons of the year as well as days of the week and months of the year.

4. _True or false?_ ___T___ Capitalize the brand name of a product, but not the kind of product it is.

5. _True or false?_ ___F___ Names of specific places should be capitalized, but languages should not be capitalized.

6. _True or false?_ ___T___ Titles of books and magazines are capitalized.

7. _True or false?_ ___T___ Names of specific school courses should be capitalized, but not names of general subject areas.

8. _True or false?_ ___F___ The opening of a letter should be capitalized, but not the closing.

Name_____   Section _____   Date _____

Score: (Number right) _____ x 5 = _____ %

➤ Capital Letters: Test 1

Underline the words that need capitalizing. Then write those words correctly in the spaces provided. The number of spaces shows how many capitals are missing in each sentence.

1. Although Jessica lives on <u>hollywood</u> <u>boulevard</u>, she claims she has never run into a movie star.

   a. _Hollywood_   b. _Boulevard_

2. Dear <u>sir</u>: Please cancel my subscription to the *Bloomington Tribune*. Sincerely yours, Clint Hart

   c. _Sir_

3. After <u>world war</u> II, Europe was in great need of assistance.

   d. _World_   e. _War_

4. The teacher asked us to write a paper titled "<u>the dangers</u> of <u>television</u>."

   f. _The_   g. _Dangers_   h. _Television_

5. One of the best-known protest songs of the 1960s is "Blowin' in the <u>wind</u>."

   i. _Wind_

6. Pedro is a member of the <u>hispanic student council</u> at his community college.

   j. _Hispanic_   k. _Student_   l. _Council_

7. Last summer, <u>mom</u> and <u>i</u> visited my aunt in New Orleans.

   m. _Mom_   n. _I_

8. The loud explosion this morning took place in my <u>chemistry</u> 101 lab.

   o. _Chemistry_

9. For dinner, Ellen bought a roast beef sandwich at <u>arby's</u>, a salad at <u>wendy's</u>, and a bottle of soda at the supermarket.

   p. _Arby's_   q. _Wendy's_

10. Tamara looked through the latest issue of *<u>sports illustrated</u>* for articles about her favorite football team, the Dallas <u>cowboys</u>.

    r. _Sports_   s. _Illustrated_   t. _Cowboys_

Name_____ Section _____ Date _____

Score: (Number right) _____ x 5 = _____%

➤ Capital Letters: Test 2

Underline the words that need capitalizing. Then write those words correctly in the spaces provided. The number of spaces shows how many capitals are missing in each sentence.

1. Vic adds <u>kellogg's</u> corn flakes to his yogurt to make it crunchy.

   a. ___*Kellogg's*___

2. Before moving into her new house, Lynn scrubbed the floors with <u>lysol</u> and washed the windows with vinegar and water.

   b. ___*Lysol*___

3. Brian foolishly complained to the police officer, "<u>but</u> sir, I never stop at that stop sign."

   c. ___*But*___

4. <u>my</u> friend Keshia enjoys <u>algebra</u> 101 but hates her gym class.

   d. ___*My*___   e. ___*Algebra*___

5. A belly dancer is the entertainment at the <u>moroccan</u> restaurant in <u>chicago</u>.

   f. ___*Moroccan*___   g. ___*Chicago*___

6. <u>bridget</u> wondered why her eleven-month-old niece needed tiny <u>reebok</u> high-tops.

   h. ___*Bridget*___   i. ___*Reebok*___

7. For our religion course, we visited <u>moslem</u> and <u>jewish</u> houses of worship.

   j. ___*Moslem*___   k. ___*Jewish*___

8. Miguel teaches <u>geology</u> 300 at a community college in <u>brooklyn</u>.

   l. ___*Geology*___   m. ___*Brooklyn*___

9. After the divorce, my mother and <u>i</u> went to live with <u>uncle</u> <u>gary</u> in Houston.

   n. ___*I*___   o. ___*Uncle*___   p. ___*Gary*___

10. Veterans <u>day</u>, observed in the United States on <u>november</u> 11, was originally called <u>armistice</u> <u>day</u>.

   q. ___*Day*___   r. ___*November*___   s. ___*Armistice*___   t. ___*Day*___

Name_____ Section _____ Date _____

Score: (Number right) _____ x 10 = _____%

➤ Capital Letters: Test 3

Underline the **two** words that require capital letters in each short passage below. Then write those words (with capital letters) in the spaces provided.

1. Last <u>may</u>, my grandmother visited Mexico City. She bought a beautiful <u>mexican</u> shawl there and claims she has never been cold since.

   a. _____*May*_____

   b. _____*Mexican*_____

2. Because <u>uncle</u> Paul has an evening class on <u>thursdays</u>, he often stays on campus for dinner. He usually packs a sandwich to eat in the student union.

   a. _____*Uncle*_____

   b. _____*Thursdays*_____

3. Roald Dahl, a <u>british</u> author, wrote some marvelous children's books in which adults get punished for their evil ways. *James and the <u>giant</u> Peach* is one of his best.

   a. _____*British*_____

   b. _____*Giant*_____

4. "The <u>stone</u> Age," said Professor Woo, "was a long period when all tools were made of stone." He continued, "<u>it</u> is the earliest known period of human culture."

   a. _____*Stone*_____

   b. _____*It*_____

5. During the class break in <u>sociology</u> 102, I asked Doris why she was moving out of her apartment. She replied, "<u>my</u> neighbors in the apartment above me are as quiet as mice—mice in combat boots, that is."

   a. _____*Sociology*_____

   b. _____*My*_____

Name _____ Section _____ Date _____

Score: (Number right) _____ x 10 = _____ %

➤ Capital Letters: Test 4

Underline the **two** words that require capital letters in each short passage below. Then write those words (with capital letters) in the spaces provided.

1. Nora is taking education courses at Rider <u>college</u>. She plans to become a high school <u>english</u> teacher.

   a. _____*College*_____

   b. _____*English*_____

2. A sleek black sports car with tinted windows came to a sudden stop on Spruce <u>street</u>. A woman and her <u>german</u> shepherd then came out of a pet store and hopped into the back seat.

   a. _____*Street*_____

   b. _____*German*_____

3. Jeremy liked his new red Nike sneakers. He told his mom, "<u>no</u> one in the world can catch me when I wear these, except maybe for you and <u>dad</u>."

   a. _____*No*_____

   b. _____*Dad*_____

4. Michael Jackson was eleven when the first <u>jackson</u> 5 recording was released in <u>november</u> of 1969. It was for the song "I Want You Back," which sold two million copies in its first six weeks.

   a. _____*Jackson*_____

   b. _____*November*_____

5. Sally and Rose have very different tastes in movies. While Rose enjoys films such as <u>*cliffhanger*</u>, Sally likes quieter ones such as *Howard's End*. They even differ in what they eat while while watching the movie. Rose loves to bring little red boxes of <u>sunkist</u> raisins, but Sally prefers popcorn.

   a. _____*Cliffhanger*_____

   b. _____*Sunkist*_____

Name_____ Section _____ Date _____

Score: (Number right) _____ x 5 = _____%

➤ Capital Letters: Test 5

The following selection contains **twenty** errors. Fifteen words need capitalizing; five words are capitalized that should not be. Cross out each wrong letter, and then write the correction above the line.

Dear New Pen Pal,

My name is Sarita Greene. I am a student at a *c*Community *c*College and hope to become a nurse. This semester I'm taking a *s*Sociology course and *P*psychology 201. I also work part-time as a salesperson at *T*thrift *D*drugstore. My favorite color is blue, and one of my favorite books is *I* *K*know *Why the Caged Bird Sings*, by *M*maya Angelou.

From the day after *C*christmas until the first day of *J*january, my family, like many African-American families, celebrates a holiday called Kwanzaa. The holiday, whose name comes from an African language called *S*swahili, was first held to celebrate the harvest of farm crops. It now celebrates family members coming together and remembering their *A*african ancestors.

This is how we celebrate Kwanzaa in our home. I braid my hair, and Mama's too, into cornrows. She and *I*i and my sisters all wear traditional African clothes. For seven days, we do not eat until sundown. *A*at that time, our relatives and friends come to our house to eat collard greens, catfish, black-eyed peas, buttermilk cornbread, and sweet potato pie. We drink to the memory of our ancestors. Sometimes *U*uncle *B*barry plays the drums, my *g*Grandfather plays the saxophone, and everybody dances. And

(Continues on next page)

on every night, we remember one of the seven principles of the holiday.

The principles are ideals like unity, self-determination, creativity, and

f
Faith. But my favorite time of Kwanzaa is when grandfather tells us
                                                           G

stories about the family's past.

I hope you will write me a letter soon telling me about yourself.

S
Sincerely,

Sarita

22 / Commas

This chapter explains six main uses of the comma:

1   Between items in a series

   • The baby needs a bottle, extra diapers, a blanket, and a rattle.

2   After introductory material

   • Although she is 70, my grandmother can do thirty pushups.

3   Around words that interrupt the flow of a sentence

   • The box of crackers, if I remember correctly, is on the nightstand.

4   Between complete thoughts connected by a joining word

   • The menu was six pages long, but my fussy son still could not find anything to order.

5   For words of direct address and short expressions

   • Children, watch your step.
   • Oh, I'd better turn off the oven before leaving the house.

6   In dates, addresses, and letters

   • Our address as of January 1, 1995, has been 26 Penn Road, Olympia, WA 98503.
   • Dear Kate,

      I hope you will join me for a very special dinner next weekend.

      Love,
      Count Dracula

A comma often marks a slight pause, or break, in a sentence. These pauses or breaks occur at the point where one of the six main comma rules applies. When you read a sentence aloud, you can often hear the points where slight pauses occur.

In general, use a comma only when a comma rule applies or when a comma is otherwise needed to help a sentence read clearly.

BETWEEN ITEMS IN A SERIES

The comma is used to separate three or more items in a series.

- The school cafeteria has learned not to serve broccoli, spinach, or Brussels sprouts.
- The letters *k*, *j*, *x*, *z*, and *q* are the least frequently used letters of the alphabet.
- Our tasks for the party are blowing up balloons, setting the table, and planning the music.

Note: Do not use a comma when the series contains only two items.

- Our tasks for the party are blowing up balloons and planning the music.

➤ **Practice 1**

In the following sentences, insert commas between items in a series.

1. President Thomas Jefferson was also an architect, inventor, and scientist.

2. Mark's summer jobs have included being a waiter, a dog walker, and a birthday party clown.

3. The student driver went through a stop sign, steered off the side of the road, and ended up in a ditch.

4. Creating booby traps, reading other people's mail, and annoying people are my brother's hobbies.

5. The zookeeper stuffed vitamins into raw meat for the lions, put fresh hay in the stables for the horses, and planned a lecture for a visiting student group.

➤ **Practice 2** *Answers will vary.*

Complete the following three sentences with a series of three or more items.

1. The little boy's pockets contained _____ *marbles, chewing gum, and* _____ *rubber bands.*

2. Three people I have had trouble relating to are my _____ *grandmother,* _____ *my older sister, and my boss.*

3. _____ *Working out, watching sports on TV,* _____ and _____ *reading* _____ are three of my favorite activities.

AFTER INTRODUCTORY MATERIAL

A comma is used to separate introductory material from the rest of the sentence.

- After taking a hot shower, Vince fell asleep on the sofa.
- When covered with chocolate syrup, frozen yogurt is no diet food.
- As the movie credits rolled, we stretched and headed toward the exits.

Read each of the above sentences aloud. You will probably pause slightly at the end of the introductory material, where the comma belongs.

Note: Short introductory material need not be followed by a comma.

- Today our cat returned home with a live baby rabbit.
- While driving I listen to self-help audio tapes.

➤ Practice 3

Insert commas after the introductory material in each of the following sentences.

1. By the end of the day, our math teacher is usually covered in chalk dust.
   ^

2. Throughout the horserace, the announcer's voice kept getting louder and higher.
   ^

3. Decorated in green flowers, the Girl Scout float won first prize.
   ^

4. When I put down the fascinating book, I realized that three hours had passed.
   ^

5. Stacked in the middle of the room, the toy blocks formed a mountain of colorful shapes.
   ^

➤ Practice 4   *Answers will vary.*

Complete the following three sentences. Remember to include a comma after the introductory material in each sentence.

1. Because Ramon was tired of studying , *he went for a walk.* _____

   _____

2. Looking under the bed , *I could see three pairs of shoes.* _____

   _____

3. When the alarm sounded , *everyone hurried toward the exits.* _____

   _____

AROUND WORDS THAT INTERRUPT THE FLOW OF A SENTENCE

Sentences sometimes contain material that interrupts the flow of thought. Such words and word groups should be set off from the rest of the sentence by commas. For example:

- Our station wagon**,** which has stickers from every state we've visited**,** seems like part of the family.

If you read this sentence out loud, you can hear that the words *which has stickers from every state we've visited* interrupt the flow of thought.

Here are some other examples of sentences with interrupters:

- Liza**, who was wearing a new dress,** yelled at the waiter who spilled wine on her.
- The waiter**, however,** was not very apologetic.
- The restaurant manager**, afraid that Liza might cause a scene,** rushed to help.

More About Interrupters

A word group that identifies another word in the sentence is not an interrupter. It is needed for the full meaning of the sentence and should not be set off with commas.* For instance, consider the boldfaced words in the following sentences:

- The man **who came to the party with Joy** says he was kidnapped by aliens.
- Harvey**, who came to the party with Joy,** says he was kidnapped by aliens.

In the first sentence, the boldfaced words are needed to identify the man. Without them, we would not know who said he was kidnapped by aliens. Such essential words are not interrupters and should not be set off with commas. In the second sentence, however, we know who said he was kidnapped by aliens even without the boldfaced words. (It was Harvey.) In that case, the boldfaced words are *not* essential to the main message of the sentence. So in the second sentence, *who came to the party with Joy* is an interrupter and should be set off by commas.

To find out whether a word group is an interrupter, try reading the sentence without it. The first sentence above would then read: "The man says he was kidnapped by aliens." This version makes us ask, "Which man?" The boldfaced words are essential to answer that question. If we read the second sentence without the boldfaced words, we would not be omitting essential information: "Harvey says he was kidnapped by aliens."

*Grammar books sometimes refer to interrupters as "nonrestrictive elements" and essential descriptions as "restrictive elements."

➤ Practice 5

Four of the following five sentences contain interrupters. Insert commas around the interrupting word groups. One sentence includes a word group that provides essential information and should not be enclosed by commas.

1. Penguins' wings,which are short and thick,are not designed for flight.

2. King Arthur,according to legend,will return some day to rule Britain.

3. My boss,it is rumored,is about to be fired.

4. The woman who sat in front of me at the concert was wearing strong perfume.

5. Grandfather likes to joke that his hometown,which has only one traffic light and two gas stations,could be missed if a traveler blinked.

➤ Practice 6   *Answers will vary.*

Write three sentences using the suggested interrupters. Add words both before and after the interrupting words. Then add the necessary commas.

1. Use the words *who is my best friend* in the middle of a sentence.

   Lisa, who is my best friend, always has time to listen to my problems.

   _____

2. Use the words *which is my favorite snack* in the middle of a sentence.

   Frozen yogurt, which is my favorite snack, is often low in calories.

   _____

3. Use the words *wearing an all-white outfit* in the middle of a sentence.

   Dolores, wearing an all-white outfit, posed at the top of the stairs.

   _____

BETWEEN COMPLETE THOUGHTS CONNECTED BY A JOINING WORD

When two complete thoughts are combined into one sentence by a joining word, a comma is used before the joining word. These are the joining words: *and, but, so, or, nor, for,* and *yet.*

- Gabe eats like a horse, **but** he is pencil-thin.

Each part of the sentence is a complete thought: *Gabe eats like a horse. He is pencil-thin.* The two complete thoughts are combined into one sentence by the joining word *but.*

Here are more sentences in which two complete thoughts are connected by a joining word:

- The student didn't want to dissect a frog, **so** he took chemistry instead of biology.
- I studied for the exam all night, **and** then I slept through it this morning.

A Note About Joining Words

Don't add a comma just because a sentence contains a joining word. Use a comma only when the joining word comes between two complete thoughts. Each of the two thoughts must have its own subject and verb.

- *Comma:* My neighbor's dog dislikes children, **and it hates** the mailman.

  Each complete thought has a subject and a verb: *dog dislikes* and *it hates.*

- *No comma:* My neighbor's dog dislikes children **and hates** the mailman.

  This sentence expresses only one complete thought: the subject *dog* has two verbs, *dislikes* and *hates.*

  ※ The use of a comma between two complete thoughts connected by a joining word is also discussed in "Sentence Types," pages 147–148.

➤ Practice 7

Insert a comma between the two complete thoughts (and before the joining word) in each of the following sentences.

1. The smoke detector was buzzing‸and we could smell something burning.

2. A severe storm was forecast‸so many people bought candles and flashlights.

3. The roast should have been ready‸but the cook had forgotten to turn on the oven.

4. Most spiders and snakes are absolutely harmless‸yet they still frighten me.

5. Members of the marching band sold oranges to raise funds for their trip to Florida‸and they sold mittens for their trip to Alaska.

➤ Practice 8   *Answers will vary.*

1. Write a sentence with two complete thoughts that are joined with a comma and the word *but.* _____

   _____

2. Write a sentence with two complete thoughts that are joined with a comma and the word *so.* _____

   _____

3. Write a sentence with two complete thoughts that are joined with a comma and the word *and*. _____

_____

FOR WORDS OF DIRECT ADDRESS AND SHORT EXPRESSIONS

For words of direct address: Use commas to set off names or other words used to address directly the person or people being spoken to.

- You, Mr. Gimble, are the lucky winner of a ballpoint pen.
- Ladies and gentlemen, the sword-swallower is unable to perform tonight due to a bad sore throat.

For short expressions: Use commas to set off words such as *well, yes, no,* and *oh.*

- No, you cannot have a raise.
- Well, I thought I would at least ask.

IN DATES, ADDRESSES, AND LETTERS

Within a date: Place commas after the the day of the week (if used), the date, and the year:

- Friday, October 13, 1995, is the date of our wedding.
- On March 7, 1876, Alexander Graham Bell received a patent for the telephone.

In an address within a sentence: Place a comma after each part of the address *except* between the state and the ZIP code.

- Send your comments about *Basic English Brushup* to Townsend Press, Pavilions at Greentree, Suite 408, Marlton, NJ 08053.

In informal letters: Place a comma after the opening and closing.

- Dear Grandma,   • With love,   • Fondly,

Note: In business letters, a colon is used after the opening, but a comma is still used after the closing.

- Dear Mr. Cramer: • Dear Homeowner: • Yours truly,

➤ Practice 9

Insert commas where needed a) to set off words of direct address and short expressions and b) in dates and addresses.

1. What are you studying at this time of day, Margaret?

2. Well, look who's coming in our direction.

3. My sister lives at 2 Dog Lane,Canine,SC 09999.
   <u> </u>^<u> </u>^

4. It's about time that you woke up,sleepy head,and got out of bed.
   <u> </u>^<u> </u>^

5. San Franciscans were surprised on the morning of April 18, 1906, by a major earthquake.
   <u> </u>^<u> </u>^

➤ Practice 10

Complete each sentence as indicated, inserting commas where needed.

1. _____ *(Answers will vary.)* _____ is my home address.
   (Fill in your address.)

2. _____ *(Answers will vary.)* _____ is the date that I was born.
   (Fill in your complete date of birth)

3. Dear <u>Susan,   </u>

   Meet me at the fountain in the mall tomorrow.

   > *Sincerely,* <u>   </u>

   > *Marco*

   (Complete the heading of the above letter with the word *Susan*, and add as a closing the word *Sincerely*.)

⁂ Another use of the comma is to set off direct quotations from the rest of a sentence, as explained in "Quotation Marks" on pages 373–375.

CHAPTER REVIEW

Answer each question by writing **T** (for *true*) or **F** (for *false*) in the space provided.

1. *True or false?* __T__ When reading out loud, you often hear a pause where a comma is written.

2. *True or false?* __T__ When three or more items are listed in a sentence, you should separate them with a comma.

3. *True or false?* __F__ When a comma separates two complete thoughts, it is placed after the joining word *and, but, so, for, or, nor,* or *yet.*

4. *True or false?* __T__ No commas are needed in the sentence "The man who is my boss just resigned."

5. *True or false?* __T__ Two commas are needed in the sentence "Howard who was my boss just resigned."

6. *True or false?* __F__ In addresses, always use a comma between the state and the ZIP code.

Name_____ Section _____ Date _____

Score: (Number right) _____ x 10 = _____%

➤ Commas: Test 1

On the lines provided, write the word or words in each sentence that need to be followed by a comma. Include each missing comma as well.

1. Peering through the bars of its cage the canary watched the cat closely.

   _____*cage,*_____

2. Annie has an older brother so all her hand-me-down baby clothes were blue.

   _____*brother,*_____

3. India ink despite its name comes from China or Egypt.

   _____*ink, . . . name,*_____

4. Hey get away from my bike!

   _____*Hey,*_____

5. Some of the dinner guests brought a houseplant a bunch of flowers or a bottle of wine to the hostess.

   ___*houseplant, . . . flowers,*___

6. It is important fellow union members to stick together during this strike.

   ___*important, . . . members,*___

7. Most Eskimos live in modern housing but igloos can still be found in some places.

   _____*housing,*_____

8. Five years after the hurricane most of the damaged houses had been repaired.

   _____*hurricane,*_____

9. The sick child a blanket draped over his shoulders slumped in his chair.

   ___*child, . . . shoulders,*___

10. False names that students have used when substitute teachers were in class include Sandy Beech Frank Furter and Ben Dover.

    ___*Beech, . . . Furter,*___

Name_____ Section _____ Date _____

Score: (Number right) _____ x 10 = _____ %

➤ Commas: Test 2

In each space, write the letter of the one comma rule that applies to the sentence. Then insert one or more commas where they belong in the sentence.

> **a** Between items in a series
> **b** After introductory material
> **c** Around interrupting words
> **d** Before a word that joins two complete thoughts
> **e** To set off words of direct address and short expressions
> **f** In dates, addresses, and letters

_a_ 1. My sister won't leave the house without her makeup, her charge card,and her boyfriend.

_b_ 2. Glaring around the room,the professor demanded silence.

_e_ 3. This bar,my friends,is a non-smoking area.

_d_ 4. I heard a siren,so I glanced up at my rear-view mirror.

_c_ 5. The campers,unused to the silence of the forest,found it hard to sleep.

_a_ 6. A fully grown porcupine has tens of thousands of quills on its head, back,sides,and tail.

_f_ 7. The final exam will be given on Wednesday, June 2.

_e_ 8. Yes,I have dated both Louise and her sister.

_b_ 9. At any given moment,there are about 1,800 thunderstorms taking place on Earth.

_d_ 10. I hopped out of the tub and ran to the phone,but the caller had hung up.

Name_____ Section _____ Date _____

➤ Commas: Test 3

On the lines provided, write out the **two** parts of each passage that need one or more commas. Include the missing commas as well.

1. After working for many months on a project Jesse finally got a vacation. He has spent his time listening to the rain trying to read and wondering what's going on at the office.

   a. _____*project, Jesse*_____

   b. _____*rain, trying to read, and*_____

2. Mammals have red blood and insects have yellow blood. The blood of lobsters believe it or not is blue.

   a. _____*blood, and*_____

   b. _____*lobsters, believe it or not,*_____

3. Tony Jane and Kareem studied for the biology final together. Each of them however got a different grade on the test.

   a. _____*Tony, Jane, and*_____

   b. _____*them, however,*_____

4. When I saw the return address on the letter my brother received I became very curious. The address was The White House 1600 Pennsylvania Avenue Washington DC 20500.

   a. _____*received, I*_____

   b. _____*House, 1600 Pennsylvania Avenue, Washington, DC*_____

5. Our first son was born on July 4 1990. We named him after his Uncle Sam and my wife painted an American flag on his bedroom wall.

   a. _____*July 4, 1990.*_____

   b. _____*Sam, and*_____

➤ Commas: Test 4

On the lines provided, write out the **two** parts of each passage that need one or more commas. Include the missing commas as well.

1. John Wilkes Booth began drinking at about three in the afternoon on April 14 1865. He left a bar at 10:15 went next door to Ford's Theater and shot President Lincoln.

   a. _____ *April 14, 1865.* _____

   b. _____ *10:15, went next door to Ford's Theater, and* _____

2. Our math teacher Ms. Jackson gives interesting tests. The problems are practical so they show the value of math in everyday life.

   a. _____ *teacher, Ms. Jackson, gives* _____

   b. _____ *practical, so* _____

3. Emily Dickinson one of America's greatest poets had only seven poems published during her lifetime. After her death in 1886 over a thousand of her poems were found in a bureau.

   a. _____ *Dickinson, one of American's greatest poets, had* _____

   b. _____ *1886, over* _____

4. The two brothers are close friends but they disagree about nearly everything. They have entirely different views on politics religion money and women.

   a. _____ *friends, but* _____

   b. _____ *politics, religion, money, and* _____

5. A study of two hundred of the Grimm brothers' fairy tales reveals an unequal treatment of the sexes. The stories for example include twenty-three evil female witches. In contrast to all the female witches only two wicked male witches are mentioned.

   a. _____ *stories, for example, include* _____

   b. _____ *witches, only* _____

Name_____ Section _____ Date _____

Score: (Number right) _____ x 5 = _____ %

➤ Commas: Test 5

Insert commas where needed in the following passage. **Twenty** commas are missing.

When a Spanish explorer by the name of Cortez marched into Mexico in 1520, he found Aztec Indians living there. The Aztecs introduced Cortez to a dark beverage that they called chocolate. Made from the beans of the cacao tree, chocolate was by itself bitter-tasting. But the Aztecs made it tasty by mixing it with honey, vanilla, and hot peppers. Yes, they actually used hot peppers! The mighty Montezuma, who was emperor of the Aztecs, drank his chocolate from golden mugs. To prove how wealthy he was, the emperor had the mugs thrown away after just one use.

Cortez took cacao beans back with him to Spain, and the drink became popular there. Instead of mixing chocolate with honey, the Spanish mixed it with sugar, but they kept the vanilla and hot peppers in the recipe. The taste for chocolate spread to England, France, and Italy, and the city of London had at least one chocolate shop by 1657.

After being used only as a hot drink until the 1840s, chocolate made a giant leap forward. Someone figured out a way to form the ground cacao beans and sugar into bars. Those first chocolate bars, however, were too bitter for many people. A solution was finally found when a Swiss man added milk to chocolate in 1875. The resulting milk chocolate bars were sweet, mild, and delicious. Chocolate is now one of the world's favorite

(Continues on next page)

flavors. Entire cookbooks are devoted to chocolate, and "chocoholic" clubs
^
offer help to people who eat too much of the delicious treat.

23 / Apostrophes

This chapter explains the two main uses of the apostrophe:

1   In contractions, to replace one or more letters that have been left out

   • I can't believe I ate the whole thing.

2   In possessives, to show that something belongs to someone or something

   • The diner's broken sign reads, "Goo Food."

This chapter also explains when *not* to use apostrophes:

1   In plurals and verbs

   • Two dogs are fighting outside.
   • Lyle collects old record album covers.

2   In possessive pronouns

   • His house is not as well-built as ours is.

THE APOSTROPHE IN CONTRACTIONS

A **contraction** is formed when two words are combined to make a new word. The apostrophe takes the place of the letter or letters omitted in forming the contraction. It goes where the missing letters used to be. For example, consider the contraction *wasn't*.

   • was + not = wasn't

Wasn't is a contraction of the two words *was not*. The apostrophe takes the place of the *o* in *not*.

Here are some other common contractions:

> I + am = **I'm** (the letter *a* in *am* has been left out)
> it + is = **it's** (the *i* in *is* has been left out)
> does + not = **doesn't** (the *o* in *not* has been left out)
> do + not = **don't** (the *o* in *not* has been left out)
> she + will = **she'll** (the *wi* in *will* has been left out)
> you + would = **you'd** (the *woul* in *would* has been left out)
> will + not = **won't** (*o* replaces *ill*; the *o* in *not* has been left out)

Contractions are commonly used in everyday speech and writing, as seen in the following passage:

Isn't this lab work going to take longer than we expected? *Shouldn't* we ask the instructor for help? Maybe he *didn't* give us the right instruments, or he *doesn't* realize how long it takes to dissect a frog. Wait, I *don't* think you were supposed to make that cut. Now we definitely *won't* get finished on time.

➤ Practice 1

Combine the following words into contractions.

1. we + are   =   *we're*   6. they + will =   *they'll*
2. you + will   =   *you'll*   7. did + not   =   *didn't*
3. could + not =   *couldn't*   8. you + are   =   *you're*
4. what + is   =   *what's*   9. can + not   =   *can't*
5. I + would   =   *I'd*   10. who + is   =   *who's*

➤ Practice 2

In the spaces provided, write the contractions of the words in parentheses.

1. The thief *(was not)* ____*wasn't*____ considered dangerous, so the judge *(did not)* ____*didn't*____ give him a jail sentence.

2. The water at that end of the lake *(is not)* ____*isn't*____ deep, but I *(do not)* ____*don't*____ think the children should play by themselves.

3. *(He would)* ____*He'd*____ rather take that children's medicine because *(it is)* ____*it's*____ covered with a fruity coating. The adult version is bitter.

4. I *(would not)* ____*wouldn't*____ force a child to take music lessons—music *(should not)* ____*shouldn't*____ be a punishment.

5. *(I would)* ____*I'd*____ like to visit my parents soon, but I *(have not)* ____*haven't*____ got any vacation time left.

➤ Practice 3

Write two sentences that include contractions. Use a different contraction in each sentence.

1. _____*Answers will vary.*_____

_____

2. _____

_____

THE APOSTROPHE IN POSSESSIVES

To show that something belongs to someone, we could say, for example, *the stereo owned by Rita*. But it's much simpler to say:

- *Rita's stereo*

To make a word possessive, add an apostrophe plus an *s*. To help you decide which word to make possessive, ask yourself the following:

1. What is owned?
2. Who is the owner?

Then put the apostrophe plus an *s* after the name of the owner. For example:

What is owned? *The stereo*

Who is the owner? *Rita*

When an apostrophe plus an *s* is added to the name of the owner, the result is the possessive form of the word: *Rita's*. That word is then followed by what is owned: *Rita's stereo*.

Here is another example:

- the waiting room belonging to the doctor

Again, ask yourself, "What is owned?" The answer is *waiting room*. Then ask, "Who is the owner?" The answer is *the doctor*. So add an apostrophe plus *s* after the name of the owner and add what is owned: *the doctor's waiting room*. The apostrophe plus *s* shows that the waiting room belongs to the doctor.

Here is a third example:

- the hopes of everyone

Again, ask yourself, "What is owned?" The answer is *hopes*. Then ask, "Who is the owner?" The answer is *everyone*. So add an apostrophe plus *s* after the name of the owner and add what is owned: *everyone's hopes*. The apostrophe plus *s* shows that the hopes belong to everyone.

➤ Practice 4

Rewrite the items below into possessives with an apostrophe plus *s*. In the first column, write the name of the owner. In the second column, write in the possessive form plus what is owned. One is done for you as an example.

	Who is the owner?	Possessive form plus what is owned
1. the bike belonging to Randy	*Randy*	*Randy's bike*
2. the purr of the cat	*cat*	*cat's purr*
3. the hobby of my father	*father*	*father's hobby*

4. the temper of our neighbor	*neighbor*	*neighbor's temper*
5. the keys belonging to someone	*someone*	*someone's keys*
6. the ending of the story	*story*	*story's ending*
7. the stinger belonging to the bee	*bee*	*bee's stinger*
8. the news of the day	*day*	*day's news*
9. the mummy belonging to the museum	*museum*	*museum's mummy*
10. the new song of Billy Joel	*Billy Joel*	*Billy Joel's new song*

➤ Practice 5

Underline the word in each sentence that needs an apostrophe plus *s*. That word is the owner. Then write the word correctly, along with what is owned, in the space provided. The first one is done for you as an example.

1. <u>Gary</u> new neighbor is from China.   *Gary's new neighbor*

2. I tracked mud on my <u>mother</u> white rug.   *mother's white rug*

3. The <u>athlete</u> knee was bothering him.   *athlete's knee*

4. <u>Vietnam</u> climate is hot and damp.   *Vietnam's climate*

5. A wallet was left at <u>Gail</u> house.   *Gail's house*

6. A <u>gorilla</u> diet is mainly vegetarian.   *gorilla's diet*

7. <u>Diane</u> nickname is Smiley.   *Diane's nickname*

8. People have searched for <u>Noah</u> ark.   *Noah's ark*

9. The <u>photographer</u> camera was stolen.   *photographer's camera*

10. The <u>bride</u> wedding dress was knee-high.   *bride's wedding dress*

➤ Practice 6

Write three sentences that include words ending in an apostrophe plus *s*.

1. _____ *Answers will vary.* _____

   _____

2. _____

   _____

3. _____

_____

Showing Possession with Singular and Plural Nouns That End in *s*

An apostrophe plus *s* is used to show possession even with a singular noun that already ends in *s*:

- Gus**'s** computer (the computer belonging to Gus)
- The boss**'s** secretary (the secretary belonging to the boss)

However, an apostrophe alone is used to show possession with a plural noun that ends in *s*:

- the contestant**s'** answers (the answers of a number of contestants)
- the three lawyer**s'** office (the office belonging to three lawyers)

➤ Practice 7

Underline the word that needs an apostrophe in each sentence below. Then write that word, adding the ' or the '*s*, in the space provided.

_____*bass's*_____ 1. Adam carefully removed the fishhook from the <u>bass</u> mouth.

_____*lions'*_____ 2. The <u>lions</u> keeper has worked with them from birth.

_____*Otis's*_____ 3. <u>Otis</u> story about being kidnapped by a flying saucer is hard to believe.

_____*twins'*_____ 4. The <u>twins</u> mother was a twin herself.

_____*Olsons'*_____ 5. The <u>Olsons</u> home has a secret passageway.

WHEN *NOT* TO USE AN APOSTROPHE: IN PLURALS AND VERBS

People sometimes confuse possessive and plural forms of nouns. Remember that a plural is formed simply by adding an *s* to a noun; no apostrophe is used. Look at the sentence below to see which words are plural and which is possessive:

- Lola's necklace has pearls and diamond chips.

The words *pearls* and *chips* are plurals—there is more than one pearl, and there is more than one diamond chip. But *Lola's*, the word with the apostrophe plus *s*, is possessive. Lola owns the necklace.

Also, many verbs end with an *s*. Do not use an apostrophe in a verb.

- Jenny **plays** poker once a week.
- She often **wins**.

➤ **Practice 8**

In the spaces provided under each sentence, correctly write the one word that needs an apostrophe. Also, explain why the other word or words ending in *s* do not get apostrophes.

Example   The patients eyelids opened slowly after surgery.

patients: _patient's, meaning "belonging to the patient"_

eyelids: _eyelids, meaning "more than one eyelid"_

1. In a new version of the fairy tale, the princes wife rescues him from fire-breathing dragons.

   princes: _prince's, meaning "belonging to the prince"_

   rescues: _rescues, verb_

   dragons: _dragons, meaning "more than one dragon"_

2. That countrys flag has blue stripes and a yellow star on a field of green.

   countrys: _country's, meaning "belonging to the country"_

   stripes: _stripes, meaning "more than one stripe"_

3. Hunters value a seals beautiful fur.

   hunters: _hunters, meaning "more than one hunter"_

   seals: _seal's, meaning "belonging to a seal"_

4. The doodles in Jacks notebook show just how much he pays attention in his history class.

   doodles: _doodles, meaning "more than one doodle"_

   Jacks: _Jack's, meaning "belonging to Jack"_

   pays: _pays, verb_

5. The grasshoppers powerful hind legs allow the insect to jump many times its own height.

   grasshoppers: _grasshopper's, meaning "belonging to the grasshopper"_

   legs: _legs, meaning "more than one leg"_

   times: _times, meaning "more than one time"_

6. The chocolates in the silver box were a gift from my mothers best friend.

   chocolates: _chocolates, meaning "more than one chocolate"_

   mothers: _mother's, meaning "belonging to my mother"_

7. It takes eight minutes for the suns light to reach Earth.

    takes: •_____ *takes, verb*_____

    minutes:_____ *minutes, meaning "more than one minute"*_____

    suns: _____ *sun's, meaning "belonging to the sun"*_____

8. The trains cars were filled with tons of coal and lumber.

    trains: _____ *train's, meaning "belonging to the train"*_____

    cars: _____ *cars, meaning "more than one car"*_____

    tons: _____ *tons, meaning "more than one ton"*_____

9. Sheer white curtains and fresh lilacs added to the rooms simple charm.

    curtains: _____ *curtains, meaning "more than one curtain"*_____

    lilacs: _____ *lilacs, meaning "more than one lilac"*_____

    rooms: _____ *room's, meaning "belonging to the room"*_____

10. The hypnotists only tools are a soothing voice and a watch that makes very loud ticks.

    hypnotists: _____ *hypnotist's, meaning "belonging to the hypnotist"*_____

    tools: _____ *tools, meaning "more than one tool"*_____

    makes: _____ *makes, verb*_____

    ticks: _____ *ticks, meaning "more than one tick"*_____

WHEN *NOT* TO USE AN APOSTROPHE: WITH POSSESSIVE PRONOUNS

Do not use an apostrophe in the possessive pronouns *his, hers, its, yours, ours, theirs*, and *whose*.

- Those seats are **ours**.
- **His** car is purple.

People often confuse certain possessive pronouns with contractions. For instance, *its* is often confused with *it's*. The following sentence includes both words:

- **It's** sad that our old tree is losing **its** leaves.

    Its means *belonging to it*—the leaves belong to it (the tree). *Its* is a possessive pronoun and does not take an apostrophe. The word *it's* is a contraction meaning *it is*. Contractions, of course, do take apostrophes.

On the next page are examples of other possessive pronouns and the contractions they are confused with.

- The Pratts rarely mow **their** lawn. **They're** not concerned about the looks of the neighborhood.

   Their means *belonging to them* (the lawn belongs to them). *They're* is a contraction that means *they are*.

- **You're** going to fall if you do not tie **your** shoelaces,

   You're is a contraction that means *you are*. *Your* means *belonging to you* (the shoelaces belong to you).

- **Who's** the person **whose** car is blocking mine?

   Who's is a contraction meaning *who is*. *Whose* means *belonging to whom* (the car belonging to whom).

➤ Practice 9

Underline the correct word within each pair of parentheses.

1. I arranged with two neighborhood boys to mow my lawn, but now (they're / <u>their</u>) father tells me (<u>they're</u> / their) not at home this weekend.

2. If (you're / <u>your</u>) homework is not done by seven o'clock, (<u>you're</u> / your) not going to watch the movie.

3. (Who's / <u>Whose</u>) turn is it to wash the dishes, and (<u>who's</u> / whose) going to dry them?

4. (<u>It's</u> / Its) difficult, if not impossible, to get toothpaste back into (it's / <u>its</u>) tube.

5. The fruit salad on the table is (hers' / <u>hers</u>), and the freshly baked bread is (ours' / <u>ours</u>).

CHAPTER REVIEW

Answer each question by circling the letter of the correct answer or by writing **T** (for *true*) or **F** (for *false*) in the space provided.

1. A contraction is two words combined into
   (a.) one word.   b. a possessive.   c. a plural.

2. In the contraction *she'll*, the apostrophe
   a. shows that *she* possesses something.   b. indicates a plural.
   (c.) takes the place of *wi*.

3. To make a possessive, an apostrophe plus an *s* is usually added to
   (a.) the name of the owner.   b. whatever is owned.

4. *True or false?* __T__ In the sentence *Barry's father loves cigars*, there is no apostrophe after *cigars* because it is simply a plural.

5. *True or false?* __F__ In the sentence *The car lost it's tailpipe*, an apostrophe is needed because *it's* means *belonging to it*.

Name_____ Section _____ Date _____

➤ Apostrophes: Test 1

Each of the sentences below contains **one** word that needs an apostrophe. Write the word, with its apostrophe, in the space provided.

1. Susans eyes were glassy with fatigue.

    _____*Susan's*_____

2. There is no bread, so well have crackers with our soup.

    _____*we'll*_____

3. Fixing drippy faucets is the landlords job.

    _____*landlord's*_____

4. I havent ever gone on a roller coaster, and I never will.

    _____*haven't*_____

5. Four tiny packages arrived in Saturdays mail.

    _____*Saturday's*_____

6. Leo knows his girlfriend is angry at him, but hes not sure why.

    _____*he's*_____

7. Many presents have been delivered to the brides home.

    _____*bride's*_____

8. You can tell by looking at me that I wasnt expecting company.

    _____*wasn't*_____

9. The keyboards plastic cover protects the keys from crumbs and dust.

    _____*keyboard's*_____

10. There are about 100,000 hairs on the average persons head.

    _____*person's*_____

➤ Apostrophes: Test 2

Each of the sentences below contains **one** word that needs an apostrophe. Write the word, with its apostrophe, in the space provided.

1. We didnt recognize our teacher at first without his beard.

   _____*didn't*_____

2. Both of Janes husbands were named Andrew.

   _____*Jane's*_____

3. Half-finished paintings filled the artists studio.

   _____*artist's*_____

4. My neighbor will water my plants while Im in the hospital.

   _____*I'm*_____

5. Floridas neighbors are Alabama and Georgia.

   _____*Florida's*_____

6. The snowflakes glittered in the flashlights glare.

   _____*flashlight's*_____

7. The farmers may lose their entire wheat crop if it doesnt rain soon.

   _____*doesn't*_____

8. Someday Ill tell you the story of Uncle Harry and the mad bull.

   _____*I'll*_____

9. The two brothers relationship has remained strong through the years.

   _____*brothers'*_____

10. The film reviewers were careful not to give away the movies surprise ending.

    _____*movie's*_____

Name_____   Section _____   Date _____

Score: (Number right) _____ x 10 = _____%

➤ Apostrophes: Test 3

Each sentence in the short passages below contains a word that needs an apostrophe. Underline the words that need apostrophes. Then write each word, with its apostrophe, in the space provided.

1. The <u>towns</u> main stoplight is broken. <u>Theres</u> a police officer directing traffic at that corner.

   a. _____*town's*_____

   b. _____*There's*_____

2. Tri Lee and his wife <u>didnt</u> date at first. She was originally his <u>sisters</u> friend.

   a. _____*didn't*_____

   b. _____*sister's*_____

3. One <u>mans</u> hiccups lasted for sixty-five years. <u>Thats</u> the longest hiccup attack known.

   a. _____*man's*_____

   b. _____*That's*_____

4. Most of us <u>cant</u> imagine how difficult being homeless can be. A homeless <u>persons</u> life is filled with frustration and danger.

   a. _____*can't*_____

   b. _____*person's*_____

5. Yesterday was my <u>weeks</u> high point. I got an A on a term paper, and a girl I really like said <u>shed</u> go out with me.

   a. _____*week's*_____

   b. _____*she'd*_____

Name_____ Section _____ Date _____

Score: (Number right) _____ x 10 = _____%

➤ Apostrophes: Test 4

Each sentence in the short passages below contains a word that needs an apostrophe. Underline the words that need apostrophes. Then write each word, with its apostrophe, in the space provided.

1. My <u>friends</u> father is the mayor of a small town. <u>Hes</u> also the animal control officer.

   a. _____*friend's*_____

   b. _____*He's*_____

2. "You <u>shouldnt</u> take my grades so seriously," said Ned to his father. "Grades are no measure of a <u>persons</u> true worth."

   a. _____*shouldn't*_____

   b. _____*person's*_____

3. <u>Wouldnt</u> you know it! The cat has been visiting the fish <u>markets</u> garbage cans again.

   a. _____*Wouldn't*_____

   b. _____*market's*_____

4. The family was sleeping and <u>hadnt</u> realized their house was burning. A <u>neighbors</u> phone call woke them up.

   a. _____*hadn't*_____

   b. _____*neighbor's*_____

5. The mountain <u>towns</u> roads are often closed by snow. Residents sometimes <u>cant</u> travel by car for weeks at a time.

   a. _____*town's*_____

   b. _____*can't*_____

Name_____ Section _____ Date _____

Score: (Number right) _____ x 10 = _____%

➤ Apostrophes: Test 5

The following passage contains **ten** errors in apostrophe use. Some apostrophes are missing, and some are used incorrectly. Underline the ten words with errors. Then above the line, write the correct form of each word.

Lots of my friends smoke. Fortunately, I have never been tempted

to—at least, not since I saw what happened to Harold. Harold was my

father's
fathers friend. He and my father worked together in the garden of a

men's
nursery. As a little girl, I was always impressed by the two mens

strength. I remember them pushing heavy wheelbarrows, the muscles in

shoulders
their shoulder's standing out. Another part of my image of Harold is his

wouldn't
ever-present cigarette. Dad used to laugh at him, saying, "I wouldnt

Harold's
recognize Harold without his little white stick." Harolds shirt pocket

always bulged with a pack of Camels.

As I grew older, I spent less time tagging along after Dad. By the

time I was a junior in high school, I had not seen Harold for ages. I had

they're
signed up with the Candy Stripers—theyre teenage volunteers at a

hospital. One night, a nurse sent me to take some juice to a patient in

Room 4. I asked if I should offer some to his roommate, too. "No," she

He's
said. "Hes too sick to drink anything." I got the glass of juice and walked

into Room 4, glancing at the sick man in the neighboring bed. It was

Harold. I stared at him in shock. Tubes fed his body oxygen and liquids.

Its
One of his arms, once so strong, lay bare on the blanket. It's loose skin

man's
hung from the bones. As I stood looking at him, the poor mans eyes

(Continues on next page)

opened and met mine. "Hi, Harold," I said, trying to sound normal. The

expression in his eyes was so sad that I knew he had seen the horror on

my face. His eyes closed again, but his lips moved. Finally he managed to

get out a gravelly whisper. "<u>D*Don't*ont</u> ever smoke," he rasped at me. And I

never have.

24 / Quotation Marks

This chapter explains the following about quotation marks:

1   How to put what someone says or writes within quotation marks

- "Is your wife home?" asked a voice on the phone.

2   When *not* to put words within quotation marks

- Someone on the phone asked if my wife was home.

3   When to use quotation marks and italics (or underlining) for titles

- The *Prevention* magazine article "Stop a Headache in 5 Minutes!" says that relaxation can fight pain.

DIRECT QUOTATIONS

A **direct quotation** is the exact words of a speaker or writer. Use quotation marks to set off all direct quotations.

- I raised my hand during the exam and said, "My pen is out of ink."

  The student's exact words are enclosed within quotation marks.

- "Your car is in big trouble," the mechanic muttered to Fred.

  The mechanic's exact words are enclosed within quotation marks.

- "We cannot solve a problem by hoping that someone else will solve it for us," wrote psychiatrist M. Scott Peck.

  The exact words that Peck wrote are enclosed in quotation marks.

How to Punctuate Simple Direct Quotations

By looking at the above examples, you should be able to complete the following statements that explain how a simple direct quotation is punctuated:

- Put quotation marks (*before* or *after?*) _____ the speaker's first word and (*before* or *after?*) _____ the speaker's last word.

- (*Capitalize* or *Do not capitalize?*) _____ the first word of the direct quotation.

- Put the comma or period that comes at the end of a quotation (*inside* or *outside?*) _____ the quotation marks.

- Use a (*period* or *comma?*) _____ to set off the direct quotation from the rest of the sentence.

Check your answers by reviewing the following guidelines for punctuating simple direct quotations:

1   Put quotation marks around the direct quotation.
2   Capitalize the first word of the quotation.
3   Always place a period or a comma that is at the end of quoted material inside the quotation marks.
4   Use a comma after a word group that introduces a quotation.

➤ Practice 1

Insert quotation marks where needed in the following sentences. Look at the example below.

Example My mother said, "Take some vitamin C for your cold."

1. "That movie is full of nonstop violence," my friend complained.
2. The operator stated, "Please deposit another quarter in order to continue this call."
3. "Do not discuss the trial during your break," the judge reminded the jury.
4. The children's voices sang, "Row, row, row your boat, gently down the stream."
5. With a grin on his face, the exterminator announced, "I'm afraid you've got carpenter ants in your walls."

➤ Practice 2

Write each sentence requested. Use a comma and quotation marks to set off a speaker's exact words. One is done for you as an example.

1. Write a sentence that begins with the words *Rosa said.*

   Rosa said, "I'm going to take a nap for an hour."

2. Write a sentence that begins with the words *Fred warned.*

   Answers will vary.

3. Write a sentence that begins with the words *My boss said.*

   _____

4. Write a sentence that ends with the words *mumbled the little boy.*

   _____

More About Punctuating Quotations

Quotations with Split Sentences

In a direct quotation, one sentence may be split into two parts:

- "After inserting the disk," said the instructor, "turn on the computer."

Note that the instructor's exact words are set off by two sets of quotation marks. The words *said the instructor* are not included in the quotation marks since they were not spoken by the instructor.

The words *turn on the computer* begin with a small letter because they are a continuation of a sentence, not a new sentence. (The full sentence spoken by the instructor is "After inserting the disk, turn on the computer.")

Commas are used to set off the quoted parts from the rest of the sentence:

- "After inserting the disk," said the instructor, "turn on the computer."

Quotations of More Than One Sentence

A direct quotation can be divided into separate sentences:

- "I really hate my job," Stan told his wife. "I think I'd better start looking for a new one."

The words *Stan told his wife* are not part of the direct quotation.

At times, a direct quotation will be more than one sentence:

- Our minister always says, "It's every citizen's responsibility to vote. If you don't vote, you shouldn't complain."

Note that only one pair of quotation marks is used. Do not use quotation marks for each new sentence as long as the quotation is not interrupted.

➤ Practice 3

Insert quotation marks where needed in the following sentences.

1. "It wasn't nice," said the little girl's mother, "to fill up the sugar bowl with salt."

2. "I don't mind if you borrow my new sweater," said my roommate, "but I don't expect to find it rolled up in a ball under your bed."

3. The newspaper editor said to the new reporter, "I'm sorry to have to tell you this. I can't use the article that you spent two weeks writing."

4. "Why don't you go to the video store," suggested Sara, "and pick up a movie for us to watch tonight."

5. "Our math teacher is unfair," complained James. "He assigns four hours of homework for each class. Does he think we have nothing else to do?"

Quotations with Question Marks and Exclamation Points

If a direct quotation is a question, place the question mark within the quotation marks:

- "Where are my red shoes?" asked Lana.

  After a question mark, no comma is used to set off the direct quotation.

If the entire sentence is a question, place the question mark after the quotation marks:

- Did you say "Thank you"?

An exclamation point also goes within quotation marks unless it applies to the whole sentence.

- The kids shouted, "Let's go to the pool!"

INDIRECT QUOTATIONS

Often we express someone's spoken or written thoughts without repeating the exact words used. When we use an **indirect quotation**, we put the message into our own words. Indirect quotations do not require quotation marks.

The following example shows how the same material could be handled as either a direct or an indirect quotation.

Direct Quotation

- The baker said, **"I forgot** to put yeast in the dough."

The words *I forgot* tell us that the baker's exact words are being used—he's referring to himself. Since his exact words are being used, they must be put in quotation marks.

Indirect Quotation

- The baker said **that he had forgotten** to put yeast in the dough.

The sentence refers to the baker as *he*, so we know that the baker's exact words are not being quoted. Quotation marks are not used for indirect quotations. The word *that* often signals an indirect quotation.

Here are a few more examples of indirect quotations:

- My boss said that I could have a day off on my birthday.
- Mom told us not to answer the front door.
- The park rangers warned us to keep our windows closed.

➤ **Practice 4**

Rewrite each of the following indirect quotations as a direct quotation. The direct quotation will include the words that someone actually spoke.

Note that you will have to change some of the words as well as add capital letters, quotation marks, and any other punctuation needed. The first one is done for you as an example.

1. The child asked if the Milky Way candy bar was really full of milk.

    The child asked, "Is the Milky Way candy bar really full of milk?"

2. My sister said that she would help me with my math homework if she could wear my new blouse.

    My sister said, "I will help you with your math homework if I can wear your

    new blouse."

3. The bookstore manager grumbled that he couldn't accept books with writing in them.

    The bookstore manager grumbled, "I can't accept books with writing in them."

    _____

4. Our boss announced that there would be no overtime this month.

    Our boss announced, "There will be no overtime this month."

    _____

5. The officer asked me if I had been drinking.

    The officer asked me, "Have you been drinking?"

    _____

QUOTATION MARKS FOR TITLES OF SHORT WORKS

Use quotation marks to set off the titles of short stories, newspaper or magazine articles, songs, poems, episodes of TV series, book chapters, and other parts of longer works.

- Our teacher assigned the short story "The Open Boat" by Stephen Crane.
- The familiar song "For He's a Jolly Good Fellow" is over two hundred years old.
- The witty poet Ogden Nash wrote a poem titled "Never Mind the Overcoat, Button Up That Lip."

Note: The titles of longer works, such as books, newspapers, magazines, plays, movies, TV series, and record albums, should be underlined when handwritten or typed. When printed, such titles should be *italicized*.

- Our assignment was to read the chapter titled "The Traits of Happy People" in a book by David Meyers, <u>The Pursuit of Happiness</u>.
- "Three Words That Can Change Your Life" was the first article I turned to in the current issue of <u>Reader's Digest</u>.

➤ **Practice 5**

Insert quotation marks or underlines where needed in the sentences below.

1. The chapter titled "Extrasensory Perception" in the textbook <u>Psychology Today</u> says there is no evidence that ESP actually exists.

2. The article "Policing the Police" in <u>Newsweek</u> magazine is about good cops who go bad.

3. The song "Whole New World" from the soundtrack of the movie <u>Aladdin</u> won the Academy Award for best song.

4. The editor of the <u>Daily Tribune</u> has received many letters supporting and opposing her editorial "Let's Ban Condoms in Schools."

CHAPTER REVIEW

Fill in each blank space with one of the choices in parentheses.

1. The exact words of (*a speaker, a writer,* or *a speaker or writer*?) _____a speaker or writer_____ must be set off with quotation marks.

2. Use a (*comma* or *period*?) _____comma_____ to set off a direct quotation from the rest of a sentence.

3. Put the comma or period that comes at the end of a quotation (*inside* or *outside*?) _____inside_____ the quotation marks.

4. (*Capitalize* or *Do not capitalize*?) _____Capitalize_____ the first word of a direct quotation.

5. A split quotation requires (*one* or *two*?) _____two_____ set(s) of quotation marks.

6. Indirect quotations (*should* or *should not*?) _____should not_____ be set off with quotation marks.

7. The titles of (*short* or *long*?) _____short_____ works should be set off in quotation marks.

Name_____ Section _____ Date _____

Score: (Number right) _____ x 12.5 = _____ %

➤ Quotation Marks: Test 1

On the lines provided, rewrite the following sentences, adding quotation marks as needed. One sentence does not need quotation marks.

1. Somebody has stuck gum all over my typewriter keys, Ted said angrily.

   "Somebody has stuck gum all over my typewriter keys," Ted said angrily.

   _____

2. One lucky caller wins a trip to Disneyland, the radio announcer promised.

   "One lucky caller wins a trip to Disneyland," the radio announcer promised.

   _____

3. I bought a truck, Julie stated, because I sit higher and feel safer.

   "I bought a truck," Julie stated, "because I sit higher and feel safer."

   _____

4. When you see me next, laughed the brunette, I'll be a blonde.

   "When you see me next," laughed the brunette, "I'll be a blonde."

   _____

5. The race car driver said he wanted a quart of milk waiting for him at the finish line.

   No quotation marks are needed.

   _____

6. More Children Alone is the title of a recent article in *The New York Times*.

   "More Children Alone" is the title of a recent article in <u>*The New York Times*</u>.

   _____

7. An hour after lunch, Rudy said, I'm starving. I hope dinner will be ready soon.

   An hour after lunch, Rudy said, "I'm starving. I hope dinner will be ready soon."

   _____

8. Go to the control panel. Then press the green button, instructed the engineer.

   "Go to the control panel. Then press the green button," instructed the engineer.

   _____

Name_____   Section _____   Date _____

Score: (Number right) _____ x 12.5 = _____%

➤ Quotation Marks: Test 2

On the lines provided, rewrite the following sentences, adding quotation marks as needed. One sentence does not need quotation marks.

1. Thanks for the lollipop, shouted the little girl to her dentist.

   "Thanks for the lollipop," shouted the little girl to her dentist.

   _____

2. The camp adviser said, Watch out for ticks.

   The camp adviser said, "Watch out for ticks."

   _____

3. I need to move back home, said Rick to his parents.

   "I need to move back home," said Rick to his parents.

   _____

4. Watching golf, complained Ann, is like watching grass grow.

   "Watching golf," complained Ann, "is like watching grass grow."

   _____

5. What If a Comet Hits the Earth? is the title of a recent article in *Time* magazine.

   "What If a Comet Hits the Earth?" is the title of a recent article in <u>Time</u> magazine.

   _____

6. The movie, said the reviewer, will scare everyone in the family.

   "The movie," said the reviewer, "will scare everyone in the family."

   _____

7. Rachel announced that she could open the locked door with a bent hanger.

   No quotation marks are needed.

   _____

8. The boss advised, Don't be late again. Or I'll have to fine you.

   The boss advised, "Don't be late again. Or I'll have to fine you."

   _____

Name_____ Section _____ Date _____

Score: (Number right) _____ x 10 = _____%

➤ Quotation Marks: Test 3

Place quotation marks where needed in the short passages that follow. Each passage needs **two** sets of quotation marks.

1. "Hospitals have odd ways," explained the patient. "Where else do they wake you up at 4:00 a.m. to make sure you're all right?"

2. After serving the couple expensive lobster dinners, the waitress was upset to find that they had left her only fifty cents for a tip. "Wait, mister," she called after the man, "you can use this more than I can."

3. The interviewer poked her head out of the office door and called out, "Please come in, Mr. Taylor." She asked him a few questions about his experience. Then she said, "We've had twenty-five applicants for this position. Tell me why you deserve to be hired rather than any of those others."

4. Scott was amazed when his friends surprised him with a birthday party. After the presents were opened, one of his friends asked him to give a speech. "I've truthfully never been so surprised," he told the gathering. "I'm probably even more surprised than you can imagine because, you see, it isn't my birthday."

5. "How do you like it?" Cindy asked, showing off her new purple fake-fur jacket.

   Her mother thought for a moment and then replied that it certainly was a cheerful color.

   Her brother was less tactful. "You look like a giant purple marshmallow, he said."

Name_____ Section _____ Date _____

Score: (Number right) _____ x 10 = _____%

➤ Quotation Marks: Test 4

Place quotation marks where needed in the short passages that follow. Each passage needs **two** sets of quotation marks.

1. Pointing to a headline in the tabloid newspaper at the supermarket counter, the boy said, "It looks as if space aliens have landed in Minnesota."

   "You'd have to be from space to believe those newspapers," stated his mother.

2. My uncle and aunt have different ways of dealing with guests who stay too long. My aunt will hint politely, "Well, it sure has been nice visiting with you." My uncle is much more direct. He says, "Let's go to bed, Norma, and let these nice people go home."

3. "This vacation was lots of fun," said the woman, "but after all of this sightseeing and shopping, I'm going to need a vacation from my vacation."

4. In an article titled "Stopping Cancer in Its Tracks," J. Madeleine Nash wrote, "Cancer is not a modern disease. Some of our apelike ancestors undoubtedly suffered from it; so did the dinosaurs."

5. The Hollywood tourist asked the handsome man in the coffee shop for his autograph. He graciously signed her menu. When she read the signature, she sputtered, "Sheldon Levine? You're nobody famous!"

   The man shrugged. "I didn't say I was. You're the one who asked for my autograph."

Name_____ Section _____ Date _____

Score: (Number right) _____ x 10 = _____%

➤ Quotation Marks: Test 5

Insert the **ten** pairs of quotation marks that are needed in the following selection.

Paul leaned against a wall, gazing at the party going on around him. Finally he selected the woman he wanted to talk to. She was tall, with short brown hair and a warm smile. Paul crossed the room to speak to her.

"Hi," he said. "Did you know that Sally Field won the Best Actress award at the Academy Awards in both 1979 and 1984? By the way, my name is Paul."

The woman looked surprised. "Uh . . . no, I didn't know that," she replied. "Nice to meet you, Paul. My name is Irene. This is a great party, isn't it?"

Paul sat down beside Irene. "Yes, it is. And are you aware," he continued, "that Mark Twain's real name was Samuel Clemens?" Paul went on to inform Helen that in 1984 the Pointer Sisters won a Grammy for their recording of the song "Jump."

Irene stared at Paul. Then she stood up and called out to Murray, a friend of hers standing nearby. When he approached, she introduced the two men. Paul said, "I'm glad to meet you, Murray. And it's interesting to note that, in the 1960s, *Bonanza* was the most popular television show in the United States. Also, Greenland's main export is fish." Irene and Murray exchanged looks. Then Irene excused herself and hurried into the other room.

(Continues on next page)

Paul looked depressed. Murray asked him, "Why were you stating those facts to Irene?"

Paul sighed and admitted, "I can never think of things to say to women. I thought if I memorized a bunch of facts out of the *World Almanac* I could keep up an interesting conversation. I guess it's back to the drawing board."

25 / Other Punctuation Marks

This chapter explains the following punctuation marks:

1   The colon (:)

2   The semicolon (;)

3   The hyphen (-)

4   The dash (—)

5   The parentheses ( )

THE COLON (:)

The colon directs attention to what follows. It has three main uses:

1   Use a colon to introduce a list.

   • On her first day of vacation, Carrie did three things: she watched a funny movie, took a long nap, and ate at her favorite restaurant.

2   Use a colon to introduce a long or a formal quotation.

   • The autobiography of Arthur Ashe begins with the following Biblical quotation: "Since we are surrounded by so great a cloud of witnesses, let us lay aside every weight, and the sin which so easily ensnares us, and let us run with endurance the race that is set before us."

3   Use a colon to introduce an explanation.

   • Bert suddenly cancelled his evening plans for a simple reason: his car was out of gas.

      ※ The use of a colon in the opening of a letter is explained on page 351.

➤ Practice 1

Add one colon to each sentence.

1. This dessert requires only three ingredients: graham crackers, marshmallows, and chocolate chips.
                                                    ^

2. The book *Anna Karenina* begins with this famous observation: "Happy families are all alike; every unhappy family is unhappy in its own way."

3. By the end of her first date with Bill, Julie was positive of one thing: there would never be a second.

4. James left the carnival loaded down with treats: cotton candy, stuffed toys, balloons, and three live goldfish.

5. Instead of the anger he expected, Darryl felt only one emotion when his son was brought home by the police: great relief.

THE SEMICOLON (;)

A semicolon indicates that the reader should pause. It has three main uses:

1 Use a semicolon to join two complete thoughts that are closely related, but are not connected by a joining word (such as *and, but*, or *so*).

- Our cat knocked over a can of Coca-Cola; the soda foamed over the white carpet.

2 Use a semicolon to join two closely related complete thoughts with a transitional word or word group (such as *afterwards, however, instead, therefore*, and *on the other hand*). Follow the transitional word or word group with a comma.

- LeQuita began school without knowing any English; nevertheless, she will graduate at the top of her class.

  ※ The use of a semicolon to join two complete thoughts is explained in "Run-Ons and Comma Splices" on pages 187–188 and "Sentence Variety and Style" on page 274.

3 Use semicolons to separate items in a series when the items themselves contain commas.

- Driving down Sunset Strip, we passed La Boutique, which sells women's clothing; The Friendly Cafe, which serves twenty different kinds of coffee; and Pet Palace, which sells snakes, parrots, and spiders.

➤ Practice 2

Add one or more semicolons to each sentence.

1. Many hopeful actors move to Hollywood; most leave disappointed.

2. I went to the airport to pick up my cousin; however, her flight had been canceled.

3. Winners in the dog show were Lady Luck, a German shepherd; Skipper's Delight, a golden retriever; and Nana, a miniature poodle.

4. The emergency room was crowded;everyone looked worried.
   ⌄

5. Hank thought the glass contained lemonade; instead, he drank pure lemon juice.
   ⌄

THE HYPHEN (-)

Hyphens are used within a word or between two words. Following are three main uses of hyphens:

1   Use a hyphen to divide a word at the end of a line of writing.

   • The lawyer put on her jacket, shoved a bundle of papers into her brief-case, and hurried to court.

   Note: Here are rules for dividing a word at the end of a line:

   a   Never divide a word which has only one syllable.

   b   Divide words only between syllables.

   c   Never divide a word in a way that leaves only one or two letters alone on a line.

   d   When dividing a word that already contains a hyphen, divide where the hyphen is.

2   Use a hyphen to join two or more words that act together to describe a noun that follows them.

   • The sports car swerved around the slow-moving truck.

3   Put a hyphen in any number from twenty-one to ninety-nine and in a fraction that is written out, such as one-fourth or two-thirds.

   Note: Words made up of two or more words are sometimes hyphenated (for example, *baby-sit* and *car-pool*). There is no clear rule to cover such cases, so when you're unsure about whether or not to hyphenate such words, check your dictionary.

➤ Practice 3

Add a hyphen to each sentence.

1. My husband takes up at least two-thirds of our bed.
   ⌄

2. You've handed in a very well-written story.
   ⌄

3. My angry-looking boss actually has a sweet personality.
   ⌄

4. Although Trudy turned thirty last month, she tells everyone she's twenty-eight.
   ⌄

5. Jose was telling me about a beautiful green-eyed girl he saw on the subway.
   ⌄

THE DASH (—)

While the hyphen is used within or between individual words, the dash is used between parts of a sentence. Following are three common uses of the dash:

1   Dashes may be used to set off and emphasize interrupting material. Use them when you wish to give special attention to words that interrupt the flow of the sentence.

- Everyone in that family—including a teenager—has a cholesterol problem.

2   Use a dash to signal the end of a list of items.

- Family support, prayer, and hope—these are what got Grady through all those months in jail.

3   A dash may be used to introduce a final element—a list of items, an explanation, or a dramatic point.

- Anne's refrigerator was packed with food for the party—trays of cold cuts, bottles of pickles, loaves of bread, and several pitchers of lemonade.
- Ravi hurriedly left work in the middle of the day—his wife was having labor pains.
- My wallet was found in a trash can—minus its cash.

Note: As mentioned above, the colon can also be used to introduce a list or an explanation. A colon tends to add more formality and less drama to a sentence than a dash.

When typing, form a dash with two hyphens, leaving no space between them; do not leave spaces before or after the dash.

➤ Practice 4

Add one or two dashes to each sentence.

1. Several papers important papers are missing from my desk.

2. A year after their divorce, Oscar and Ruby did something surprising they got married again.

3. Aggression, deceit, and violence these are useful things in football.

4. The maple tree in our front yard it had been standing there for sixty years blew down last night.

5. Harold walked into the room wearing an odd outfit an elegant tuxedo, a rose in his buttonhole, and cheap rubber sandals.

PARENTHESES ( )

Here are two common uses of parentheses:

1   Use parentheses to set off material that interrupts the flow of a sentence. While dashes are used to emphasize interrupting material, parentheses are generally used for material you do not wish to emphasize.

   • Aunt Fern (who arrived two hours late) brought the biggest gift.

2   Place parentheses around numbers that introduce items in a list within a sentence.

   • Ron's work for the evening is as follows: (1) finish a history term paper, (2) read a chapter in the psychology text, and (3) wash a load of laundry.

> Practice 5

Add one set of parentheses to each sentence.

1. The tree by our front door (a sycamore) is home to a family of robins.

2. My mother (whose maiden name is Wojcik) was born in a small town in Poland.

3. The Twice Around Resale Shop (it's at Fifth and Maple) has wonderful clothing bargains.

4. To perform this magic trick, you need (1) a styrofoam cup, (2) a rubber band, and (3) two feet of thread.

5. Harvey Whitman and Erica Whitman (they're not related) will conduct a seminar on leadership for company managers.

> Practice 6

At the appropriate place or places, insert the punctuation mark(s) shown in the margin.

-    1. I do the same job Ralph does for two-thirds of his salary.

;   2. The soup simmered all morning; its delicious aroma filled the house.

( )   3. Thea drives her car (an old Chevy Impala) nearly five hundred miles every week.

—   4. When I got to the bathtub, I discovered something had gotten there before me—a baby alligator.

-    5. The story of Ferdinand is about a fierce-looking bull who loves flowers.

:   6. After a bump on the head, be on the lookout for these symptoms*:* sleepiness, dizziness, and vomiting.

—   7. Old newspapers, sponges, and some paint that's all you need to create some pretty and inexpensive wrapping paper.

( )   8. The last movie I saw (it was at least two months ago) was a romantic comedy starring Meg Ryan.

;   9. This morning I have to go to the hardware store to buy lightbulbs, duct tape, and a screwdriver; the bank to cash a check; and the grocery store to pick up bread, milk, cheese, and eggs.

:   10. Eleanor Roosevelt wrote this about courage: "You gain strength, courage and confidence by every experience in which you really stop to look fear in the face. You are able to say to yourself, 'I lived through this horror. I can take the next thing that comes along.'"

CHAPTER REVIEW

Circle the letter of the correct answer to each question.

1. A colon can
   a. join two complete thoughts.
   (b.) introduce a list, quotation, or explanation.
   c. emphasize interrupting material.

2. A semicolon can
   a. introduce a long or formal quotation.
   b. introduce a final element.
   (c.) separate items in a series in which the items contains commas.

3. A hyphen can
   (a.) join two or more words that act together to describe a noun that follows.
   b. signal the end of a list of items.
   c. introduce a list of items, an explanation, or a dramatic point.

4. A dash can
   a. be used within any number from twenty-one to ninety-nine and in fractions that are written out.
   b. separate items in a series.
   (c.) introduce a final element in a sentence.

5. Parentheses can
   (a.) set off material that interrupts the flow of a sentence.
   b. separate items in a series in which the items contain commas.
   c. introduce a list, quotation, or explanation.

Name_____ Section _____ Date _____

Score: (Number right) _____ x 10 = _____%

➤ Other Punctuation Marks: Test 1

At the appropriate place or places, insert the punctuation mark(s) shown in the margin.

; 1. The beach was clean and inviting;the water was cool and blue.

- 2. One well-built home survived the earthquake with barely a scratch.

— 3. Goldilocks, Cinderella, and Angel these are the names of my brother's three cocker spaniels.

( ) 4. My Aunt Amelia(actually she's my great-aunt)will be visiting us over the holidays.

: 5. There will be auditions tomorrow for three parts in the play: the father, the mother, and the twelve-year-old daughter.

- 6. Wolfgang Amadeus Mozart, a musical genius, died when he was only thirty-four years old.

— 7. Melissa's purse a large handbag covered with beads weighs two pounds when it's empty.

; 8. Pizza would be good tonight; on the other hand, I haven't had Chinese food for a long time.

( ) 9. There are three reasons I won't buy you a set of toy hand grenades: (1) I don't like war toys, (2) you don't need them, and (3) they are ridiculously expensive.

: 10. Mark Twain had this to say about cats:"If man could be crossed with the cat it would improve man, but it would deteriorate the cat."

➤ Other Punctuation Marks: Test 2

At the appropriate places in the following paragraphs, insert the punctuation marks shown in the margin.

; :   1. Lisa didn't want to give her brother a loan;he had borrowed money before and never paid it back. So she read him a piece of advice from Benjamin Franklin:"Neither a borrower nor a lender be."

; ( )   2. I usually like my job;however, today was an exception. I spent the morning trying to get rid of a pushy salesman (a man named Roy) who wanted me to buy a new office copier.

- —   3. A fast-talking pal of mine convinced me to try a camping trip. We spent three nights in a damp tent with flies, mosquitoes and an unappealing neighbor—a huge bear.

( ) -   4. My photography class (twenty students) spent a morning taking pictures at a playground. The camera-loving children there were great subjects. They competed for our attention, smiling and doing endless tricks.

: —   5. My roommate described all her new boyfriend's wonderful qualities: kindness, sensitivity, charm, and intelligence. I couldn't wait to meet him when he picked her up for their date that night. When he knocked on the door, I opened it and found myself facing someone familiar—my ex-husband!

Name_____   Section _____   Date _____

Score: (Number right) _____ x 10 = _____%

➤ Other Punctuation Marks: Test 3

In the following selection, add **one** punctuation mark or a pair of parentheses to each of the ten sentences named in the boxes on this and the next page. Choose from the punctuation marks listed for each sentence.

Sentence 1: Add a colon, semicolon, or hyphen.
Sentence 2: Add a semicolon, hyphen, or dash.
Sentence 3: Add a colon, semicolon, or hyphen.
Sentence 4: Add a semicolon, hyphen, or pair of parentheses.
Sentence 6: Add a semicolon, hyphen, or a pair of parentheses.
Sentence 9: Add a semicolon, a hyphen, or a dash.
Sentence 10: Add a colon, a semicolon, or a hyphen.

---

[1]More than four hundred years ago in Russia, there lived a cruel ruler:Ivan the Terrible. [2]Ivan was famous for certain things intelligence, charm and ruthless acts of violence. [3]During his reign of fifty-one years, he murdered countless Russians for a variety of offenses, real and imagined. [4]Today, it seems clear that Ivan was not just an evil man;he surely suffered from severe mental illness.

[5]Ivan was born in 1530. [6]When he was three, his father died, making little Ivan the czar(that is, the king). [7]His mother ruled for him. [8]When Ivan was seven, his mother died, probably poisoned by political enemies. [9]As a child, Ivan enjoyed cruel hobbies throwing puppies from high castle towers and putting out the eyes of cats. [10]As a teenager, he would ride into villages;his "sport" there was raping peasant women and beating their husbands. [11]When he was seventeen, Ivan married a woman named

(Continues on next page)

Sentence 12: Add a semicolon, a hyphen, or a pair of parentheses.
Sentence 14: Add a semicolon, a hyphen, or a dash.
Sentence 18: Add a colon, a semicolon, or a hyphen.

Anastasia and seemed to recover his senses for a while. [12]He chose good advisers and began making much-needed changes in Russia. [13]But when Anastasia died, Ivan fell apart. [14]He ordered the deaths of people he had relied upon friends and military commanders. [15]Later he decided that the people of Novgorod were plotting against him. [16]Ivan spent five weeks in the city listening to pleas for mercy and passing death sentences. [17]He had so many killed that a nearby river was clogged with their bodies. [18]Ivan even beat his son to death with a spear; his howls of grief could be heard outside the palace for months afterwards. [19]Two years later, Ivan died, probably poisoned by palace officials who feared what further evil their mad ruler might do.

26 / Numbers and Abbreviations

This chapter explains the following:

1   When to write out numbers (*one*, *two*) and when to use numerals (*1, 2*)

2   When to use abbreviations and which ones to use

NUMBERS

Here are guidelines to follow when using numbers.

1   Spell out any number that can be written in one or two words. Otherwise, use numerals.

- When my grandmother turned **sixty-nine**, she went on a **fifteen**-day trip across **nine** states.
- The mail carrier delivered **512** pieces of mail today.

Note: When written out, numbers twenty-one through ninety-nine are hyphenated.

2   Spell out any number that begins a sentence.

- **Eight hundred and seventy-one** dollars were found in the briefcase.

To avoid writing out a long number, you can rewrite the sentence:

- The briefcase contained **$871**.

3   If one or more numbers in a series need to be written as numerals, write all the numbers as numerals.

- The movie theater sold **137** tickets to a horror movie, **64** to a comedy, and **17** to a romance.

4   Use numerals to write the following.

    a Dates:

- My grandfather was born on July **4, 1909**.

    b Times of the day:

- The last guest left at **1:45** a.m.

But: When the word *o'clock* is used, the time is spelled out:

- I got home at **six o'clock**.

Also spell out the numbers when describing amounts of time:

- I worked **fifty** hours last week.

    c Addresses:

- The bookstore is located at **1216** North **48th** Street.

    d Percentages:

- Nearly **70** percent of my class donated blood.

    e Pages and sections of a book:

- Jeff read pages **40-97** of the novel, which includes chapters **2** and **3**.

    f Exact amounts of money that include change:

- My restaurant bill came to **$8.49**.

    g Scores:

- The New York Knicks beat the Indiana Pacers **94-90**.
- People with an IQ between **20** and **35** are considered severely retarded.

5   When writing numerals, use commas to indicate thousands.

- Angie has **1,243** pennies in a jar.
- The number that comes after **999,999** is **1,000,000**.

But: Do not use commas in telephone numbers (555-1234), zip codes (08043), street numbers (3244 Oak Street), social security numbers (372-45-0985), or years (1995).

➤ Practice 1

Cross out the one number mistake in each sentence. Then write the correction in the space provided.

    _____50_____   1. No wonder these cookies cost $5.25—they're ~~fifty~~ percent butter!

_____two_____ 2. The pro football player wore a gold earring and ~~2~~ diamond rings.

_____seven_____ 3. By ~~7~~ o'clock, the temperature had dipped below freezing.

_____1994_____ 4. I began working at my present job in ~~nineteen hundred and ninety four~~.

_____40_____ 5. For next week, please read pages 1–~~forty~~ in Chapter 1.

_____Twenty-six_____ 6. ~~26~~ students helped out at the homeless shelter at 31 South Lake Street.

_____2:45_____ 7. Last night I woke up at midnight and didn't fall asleep again until ~~two forty-five~~.

_____ten_____ 8. Did you know that an official baseball weighs about five ounces and a regulation basketball hoop is ~~10~~ feet above the floor?

_____50_____ 9. For our wedding in 1980, we invited 260 people, 210 of my wife's friends and relatives and ~~fifty~~ of mine.

_____2,456_____ 10. In the mayoral election, the winner received ~~two thousand four hundred and fifty six~~ more votes than her nearest opponent.

ABBREVIATIONS

Abbreviations can save you time when taking notes. However, you should avoid abbreviations in papers you write for classes. The following are among the few that are acceptable in formal writing.

1 Titles that are used before and after people's names:

- **Ms.** Glenda Oaks
- **Dr.** Huang
- Keith Rodham, **Sr.**

2 Initials in a person's name:

- Daphne **A.** Miller
- **T.** Martin Sawyer

3 Time and date references:

- The exam ended at 4:45 **p.m.**
- Cleopatra lived from about 69 to 30 **B.C.**

4 Organizations, agencies, technical words, countries, or corporations known by their initials. They are usually written in all capital letters and without periods:

- USA
- VCR
- YMCA
- FBI
- AIDS
- NBC

➤ **Practice 2**

Cross out the one abbreviation mistake in each sentence. Then write the correction in the space provided.

century   1. Buddhism was founded in the sixth ~~cent.~~ B.C. by Buddha.

Philadelphia   2. Dr. Diamond works for the YMCA in ~~Phila.~~

Canada   3. Mr. Ostrow emigrated from the USSR to ~~Can.~~ in 1995.

Monday   4. On ~~Mon.,~~ I have an appointment at IBM with Ms. Janice Grant.

Kansas   5. Dwight D. Eisenhower was born in Abilene, ~~Kan.,~~ in 1890.

William   6. My brother ~~Wm.~~ tried to get his VCR to record a show at 5:30 p.m.

retired   7. When my grandfather ~~retd.,~~ he volunteered to work with a local AIDS group.

number   8. In 1970, the FBI expanded the ~~nmbr.~~ of criminals on its most-wanted list from ten to sixteen.

California   9. My cousin is getting married at 9:30 a.m. on the beach in Santa Cruz, ~~Calif.~~

college   10. According to an NBC reporter, many of today's ~~coll.~~ students drink in binges.

CHAPTER REVIEW

A. Put a check (✓) by the items for which numerals can be used.

  _____ Any number that can be written in one or two words

  _____ Any number that begins a sentence

  _✓_ Dates

  _✓_ Pages of a book

B. Put a check (✓) by the items that can be abbreviated in formal writing.

  _✓_ Titles with people's names

  _____ Names of months and days of the week

  _✓_ Time and date references

  _____ Common words, such as _appt._ (for _appointment_)

Name_____ Section _____ Date _____

➤ Numbers and Abbreviations: Test 1

Cross out the **one** number or abbreviation mistake in each of the following sentences. Then write the correction on the line provided.

One hundred and two
1. ~~102~~ patients visited Dr. Jamison's clinic today.

three
2. I wrote ~~3~~ protest letters to CBS when my favorite show was cancelled.

university
3. That ~~univ.~~ has 143 professors and 894 students.

population
4. Davenport, Iowa, has a ~~pop.~~ of over 100,000.

hospital
5. The ~~hosp.~~ has treated eighteen patients with AIDS.

superintendent
6. Mr. Pidora has been ~~supt.~~ of schools for the past nine years.

eight
7. We finally reached the outskirts of New York City at ~~8~~ o'clock.

thirteen
8. Only ~~thirteen~~ percent of the customers preferred the new brand of cereal.

$1,220
9. The IRS says I owe ~~one thousand, two hundred and twenty dollars~~ on back taxes.

sandwich
10. I got up at 2:30 a.m. and made myself a tuna ~~sand.~~ on rye.

Name_____ Section _____ Date _____

Score: (Number right) _____ x 10 = _____%

➤ Numbers and Abbreviations: Test 2

Cross out the **one** number or abbreviation mistake in each of the following sentences. Then write the correction on the line provided.

_____*five*_____ 1. Ms. Bradley begins her day at ~~5~~ o'clock.

_____*January*_____ 2. An officer of the NAACP will speak on campus in ~~Jan.~~

_____*thirty*_____ 3. Shelly watched a program on PBS for ~~30~~ minutes before going to work.

_____*reference*_____ 4. I listed Dr. Keenan as a ~~ref.~~ on my résumé.

_____*80*_____ 5. The vendors sold ~~eighty~~ soft pretzels, 145 soft drinks, and 106 hot dogs.

_____*Francisco*_____ 6. While in San ~~Fran.,~~ we were part of a six-car accident on the Golden Gate Bridge.

_____*America*_____ 7. The twenty-seven students in Mrs. Greene's class are learning about South ~~Amer.~~

_____*Boulevard*_____ 8. The YWCA on Waverly ~~Blvd.~~ is having an open house in two weeks.

_____*$1.50*_____ 9. Since the meal was about ten dollars, the tip should be at least ~~one dollar and fifty cents~~.

_____*19*_____ 10. On September ~~nineteen~~, 1893, New Zealand became the first nation to give women the right to vote.

Name_____ Section _____ Date _____

Score: (Number right) _____ x 10 = _____%

➤ Numbers and Abbreviations: Test 3

The following passage contains **ten** number or abbreviation errors. Cross out each one, and write the correction above the line.

People with mental retardation usually have trouble handling complicated ideas. They are generally "slower" than people with normal *intelligence* ~~intell~~. However, surprisingly, there is occasionally a retarded person who has amazing ability in one particular area. Such a person is known as a savant. Most savants score under 70 on intelligence tests. (A score of 100 *24* is considered average. About ~~twenty-four~~ percent of the population scores *95* *three* between ~~ninety-five~~ and 104 on intelligence tests.) About ~~3~~ times as many men as women are savants.

The most common type of savant is a person who might be described as a walking calendar. Such a savant, for example, could tell you in a *1328* moment what day of the week July 2, ~~thirteen hundred and twenty-eight~~ fell on. Other savants can perform remarkable mathematical problems in *multiply* their heads. That kind of savant could be asked to ~~mult.~~ 524 by 978 and instantly reply, "512,472." Dustin Hoffman played the role of such a *mathematics* ~~math.~~ savant in the movie *Rain Man*. Still other savants are gifted with musical ability. Such a savant was Leslie Lemke, who was blind, *nineteen* mentally retarded, and had cerebral palsy. When he was ~~19~~, Lemke sat down at a piano for the first time. He played through Tchaikovsky's First *Five* Piano Concerto after having heard it on the radio a single time. ~~5~~-year-old savant Nadia (her parents don't want her last name released) is a

(Continues on next page)

gifted artist. Her drawings of animals in motion can only be called
astonishing. Scientists cannot explain how an otherwise ~~ret.~~ *retarded* person can
be brilliant in one area. Savants serve as a reminder that, for all our
discoveries, the human brain holds many mysteries.

Proofreading

An important step in becoming a good writer is learning to proofread. When you proofread, you check the next-to-final draft of a paper for grammar, punctuation, and other mistakes. Such mistakes are ones you did not find and fix in earlier drafts of a paper because you were working on content.

All too often, students skip the key step of proofreading in their rush to hand in a paper. As a result, their writing may contain careless errors that leave a bad impression and result in a lower grade. This chapter explains how to proofread effectively and suggests a sequence to follow when proofreading. The chapter also provides a series of practices to improve your proofreading skills.

HOW TO PROOFREAD

1   Proofreading is a special kind of reading that should not be rushed. Don't try to proofread a paper minutes before it is due. If you do, you are likely to see what you intended to write, not what is actually on the page. Instead, do one of the following:

- Read your writing out loud.
- Alternatively, do the reading "aloud" in your head, perhaps mouthing it as you read.

In either case, listen for spots that do not read smoothly and clearly. You will probably be able to hear where your sentences should begin and end. You will then be more likely to find any fragments and run-ons that are present. Other spots that do not read smoothly may reveal other grammar or punctuation errors. Take the time needed to check such spots closely.

2   Read through your paper several times, looking for different types of errors in each reading. Here is a good sequence to follow:

- Look for sentence fragments, run-ons, and comma splices.
- Look for verb mistakes.
- Look for capital letter and punctuation mistakes.
- Look for missing words or missing -s endings.
- Look for spelling mistakes, including errors in homonyms.

This chapter will give you practice in proofreading for the above kinds of mistakes. In addition, as you proofread your own work, also watch for problems with pronoun and modifier use, word choice, and parallelism.

(For other proofreading suggestions, see pages 17–18 in "A Brief Guide to Effective Writing.")

SENTENCE FRAGMENTS, RUN-ONS, AND COMMA SPLICES

Sentence Fragments

When proofreading for sentence fragments, remember to look for:

- Dependent-word fragments
- Fragments without subjects
- Fragments without a subject and a verb (*-ing* and *to* fragments, example fragments)

In general, correct a fragment by doing one of the following:

1. Connect the fragment to the sentence that comes before or after it.
2. Create a completely new sentence by adding a subject and/or a verb.

(To further refresh your memory about fragments, turn to pages 163–174.)

Run-On Sentences and Comma Splices

When proofreading for run-on sentences and comma splices, keep the following definitions in mind:

- A **run-on sentence** results when one complete thought is immediately followed by another, with nothing between them.
- A **comma splice** is made up of two complete thoughts that are incorrectly joined by only a comma.

To correct run-on sentences and comma splices, do one of the following:

1. Use a period and a capital letter to create separate sentences.
2. Use a comma plus a joining word (such as *and*, *but*, or *so*) to connect the two complete thoughts into one compound sentence.
3. Use a dependent word to make one of the complete thoughts dependent upon the other one.
4. Use a semicolon to connect the two complete thoughts.

(To further refresh your memory about run-on sentences and comma splices, turn to pages 181–190.)

➤ Practice 1   *Corrections may vary.*

Read each of the following short passages aloud to yourself. Each passage contains a sentence fragment, a run-on, or a comma splice. Find and underline the error. Then correct it in the space provided.

1. <u>That bookcase is too heavy on top it could fall over.</u> Take some of the big books off the highest shelf and put them on the bottom one.

   That bookcase is too heavy on top, so it could fall over.
   _____

2. The detective asked everyone to gather in the library. He announced that he had solved the mystery. <u>And would soon reveal the name of the murderer.</u> Suddenly the lights went out.

   He announced that he had solved the mystery and would soon reveal the name

   of the murderer.

3. That rocking chair is very old. <u>It belonged to my great-grandfather, he brought it to the United States from Norway.</u> I like to think about all the people who have sat in it over the years.

   It belonged to my great-grandfather; he brought it to the United States from

   Norway.

4. <u>Before you leave the house.</u> Please close all the windows in case it rains. I don't want the carpet to get soaked.

   Before you leave the house, please close all the windows in case it rains.
   _____

5. For vacation this year, we are going to rent a cabin. <u>It is on a lake in the mountains we can swim, fish, and sunbathe there.</u> Everyone in the family is looking forward to that week.

   Because it is on a lake in the mountains, we can swim, fish, and sunbathe

   there.

6. My aunt took a trip on a boat off the coast of California. She wanted to see whales. Whales are always sighted there. <u>At a certain time of the year.</u>

   Whales are always sighted there at a certain time of the year.
   _____

7. Hsia is from Taiwan, she uses the English name Shirley, which is easier for her American friends to say. Everyone in her family has both a Chinese and an English name.

Hsia is from Taiwan. She uses the English name Shirley, which is easier for her

American friends to say.

8. Rosalie went to the beauty parlor on Friday. Intending to get her long hair trimmed just a little. However, she changed her mind and had it cut very short.

Rosalie went to the beauty parlor on Friday intending to get her long hair

trimmed just a little.

9. The Webbs put a white carpet in their living room. Now they feel that was a foolish choice. Every smudge of dirt or spill of food shows on the white surface. And is nearly impossible to get rid of.

Every smudge of dirt or spill of food shows on the white surface and is nearly

impossible to get rid of.

10. That waiter is quick and hard-working, he is not friendly with customers. For that reason he doesn't get very good tips. His boss tells him to smile and be more pleasant, but he doesn't seem to listen.

That waiter is quick and hard-working, but he is not friendly with customers.

COMMON VERB MISTAKES

When proofreading, look for the following common verb mistakes:

- Needless shifts of verb tense
- The wrong past or past participle forms of irregular verbs
- Lack of subject-verb agreement

(To further refresh your memory about common verb mistakes, turn to pages 103–110, pages 117–124, and pages 129–138.)

➤ Practice 2

Read each of the following sentences aloud to yourself. Each contains a verb mistake. Find and cross out the error. Then correct it in the space provided.

_____swam_____ 1. The girls ~~swimmed~~ all the way to the raft.

_____wear_____ 2. The rock climbers ~~wears~~ safety ropes in case they fall.

did   3. Because my brother studied hard, he <u>does</u> very well on the exam.

grew   4. When he <u>growed</u> up, Neil married his babysitter.

is   5. Neither of our cars <u>are</u> working right now.

answered   6. The phone rang twenty times before someone went and <u>answers</u> it.

are   7. The public swimming pools in the city <u>is</u> not open yet.

slept   8. After being out all night, Lee Ann <u>sleeped</u> until noon.

is   9. There <u>are</u> poison ivy growing all over that empty lot.

claims   10. Gerald tells everybody it's his birthday and then <u>claimed</u> he doesn't want presents.

CAPITAL LETTER AND PUNCTUATION MISTAKES

When proofreading, be sure the following begin with **capital letters**:

- The first word in a sentence or direct quotation
- The word *I* and people's names
- Family names
- Names of specific places and languages
- Names of specific groups
- Names of days of the week, months and holidays (but not the seasons)
- Brand names
- Titles
- Names of specific school courses
- Names of historic periods and well-known events
- Opening and closing of a letter

When proofreading, look for **commas** in the following places:

- Between items in a series
- After introductory material
- Around words that interrupt the flow of a sentence
- Between complete thoughts connected by a joining word
- Before and/or after words of direct address and short expressions
- In dates, addresses and letters

When proofreading, be sure **apostrophes** are used in the following:

- Contractions
- Possessives (but not in plurals or verbs)

When proofreading, look for **quotation marks** around direct quotations. Eliminate any quotation marks around indirect quotations.

Finally, remember to also watch for problems with **colons, semicolons, hyphens, dashes,** and **parentheses.**

(To further refresh your memory, turn to "Capital Letters," pages 333–338; "Commas," pages 345–352; "Apostrophes," pages 359–366; "Quotation Marks," pages 373–378; and "Other Punctuation Marks," pages 385–390.)

➤ Practice 3

Read each of the following sentences aloud to yourself. Each sentence contains an error in capitalization, an error in comma or apostrophe use, or two missing quotation marks. Find the mistake, and correct it in the space provided.

_____*sauce,*_____ 1. I loaded up my low-fat frozen yogurt with fudge sauce peanuts, cherries, and whipped cream.

_____*Bob's*_____ 2. Bobs uncle is an actor in a soap opera.

_____*yelled,*_____ 3. The deli clerk yelled "Who's next?"

_____*Chicago*_____ 4. Our flight to chicago was delayed two hours because of mechanical problems.

"Please . . . Tom," 5. Please call me Tom, our business instructor said.

_____*summer*_____ 6. I dread the Summer because I get hay fever so badly.

_____*doesn't*_____ 7. A person doesnt have to be great at a sport to be a great coach.

_____*character,*_____ 8. Although he's only a cartoon character Mickey Mouse is loved by millions.

_____*watermelons*_____ 9. The fresh watermelon's in the supermarket look delicious.

*question," . . . "I* 10. "I'd like to ask you a question, Marvin told June. I hope you don't think it's too personal."

MISSING -*S* ENDINGS AND MISSING WORDS

Since you know what you meant when you wrote something, it is easy for you not to notice when a word ending or a word is missing. The following two sections will give you practice in proofreading for such omissions.

Missing -s Endings

When you proofread, remember the following about noun and verb endings:

- The plural form of most nouns ends in *s* (for example, two *cups* of coffee).

- Present tense verbs for the singular third-person subjects end with an *s*.

(To further refresh your memory about the present tense, turn to page 87.)

➤ **Practice 4**

Read each of the following sentences aloud to yourself. In each case an *-s* ending is needed on one of the nouns or verbs in the sentence. Find and cross out the error. Then correct it in the space provided, being sure to add the *s* to the word.

_____*telephones*_____ 1. All of the pay ~~telephone~~ are being used.

_____*looks*_____ 2. You should check your front left tire because it ~~look~~ a little flat.

_____*jokes*_____ 3. My uncle is always telling terrible ~~joke~~.

_____*barns*_____ 4. Most ~~barn~~ are painted a dark red color.

_____*makes*_____ 5. Ella ~~make~~ new friends quite easily.

_____*speaks*_____ 6. Luis got his job because he ~~speak~~ Spanish and English equally well.

_____*closes*_____ 7. The drugstore ~~close~~ at nine o'clock, but the other mall stores stay open till ten.

_____*grows*_____ 8. The grass always ~~grow~~ faster whenever we have a heavy summer rain.

_____*cans*_____ 9. There are two ~~can~~ of soda hidden on the bottom shelf of the refrigerator.

_____*freckles*_____ 10. Many red-haired people have ~~freckle~~ on their skin and also get sunburned quickly.

Missing Words

When you proofread, look for places where you may have omitted such short words as *a*, *of*, *the*, or *to*.

➤ **Practice 5**

Read each of the following sentences aloud. In each sentence, one of the following little words has been omitted:

a   and   by   of   the   to   with

Add a caret (∧) at the spot where the word is missing. Then write the word in the space provided.

Example ___*the*___ All sections of ∧ course that I wanted to take were closed.

___*of*___ 1. Several pieces ∧ this puzzle are missing.

___*to*___ 2. When she went to the grocery store, Louise forget ∧ buy bread.

___*of*___ 3. Some ∧ the programs on TV are too violent for children.

___*with*___ 4. That orange shirt looks great ∧ the black pants.

___*a*___ 5. Not a single lottery ticket that I bought last year won ∧ prize.

___*and*___ 6. Paul plays both the piano ∧ the bass guitar.

___*the*___ 7. Sandra became tired climbing up ∧ steep hill.

___*by*___ 8. Everyone was surprised ∧ Helen and Stan's divorce.

___*with*___ 9. Do you drink your coffee ∧ cream or just sugar?

___*to*___ 10. It's hard ∧ pay attention to a boring speaker.

HOMONYM MISTAKES

When proofreading, pay special attention to the spelling of words that are easily confused with other words. (To refresh your memory of the homonyms listed in this book, turn to pages 311–324.)

➤ **Practice 6**

Read each of the following sentences aloud. Each sentence contains a mistake in a commonly confused word. Find and cross out the error. Then correct it in the space provided.

___*too*___ 1. We left the beach early because there were ~~to~~ many flies.

___*your*___ 2. It's ~~you're~~ own fault that you missed the deadline.

___*whose*___ 3. No one knows ~~who's~~ sweatshirt this is.

___*you're*___ 4. If ~~your~~ hungry, fix yourself something to eat.

___*its*___ 5. I can't get close enough to the stray dog to read the tag on ~~it's~~ collar.

_____*they're*_____ 6. My cousins have promised that ~~their~~ coming here soon for a visit.

_____*two*_____ 7. I can think of ~~too~~ practical reasons for staying in school: to improve your skills and to prepare for a better job.

_____*their*_____ 8. These greeting cards have pictures on ~~they're~~ covers, but there's no message inside.

_____*it's*_____ 9. Although ~~its~~ tempting to keep the money, you should return it to the man whose name appears in the wallet.

_____*passed*_____ 10. As we waited in the emergency room to hear whether our sick friend would be okay, time ~~past~~ slowly.

A NOTE ON MAKING CORRECTIONS IN YOUR PAPERS

You can add several corrections to a paper and still hand it in. Just make the corrections neatly. Add missing punctuation marks right in the text, exactly where they belong. Draw a straight line through any words or punctuation you wish to eliminate or correct. Add new material by inserting a caret (∧) at the point where the addition should be. Then write the new word or words above the line at that point. Here's an example of a sentence that was corrected during proofreading:

> • Some Hondas are made in ~~japan,~~ *Japan* but others are made *in* this country.
>   ∧

Retype or recopy a paper if you discover a number of errors.

➤ **Practice 7**   *Corrections in sentences 2 and 5 may vary.*

Here are five sentences, each of which contains **two** of the types of errors covered in this chapter. Correct the errors right on the lines by crossing out or adding words or punctuation marks, as in the example above.

1. Helena is taking two ~~english course~~ *English courses* in school this semester.

2. I feel sorry for ~~Donnas dog, it~~ *Donna's dog. It* lost a leg in a car accident.

3. Rusty cans, plastic bags, and scraps of wood washed up on *the* deserted beach.
   ∧

4. My mother ~~take~~ *takes* night classes at college, ~~wear~~ *where* she is learning to use a

   computer.

5. Because of an anonymous ~~tip. Police~~ *tip, police* were able to raid the drug house, *and*
   ∧
   they made five arrests.
   ∧

CHAPTER REVIEW

Fill in the correct word or words in each space provided.

1. Proofreading is reading done to find any _____*errors*_____ you missed in previous drafts of a paper.

2. Proofreading is best done (*aloud, quickly,* or *right before the paper is due?*) _____*aloud*_____.

3. You can find sentence fragments, run-ons, and comma splices in a paper by hearing where _____*sentences*_____ should begin and end.

4. It's best to proofread your paper carefully (*once* or *several times?*) _____*several times*_____.

5. When correcting a paper, insert a caret where you wish to (*add* or *remove?*) _____*add*_____ material.

Name_____ Section _____ Date _____

Score: (Number right) _____ x 20 = _____%

➤ Proofreading: Test 1

Read the following passage aloud to yourself, looking in turn for each of the following **five** mistakes:

---

1 missing capital letter	**1 comma splice**	**1 verb error**
1 sentence fragment	**1 missing apostrophe**	

Correct the mistakes, crossing out or adding words or punctuation marks as needed.

Corrections of the fragment and comma splice may vary.

¹When I was 19, I lived in Costa ~~r~~ica for a few months. [*R* inserted above] ²The country

is very beautiful; fruits and flowers are growing everywhere. ³The

country is also blessed with beautiful rain forests, mountains, and

inactive volcanoes. ⁴One of my favorite memories ~~are~~ [*is*] of a time I was

staying overnight on the beach with some friends. ⁵At about midnight, we

decided to stand waist-deep in the warm ocean water. ⁶A gentle rain

began to fall, and we could see lightning flashing in the clouds many

miles away. ⁷Suddenly, we all gasped in amazement. ⁸Lines of flickering

green light were dancing across the tops of the ~~waves. ⁹As~~ [*waves as*] they rolled

toward us. ¹⁰We learned later that the light was caused by tiny glowing

animals which live on the ocean's surface. ¹¹That night was a magical time

for us.

Name_____ Section _____ Date _____

➤ Proofreading: Test 2

Read the following passage aloud to yourself, looking in turn for each of the following **five** mistakes:

---

1 comma splice   **1 capital letter mistake**   **1 verb mistake**
1 missing -s ending   **1 quotation mark mistake**

Correct the mistakes, crossing out or adding words or punctuation marks as needed.

Correction of the comma splice may vary.

[1]Elaine and Don were on a long drive. [2]They stopped at a convenience store to buy something to drink. [3]While Elaine picked up

Pepsi
cans of ~~pepsi~~ and fruit juice, Don browsed through the snacks. [4]He decided that it would be fun to try something new and unusual, so he bought pickled hard-boiled eggs, a bag of pork rinds, and a tasty-looking

nibbled
sausage. [5]Back in the car, Elaine ~~nibbles~~ on a pickled egg. [6]"Hey, I like

answer.
this," she said. [7]"What are you going to try first?" [8]But Don didn't ~~answer,~~
He   *sounds*
~~he~~ just made choking ~~sound~~ as he hurriedly opened a can and gulped

down some soda. [9]"Don't eat that sausage!" he finally gasped. [10]Elaine

picked up the sausage package and read the label. [11]"Fire-Eater's

Favorite Chili Sausage," she said. [12]"Maybe you should have read the

label first."

Name_____ Section _____ Date _____

➤ **Proofreading: Test 3**

Read the following passage aloud to yourself, looking in turn for each of the following **five** mistakes:

| 1 fragment | 1 missing apostrophe | 1 run-on |
| 1 homonym mistake | 1 missing quotation mark | |

Correct the mistakes, crossing out or adding words or punctuation marks as needed.

Corrections of the fragment and run-on may vary.

¹Last week, a girl I dated in high school called me. ²She and her new

town, and she

husband had just moved to ~~town she~~ wanted us to meet them for dinner.

³"Sherry is really nice, and I'm sure her husband is also," I told my wife.

"
⁴We'll have a good time." ⁵Boy, was I wrong. ⁶We met Sherry and Jake at
^

Jake's

a crowded restaurant. ⁷"Wow, aren't you a babe," was ~~Jakes~~ first remark

to my wife. ⁸Next he decided that our waiter was gay. ⁹He kept making

remarks about

loud ~~remarks.~~ ¹⁰~~About~~ "queers" and "fairies." ¹¹When a black woman and

white man sat down nearby, Jake started complaining about "race

mixing." ¹²By that time, my wife had had enough. ¹³She stood up and

Then

said, "Sorry, Jake. I don't eat with people like you." ¹⁴~~Than~~ she stormed

out of the restaurant.

Name_____ Section _____ Date _____

Score: (Number right) _____ x 20 = _____ %

➤ Proofreading: Test 4

Read the following passage aloud to yourself, looking in turn for each of the following **five** mistakes:

1 fragment	**1 comma splice**	**1 verb mistake**
1 comma mistake	**1 missing apostrophe**	

Correct the mistakes, crossing out or adding words or punctuation marks as needed.

Corrections of the fragment and comma splice may vary.

^{1}When a group of rare white lions arrived at the Philadelphia ~~Zoo.~~ *Zoo, it* ^{2}~~It~~ was an exciting event. ^{3}The lions were the only ones of their kind in North America, *and* they soon became the zoo's most popular exhibit. ^{4}The lions are native to southern Africa. ^{5}They are so rare because of a problem caused by their unusual color. ^{6}Most lions, with their golden-brown color, can sneak through grass and trees without being detected. ^{7}But the moonlight shining on the white lions' coats ~~make~~ *makes* it difficult for them to hunt at night. ^{8}~~Its~~ *It's* too easy for other animals to see them. ^{9}Therefore, most white lions in the wild starve to death. ^{10}Although all the white lions in Philadelphia are female, the zoo is hoping to get a white male soon and raise a family of white lion cubs.

Name_____ Section _____ Date _____

Score: (Number right) _____ x 10 = _____%

➤ Proofreading: Test 5

Read the following passage aloud to yourself, looking in turn for each of the following **ten** mistakes:

2 fragments	**1 missing apostrophe**	**2 verb mistakes**
2 comma mistakes	**1 comma splice**	
1 run-on sentence	**1 homonym mistake**	

Correct the mistakes, crossing out or adding words or punctuation marks as needed.

Corrections of the fragments, run-on, and comma splice may vary.

¹The city of Seattle, Washington, is known for its beauty. ²It has a cool, pleasant climate and is surrounded by spectacular mountain ranges.

³Seattle is home to the University of Washington, professional theater companies, an opera company, and several museums. ⁴That's the good news. ⁵On the other hand, the region around Seattle is also known for its enormous slugs. ⁶While ~~their~~ *there* are slugs in other parts of the U.S., they ~~dont~~ *don't* compare to the Seattle variety. ⁷Seattle slugs average four to five inches in length, and they come in a rainbow assortment of ~~colors.~~ *colors, including* ⁸~~Including~~ green with yellow spots. ⁹When a pack of slugs moves into a Seattle ~~garden.~~ *garden, it* ¹⁰~~It~~ can clean out a lettuce crop overnight.

¹¹The residents of the Seattle region have ~~thinked~~ *thought* up some creative ways to deal with the giant slugs. ¹²Most of that creativity is devoted to finding ways to kill them. ¹³The most effective method, they say, is to sprinkle the slugs with salt *because* the salted slugs dissolve on the spot.

(Continues on next page)

[14]Another popular method is to fill a pie tin with half an inch of beer.

[15]The slugs crawl in, drink the beer, pass out, and drown.

[16]But others say you can learn to live with, and even love, the slimy

slugs. [17]Residents of the nearby town of Elma, Washington, ~~has~~ *have* an

annual slug festival. [18]They dress the slugs up in little costumes and have

slug races. [19]There are even rumors of slug cookbooks available in and

around ~~Seattle, they~~ *Seattle. They* are for people who *really* love the creepy crawlers.

Appendix A: Parts of Speech

Words—the building blocks of sentences—can be divided into eight parts of speech. **Parts of speech** are classifications of words according to their meaning and use in a sentence.

This chapter will explain the eight parts of speech:

nouns	**prepositions**	**conjunctions**
pronouns	**adjectives**	**interjections**
verbs	**adverbs**	

NOUNS

A **noun** is a word that is used to name something: a person, a place, an object, or an idea. Here are some examples of nouns:

Nouns

woman	city	pancake	freedom
Alice Walker	street	diamond	possibility
Steve Martin	Chicago	Corvette	mystery

Most nouns begin with a lowercase letter and are known as **common nouns**. These nouns name general things. Some nouns, however, begin with a capital letter. They are called **proper nouns**. While a common noun refers to a person or thing in general, a proper noun names someone or something specific. For example, *woman* is a common noun—it doesn't name a particular woman. On the other hand, *Alice Walker* is a proper noun because it names a specific woman.

➤ Practice 1   *Answers will vary.*

Insert any appropriate noun into each of the following blanks.

1. The shoplifter stole a(n) _____*jacket*_____ from the department store.

2. _____*Randall*_____ threw the football to me.

3. Tiny messages were scrawled on the _____*paper*_____.

4. A _____*rock*_____ crashed through the window.

5. Give the _____*job*_____ to Ellen.

Singular and Plural Nouns

Singular nouns name one person, place, object, or idea. **Plural nouns** refer to two or more persons, places, objects, or ideas. Most singular nouns can be made plural with the addition of an *s*.

Some nouns, like *box*, have irregular plurals. You can check the plural of nouns you think may be irregular by looking up the singular form in a dictionary.

Singular and Plural Nouns

Singular	Plural
goat	goats
alley	alleys
friend	friends
truth	truths
box	boxes

※ For more information on nouns, see "Subjects and Verbs," pages 67–68.

➤ **Practice 2**

Underline the three nouns in each sentence. Some are singular, and some are plural.

1. Two <u>bats</u> swooped over the <u>heads</u> of the frightened <u>children</u>.

2. The <u>artist</u> has purple <u>paint</u> on her <u>sleeve</u>.

3. The lost <u>dog</u> has <u>fleas</u> and a broken <u>leg</u>.

4. <u>Gwen</u> does her <u>homework</u> in green <u>ink</u>.

5. Some <u>farmers</u> plant <u>seeds</u> by <u>moonlight</u>.

PRONOUNS

A **pronoun** is a word that stands for a noun. Pronouns eliminate the need for constant repetition. Look at the following sentences:

• The phone rang, and Bill answered the phone.

• Lisa met Lisa's friends in the record store at the mall. Lisa meets Lisa's friends there every Saturday.

- The waiter rushed over to the new customers. The new customers asked the waiter for menus and coffee.

Now look at how much clearer and smoother the sentences sound with pronouns.

- The phone rang, and Bill answered **it**.

  The pronoun *it* is used to replace the word *phone*.

- Lisa met **her** friends in the record store at the mall. **She** meets **them** there every Saturday.

  The pronoun *her* is used to replace the word *Lisa's*. The pronoun *she* replaces *Lisa*. The pronoun *them* replaces the words *Lisa's friends*.

- The waiter rushed over to the new customers. **They** asked **him** for menus and coffee.

  The pronoun *they* is used to replace the words *the new customers*. The pronoun *him* replaces the words *the waiter*.

Following is a list of commonly used pronouns known as **personal pronouns**:

Personal Pronouns

I	you	he	she	it	we	they
me	your	him	her	its	us	them
my	yours	his	hers		our	their

➤ Practice 3

Fill in each blank with the appropriate personal pronoun.

1. Andrew feeds his pet lizard every day before school. _____*He*_____ also gives _____*it*_____ flies in the afternoon.

2. The female reporter interviewed the striking workers. _____*They*_____ told _____*her*_____ about their demand for higher wages and longer breaks.

3. Students should save all returned tests. _____*They*_____ should also keep _____*their*_____ review sheets.

4. The pilot announced that we would fly through some air pockets. _____*He* (or *She*)_____ said that we should be past _____*them*_____ soon.

5. Randy returned the calculator to Sheila last Friday. But Sheila insists _____*she*_____ never got _____*it*_____ back.

There are a number of types of pronouns. For convenient reference, they are described briefly in the box below.

Types of Pronouns

Personal pronouns can act in a sentence as subjects, objects, or possessives.

Singular: I, me, my, mine, you, your, yours, he, him, his, she, her, hers, it, its

Plural: we, us, our, ours, you, your, yours, they, them, their, theirs

Relative pronouns refer to someone or something already mentioned in the sentence.

who, whose, whom, which, that

Interrogative pronouns are used to ask questions.

who, whose, whom, which, what

Demonstrative pronouns are used to point out particular persons or things.

this, that, these, those

Note: Do not use *them* (as in *them* shoes), *this here, that there, these here* or *those there* to point out.

Reflexive pronouns are those that end in *-self* or *-selves*. A reflexive pronoun is used as the object of a verb (as in *Cary cut **herself**)* or the object of a preposition (as in *Jack sent a birthday card to **himself**)* when the subject of the verb is the same as the object.

Singular: myself, yourself, himself, herself, itself
Plural: ourselves, yourselves, themselves

Intensive pronouns have exactly the same forms as reflexive pronouns. The difference is in how they are used. Intensive pronouns are used to add emphasis. (*I **myself** will need to read the contract before I sign it.*)

Indefinite pronouns do not refer to a particular person or thing.

each, either, everyone, nothing, both, several, all, any, most, none

Reciprocal pronouns express shared actions or feelings.

each other, one another

※ For more information on pronouns, see "Pronoun Forms," pages 197–204, and "Pronoun Problems," pages 211–220. For information on indefinite pronouns, see also "Subject-Verb Agreement," pages 134–135.

VERBS

Every complete sentence must contain at least one verb. There are two types of verbs: action verbs and linking verbs.

Action Verbs

An **action verb** tells what is being done in a sentence. For example, look at the following sentences:

- Mr. Jensen **swatted** at the bee with his hand.
- Rainwater **poured** into the storm sewer.
- The children **chanted** the words to the song.

In these sentences, the verbs are *swatted, poured*, and *chanted*. These words are all action verbs; they tell what is happening in each sentence.

> ⁂ For more about action verbs, see "Subjects and Verbs," pages 71–72.

➤ Practice 4   *Answers will vary.*

Insert an appropriate word into each blank. That word will be an action verb; it will tell what is happening in the sentence.

1. The surgeon _____*cut*_____ through the first layer of skin.

2. The animals in the cage _____*sleep*_____ all day.

3. An elderly woman on the street _____*asked*_____ me for directions.

4. The boy next door _____*mows*_____ our lawn every other week.

5. Our instructor _____*graded*_____ our papers over the weekend.

Linking Verbs

Some verbs are **linking verbs**. These verbs link (or join) a noun to something that is said about it. For example, look at the following sentence:

- The clouds **are** steel gray.

In this sentence, *are* is a linking verb. It joins the noun *clouds* to words that describe it: *steel gray*.

Other common linking verbs include *am, is, was, were, look, feel, sound, appear, seem*, and *become*.

> ⁂ For more about linking verbs, see "Subjects and Verbs," pages 73–74.

➤ **Practice 5**

Into each slot, insert one of the following linking verbs: *am, feel, is, look, were.*
Use each linking verb once.

1. The important papers _____*were*_____ in a desk drawer.

2. I _____*am*_____ anxious to get my test back.

3. The bananas _____*look*_____ ripe.

4. The grocery store _____*is*_____ open until 11 p.m.

5. Whenever I _____*feel*_____ angry, I go off by myself to calm down.

Helping Verbs

Sometimes the verb of a sentence consists of more than one word. In these cases, the main verb will be joined by one or more **helping verbs**. Look at the following sentence.

• The basketball team **will be leaving** for their game at six o'clock.

In this sentence, the main verb is *leaving*. The helping verbs are *will* and *be*.

Other helping verbs include *do, has, have, may, would, can, must, could,* and *should.*

※ For more information about helping verbs, see "Subjects and Verbs," pages 75–76; "Verb Tenses," pages 89–95; and "More About Verbs," page 119.

➤ **Practice 6**

Into each slot, insert one of the following helping verbs: *does, must, should, could,* and *has been.* Use each helping verb once.

1. You _____*should*_____ start writing your paper this weekend.

2. The victim _____*could*_____ describe her attacker in great detail.

3. You _____*must*_____ rinse the dishes before putting them into the dishwasher.

4. My neighbor _____*has been*_____ arrested for drunk driving.

5. The bus driver _____*does*_____ not make any extra stops.

PREPOSITIONS

A **preposition** is a word that connects a noun or a pronoun to another word in the sentence. For example, look at the following sentence:

- A man **in** the bus was snoring loudly.

In is a preposition. It connects the noun *bus* to *man*. Here is a list of common prepositions:

Prepositions

about	before	down	like	to
above	behind	during	of	toward
across	below	except	off	under
after	beneath	for	on	up
among	beside	from	over	with
around	between	in	since	without
at	by	into	through	

The noun or pronoun that a preposition connects to another word in the sentence is called the **object** of the preposition. A group of words that begins with a preposition and ends with its object is called a **prepositional phrase**. The words *in the bus*, for example, are a prepositional phrase.

Now read the following sentences and explanations.

- An ant was crawling **up the teacher's leg**.

   The noun *leg* is the object of the preposition *up*. *Up* connects *leg* with the word *crawling*. The prepositional phrase *up the teacher's leg* describes *crawling*. It tells just where the ant was crawling.

- The man **with the black moustache** left the restaurant quickly.

   The noun *moustache* is the object of the preposition *with*. The prepositional phrase *with the black moustache* describes the word *man*. It tells us exactly which man left the restaurant quickly.

- The plant **on the windowsill** was a present **from my mother**.

   The noun *windowsill* is the object of the preposition *on*. The prepositional phrase *on the windowsill* describes the word *plant*. It describes exactly which plant was a present.

   There is a second prepositional phrase in this sentence. The preposition is *from*, and its object is *mother*. The prepositional phrase *from my mother* explains *present*. It tells who gave the present.

▓ For more about prepositions, see "Subjects and Verbs," pages 69–70, and "Subject-Verb Agreement," pages 129–130.

➤ Practice 7

Into each slot, insert one of the following prepositions: *of, by, with, in,* and *without.* Use each preposition once.

1. The letter from his girlfriend had been sprayed _____*with*_____ perfume.

2. The weedkiller quickly killed the dandelions _____*in*_____ our lawn.

3. _____*Without*_____ giving any notice, the tenant moved out of the expensive apartment.

4. Donald hungrily ate three scoops _____*of*_____ ice cream and an order of French fries.

5. The crates _____*by*_____ the back door contain glass bottles and old newspapers.

ADJECTIVES

An **adjective** is a word that describes a noun (the name of a person, place, or thing). Look at the following sentence.

• The dog lay down on a mat in front of the fireplace.

Now look at this sentence when adjectives have been inserted.

• The **shaggy** dog lay down on a **worn** mat in front of the fireplace.

The adjective *shaggy* describes the noun *dog*; the adjective *worn* describes the noun *mat*. Adjectives add spice to our writing. They also help us to identify particular people, places, or things.

Adjectives can be found in two places:

1   An adjective may come before the word it describes (a **damp** night, the **moldy** bread, a **striped** umbrella).

2   An adjective that describes the subject of a sentence may come after a linking verb. The linking verb may be a form of the verb *be* (he *is* **furious**, I *am* **exhausted**, they *are* **hungry**). Other linking verbs include *feel, look, sound, smell, taste, appear, seem,* and *become* (the soup *tastes* **salty**, your hands *feel* **dry**, the dog *seems* **lost**).

Note: The words *a, an,* and *the* (called **articles**) are generally classified as adjectives.

※ For more information on adjectives, see "Adjectives and Adverbs," pages 227–228 and 230–234.

➤ Practice 8   *Answers will vary.*

Write any appropriate adjective in each slot.

1. The _____*large*_____ pizza was eaten greedily by the _____*hungry*_____ teenagers.

2. Melissa gave away the sofa because it was _____*old*_____ and _____*worn*_____.

3. Although the alley is _____*dark*_____ and _____*lonely*_____, Karen often takes it as a shortcut home.

4. The restaurant throws away lettuce that is _____*wilted*_____ and tomatoes that are _____*overripe*_____.

5. When I woke up in the morning, I had a(n) _____*slight*_____ fever and a(n) _____*sore*_____ throat.

ADVERBS

An **adverb** is a word that describes a verb, an adjective, or another adverb. Many adverbs end in the letters *ly*. Look at the following sentence:

- The canary sang in the pet store window as the shoppers greeted each other.

Now look at this sentence after adverbs have been inserted.

- The canary sang **softly** in the pet store window as the shoppers **loudly** greeted each other.

The adverbs add details to the sentence. They also allow the reader to contrast the singing of the canary to the noise the shoppers are making.

Look at the following sentences and the explanations of how adverbs are used in each case.

- The chef yelled **angrily** at the young waiter.

  The adverb *angrily* describes the verb *yelled*.

- My mother has an **extremely** busy schedule on Tuesdays.

  The adverb *extremely* describes the adjective *busy*.

- The sick man spoke **very** faintly to his loyal nurse.

  The adverb *very* describes the adverb *faintly*.

Some adverbs do not end in -*ly*. Examples include *very, often, never, always*, and *well*.

※ For more information on adverbs, see "Adjectives and Adverbs," pages 228–235, and "Subjects and Verbs," page 77.

➤ Practice 9 *Answers will vary.*

Fill in each slot with any appropriate adverb.

1. The water in the pot boiled _____*quickly*_____.

2. Carla _____*carefully*_____ drove the car through _____*slowly*_____ moving traffic.

3. The telephone operator spoke _____*softly*_____ to the young child.

4. The game show contestant waved _____*happily*_____ to his family in the audience.

5. Wes _____*rarely*_____ studies, so it's no surprise that he did _____*very*_____ poorly on his finals.

CONJUNCTIONS

Conjunctions are words that connect. There are two types of conjunctions, coordinating and subordinating.

Coordinating Conjunctions (Joining Words)

Coordinating conjunctions join two equal ideas. Look at the following sentence:

- Kevin **and** Steve interviewed for the job, **but** their friend Anne got it.

In this sentence, the coordinating conjunction *and* connects the proper nouns *Kevin* and *Steve*. The coordinating conjunction *but* connects the first part of the sentence, *Kevin and Steve interviewed for the job*, to the second part, *their friend Anne got it*.

Following is a list of all the coordinating conjunctions. In this book, they are simply called *joining words*.

Coordinating Conjunctions (Joining Words)

and	so	nor	yet
but	or	for	

※ For more on coordinating conjunctions, see information on joining words in "Sentence Types," pages 147–148, and "Run-Ons and Comma Splices," page 184.

➤ Practice 10

Write a coordinating conjunction in each slot. Choose from the following: *and, but, so, or,* and *nor.* Use each conjunction once.

1. Either Jerome ___*or*___ Alex scored the winning touchdown.

2. I expected roses for my birthday, ___*but*___ I received a vase of plastic tulips from the discount store.

3. The cafeteria was serving liver and onions for lunch, ___*so*___ I bought a sandwich at the corner deli.

4. Marian brought a pack of playing cards ___*and*___ a pan of brownies to the company picnic.

5. Neither my sofa ___*nor*___ my armchair matches the rug in my living room.

Subordinating Conjunctions

When a **subordinating conjunction** is added to a word group, the words can no longer stand alone as an independent sentence. They are no longer a complete thought. For example, look at the following sentence:

• Karen fainted in class.

The word group *Karen fainted in class* is a complete thought. It can stand alone as a sentence. See what happens when a subordinating conjunction is added to a complete thought:

• When Karen fainted in class

Now the words cannot stand alone as a sentence. They are dependent on other words to complete the thought:

• When Karen fainted in class, we put her feet up on some books.

In this book, a word that begins a dependent word group is called a *dependent word.* Subordinating conjunctions are common dependent words. Below are some subordinating conjunctions.

Subordinating Conjunctions

after	even if	unless	where
although	even though	until	wherever
as	if	when	whether
because	since	whenever	while
before	though		

Following are some more sentences with subordinating conjunctions:

- **After** she finished her last exam, Joanne said, "Now I can relax."

  After she finished her last exam is not a complete thought. It is dependent on the rest of the words to make up a complete sentence.

- Lamont listens to books on tape **while** he drives to work.

  While he drives to work cannot stand by itself as a sentence. It depends on the rest of the sentence to make up a complete thought.

- **Since** apples were on sale, we decided to make an apple pie for dessert.

  Since apples were on sale is not a complete sentence. It depends on *we decided to make an apple pie for dessert* to complete the thought.

  ⁂ For more information on subordinating conjunctions, see information on dependent words in "Sentence Types," page 151; "Sentence Fragments," pages 163–166; and "Run-Ons and Comma Splices," page 185.

➤ Practice 11

Write a logical subordinating conjunction in each slot. Choose from the following: *even though, because, until, when,* and *before*. Use each conjunction once.

1. The bank was closed down by federal regulators _____*because*_____ it lost more money than it earned.

2. _____*When*_____ Paula wants to look mysterious, she wears dark sunglasses and a scarf.

3. _____*Even though*_____ the restaurant was closing in fifteen minutes, customers sipped their coffee slowly and continued to talk.

4. _____*Before*_____ anyone else could answer it, Carl rushed to the phone and whispered, "It's me."

5. The waiter was instructed not to serve any food _____*until*_____ the guest of honor arrived.

INTERJECTIONS

Interjections are words that can stand independently and are used to express emotion. Examples are *oh, wow, ouch,* and *oops*. These words are usually not found in formal writing.

- **"Hey!"** yelled Maggie. "That's my bike."
- **Oh**, we're late for class.

A Final Note

A word may function as more than one part of speech. For example, the word *dust* can be a verb or a noun, depending on its role in the sentence.

- I **dust** my bedroom once a month, whether it needs it or not. *(verb)*
- The top of my refrigerator is covered with an inch of **dust**. *(noun)*

Appendix B: Dictionary Use

OWNING A GOOD DICTIONARY

It is a good idea to own two dictionaries. The first dictionary should be a paperback that you can carry with you. Any of the following would be an excellent choice:

The American Heritage Dictionary, Paperback Edition

The Random House Dictionary, Paperback Edition

Webster's New World Dictionary, Paperback Edition

Your second dictionary should be a full-sized, hardcover edition which should be kept in the room where you study. All the above dictionaries come in hardbound versions, which contain a good deal more information than the paperback editions.

UNDERSTANDING DICTIONARY ENTRIES

Each word listed alphabetically in a dictionary is called an **entry word**. Here are an entry word and definitions taken from *The American Heritage Dictionary* (abbreviated in the rest of this section as the *AHD*)*:

---

thun·der (thŭn′dər) *n.* **1.** The booming sound produced by rapidly expanding air along the path of the electrical discharge of lightning. **2.** A sound resembling thunder. —*v.* **1.** To produce thunder or similar sounds. **2.** To utter loud remarks or threats.

Spelling and Syllables

The dictionary first gives the correct spelling and syllable breakdown of a word. Dots separate the words into syllables. Each syllable is a separate sound, and each sound includes a vowel. In the entry shown above, *thunder* is divided into two syllables.

*Reproduced by permission from *The American Heritage Dictionary, Third Paperback Edition*. Copyright © 1994 by Houghton Mifflin Company.

➤ Practice 1

Use your dictionary to separate the following words into syllables. Put a slash (/) between each syllable and the next. Then write the number of syllables in each word. The first one is done for you as an example.

1. g u a r / a n / t e e   _3_ syllables

2. m o l / e / c u l e   _3_ syllables

3. v o / c a b / u / l a r / y   _5_ syllables

4. c a u / l i / f l o w / e r   _4_ syllables

Pronunciation Symbols and Accent Marks

Most dictionary entry words are followed first by a pronunciation guide in parentheses, as in the entry for *thunder:*

thun·der (thŭn′dər)

The information in parentheses includes two kinds of symbols: pronunciation symbols and accent marks. Following is an explanation of each.

Pronunciation Symbols

The pronunciation symbols tell the sounds of consonants and vowels in a word. The sounds of the consonants are probably familiar to you, but you may find it helpful to review the vowel sounds. Vowels are the letters *a, e, i, o, u,* and sometimes *y.* To know how to pronounce the vowel sounds, use the **pronunciation key** in your dictionary. Such a key typically appears at the front of a dictionary or at the bottom of every other page of the dictionary. Here is a pronunciation key (drawn from the *AHD*'s) for the vowels and a few other sounds that often confuse dictionary users.

Pronunciation Key

ă pat	ā pay	â care	ä father	ĕ pet	ē bee	ĭ pit
ī pie, by	î pier	ŏ pot	ō toe	ô paw, for		oi noise
ŏŏ took	ōō boot	ou out	th thin	*th* this		ŭ cut
ûr urge	yōō abuse	zh vision	ə about, item, edible, gallop, circus			

The key tells you, for instance, that the sound of ă (called "short a") is pronounced like the *a* in *pat,* the sound of ā (called "long a") is pronounced like the *ay* in *pay,* and so on. All the vowels with a cup-shaped symbol above them are called short vowels. All the vowels with a horizontal line above them are called long vowels. Note that long vowels have the sound of their own name. For example, long *a* sounds like the name of the letter *a.*

To use the above key, first find the symbol of the sound you wish to pronounce. For example, suppose you want to pronounce the short *i* sound.

Locate the short *i* in the key and note how the sound is pronounced in the short word *(pit)* that appears next to the short *i*. This tells you that the short *i* has the sound of the *i* in the word *pit*. The key also tells you, for instance, that the short *e* has the sound of the *e* in the word *pet*, that the short *o* has the sound of the *o* in the word *pot*, and so on.

Finally, note that the last pronunciation symbol in the key looks like an upside-down *e:* ə. This symbol is known as the **schwa**. As you can see by the words that follow it, the schwa has a very short sound that sounds much like "uh" (as in *about*, *gallop*, and *circus*) or "ih" (as in *item* and *edible*).

➤ Practice 2

Refer to the pronunciation key to answer the questions about the following words. Circle the letter of each of your answers.

1. **hic·cup** (hĭk′ŭp)

   The *i* in *hiccup* sounds like the *i* in

   ⓐ *pit.*   b. *pie.*

2. **si·lent** (sī′lənt)

   The *i* in *silent* sounds like the *i* in

   a. *pit.*   ⓑ *pie.*

3. **na·tive** (nā′tĭv)

   The *a* in *native* sounds like the *a* in

   a. *father.*   ⓑ *pay.*

4. **lot·ter·y** (lŏt′ə-rē)

   The *o* in *lottery* sounds like the *o* in

   ⓐ *pot.*   b. *for.*

➤ Practice 3

Use your dictionary to find and write in the pronunciation symbols for the following words. Make sure you can pronounce each word. The first word has been done for you as an example.

1. reluctant   *rĭ-lŭk′tənt*

2. homicide   *hŏm′ĭ-sīd′*

3. extravagant   *ĭk-străv′ə-gənt*

4. unanimous   *yōō-năn′ə-məs*

Accent Marks

Notice the mark in the pronunciation guide for *thunder* that is similar to an apostrophe:

thun·der (thŭn′dər)

The dark mark (′) is a bold accent mark, and it shows which syllable has the stronger stress. That means the syllable it follows is pronounced a little louder than the others. Syllables without an accent mark are unstressed. Some syllables are in between, and they are marked with a lighter accent mark (′).

The word *recognize*, for example, is accented like this:

rec·og·nize (rĕk′əg-nīz′)

Say *recognize* to yourself. Can you hear that the strongest accent is on *rec*, the first syllable? Can you hear that the last syllable, *nize*, is also accented but not as strongly? If not, say the word to yourself again until you hear the differences in accent sounds.

➤ Practice 4

Answer the questions following each of the words below.

1. **pep·per·mint** (pĕp′ər-mĭnt′)
   a. How many syllables are in *peppermint*? _____3_____
   b. Which syllable is most strongly accented? ___first___

2. **in·ter·me·di·ate** (ĭn′tər-mē′dē-ĭt)
   a. How many syllables are in *intermediate*? _____5_____
   b. Which syllable is most strongly accented? ___third___

3. **in·her·it** (ĭn-hĕr′ĭt)
   a. How many syllables are in *inherit*? _____3_____
   b. Which syllable is accented? ___second___

4. **con·tra·dic·tion** (kŏn′trə-dĭk′shən)
   a. How many syllables are in *contradiction*? _____4_____
   b. Which syllable is most strongly accented? ___third___

Parts of Speech

Every word in the dictionary is either a noun, a verb, an adjective, or another part of speech. In dictionary entries, the parts of speech are shown by abbreviations in italics. In the entry for *thunder*, for example, the abbreviations *n.* and *v.* tell us that *thunder* can be both a noun and a verb.

When a word is more than one part of speech, the dictionary gives the definitions for each part of speech separately. In the above entry for *thunder*, the abbreviation telling us that *thunder* is a noun comes right after the pronunciation symbols; the two noun definitions follow. When the noun meanings end, the abbreviation *v.* tells us that the verb definitions will follow.

Parts of speech are abbreviated in order to save space. Following are common abbreviations for parts of speech.

n.—noun	*v.*—verb
pron.—pronoun	*conj.*—conjunction
adj.—adjective	*prep.*—preposition
adv.—adverb	*interj.*—interjection

Irregular Verb Forms and Irregular Spellings

After the part of speech, special information is given in entries for irregular verbs, for adjectives with irregularly spelled forms, and for irregularly spelled plurals.

For irregular verbs, the dictionary gives the past tense, the past participle, and the present participle. For example, the entry for *blow* shows that *blew* is the past tense, *blown* is the past participle, and *blowing* is the present participle.

blow (blō) *v.* **blew** (bloo), **blown** (blōn), **blowing**.

For adjectives with irregularly spelled forms, the comparative (used when comparing two things) and the superlative (used when comparing three or more things) are shown after the part of speech. The entry for *skinny*, for instance, shows that the comparative form of that adjective is *skinnier* and the superlative form is *skinniest*.

skin·ny (skĭn′ē) *adj.* **-ni·er, -ni·est**.

Irregular plural spellings are also included in this spot in an entry. For example, after the part of speech, the entry for *party* tells us that this word's plural ends in *-ies*.

par·ty (pär′tē) *n., pl.* **-ties**.

Definitions

Words often have more than one meaning. When they do, their definitions may be numbered in the dictionary. You can tell which definition of a word fits a given sentence by the meaning of the sentence. For example, the following are the definitions in the *AHD* for the verb form of *surprise*:

1. To encounter suddenly or unexpectedly.

2. To attack or capture suddenly and without warning.

3. To astonish by the unanticipated.

Which of these definitions best fits the sentence below?

> The soldiers *surprised* the enemy troops, who had bedded down for the night.

The answer is definition 2: The soldiers *suddenly attacked* the enemy troops.

➤ **Practice 5**

A. Use your dictionary to answer the questions below about *obstinate*.

1. Which syllable in *obstinate* is most strongly accented? __*first*__

2. How many syllables are in the word *obstinate*? __3__

3. How many *schwa* sounds are in the word *obstinate*? __1__

4. Does the first syllable in *obstinate* have a long or a short *o* sound?
   __short__

5. Which definition of *obstinate* applies in the following sentence? (Write out the full definition from your dictionary.)

   Felicia stayed home all week with an *obstinate* case of the flu.

   Definition: _____ difficult to alleviate or cure _____

   _____

B. Use your dictionary to answer the questions below about *solitary*.

6. How many syllables are in the word *solitary*? __4__

7. Which syllable in *solitary* is most strongly accented? __*first*__

8. Does the first syllable in *solitary* have a long or a short *o* sound?
   __short__

9. Which definition of *solitary* applies in the following sentence? (Write out the definition from your dictionary.)

   The box of cookies was bought yesterday, and today there's only a *solitary* cookie remaining.

   Definition: _____ single; sole _____

   _____

10. Which definition of *solitary* applies in the following sentence? (Write out the definition from your dictionary.)

    Some people like to study in groups, but Sarita prefers *solitary* study.

    Definition: _____ happening or done alone _____

    _____

Index